Ballroom, Boogie, Shimmy Sham, Shake

Ballroom, Boogie, Shimmy Sham, Shake

A Social and Popular Dance Reader

Edited by

Julie Malnig

University of Illinois Press
Urbana and Chicago

Juliet McMains's chapter, "Dancing Latin/Latin Dancing: Salsa and DanceSport," includes sections from "Brownface: Representations of Latin-ness in Dancesport," "Social and Popular Dance," special issue, *Dance Research Journal* 33, no. 2 (Winter 2001), and *Glamour Addiction: Inside the American Ballroom Dance Industry* (Middletown, Conn.: Wesleyan University Press, 2006). Earlier versions of Lisa Doolittle's chapter, "The Trianon and On: Reading Mass Social Dancing in the 1930s and 1940s in Alberta, Canada," and Sally R. Sommer's chapter, "C'mon to My House: Underground House Dancing," appeared in "Social and Popular Dance," special issue, *Dance Research Journal* 33, no. 2 (Winter 2001).

Library of Congress Cataloging-in-Publication Data
Ballroom, boogie, shimmy sham, shake : a social and popular
dance reader / edited by Julie Malnig.
    p. cm.
Includes index.
ISBN 978-0-252-03363-6 (cloth : alk. paper) —
ISBN 978-0-252-07565-0 (pbk. : alk. paper)
  1. Dance—History. 2. Dance—Social aspects.
I. Malnig, Julie.
GV1781.B35   2009
792.309—dc22   2008009043

In memory of my father,
Lawrence R. Malnig—
professor, counselor, mentor,
friend

Contents

Acknowledgments

Many people have contributed to the evolution of this book project, and I am pleased to thank them here. First and foremost, I wish to heartily thank all of the authors who lent their time, energy, and expertise to the collection. I thank you for your graciousness and good cheer in responding to my many queries and for adding immeasurably to our understanding of the field of social and popular dance. I have been inspired by your knowledge and dedication. For their assistance in helping track down photographs and securing permissions, I am grateful to Susan Curtis, Jackie Danois, Annette Macdonald, Carol Martin, Terry Monaghan, Robin Moore, Ron Seymour, Deirdre Towers, and Pat Rader and the staff of the Jerome Robbins Dance Division of The New York Public Library for the Performing Arts. I am grateful to Waring Abbott, Philip Gould, and Jonathan Marion for generously allowing us to include their photographs. I am indebted to Barbara Cohen-Stratyner and Leslie Satin for reading early drafts of my introduction and essay as well as my sister Anita Malnig, who provided indispensable editorial assistance and wisdom. Thanks to my mother, Laura Malnig, as well, for her consistence encouragement and abiding faith in my work. For providing support of many kinds throughout the process, I wish to thank Sharon Friedman, Edwin R. Robbins, Sally R. Sommer, J M Stifle, and also my dear pal, Homen.

I want to thank several graduate assistants who worked on the manuscript at various stages: Vanessa Manko, Cristina Huebner, and especially Catherine Massey, an indefatigable worker, who brilliantly executed an extraordinary number of details with characteristic calm and assurance. She made completion of the project a most pleasurable experience. The Gallatin Faculty Enrichment Fund at the Gallatin School of New York University helped provide material and financial assistance for which I am very grateful. I also wish to thank the board members of the Congress on Research in Dance (CORD) for their encouragement of a theme issue of *Dance Research Journal*, which planted the seed for this volume.

I owe many thanks to my editor, Joan Catapano, who was enthusiastic about this project from the start and has provided ongoing expert assistance and guidance. I would also like to extend my deep thanks to Managing Editor Rebecca Crist and Assistant Managing Editor Jennifer Clark for carefully attending to the manuscript at various stages of the editorial process, as well as Art Director Copenhaver Cumpston for overseeing the book's lovely design. Two longtime mentors from the Department of Performance Studies at New York University deserve a special note of thanks: professors Brooks McNamara, who got me hooked on the history of popular entertainments, and Barbara Kirshenblatt-Gimblett, for lighting my intellectual fires. And, finally, and certainly not least, thanks go to my husband, Ogden Goelet, for his endless enthusiasm for the topic, his astute editorial suggestions, and his tolerance for interruptions from his own scholarly work to read yet another draft, listen to another thought, or calm an anxious worry. I am deeply grateful for his support.

Ballroom, Boogie, Shimmy Sham, Shake

Introduction

Julie Malnig

In the late 1970s, when the field of popular entertainment was struggling for legitimacy, noted performance scholar Brooks McNamara made a plea to historians to examine not only the "great moments" in theater history, but those less well-documented theatrical occasions, sometimes hidden in the recesses of culture where scholars had seldom tread. This traditional approach to studying the theatrical past, suggested McNamara, "leaves the student with the impression that a kind of mysterious hierarchy of performance exists, crowned by 'greatest achievements' which tower over a series of unrelated and vaguely defined 'minor forms' and crude folkish attempts at theatre."[1] This "tidy view" toward history, he noted, overlooked how "performance in a culture during a given period is certainly no less than the sum of all its parts."[2]

In many respects, McNamara's observations about the status of popular entertainments reflected a similar situation in the study of social, vernacular, and popular dance, considered a kind of poor relation within the scholarly hierarchy. Until fairly recently, the traditional periodization of dance studies neglected these forms, favoring instead the study of concert dance and well-known dancers and choreographers. Perhaps because dance, as scholars Ellen W. Goellner and Geraldine Shea Murphy point out, was for so long "viewed as unintellectual, intuitive, and uncritically expressive,"[3] the "greatest moments" approach was understandable as the field struggled to establish itself and legitimize its own history. Part of this omission, too, stemmed from the long-standing bias within the academy generally (as McNamara recognized), toward "high" versus "low" forms of entertainment. And to be fair, the lack of sustained attention to the study of social and popular dance forms reflected the fact that in the 1970s and early 1980s, much of this history had yet to be written.

Thankfully, though, this landscape is changing. The widespread efforts in the 1980s to expand the traditional literary, artistic, and historical canons carried over into dance studies, in which there has been much rethinking of how we critique, conceptualize, and theorize about dance. Also, over the last ten to fifteen years we have seen a flourishing of writing on social, vernacular, and popular dance forms, the result of scholars who have been engaged in an ongoing process of excavation and analysis. In many cases, this has meant taking the time to steep ourselves in new, interdisciplinary inquiries to develop the tools necessary to understand and assess these forms within their larger cultural and social contexts.[4]

Although my 1987 dissertation on the history of American exhibition ballroom dance was viewed with skepticism by some as a kind of sideline curio within the dance and performance worlds, today many more doctoral students are producing, and are encouraged to produce, analytical studies on a wide range of social and popular dance-related topics from break dancing to raves.[5] Also, in the past decade several influential anthologies have emerged which, although not focused exclusively on social and popular dance, include significant essays on the subject, such as Helen Thomas's *Dance in the City*, Jane C. Desmond's *Dancing Desires: Choreographing Sexualities On and Off the Stage*, and Thomas F. DeFrantz's *Dancing Many Drums: Excavations in African American Dance*.[6] Individual authors, too, have contributed several pioneering books spanning subjects from club culture, to punk rock, to competitive ballroom dance.[7]

Buoyed by the boom in critical dance scholarship and the new interest in cultural studies, what the majority of these works share is a commitment to expanding the borders of our investigations and exploring dance as integral to cultural practice. *Ballroom, Boogie, Shimmy Sham, Shake: A Social and Popular Dance Reader* intends to add to these ongoing inquiries. My aims in creating this Reader (the first full collection of social and popular dance essays) are to provide a platform for further research and to make possible more concerted study of the cultural significance of social and ballroom forms within the college dance curricula.

Because social dance covers such a large and sweeping historical and geographic terrain, one must invariably be selective in compiling an anthology of this sort. My main focus is on the secular tradition of American social dance performed by the public in a variety of social and recreational gatherings—ballrooms, cabarets, nightclubs, dance halls, discotheques, the street—from approximately the late eighteenth century through the early twenty-first century. The broad goals of the Reader are twofold: to explore various styles of social and popular dance developed as a result of the rich fusions of West African, African American, Euro-American, and Latin American forms of dance within the United States, Canada, and the Caribbean and to analyze these dance forms within their wider social, political, cultural, and economic contexts. Although it is not possible, of course, to include all of the many stylistic variations of these dances, the collection nonetheless spotlights some particularly key dance forms and phenomena and considers the reasons for their cultural resonance and appeal.

The anthology is divided into four sections: "Historical Precedents," "Evolving Styles," "Theatricalizations of Social Dance Forms," and "The Contemporary Scene." Many of the issues and concerns central to one section, however, spill over into others. Therefore readers are urged to seek out connections between chapters, beyond their categorical groupings. The topical-chronological approach is not meant to suggest a neat or orderly progression, necessarily, from the Cakewalk to hip-hop, but rather to consider how multifaceted these dance forms are; how Old World and New World forms have collided, borrowed from, and added to one another in a dynamic and constantly evolving process of invention and change. The chapters themselves aim to merge close, physical description of the dances with contextual, cultural analysis. I asked authors to consider the "fabric" of the dances—Who performed them? How? In what contexts? And under what social and historical circumstances?—and to locate how those dances are embedded within the existing conventions and "codes" governing that culture's understandings of movement and the body.[8]

In recognizing social and popular dance both as an *experience* of movement and as "a form of life or as a way of being," in dance sociologist Andrew Ward's words,[9] these chapters adopt a wide range of strategies, many used in combination, that university students are now apt to encounter in the course of their studies in dance history and theory. These include genre and stylistic analysis, anthropological analysis, sociocultural analysis, social history, theories of popular culture and mass leisure, intertextual analysis, race and gender theory, transnational analysis, and ritual theory, among others. This diversity of approaches speaks, in part, to the increasing interdisciplinarity of dance studies and, in part, to the need for more sustained attention to social and popular dance topics in related disciplines.[10]

A particularly underexplored relationship has been that between social dance and music, both of which historically have been inextricably linked. Although the majority of contributors are dance historians, dance anthropologists, and performance studies scholars, several are scholars and writers from the areas of ethnomusicology and mass media studies. Far too often, dance scholars have de-emphasized the role of music, and musicologists (who have examined forms such as salsa, mambo, and hip-hop) have not looked as closely as they might at the connections between those musical forms and how they are made possible by the rhythmic variations of the dances. I hope these chapters gesture toward bridging that gap.

A Few Words about Form and Terms

The labels "social," "vernacular," and "popular" are used interchangeably and often inconsistently in the social dance literature. Without becoming overly prescriptive (our authors express best the ways that we may understand these distinctions), I do offer a few, brief thoughts about how I have conceptualized these terms for the sake of the collection and how the forms themselves share many similarities yet maintain important differences. Part of the difficulty in pinning down social and popular dance is that it is constantly in flux. New forms spring up; others disappear; and what may have been considered elitist in one generation, in the next may become "popular" or widely heralded.[11] Most of the social dances discussed in this volume are essentially vernacular in the sense that they spring from the lifeblood of communities and subcultures and are generally learned informally, through cultural and social networks. In describing the black vernacular tradition, which has been crucial to the story of American social dance, dance scholar Jacqui Malone sees it as "an evolving tradition and a vital process of cultural production."[12] She quotes Ralph Ellison, whose description of the vernacular reflects the mode of transmission characteristic of many of the dances referred to in these chapters. He refers to it "as a dynamic process in which the most refined styles from the past are continually merged with the play-it-by-eye-and-by-ear improvisations."[13] In the vernacular tradition, performers draw on and embellish existing forms of dance that, as dance ethnographer LeeEllen Friedland notes, generally grow out of a group's "shared knowledge of movement repertoire" emerging from its geography and social circumstance.[14]

In this volume, however, I prefer to use the term "social" dance primarily, in part to distinguish it from other forms of vernacular dance, such as folk dance, which tend to involve like-minded or homogeneous communities of dancers interested primarily in the preservation of heritage and group traditions. In social dancing, a sense of community often derives less from preexisting groups brought together by shared social and cultural interests than from a community created *as a result* of the dancing.[15] Whether in cabarets of the 1910s or house clubs of the 1990s, it is often the sheer physicality of the dancing itself, the energy of the surroundings, and the eclectic mix of individuals that bring diffuse groups of individuals together into a collective, social bond. Unlike ceremonial or ritual dances designed to mark or commemorate special occasions or events or to produce specific outcomes (harvesting rituals, weddings ceremonies, and the like), the forms of modern social dance represented here are symbolic or *expressive* of a host of social and cultural values (regarding individual or group identity, sexuality, or class interests, for instance) *particular to* their time, place, and historical contexts. Whether a society ballroom dance, a disco dance, or a house party, different rules of behavior and propriety apply. To each of these venues, dancers bring their own individual backgrounds, tastes, and personal attitudes, all of which color the totality of the dance experience.

Popular dance can also be synonymous with social dance, in that it is accessible to and enjoyed by a large swath of the population and, like social dance, is generally seen as a counterpoint to what have typically been considered "high" culture or classical forms of dance aimed at privileged audiences. In the collection, though, popular dance is also identified according to a specific *process* by which local, vernacular, and social dance traditions become popularized in the public sphere.[16] A salient quality of social dances is their ability to spread beyond local contexts to become, in many cases, national or worldwide dance phenomena. Punk and hip-hop are examples of what began as subcultural dance forms only to become more fully incorporated into (some would argue appropriated by) mainstream culture. Thus, how dances have become commercialized, marketed, and sold for public consumption is a large part of the story of the relationship between social and popular dance in North American contexts. Whether through dance-song instructions, radio-dance lessons, etiquette manuals, daily newspapers, sound recordings, or MTV, media forces of many kinds have shaped the look, style, and popularity of social dance from the late nineteenth century to the present day.

Part of the defining process of social and popular dance must also take into account the fluidity in levels of expertise among dancers. Although social dancers may begin as amateurs (and many of course remain that way), there is no question that much social dancing may certainly rise to a level of sophistication, style, and skill often equal to that of professionals. What many of the chapters bear out is how both social and popular dance forms exist on a continuum from the purely recreational to more theatrical and theatricalized styles. The spatial configurations in many social and popular dance settings, in fact, enhance the performative and often competitive nature of the dances as in the three-quarter circle (or cipher) in break dance and house styles in which dancers take off on flights of imaginative improvisation before their peers, or designated corners of ballrooms and clubs (such as the northeast corner of the Savoy Ballroom), designed to showcase the talents of elite dancers. In these environments, participants become spectators and vice versa, as dancers continually shift "from viewer to doer," as dance scholar Linda Tomko has noted, in an active presentation of self.[17]

Chapters and Issues

In her 1991 essay, "Dance Narratives and Fantasies of Achievement," dance theorist and sociologist Angela McRobbie urged scholars and writers to begin to consider dance "as a social activity, a participative form enjoyed by people in leisure, a sexual ritual, a form of self-expression, a kind of exercise and a way of speaking through the body."[18] Of course, of all forms of dance, whether recreational or staged, performance dance may be viewed from these sociological perspectives; social dance, in particular, though, cries out for such analysis as it is so rooted in the materiality of everyday life. Our authors, I believe, take up McRobbie's challenge and address the myriad ways that social and popular dance reflects and absorbs daily life as well as shapes, informs, and influences social patterns and behaviors. Because a subject such as social and popular dance is by definition concerned with questions of "sociality," it stands to reason that these chapters touch on a host of social issues and cultural concerns.

Race and racial issues, for one, figure prominently in this collection. To talk about American social, vernacular, and popular forms means discussing the prominence of African and African American forms and their transformative influence on American social dance. As dance theorist Brenda Dixon Gottschild has said of what she calls the "Africanist" presence in dance, "Like electricity through the wires, we draw from it all the time but few of us are aware of its source."[19] A major characteristic of social and popular dance is that it is constantly changing, morphing, and evolving as it absorbs different dance rhythms and different cultural traditions. As one of the anthology's authors, Yvonne Daniel, notes of the trajectory of popular dance generally, "It is always borrowing, returning, imitating, shifting, reversing, inverting, improvising, and in the process shaping and polishing yet another named creation of the current day." Often, however, those creations have gone unnamed, their racial roots ignored or unaccounted for. Several authors in the collection bring to the historical record traditions not previously fully acknowledged and uncover the rich cross-fertilizations between black and white, and black and Latin, inventions that have created some of our most popular social dances. Others theorize that these historical erasures occur when black-derived dances enter the white marketplace, where their origins become obscured and the price of popularity often means dilution of the form.

In "Our National Poetry: The Afro-Chesapeake Inventions of American Dance," which opens this collection, Jurretta Jordan Heckscher notes that "if we are to begin to understand American vernacular dance and movement, we must come to terms with its Africanity." Heckscher examines Chesapeake-area dance of the colonial era, which not only solidified a powerful and vibrant African American dance tradition but also produced some of the richest black and white cultural exchanges that would come to influence the trajectory of American social dance. Drawing on approaches from anthropology and American studies, Heckscher uses the development of the Virginia jig to trace a three-step cultural process of creolization that ultimately conjoined African and European movement systems.

In "Louisiana Gumbo: Retention, Creolization, and Innovation in Contemporary Cajun and Zydeco Dance," May Gwin Waggoner also traces the confluence of traditions, in this case of the Afro-Creoles, Anglophone African Americans, and French and Anglo-Acadians. In her stylistic and cultural analysis of Louisiana's popular dances, Waggoner points to the persistence of these groups' dance and musical traditions despite slavery, segregation, and language discrimination. Critic and novelist Wole Soyinka, writing about the resilience of West African drama in his 1982 essay, has described how cultural conditions may demand that certain forms become transformed to preserve their threatened status.[20] So, too, with the Cajun and Creole traditions in which, as Waggoner explains, "innovation" secured cultural survival, and "the dances were modified as different ethnic groups sought a common denominator on the dance floor."

In her chapter "'Just Like Being at the Zoo': Primitivity and Ragtime Dance" (whose title refers to a quote by African American dance chronicler Mura Dehn), Nadine George-Graves traces the "physical vocabulary" of Southern black dances of the nineteenth century and their impact on Northern ragtime dance. At the same time, she draws on critical race theory to explore the systematic exclusion of these dances when transferred to white venues and the complex ways in which ragtime dance's association with the "primitive" constrained a fuller appreciation of those dances—even to the present day. In "Negotiating Compromise on a Burnished Wood Floor: Social Dancing at the Savoy," Karen Hubbard and Terry Monaghan explore the Lindy Hop as "a major reordering of almost the entire African American social dance experience." Their cultural history reconsiders traditional accounts of the famed Harlem dance club to explore how the Savoy was not only an exalted showcase for highly celebrated bands and dancers but also a venue for "the mass social dance aspirations of the predominantly black local community."

Latin American influences on North American social dance have been equally profound; in "Rumba Then and Now: *Quindembo*," Yvonne Daniel provides us with an evocative rendering of the dance from its roots in nineteenth-century Cuba through its sensational rise in the United States in the 1950s. *Quindembo* means "mixture," and indeed rumba was never just *one* dance, but a complex mixture of dance styles and fads (along with singing, feasting, and music making). Daniel traces the rumba in all its complexity and demonstrates what was lost and gained as it migrated from Cuba to North America. Like Daniel, David F. García employs race and class perspectives as well as a transnational approach in "Embodying Music/Disciplining Dance: The Mambo Body in Havana and New York City." Here he compares how the commercialization of mambo in both cities partook of racialized stereotypes that appealed to white, primal fantasies and illustrates how at least one highly influential Palladium team, Cuban Pete and Millie Donay (a Puerto Rican and an Italian American), broke free of these constraints and helped restructure "sexual comportment and interracial relations."

Although social and popular dance incorporates and reinforces social values, it may also transcend and defy them, depending on the historical, cultural, and political circumstances of the given time. Rock-'n'-roll dance, for instance, represents a curious instance of both acquiescence to and flaunting of social norms. In "Rocking Around the Clock: Teenage Dance Fads from 1955 to 1965," Tim Wall explores white youth's fascination with black-derived rhythm-and-blues music and how one's competence in the dances ensured peer acceptance. Yet at the same time, the dancers' adoption of "stylized movement imbued with the insolence and understated swagger of youth," enabled them to take a stance against the social decorum associated with previous eras of dance.

In "Beyond the Hustle: 1970s Social Dancing, Discotheque Culture, and the Emergence of the Contemporary Club Dancer," Tim Lawrence discusses how social dancing of this era, with its sustained, propulsive beats and amplified sound, was an often transcendent means of asserting individual (and group) identity. As he notes, "Riding on the back of gay liberation, feminism, and civil rights, the core dancers of the disco era were also engaging in the development of new social forms and cultural expression, and the floor provided them with a relatively safe space in which they could work out their concerns and articulate their emotions and desires."

In "Dancing Latin/Latin Dancing: Salsa and DanceSport," Juliet McMains highlights another facet of group identity in competitive ballroom dance, a form that straddles both social and theatrical dance styles. Here McMains examines the ways that Latin dance is practiced in two different theatrical and cultural arenas: semiprofessional, theatricalized DanceSport competitions and salsa club dancing (the studio versus the street). What is "at stake," McMains notes, are two versions of Latin dance, "as predetermined choreography versus improvisational movement." One represents the professionalization of Latin American social dance, the other a concept of pan-Latino identity. McMains attempts to sort out each group's competing claims of "authenticity."

Not to be overlooked in social dance's ability to create and shape identity is the notion of *pleasure* experienced in the act of dancing alongside other moving bodies. Writing about the physical and psychic effects of popular music in *Urban Rhythms: Pop Music and Popular Culture*, critic Iain Chambers explains how popular dancing may express the simple pleasures of "'letting off steam,' 'a well-earned break,' [and] 'enjoying oneself,'" yet those same pleasures may elicit moments of self-realization.[21] Sally R. Sommer, in "'C'mon to My House': Underground House Dancing," writes of the essentialness of the "vibe" in house dance, a popular form of club dance (and an offshoot of disco) performed to propulsive, nonstop music.[22] The vibe, she notes, "is an active communal force, a feeling, a rhythm created by the mix of dancers, the balance of loud music, the effects of darkness and light and physical/psychical energy." Invoking anthropologist Victor Turner, Sommer describes how the combination of "hard" dancing, sonic energy, and the repetitive, incantatory-like song lyrics of house dance, may induce a transformative spirit of *communitas* or grace.

Social and popular dance is typically associated with leisure and recreation—what people do in their off time. As the field of leisure studies itself has grown, though, scholars are now exploring popular pastimes that occur apart from the world of work not merely as diversionary activities but as spaces for rejuvenation, testing of behaviors, and assertions of identity outside the confines of the ordered, everyday world. In "The Multiringed Cosmos of Krumping: Hip-Hop Dance at the Intersections of Battle, Media, and Spirit," Christina Zanfagna also invokes Turner and reformulates his concept of "liminality" to analyze how krumping—a twenty-first-century incarnation of break dancing—embodies both competitive and spiritual dimensions that manifest in the circle or "ring" (harkening back to the African American ring shout). Zanfagna describes krumping as "a combination of street fighting, moshing, sanctified church spirit possession, and aerobic striptease," a type of "serious play" in which dancers may confront anger, pain, and sadness.

The dance marathons of the 1920s and 1930s were surely another type of "serious play" that tapped the yearnings and fears of Depression-era Americans. Here, fox trots, waltzes, and the Charleston, among other dances, became contests of fortitude for primarily working-class Americans. As Carol Martin illustrates in "Reality Dance: American Dance Marathons," these spectacles, which blurred the lines between reality and fiction, presented the "struggle to survive" as an animating narrative to help spectators make sense of deprivation and loss. Here, leisure, as Martin notes, "became an escape, an expanse of time no longer related to respite from labor, but respite from lack of labor."

If social and popular dance forms are indeed a way of "speaking through the body," then it is not surprising that attitudes about morality, sexuality, and gender loom large in these discussions. Several chapters also illustrate how these concerns intersect with those of class. In "The Civilizing of America's Ballrooms: The Revolutionary War to 1890," Elizabeth Aldrich's historical and cultural analysis of the experience of immigrant and middle-class colonial settlers, social dancing and its attendant rituals of etiquette and proper decorum were a means of gaining entry into a new society. Aldrich charts the evolution from courtly couple dances to the egalitarian group-oriented cotillions, reels, and English country dances and "the struggle of the middle class as it established a code of manners for the ceremonious aspects of daily life, including evenings dedicated to dance."

In "Apaches, Tangos, and Other Indecencies: Women, Dance, and New York Nightlife of the 1910s," I explore the ways that social dancing of the 1910s, an era of heightened attention to the female body, can be read as a means of engaging working- and middle-class women with contemporary ideas about equality, sexuality, and women's identity. At the same time, I consider the moral and religious injunctions against the dances (a fact that has plagued social dance throughout its history) and how women of both classes performed "in dialogue" with these prohibitions and used popular ragtime dances as a means of testing new modes of heterosexual courtship and personal expressions of self. Both Elizabeth Aldrich and I consider the important ways that social and popular dance forms have served a didactic function within society. The courtesy literature of the nineteenth century and the dance instructional manuals of the 1910s, for instance, helped impart what were considered requisite social skills and appropriate deportment that might be attained through dance.

Lisa Doolittle considers how social dance is expressive of gender, class, and geography in her ethnographically based "The Trianon and On: Reading Mass Social Dancing in the 1930s and 1940s in Alberta, Canada." In this New Historicist reading, Doolittle brings to light the recollections of former dancers, now octogenarians, to reveal how social dancing in western Canada during the World War II years became "a crucial territory for staging of choreographies of community cultural values." Doolittle analyzes how mass migration from the provinces to the cities, sudden encounters between regional groups, and accompanying qualms about what constituted acceptable dance behavior (especially for women) all accounted for the emergence of specific dance styles and practices. Doolittle, too, offers important insights into the challenges of researching social dance, an elusive, often evanescent form too often ignored in the documentary records.

An exploration of social and popular dance would not be complete without some discussion of its symbiotic relationship with more formal staged dances. From ballet to Broadway, social and vernacular forms have long served as deep reservoirs of inspiration for directors and choreographers. As dance critic Marcia B. Siegel has observed in *The Shapes of Change: Images of American Dance,* "This constant stream of vernacular and popular material flowing into our art dance, sometimes by design and sometimes inadvertently, is one of the major sources of the creativity of the American dance."[23] Vernacular and theatrical stage forms have continually floated back and forth, feeding and informing one another, often giving rise to yet new forms. Social dances get picked up and transformed as staged dances; those staged dances, in turn, circulate back into social realms in yet other modified forms. It is a kind of endless loop of creativity in which steps and styles are continually recycled, recombined, and reborn. The chapters in section III, "Theatricalizations of Social Dance Forms," explore social and vernacular dances as they have developed in four distinct theatrical arenas: Broadway musical theater of the 1910s and 1920s, nightclub entertainment of the 1930s and 1940s, contemporary music video, and the modern-dance concert stage. In "'A Thousand Raggy, Draggy Dances': Social Dance in Broadway Musical Comedy in the 1920s," Barbara Cohen-Stratyner looks at the intricate ways that the Charleston and Black Bottom were transformed from their black vernacular roots into stylized stage dances. She explores how the design and placement of these dances underscored their primarily middle-class audience's preoccupations with a new consumer culture, women's entry in the work world, and new patterns of courtship and marriage. Knowledge of popular social dances of the day, learned through musical shows, helped people define their place in society. As Stratyner notes, "In 1920s New York, you were what you danced."

In "From Bharata Natyam to Bop: Jack Cole's 'Modern' Jazz Dance," Constance Valis Hill traces the work of legendary jazz choreographer Jack Cole and one of his most notable dance numbers, "Sing, Sing, Sing," performed to Benny Goodman's famed composition. "More than a step," Valis Hill writes, "the jitterbug was a style, a state of mind: a violent, even frenzied athleticism." In her detailed choreographic analysis, Valis Hill describes how Cole captured the essential jitterbug in an eclectic style that combined steps from African American-based vernacular forms, East Indian dance, and the rhythms of bebop. Cole's work is a testament to the influence of social dance forms in helping forge new theatrical traditions—in this case modern jazz dance—that have been influential to this day.

Music television video (MTV), popular since the 1980s, has been rife with variations on forms of social and vernacular dance from moshing to voguing to krumping. Sherril Dodds, in "From Busby Berkeley to Madonna: Music Video and Popular Dance," spotlights some of the earliest examples of filmed dance in the work of legendary choreographers Busby Berkeley and Fred Astaire and discusses how many of these screen-dance traditions are still alive in the music videos of Madonna, Michael Jackson, and others. Dodds also delves into the complicated interplay between music video's role as a promotional tool for recording artists and a breeding ground for new dance styles. She notes that music video functions in "a sophisticated circuit of reinvention." Although it feeds off existing social dance traditions, and in many respects exploits them, it also "serves as a pedagogical tool that circulates and distributes dance styles that audience are keen to adopt and develop."

As several chapters illustrate, hip-hop and break-dancing styles have become commercialized in a variety of popular media, including music, film, and television advertisements. Halifu Osumare turns our sights to the ways these forms have become theatricalized on the concert stage. In "The Dance Archaeology of Rennie Harris: Hip-Hop or Postmodern?" she reveals how modern dance choreographer Rennie Harris, whose work combines elements of the postmodern dance aesthetic with the African American vernacular, has shattered the distinction between "high" and "low" art dance forms. Osumare, who interviewed Harris for this chapter, concludes that he is creating a new kind of so-called theatrical ritualization, "transform[ing] a dance form meant as virtuosic spectacle into an often delicate and subtle, pared down, concert-oriented movement that explores the human condition."

The range of material in social dance, both historical and contemporary, is far-reaching and the variety of styles great. Of the chapters included here, my hope is that they may be read in multiple ways: chronologically, methodologically, stylistically, and culturally. Because of the interdisciplinary nature of the subject, instructors in fields other than dance may turn to the collection to explore how dance is a crucial element in understanding the art and culture of any given era. A student writing about the novelist F. Scott Fitzgerald or Edith Wharton, for instance, might fill in her knowledge and understanding of the Jazz Age and the vital role that dance and music played in the cultural life of that time; likewise, a student studying etiquette in the Gilded Age might profit from the discussions on nineteenth-century dance and social mores. Readers are also urged to follow up on the rich bibliographic sources as guides to inform their inquiries. Still to be explored are other historical forms of social dance, non-U.S. forms, and contemporary cross-cultural variations of social, vernacular, and popular forms that have taken root globally. I hope this volume, which has begun to illuminate one corner of the social and popular dance world, will stimulate our collective imaginations and spur further investigations into this perpetually fascinating, ever culturally rich, and truly generative art form and social practice.

Notes

1. Brooks McNamara, "The Invisible Theatre: The Folk and Festival Tradition in America," in *Theatre Byways: Essays in Honor of Claude L. Shaver*, ed. C. J. Stevens and Joseph Aurbach (New Orleans: Polyanthos, 1978), 7.

2. Ibid.

3. See Ellen W. Goellner and Jacqueline Shea Murphy, eds., *Bodies of the Text: Dance as Theory, Literature as Dance* (New Brunswick, NJ: Rutgers University Press, 1995), 3.

4. See Sally Banes, "Criticism as Ethnography," in *Writing Dancing in the Age of Postmodernism* (Middletown, CT: Wesleyan University Press, 1994), 16–24. Banes discusses her challenges as a young critic covering the new hip-hop dance scene. To fully understand the dance form, like an anthropologist, she took to the South Bronx to immerse herself in hip-hop culture.

5. Some of these include Danielle Robinson, "Race in Motion: Reconstructing the Practice, Profession, and Politics of Social Dancing, New York City, 1900–1930" (PhD diss., University of California, Riverside, 2004); Carrie Stern, "Shall We Dance?: The Participant as Performer/Spectator in Ballroom Dancing" (PhD diss., New York University, 1998); as well as books originally written as dissertations, among them Juliet McMains, *Glamour Addiction: Inside the American Ballroom Dance Industry* (Middletown, CT: Wesleyan University Press, 2006); and Fiona Buckland, *Impossible Dance: Club Culture and Queer World-Making* (Middletown, CT: Wesleyan University Press, 2002).

6. See Helen Thomas, ed., *Dance in the City* (St. Martin's Press, 1997); Jane C. Desmond, ed, *Dancing Desires* (Madison: University of Wisconsin Press, 2001); and Thomas F. DeFrantz, ed., *Dancing Many Drums* (Madison: University of Wisconsin Press, 2002). Other important and influential anthologies containing essays on social and popular dance subjects include Lisa Doolittle and Anne Flynn's *Dancing Bodies and Living History: New Writings about Dance and Culture* (Banff, Alberta: Banff Centre Press, 2000);

Ann Dils and Ann Cooper Albright's *Moving History/Dancing Cultures: A Dance History Reader* (Middletown, CT: Wesleyan University Press, 2001); and Maureen Needham's *I See America Dancing: Selected Readings, 1685–Present* (Urbana: University of Illinois Press, 2002).

7. Some of these include Tricia Henry Young, *Break All Rules: Punk Rock and the Making of a Style* (Ann Arbor, MI: UMI Research Press, 1989); Barbara Browning, *Samba: Resistance in Motion* (Bloomington: Indiana University Press, 1995); Yvonne Daniel, *Rumba: Dance and Social Change in Contemporary Cuba* (Bloomington: Indiana University Press, 1995); Marta Savigliano, *Tango and the Political Economy of Passion* (Boulder, CO: Westview Press, 1995); Julie Taylor, *Paper Tangos* (Durham, NC: Duke University Press, 1998); and Linda Tomko, *Dancing Class: Gender, Ethnicity, and Social Divides in American Dance, 1890–1920* (Bloomington: Indiana University Press, 1999). See also McMains, *Glamour Addiction,* and Buckland, *Impossible Dance.*

8. Dance scholar Jane Desmond notes that "every dance exists in a complex network of relationships to other dances and other nondance ways of using the body. . . . Its meaning is situated both in the context of other socially prescribed and socially meaningful ways of moving and in the context of the history of dance forms in specific societies." See Jane Desmond, "Embodying Difference: Issues in Dance and Cultural Studies," in *Meaning in Motion: New Cultural Studies of Dance,* ed. Jane Desmond (Durham, NC: Duke University Press, 1997), 31. Desmond's groundbreaking anthology makes a cogent case for the inherent relationship between dance and cultural studies.

9. Andrew Ward, "Dancing around Meaning (and the Meaning around Dance)," in Helen Thomas, *Dance in the City,* 18.

10. Several scholars have discussed the status of dance studies and its development over the past twenty to thirty years. Although some argue that the field must adopt its own disciplinary methods and frameworks, others maintain that interdisciplinary approaches not only enhance the field but ensure its perceived legitimacy within the academy. On the other hand, Jane Desmond points out how fields such as cultural studies have been slow to incorporate the study of dance in their discussions of various forms of cultural expression. It could be argued, then, that dance scholars' insistence on interdisciplinary approaches might help make a case for the further inclusion of dance in these and other fields. See Jane Desmond, "Embodying Difference," in *Meaning in Motion,* 29–31. For further illumination of some of these debates, see Gay Morris's introduction in her anthology *Moving Words: Re-Writing Dance* (London: Routledge, 1996), 2–12; and Goellner and Murphy, "Introduction: Movement Movements," in *Bodies of the Text,* 1–18.

11. For another perspective on the distinctions between social, vernacular, and popular dance traditions, see Barbara Cohen-Stratyner, "Dialogues: Issues in Social and Vernacular Dance," in "Social and Popular Dance," special issue, *Dance Research Journal* 33, no. 2 (Winter 2001): 121–24.

12. Jacqui Malone, *Steppin' on the Blues: The Visible Rhythms of African American Dance* (Urbana: University of Illinois Press, 1996), 2.

13. Ibid.

14. LeeEllen Friedland, "Disco: Afro-American Vernacular Performance," *Dance Research Journal* 15, no. 2 (Spring 1983): 33.

15. For a distinction between folk and popular dance forms, see LeeEllen Friedland, "Dance: Popular and Folk Dance," in *The Encyclopedia of Religion,* chief ed. Mircea Eliade (New York: Macmillan, 1987). She notes, "Folk dance was believed to be a pure expression of national identity, whereas popular dance was a commodity in the mar-

ketplace of a heterogeneous, multicultural society" (215). For a discussion of some of the distinctions between folk and vernacular dance, see Susan Spalding, *Communities in Motion: Dance, Community, and Tradition in America's Southeast and Beyond* (Westport, CT: Greenwood Press, 1995), 2.

16. Media theorist Sarah Thornton also discusses how those cultural forms and practices that become popular do so also as a result of issues of taste; they may become "approved" or "preferred" by segments of society. See Sarah Thornton, *Club Cultures: Music, Media and Subcultural Capital* (Middletown, CT: Wesleyan University Press, 1996), 164.

17. Tomko, *Dancing Class*, 27. For more on the performer-audience relationship in ballroom dance, see Stern, "Shall We Dance," 16–17, 74–5.

18. Angela McRobbie, "Dance Narratives and Fantasies of Achievement," in *Meaning in Motion*, 211.

19. Brenda Dixon Gottschild, *Digging the Africanist Presence in American Performance: Dance and Other Contexts* (Westport, CT: Greenwood Press), 23.

20. Wole Soyinka, "Theatre in African Traditional Cultures: Survival Patterns," in *The Twentieth-Century Performance Reader*, ed. Michael Huxley and Noel Witts (London: Routledge, 1996), 342. Previously published in *Art, Dialogue and Outrage*, ed. B. Jeyifo (London: Methuen, 1982).

21. Iain Chambers, *Urban Rhythms: Pop Music and Popular Culture* (New York: St. Martin's Press, 1985), 17.

22. In their respective chapters, Sally R. Sommer and Tim Lawrence maintain slightly different slants on the definition and trajectory of house dance. Please see their notes for further clarification of these distinctions.

23. Marcia B. Siegel, *The Shapes of Change: Images of American Dance* (New York: Avon, 1979), 3.

Section 1

Historical
Precedents

1

Our
National Poetry

The Afro-Chesapeake
Inventions of
American Dance

Jurretta Jordan Heckscher

Dance and body movement are an African contribution of profound, if almost entirely hidden, importance to American cultural identity. Because dance is difficult to describe, it is elusive in the historical record. Its deeper cultural implications are even harder to trace, for dancing cannot be separated from the larger web of a culture's movement system—the way people within that culture move, which is as characteristic and culturally specific as the way they speak, and far more difficult to document. Yet if we are to begin to understand American vernacular dance and movement, we must come to terms with its Africanity and, in particular, with what happened between about 1700 and 1865 in the region embracing Virginia, Maryland, the District of Columbia, and much of North Carolina that might be called the Greater Chesapeake. For that area witnessed the earliest, most extensive, and arguably most influential black-white cultural interchange on the North American continent, and out of that interchange came a powerfully Africanized tradition of dance and movement that informs American bodily expression to this day.[1]

North American slavery flourished first in the Chesapeake, and abundant evidence demonstrates dancing's great importance to the enslaved throughout the decades of captivity. "[W]hen I was a girl guess I'd ruther dance than eat," recalled Sally Ashton of her antebellum girlhood; whereas James Campbell, like many others, remembered dancing "long as de can'les lasted" nearly every Saturday night.[2] White observers wrote that "the Negroes have a mania" for dancing and that dance skill was an "indispensable acquirement" of black youth.[3] Identical observations were made of Chesapeake whites, especially the slaveholding elite. In the early eighteenth century, William Byrd boasted that his year-old daughter could dance before she could walk and wrote of the "old women" at Williamsburg balls, reflecting a culture in which dancing was a lifelong preoccupation.[4] "If a man can dance he is with [Virginians] a damn'd fine fellow," observed one British immigrant in the 1760s; ". . . it is the principal characteristic of a fine gentleman . . . [t]he first knowledge they acquire, and the last that forsakes them."[5] To the close of the Civil War, others documented the importance of multigenerational dance events with "large crowds" that lasted "until the roosters crowed in the morning."[6]

In neither community, moreover, was the evangelical tide that flowed strong from the mid-eighteenth century and transformed culture in the nineteenth sufficient to quench the love of dancing, however it might dampen it. Enslaved African Americans opened their homes to dances and prayer meetings alike and made the ring shout the unacknowledged vessel of dance and worship together; in the 1830s, pious whites held "Baptist dancing parties" at which "they danced nearly all night."[7] Dancing was also the locus of mutual exchange between African and European cultures and an instrument and expression of cultural transformation. And because the Greater Chesapeake was the major source area for the vast migration to the Deep South between the Revolutionary War and the Civil War, the region's cross-fertilization of African and European dance traditions helped shape a distinctive set of Southern and ultimately American bodily and movement identities in ways that went largely unacknowledged at the time and have been unrecognized since. To these identities, Africans and African Americans made a definitive contribution.

Fortunately for historians, in most obvious respects elite white dance in the Greater Chesapeake remained part of an extensively documented European tradition. Visitors from beyond the region between 1700 and 1865 typically found familiar forms: the minuet, the reel, assorted country dances, the quadrille, the lancers, the waltz, and the polka, among others.[8] Such dance forms were broadly characterized by linearity and geometric regularity, vertical physicality, and the balance and symmetry of complements: floor patterns in parallel lines, serpentine lines, diagonals, rectangles, squares, and circles; a strongly vertical disposition of the body enacted in an upright torso moving as a unit from shoulders to hips, its upward line broken only occasionally and unemphatically at the waist, the verticality reinforced also by buoyant footwork and a range of limb movement close to the vertical axis; and a constant, insistent exploitation of both terms of the complementary and symmetrical pairings of left and right, forward and back, and—underlying all—male and female.[9]

The corresponding black tradition is far more elusive. It is all but certain, however, that except on a limited local basis, the captive Africans who poured into the Chesapeake from the late seventeenth to the late eighteenth century could not have danced together simply by re-creating a single shared tradition. Most historians believe that no single African ethnicity defined black Chesapeake culture; instead, slaves came from numerous societies in several African regions.[10] Yet there is abundant reason to suppose that dancing was a significant phenomenon in most, if not all, of their native lands. "We are almost a nation of dancers," Olaudah Equiano remembered—or remembered being told—of his ancestral Igbo homeland, and "every great event . . . is celebrated in public dances."[11] He could have been speaking for most West and Central Africans, for whom dance also marked the great passages in the individual life cycle, serving as symbol and instrument of morally legitimate community and shaping the enactment of socially integrated personhood.[12]

With such a heritage, the need to order personal and communal life through dancing would surely have persisted even—or perhaps especially—within the trauma and upheaval of enslavement. Given their cultural heterogeneity, Africans in the Greater Chesapeake most likely learned to dance together by drawing on the "grammar of culture" shared across much of West and Central Africa: the common set of deep structural principles that relate cultural forms in different ethnic groups to each other and explain their "underlying similarities."[13] Like the grammar that orders a language, these principles almost certainly provided slaves from many African nations with a common generative foundation on which to order their creolized African American cultural systems, including movement and dance. Out of such African commonalities, perhaps not long before the eighteenth century had become the nineteenth, they built something like a regional Chesapeake tradition, something that the African Americans who were by then the dancers recognized as their parents' way of dancing, and therefore their own.

The result was a thing entirely novel in European eyes. In Maryland in 1774, a young Englishman struggled to find words for the "Negro Ball" he

witnessed: "Their Dancing is most violent exercise, but so irregular and grotesque. I am not able to describe it." A decade later, a Virginia traveler noted
that each participant at an all-night "negroe dance" typically "performs
with astonishing agility, and the most vigorous exertions, keeping time and
cadence, most exactly . . . until he exhausts himself."[14] Such fragmentary
evidence, almost entirely filtered through uncomprehending white eyes,
nevertheless suggests basic qualities of eighteenth-century black dance: an-
gularity and asymmetry, rhythmic precision, long duration, physical virtuosity, and dynamic intensity.[15]

What was wrought by Africans and their children in the early Chesapeake,
as in the kindred dance traditions simultaneously created by other peoples
of African descent throughout the Americas, was a primary creolization that
undergirds much of the subsequent development of American vernacular
dance: the creation of a new choreographic tradition out of disparate African
ancestral lineages. It was the first of three creolizing processes that shaped the
region's—and much of the nation's—vernacular dance heritage. And because
it arose from conditions unique to the Western Hemisphere, it was surely in
the broadest sense among the first distinctively American forms of art.

Within one or two generations of establishing a dance culture in the
eighteenth century, and possibly almost simultaneously with that achievement, Chesapeake slaves had gradually begun to reinvent their African dance
heritage through creative adaptation of the dances of their oppressors. In so
doing, they began to effect the second fundamental creolization that guided
the creation of a continental North American dance identity, gradually fash-
ioning a mature and immensely influential African American tradition that
reached its zenith between approximately 1800 and 1865. Fortunately, that
tradition is far better documented than its eighteenth-century antecedents,
and much of the record comes from African Americans themselves.

Such evidence leaves no doubt that black dancing continued to be generated by an African movement grammar in definitive ways. Even some of the
elements that mirrored European practices were at least as likely to have represented continuations or revivifications of African movement preferences as
the adoption of white norms. Thus, if, as the limited pictorial record suggests,
the typical African practice of bending the torso emphatically at the waist
and hips gave way by the nineteenth century to a general preference for a
straighter and more upright spine, such verticality may well have been less a
European-influenced innovation than an inflection of the African movement
preference for the strong, balancing spine that enabled enslaved women in
the Greater Chesapeake to carry heavy loads on their heads like their African

foremothers and enslaved dancers to make balancing a glass of water on the head a powerful motif of contest and virtuosic accomplishment.[16]

Other formative elements of the nineteenth-century tradition were unmistakably African. They included a strong preference for angular and asymmetrical dispositions of the body, enabling the dancer to emphasize the independence of different body parts and thereby serve the articulation of simultaneous multiple body rhythms—polyrhythms—in the African mode; the carriage of the body's center of gravity low, in the hips and pelvis, rather than high in the abdomen and solar plexus as in European classical dance, a practice that loosened the waist to mediate contrasting rhythmic impulses in the upper and lower torso; the extensive use of certain spatial formations with clear African antecedents, such as a ring encircling a soloist, or the "apart dancing" of two dancers paired without touching as they relate playfully to each other and to the same rhythmic impulses; abundant scope for competitive individuality and improvisation; and a dynamic intensity and inventive range embracing movements "of every imaginable description" from lavish "contortions, flings, kicks, gyrations" and leaps to exquisitely subtle articulations of the muscles of the face.[17]

In its seamless integration with music, too, this tradition, like so many others from African wellsprings, made music and dance "conceptually inseparable," perhaps most obviously in the rhythmic slapping of the body known as "patting juba," which was both a form of music and a form of dance and may have been other dancing's most frequent accompaniment.[18] The core of the Afro-Chesapeake dance/music complex was virtuosic rhythmic exactitude, rhythm's emphatic articulation in the motions of the body and the sounds of the feet, whose intricate diversity of motion—from smooth "shuffles" to percussive "toe-and-heelings"—already manifested the range that came to characterize the jazz-tap tradition. The visual uniformity of European dance was unnecessary, for with "everyone [moving] after his or her own fashion, but keeping time to the beat," rhythm itself was the unifying force field even amid the individualities of improvisation. By shaping each movement with the vital beat, black dancers in the Chesapeake carried forward a fundamental African contribution to American vernacular dance.[19] Yet at some point between the time when Africans in the Greater Chesapeake first began to dance together and the time when their descendants' dancing is extensively documented in the first part of the nineteenth century, something fundamental also changed in black dance practice—and this change was of immense historical importance, for it involved the creolization of European and African forms.

Momentous shifts in human culture can sometimes be marked in small things. Something as slight as the shift to dancing frequently on the balls of the feet may have indexed the grafting of European elements onto African dance, for no such footwork surfaces in the scant records remaining of African dancing in the seventeenth and eighteenth centuries, nor is it characteristic of traditional dance today in areas of Africa from which most Chesapeake slaves came. Yet both the pictorial and the written record document its prevalence in the nineteenth century.[20] Like the use of upright posture, elevated footwork may have been adopted from white dance forms. What is indisputable is that other elements fundamental to the antebellum black dance tradition were indeed adopted from European practices: a range of set-dance forms that became standard at black dance events and male-female partnering in which the partners often touched (figure 1.1).

The most significant of these incorporations, both because it represented a fundamental break with African traditions and because the integration of white set-dance forms depended on it, was the practice of heterosexual partnering: the adoption of the male-female dyad as the normative, though certainly never the exclusive, structural unit of dance. It is difficult to establish when such partnering became a standard practice, though that had clearly happened at least by the late 1820s and early 1830s.[21] The earliest evidence for it, however, is the historically pivotal dance form that can best be designated the Virginia jig.[22]

At some point no later than the mid-eighteenth century, black people in the Greater Chesapeake invented a dance type that set a succession of male-female couples in physically demanding encounters within a circle of participant onlookers. The partners danced responsively, face to face, but without touching; their movement choices apparently required a degree of improvisation; and whether between partners or in the succession of performers, there were unmistakable elements of flamboyant exhibition and contest. This was the Virginia jig, and the evidence suggests that it continued to be a staple of the black dance repertoire for the better part of a century.[23]

Structurally and historically, the Virginia jig is clearly related to a whole family of dances originally fashioned by peoples of African descent that achieved broad popularity throughout Latin America, the Caribbean, and Louisiana, including the chica—the name of which may possibly have been corrupted into the familiar English word "jig"—and the major Latin American dance category that John Charles Chasteen calls simply "the dance-of-two."[24] The Virginia jig was the northernmost example of a choreographic phenomenon that spanned much of the Western Hemisphere. Yet in British

Figure 1.1: The oil painting *Kitchen Ball at White Sulpher Springs, Virginia,* by Christian Mayr, 1838. African Americans, dancing in the service area at an elite resort, display the mature creolized forms that marked black dance in the region by the antebellum era. Courtesy of the North Carolina Museum of Art, Raleigh.

North America, as its name suggests, it was identified primarily with the Greater Chesapeake, the North American slave society where black-white interaction was earlier, more thorough, and more habitual than in any other. In a dance emblematic of Chesapeake creolization, the African contributions are perhaps most obvious. They include the competitive element, the use of improvisation, apart dancing, the integral participation of an encircling company, the dance's typically long duration, and the texture of the steps and gestures, leading white observers from outside the region to term them "irregular," "eccentric," or "grotesque."[25] Yet in one profoundly important sense, the Virginia jig developed by first- and second-generation Africans in the Chesapeake was irreducibly European; it brought individual men and women together as partners whose stylized coupling was the literal center and subject of the dance.

It is difficult for us to imagine what a radical departure from African tradition this almost certainly was. Though men and women sometimes danced together in parallel group formations, in all the vast riches of the sub-Saharan African dance heritage there seems to be no evidence for sustained one-on-one male-female partner dancing anywhere before the late colonial era—and even then, it was apparently often regarded as a European peculiarity in distinctly poor taste.[26] By placing a man and a woman together against this background, the Virginia jig may well have been the earliest North American black dance form to incorporate a striking innovation that has since become a hallmark of all African American dance.

Why might black dancers in the Chesapeake have chosen to depart so radically from their ancestral heritage? Perhaps because dance events there were what the anthropologist Victor Turner calls "dominant genres of cultural performance," enabling those who danced or witnessed dancing to imagine and reimagine certain vital dimensions of a shared identity in vividly important ways.[27] It seems highly probable that the Virginia jig provided both a means of acknowledging and reimagining the provocative presence of European dance forms in the new American milieu and a means of expressing perhaps the greatest change in social ideals that marked the transition from Africa to America: the passage from a polygynous to a monogamous paradigm of marriage that had taken place by the late eighteenth century.

Consider that the vast majority of sub-Saharan African societies held to an ideal of polygyny, which not all could achieve but to which all might aspire.[28] Yet in the Greater Chesapeake, as throughout the South, for reasons that historians have only partially unraveled and that surely bore some unfathomably complex relation to the white example, the monogamy initially enforced by sexual imbalances quickly became neither a demographic necessity nor the white man's imposition but an inherently black ideal.[29] Centrally coupled choreographies may well have offered a concrete way of imaging and playfully honoring those bonds of monogamous love that came often to be forged so strong that they endured through decades of separation.[30]

African Americans continued to dance the Virginia jig well into the nineteenth century, by which time heterosexual partnering pervaded their dancing, and they had thoroughly absorbed and incorporated many white dance types: solo jigs and hornpipes, and couple dances such as reels, waltzes, and the broad genres identified simply as "country dances" and "square dances," among others.[31] The couple dances required the partners to touch; the later ones even set them in stylized embrace. The innovations of the Virginia jig, and the choreographic and cultural transformations they announced, became integral to black dance.

Beginning in the crucible of the eighteenth century, then, and continuing into mature form in the nineteenth, African American dance in the Greater Chesapeake—like a number of other black dance traditions developed contemporaneously elsewhere in the Americas—came to exemplify something truly new in the history of human culture: a genuine creolization of African and European expressive movement systems. "Sech a dancin' you never seed befo'," Nancy Williams said of the dancing she remembered from her youth in antebellum Virginia, and she was correct in ways she herself probably did not recognize.[32] Yet the new dance tradition, the outcome of the second momentous process of creolization, reframed without obliterating the fundamental Africanity that was the dancers' ancestral heritage. One can more easily identify the European elements in nineteenth-century Greater Chesapeake black dance—extensive and focal heterosexual partnering, specific dance types, the footwork stylings and perhaps the postures that sustained them—than the African, because the latter are both more pervasive and more subtle, involving values and processes—such as improvisation, the centrality of rhythm, dynamic intensity, and competitive individuality—no less than form. What is European has been added without obscuring or diminishing what is African, which persists like the generative rhythm at the dance's core.

The Virginia jig is vital evidence of yet a third process of creolization that came to define the Chesapeake's dance traditions. By the middle of the eighteenth century—perhaps not long after Africans and African Americans had created it—this seminal black dance type had been equally widely adopted by elite whites, to the bemusement and consternation of visiting Europeans. "Towards the close of an evening," wrote an Englishman visiting Virginia in 1759, "when the company are pretty well tired with country dances, it is usual to dance jiggs; a practice originally borrowed, I am informed, from the Negroes." He went on to describe the Virginia jig.[33] For several decades between the middle of the eighteenth century and the early years of the nineteenth, Virginia jigs were frequently the culmination of major elite dance events in the Chesapeake, serving as a decisive departure from the minuets, reels, and country dances that preceded them and as an irresistible invitation into a more lavish realm of play. In Richmond around 1800, the sequence of forms on great occasions was invariable: "The ball was opened . . . with a *minuet de la Cour*. . . . Then commenced the reel. . . . Contra dances followed, and sometimes a congo, or a hornpipe; and when 'the music grew fast and furious,' and the most stately of the company had retired, a jig would wind up the evening."[34]

As the reference to the "congo" suggests, the Virginia jig was evidently not the only elite dance type adopted from the black repertoire. The middle of the eighteenth century saw references to "congo minuets," while the dance called simply the Congo is mentioned repeatedly in accounts of elite dance events in Richmond around the turn of the nineteenth century. Documents from the same period refer to members of the elite dancing the "pigeon wing," which emerged as a favorite dance step or type in the black community and almost certainly originated there.[35] From at least the mid-eighteenth century to the first decade or so of the nineteenth, then, the slaveholding elite habitually danced in ways that they themselves acknowledged had been invented by those they enslaved.

And then, gradually but unmistakably, they entirely ceased to do so. One looks in vain after the 1820s for any aspect of wealthy whites' dance that they were willing to attribute to the black aesthetic. It may not be coincidence that black forms disappeared from the white repertoire at precisely the time when white identity in the Chesapeake and elsewhere came to be tied explicitly to the emerging ideology of race.[36] Dance remained central to elite culture at least until the Civil War, but the evolving rationalization and increasing ossification of racism and racial categories may well have rendered obvious African American elements an impermissibly dangerous form of imaginative play.

The apparent disappearance of black forms signified less than white people may have wished to believe, however, for there can be little doubt that the powerful influence of black dance culture persisted at the roots of white movement expression, underground and unacknowledged both then and now. What other conclusion can one draw from the undeniable fact that elite white Chesapeake dancing until the Civil War was almost invariably shaped by the artistry of black fiddlers, whose music was overwhelmingly preferred to that of white? Such men (and they were always men) often played for both black and white dance events, and what made their music uniquely desirable to white dancers was surely its African and African American nuances.[37] The Chesapeake gentry may not have acknowledged the degree to which their dancing depended on black musicians who knew music and dancing as a single whole, but the cultural historian is under no such disability. In dance, the antebellum elite could exult bodily in a thoroughly creolized identity that their racist self-image required that their minds suppress.

The influence of black movement culture on the dance and kinetic identity at the heart of much white culture was also decisively shaped by the enslaved nurses or "mammies" who were the primary caretakers of white infants and small children in wealthier households and by the enslaved playmates, the children of household and agricultural workers, who surrounded, constantly interacted with, and almost invariably outnumbered the sons and daughters of the gentry throughout their childhoods in the plantation milieu. When a young mother from New York fretted that her North Carolinian daughter was learning "things I do not like" from "[t]he little negroes," because "[i]f she sees one of them kicking up her heels, up hers must go too. She imitates everything and every body"; when a New Englander complained that it was slave women who "molded" white children in Virginia; when Frederick Law Olmsted expressed astonishment at "negro women . . . carrying black and white babies together in their arms; black and white children . . . playing together"; they were unwittingly identifying something fundamental about the influence of black culture on the white self, in bodily habits of being no less than in habits of mind.[38]

By "molding" them as surrogate mothers in their formative years, by dancing and playing with them in childhood, by making the music that defined and guided their most cherished form of collective expression, the enslaved people of the Greater Chesapeake in the end created for their white masters a distinctive creolized kinetic identity profoundly influenced by the African American cultural system of movement and dance. The result was that by the antebellum era, members of the white elite could seem as utterly alien to their Northern peers as any foreigner. When Ellen Randolph Coolidge, nurtured by an enslaved "mammy" in Virginia, moved to Boston as a bride in 1825, paralyzing self-consciousness engulfed her: "I fear it will take me a long time to get reconciled to the habits and customs of my new country-men. I move like one who is fettered in every limb. The perpetual fear of violating some established rule, of sinning against the laws of propriety as they are understood here, hangs like a dark cloud over me . . . and yet I do my best to bring myself within the pale of pro-priety. I weigh every word before I utter it, curb every sally of imagination, regulate my very countenance, and try to look, speak walk, and sit just as I ought to do."[39]

If such mutual alienation existed between the conventions of movement identity in the cultures of the Yankee and Chesapeake elites, if the latter were indeed to their Northern kin as an incomprehensibly foreign tribe, it becomes not only possible but necessary to ask whether this estrangement at the most elemental levels of self and culture made it easier for each to see the other not only as alien but ultimately as enemy. If that be so, it could also be said that the slaves' cultural influence on the master class through movement and dance ironically helped lay the groundwork for the cleansing cataclysm that liberated them at last from slavery. For the moment, at least, such reflections must necessarily remain speculative. But if the influence of black movement culture on white dance, movement, and cultural identity in the Greater Chesapeake is both certain and elusive, its part in the broader streams of American culture is easier to trace.

By the end of the eighteenth century, African Americans in the Greater Chesapeake were caught up in a diaspora scarcely less brutal than the Middle Passage. By the eve of the Civil War, almost 69 percent of the interstate slave trade's more than 1 million victims had come directly from the Greater Chesapeake, and many others from states such as Kentucky or Tennessee whose African American populations were largely of Chesapeake heritage.[40] The result, as one former slave noted bitterly, is that "Virginia was the mother of slavery."[41] Yet it was the domestic slave trade that made the Greater Chesapeake a fountainhead of African American culture. "The greater portion of our national poetry originates in Virginia, or among involuntary Virginia emigrants," declared J. Kinnard in 1845, because "[e]very year thousands are sent to the far south and southwest for sale. The Virginian type of negro character therefore has come to prevail throughout the slave states, with the exception of some portions of Louisiana and Florida. Thus everywhere you may hear much the same songs and tunes, and see the same dances, with little variety, and no radical difference."[42] Dance practices formed in the Greater Chesapeake rode the currents of black migration through the South in the nineteenth century and from the South throughout the nation in the twentieth, becoming thereby a heritage for all African American dancing.

And for more than a century, the history of American vernacular dance has been the history of the ascendant black tradition. From the white vogue for the Cakewalk around 1900 to the rock 'n' roll revolution and all the forms it has generated, the dancing of African Americans has become the dance vernacular of nearly all Americans, tracing a trajectory of cultural domination that has revolutionized human movement and cultural identity.[43] Dance and its related systems of body movement are not only one of Africa's great legacies to America, they are also a legacy to humanity, for mass media and cultural globalization have made American dance the world's.

Notes

1. For the "Greater Chesapeake" and its significance as a culture hearth, see Jurretta Jordan Heckscher, "'All the Mazes of the Dance': Black Dancing, Culture, and Identity in the Greater Chesapeake World from the Early Eighteenth Century to the Civil War" (PhD diss., George Washington University, 2000), chapter 1 and afterword. For dance as part of a culture's movement system, see Ray L. Birdwhistell, *Kinesics and Context: Essays on Body Motion Communication* (Philadelphia: University of Pennsylvania Press, 1970), 107–8; Alfred Gell, "Style and Meaning in Umeda Dance," in *Society and the Dance: The Social Anthropology of Process and Performance*, ed. Paul Spencer (Cambridge: Cambridge University Press, 1985), 203–4; Adrienne L. Kaeppler, "Structured Movement Systems in Tonga," in *Society and the Dance*, 92–94; Joann Marie Wheeler Kealiinohomoku, "Theory and Methods for an Anthropological Study of Dance" (PhD diss., Indiana University, 1976), 160–62; and Gertrude Prokosch Kurath, "Panorama of Dance Ethnology," *Current Anthropology* 1, no. 3 (May 1960): 234–35.

2. Sally Ashton, interview in Charles L. Perdue Jr., Thomas E. Barden, and Robert K. Phillips, eds., *Weevils in the Wheat: Interviews with Virginia Ex-Slaves* (Charlottesville: University Press of Virginia, 1976), 14; James Campbell, interview in George P. Rawick, ed., *The American Slave: A Composite Autobiography*, series 2, vol. 16, *Kansas, Kentucky, Maryland, Ohio, Virginia, and Tennessee Narratives* (Westport, CT: Greenwood, 1972), Ohio section, 20.

3. Médéric-Louis-Élie Moreau de St. Méry, *Moreau de St. Méry's American Journey [1793–1798]*, trans. and ed. Kenneth Roberts and Anna M. Roberts (Garden City, NY: Doubleday, 1947), 60; "Letter from Newbern," *The Liberator*, December 12, 1862.

4. William Byrd II to Charles Boyle, Earl of Orrery, February 5, 1727/8, in Marion Tinling, ed., *The Correspondence of the Three William Byrds of Westover, Virginia, 1684–1776* (Charlottesville: University Press of Virginia for the Virginia Historical Society, 1977), 1:370; William Byrd II to Jane Pratt Taylor, October 10, 1735, in *The Correspondence of the Three William Byrds of Westover, Virginia, 1684–1776*, 2:462.

5. James Reid, "The Religion of the Bible and the Religion of K[ing] W[illiam] County Compared," in "The Colonial Virginia Satirist: Mid-Eighteenth-Century Commentaries on Politics, Religion, and Society," ed. Richard Beale Davis, special issue, *Transactions of the American Philosophical Society*, New Series, 57, Part 1 (March 1967): 57.

6. C. A. Bryce, "Dusky 'Fiddlers' of Olden Days Tenderly Recalled by Writer," *Richmond Times-Dispatch*, May 22, 1921, sec. 2, 5.

7. Nelson Stewart, interview in Rawick, *The American Slave*, series 1, vol. 11, *North Carolina and South Carolina Narratives* (Westport, CT: Greenwood Press, 1977), 49; John Dixon Long, *Pictures of Slavery in Church and State* (Philadelphia: the Author, 1857), 383–84; C. C. Coffin, "The First Day of Freedom," *Watchman and Reflector*, n.d., reprinted in *National Anti-Slavery Standard*, August 13, 1864, 4; Jesse F[rayser] Clarke to Augustus Clarke, December 31, 1838, Clarke Family Papers, Virginia Historical Society.

8. Among many examples: Philip Vickers Fithian, *Journal and Letters of Philip Vickers Fithian, 1773–1774: A Plantation Tutor of the Old Dominion*, ed. Hunter Dickinson Farish (Charlottesville: University Press of Virginia, 1968), 56–57; James Battle Avirett, *The Old Plantation: How We Lived in Great House and Cabin before the War* (New York: F. Tennyson Neely, 1901), 98; Mrs. Roger A. Pryor [Sarah Agnes Rice Pryor], *My Day: Reminiscences of a Long Life* (New York: Macmillan, 1909), 187–88.

9. This European and European American dance tradition is extensively documented

in the Library of Congress online collection "An American Ballroom Companion: Dance Instruction Manuals, ca. 1490–1920," available at http://memory.loc.gov/ammem/dihtml/dihome.html.

10. For a good recent summary of what is currently a dynamic area of research, see Lorena S. Walsh, "The Transatlantic Slave Trade and Colonial Chesapeake Slavery," *OAH Magazine of History* 17, no. 3 (April 2003): 11–15.

11. Olaudah Equiano, *The Interesting Narrative of the Life of Olaudah Equiano, Written by Himself*, ed. Robert J. Allison (Boston: Bedford Books, 1995), 36. For newly discovered evidence that Equiano was not himself born in Africa, see Vincent Carretta, *Equiano, the African: Biography of a Self-Made Man* (Athens: University of Georgia Press, 2005), xiv, 80, 146–49.

12. Heckscher, "'All the Mazes of the Dance,'" 28–34.

13. For the African grammar of culture, see Melville J. Herskovits, *The Myth of the Negro Past* (Boston: Beacon Press, 1941), 61–85, 294–96, quotations on 81 and 85.

14. Nicholas Cresswell, *The Journal of Nicholas Cresswell, 1774–1777* (New York: Lincoln MacVeagh/The Dial Press, 1924), 18–19; J. F. D. Smyth, *A Tour in the United States of America* (Dublin: G. Perrin, 1784), 1:27–28.

15. Heckscher, "'All the Mazes of the Dance,'" 72–95.

16. The pictorial record includes Christian Mayr, *Kitchen Ball at White Sulphur Springs, Virginia*, 1838 (North Carolina Museum of Art, Raleigh); Lewis Miller, *Lynchburg—Negro Dance, August 18th, 1853* (Abby Aldrich Rockefeller Folk Art Center, Williamsburg, VA); A. W. Thompson, "Registration at the South—Scene at Asheville, North Carolina," *Harper's Weekly*, September 28, 1867, 621; and Eastman Johnson, *Negro Life at the South*, 1859 (The New-York Historical Society, New York, NY), which depicts a scene in Washington, DC. For the straight, balancing spine in West African movement and dance, see, for example, Peggy Harper, "Dance in Nigeria," *Ethnomusicology* 13 (1969): 288–89. Numerous images depict black women in the early Chesapeake carrying loads on their heads; see, for example, the woodcut by an unidentified artist, possibly Alexander Anderson, *Life in Eastern Virginia: The Home of the Planter*, probably 1840s, Museum Folder "African American Engravings," Library of the Virginia Historical Society. For dances balancing water on the head, see, for example, Fannie Berry, interview in Perdue, Barden, and Phillips, *Weevils in the Wheat*, 50; and Nancy Williams, interview in Perdue, Barden, and Phillips, *Weevils in the Wheat*, 316.

17. Heckscher, "'All the Mazes of the Dance,'" 179–213; quotations, Edward Warren, *A Doctor's Experiences on Three Continents* (Baltimore: Cushings and Bailey, 1885), 202. For apart dancing, see Robert Farris Thompson, "An Aesthetic of the Cool: West African Dance," *African Forum* 2 (Fall 1966): 94; for polyrhythm in earlier African dance, see Heckscher, "'All the Mazes of the Dance,'" 41–43.

18. Alan P. Merriam, *African Music in Perspective* (New York: Garland, 1982), 110. On patting juba, see Heckscher, "'All the Mazes of the Dance,'" 169–77. Robert Farris Thompson persuasively argues that patting juba derives directly from the Kongo *Zuba* in *Tango: The Art History of Love* (New York: Pantheon Books, 2005), 64–65.

19. Heckscher, "'All the Mazes of the Dance,'" 138–43, 199–204; quotations, "Letter from Newbern," *The Liberator*, December 12, 1862; James Hungerford, *The Old Plantation, and What I Gathered There in an Autumn Month* (New York: Harper and Brothers, 1859), 196.

20. The pictorial record includes Mayr, *Kitchen Ball*; Miller, *Lynchburg—Negro Dance*; and Thompson, "Registration"; the written record includes the sources cited in Heckscher, "'All the Mazes of the Dance,'" 202–4.

21. Jacob D. Green, *Narrative of the Life of J. D. Green, a Runaway Slave* (Huddersfield,

England: Henry Fielding, 1864), 11–12; [Fields Cook], "Fields's Observations: The Slave Narrative of a Nineteenth-Century Virginian," ed. Mary J. Bratton, *Virginia Magazine of History and Biography* 88 (1980): 82; William B. Smith, "The Persimmon Tree and the Beer Dance," *Farmer's Register* 6 (April 1838), reprinted in *The Negro and His Folklore in Nineteenth-Century Periodicals,* ed. Bruce Jackson (Austin: University of Texas Press, 1967), 5.

22. It is so named by "Dick the negro" in John Davis, *Travels of Four Years and a Half in the United States of America* (Bristol, England: R. Edwards, 1803), 380; and by Luigi Castiglioni, *Luigi Castiglioni's Viaggio = Travels in the United States of North America, 1785–87,* trans. and ed. Antonio Pace (Syracuse, NY: Syracuse University Press, 1983), 196, 304 n. 51, among others. Also known as the Negro jig or simply the jig, it should not be confused with the generic solo dance type called the jig inherited from the British Isles that was also perpetuated by both blacks and whites in the Greater Chesapeake throughout the era of slavery.

23. John Bernard, *Retrospections of America, 1797–1811,* ed. Mrs. Bayle Bernard (New York: Harper and Brothers, 1887), 208–9; Andrew Burnaby, *Travels through the Middle Settlements in North-America,* 2nd ed. (London: T. Payne, 1775), 21–22; Green, *Narrative of the Life of J. D. Green,* 12; Hungerford, *The Old Plantation,* 195, 198–99; [John Pendleton Kennedy], *Swallow Barn, or A Sojourn in the Old Dominion* (Philadelphia: Carey and Lea, 1832), 1:113; John Williamson Palmer, "Old Maryland Homes and Ways," *Century Magazine* 49 (December 1894): 260; Henry W. Ravenel, "Recollections of Southern Plantation Life," *Yale Review* 25 (1936): 768 (though set in South Carolina, this account unquestionably depicts the Virginia jig); and Smith, "The Persimmon Tree," 5–9.

24. For similar dance forms in the Caribbean and Louisiana, see the material compiled in Lynne Fauley Emery, *Black Dance from 1619 to Today,* 2nd ed. (Princeton, NJ: Princeton Book, 1988), 15–29, 147–49, 154–66, 172–73; for the dance-of-two in Latin America, see John Charles Chasteen, *National Rhythms, African Roots: The Deep History of Latin American Popular Dance* (Albuquerque: University of New Mexico Press, 2004), passim.

25. For the three terms quoted, see the passages from Burnaby, Bernard, and Ravenel cited in note 23.

26. Léopold Sédar Senghor, "African-Negro Aesthetics," *Diogenes* 16 (Winter 1956): 33, quoted in Marshall Stearns and Jean Stearns, *Jazz Dance: The Story of American Vernacular Dance* (New York: Schirmer, 1968), 12; Gertrude Prokosch Kurath and Nadia Chilkovsky, "Jazz Choreology," in *Mother Wit from the Laughing Barrel: Readings in the Interpretation of Afro-American Folklore,* ed. Alan Dundes (Englewood Cliffs, NJ: Prentice-Hall, 1973), 107; and Herskovits, *The Myth of the Negro Past,* 271. The apparent absence of sustained one-on-one couple partnering in precolonial Africa merits ongoing research, bearing in mind the very few sources that are ever likely to come to light.

27. Victor Turner, *The Anthropology of Performance* (New York: PAJ, 1987), 21 (the term is originally Milton Singer's).

28. It was recently estimated that 98 percent of African societies still hold a polygynous ideal, although because of economic and other constraints, polygyny rates of only 25 to 30 percent are typically realized; James H. Vaughan, "Population and Social Organization," in *Africa,* ed. Phyllis M. Martin and Patrick O'Meara, 2nd ed. (Bloomington: Indiana University Press, 1986), 166.

29. The scholarship that established the strength of the monogamous family ideal under slavery is Herbert G. Gutman, *The Black Family in Slavery and Freedom, 1750–1925* (New York: Vintage Books, 1976).

30. For a fuller exploration of this transition and its manifestations in dance, see Heckscher, "'All the Mazes of the Dance,'" 325–35.

31. For example, Charles H. Anderson, interview in Rawick, *The American Slave*, series 2, vol. 16 (Ohio), 3; Fannie Berry, interview in Perdue, Barden, and Phillips, *Weevils in the Wheat*, 36; Lucy Chase to "Dear Ones at Home," September 30, 1863, in Lucy Chase and Sarah Chase, *Dear Ones at Home: Letters from Contraband Camps*, ed. Henry L. Swint (Nashville, TN: Vanderbilt University Press, 1966), 89–90; Daniel Webster Davis, "Echoes from a Plantation Party," *The Southern Workman and Hampton School Record* 28 (1899): 56; and Matilda Henrietta Perry, interview in Perdue, Barden, and Phillips, *Weevils in the Wheat*, 225–26. For the broader context and significance of such adaptations by black dancers throughout the Americas, see John F. Szwed and Morton Marks, "The Afro-American Transformation of European Set Dances and Dance Suites," *Dance Research Journal* 20, no. 1 (Summer 1988): 29–36.

32. Nancy Williams, interview in Perdue, Barden, and Phillips, *Weevils in the Wheat*, 318.

33. Burnaby, *Travels through the Middle Settlements*, 21.

34. [Samuel Mordecai], *Richmond in By-Gone Days; Being Reminiscences of an Old Citizen* (Richmond, VA: George M. West, 1856), 179–80.

35. Davis, *Travels of Four Years and a Half*, 380; [Mordecai], *Richmond in By-Gone Days*, 35, 179–80; Benjamin Howard to David Watson, January 30, 1799, in Joseph Shelton Watson et al., "Letters from William and Mary, 1795–1799," *Virginia Magazine of History and Biography* 30 (1922): 249. For the pigeon wing at black dance events, see, for example, Avirett, *The Old Plantation*, 120–21; and Palmer, "Old Maryland Homes and Ways," 260; although these and other instances refer to a later period than the white references, both the step's name—reflecting the animal allusions typical of black dance names—and its popularity in the black community make it likely that it was a black invention, and its absence from earlier black dance records may be attributed to those records' scarcity.

36. See, for example, George M. Frederickson, *The Black Image in the White Mind: The Debate on Afro-American Character and Destiny, 1817–1914* (Middletown, CT: Wesleyan University Press, 1971), especially 1–27, 43–70; and Ira Berlin, *Many Thousands Gone: The First Two Centuries of Slavery in North America* (Cambridge, MA: Belknap Press of Harvard University Press, 1998), 363–64.

37. For two examples among an almost inexhaustible number, see Bryce, "Dusky 'Fiddlers,'" 5; and Castiglioni, *Luigi Castiglioni's Viaggio*, 196, 304 n. 51. For individuals who played for dances in both communities, see, for example, Sally Ashton, interview in Perdue, Barden, and Phillips, *Weevils in the Wheat*, 14; and Avirett, *The Old Plantation*, 99–104, 120–21, 136–37, 189–93.

38. Sarah F. H. Williams to [Sarah and Samuel Hicks?], January 3, 1856, in "Plantation Experiences of a New York Woman," ed. James C. Bonner, *North Carolina Historical Review* 33 (1956): 411; Ephraim Adams, *Ephraim Adams' Sketch Book* (San Francisco: Sorg, 1968), 68–69; Frederick Law Olmsted, *A Journey in the Seaboard Slave States* (New York: Dix and Edwards, 1856), 17–18.

39. Transcript of letter from Ellen Wayles Randolph Coolidge to Martha Jefferson Randolph, [August 1825], in the Ellen Wayles Randolph Coolidge Correspondence, Albert and Shirley Small Special Collections Library, University of Virginia, viewed online in the Family Letters Project, Thomas Jefferson Foundation, available at http://familyletters.dataformat.com. Several letters in this online collection refer to Coolidge's "mammy," Priscilla Hemings.

40. For the statistical analysis supporting this sentence, see Heckscher, "'All the

Mazes of the Dance,'" 409 n. 11. As David Hackett Fischer and James C. Kelly note, "Throughout the history of American slavery . . . by far the largest slave exporter was Virginia, which even as late as the 1850s nearly equaled the next two largest slave-exporting states combined. Furthermore, much of the slave trade from other states consisted of the children of emigrants from Virginia"; David Hackett Fischer and James C. Kelly, *Bound Away: Virginia and the Westward Movement* (Charlottesville: University Press of Virginia, 2000), 231.

41. Louis Hughes, *Thirty Years a Slave* (Milwaukee: South Side Printing, 1897), 11.

42. J. Kinnard Jr., "Who Are Our National Poets?" *Knickerbocker Magazine* 36 (October 1845), reprinted in *The Negro and His Folklore in Nineteenth-Century Periodicals,* ed. Bruce Jackson (Austin: University of Texas Press, 1967), 27.

43. Stearns and Stearns, *Jazz Dance,* 1–7, 17, 24, 83–84, 95–114, 315–34, 358; Sharon Leigh Clark, "Rock Dance in the United States, 1960–1970: Its Origins, Forms, and Patterns" (PhD diss., New York University, 1973); Brenda Dixon-Stowell, "Popular Dance in the Twentieth Century," in Emery, *Black Dance from 1619 to Today,* 343, 351–54, 356, 359; Kurath and Chilkovsky, "Jazz Choreology," 107–9; and Jacqui Malone, *Steppin' on the Blues: The Visible Rhythms of African American Dance* (Urbana: University of Illinois Press, 1996), 118–25, 128, 142–43.

2

The Civilizing of America's Ballrooms

The Revolutionary War to 1890

Elizabeth Aldrich

Many of the immigrants who crossed the ocean to settle colonial America were lower and middle-class people, seeking a new life free of religious persecution or because they were unable to improve their status in their homelands. Thus, they were not necessarily familiar with the rules of "society," and, unlike Europe, America had no aristocratic class to set standards of behavior. Consequently, classes rose that, in turn, looked down on yet lower classes for examples of crude or offensive behavior.

During the nineteenth century, Americans pushed westward while many more crowded into Eastern urban centers. Eighteenth-century traditions, in which men and women worked side by side, directly involved in all stages of care for the family unit, disintegrated in these urban confines as workers became less independent and more dependent upon a new, rising merchant class. It was now no longer socially sanctioned for middle-class women to work outside the home. As a consequence, women assumed the role of arbiters of conduct, a duty thought to be in accord with the leisurely life of urban middle-class women. To address these responsibilities, which were aimed primarily at the rapidly expanding middle class, book publishers disseminated courtesy literature, including cookbooks, which provided recipes as well as medical remedies; manuals devoted to setting the table and other topics concerning the dining room; information on fashion, beauty tips, and manners; and manuals that described evenings of entertainment, including tableaux, theatricals, song books, instructions for card games, books on fortune-telling, and how to organize evenings devoted to dance.

This chapter concentrates on the latter activity: the ritual of the ballroom, which, as described throughout the published advice literature, was a richly detailed ceremony. Interpretation and information on social dancing during the latter eighteenth century is difficult, but we can glimpse at its vibrancy through contemporary French and English manuals, supplemented by numerous letters, diaries, and the writings of the many European visitors who came to these shores to experience, firsthand, the American "experiment" in democracy. The amount of existing advice literature that circulated throughout nineteenth-century America is significant, reflecting the struggle of the middle class as it established a code of manners for the ceremonious aspects of daily life, including evenings dedicated to dance.

Late-Eighteenth-Century Ballrooms

Social dancing in eighteenth-century America was based on traditions that originated in Great Britain and France, and, although many questions remain concerning performance practices in the new American colonies, descriptions of dance in letters, diaries, and journals frequently refer to dances and balls using terms such as "the most fashionable" or the "latest."[1] Indeed, research has demonstrated that, "cultivated dancing was part and parcel of a genteel education in America."[2] Although English country dances and reels were British, cotillions, contra dances, and the minuet were French. Numerous French dancing masters—or, at least those who adopted French names in order to secure students—traveled throughout America, and the use of French dance terminology continued to be used by dancing masters and in published dance manuals and manuscripts throughout the nineteenth century.

Manners and Etiquette Manuals in Colonial America

Although fashioned after the rank-order structure of English society, class definitions in colonial America were radically different than those in England. In America, which lacked a class of nobility that determined structure of society, planters and merchants established themselves as the "upper class," and they attempted to emulate the fashion and manners of their British counterparts. Etiquette books that circulated throughout colonial America were reprints of much older English or French works that emphasized appropriate behavior toward "superiors" and "inferiors" in terms that later generations would consider appallingly vulgar.[3] For example, one of the most popular manuals, *The School of Good Manners,* was based on a 1564 French treatise that was translated into English in 1595. The first American edition appeared in 1715, and the 1786 edition reminded its readers to "spit not in the room but in the corner" and "Put not thy hand in the presence of others to any part of thy body not ordinarily discovered."[4] It was reprinted in thirty-four editions until 1847. These publications point to a more comfortable acceptance of the discussion of bodily functions that quickly disappeared as the middle class of the nineteenth century deemed discussions of this kind to be distasteful.

During the course of the eighteenth century, an expanding market economy forced rural people to rely less and less on home-produced products and diminished the importance of close familial and community relationships—traditional structures that passed down matters of etiquette and appropriate behavior via parent to child or through apprenticeships. By the end of the eighteenth century, great waves of rural populace began to migrate to the anonymity of the expanding urban landscape, thus setting the stage for the nineteenth-century profusion of courtesy literature (including dance manuals) that was required to define the boundaries of polite society.

Popular Dances in Colonial America

Courtly dances that allowed one couple at a time to demonstrate their proficiency were the dominant form of social dance for the first half of the eighteenth century, but by the end of the century they gave way to the more egalitarian group dances that appealed to the middle class, specifically English country dances, cotillions, and reels. Even the minuet, the most formal of the solo couple dances, continued to be performed by the middle class but was transformed into a more democratic group dance of lines or circles.

The most popular dance of this era was the English country dance, which was performed by two lines of dancers, men facing women. A highly social dance, country dances allow each couple to interact with everybody in the line. English country dances are well documented in eighteenth-century America with more than 2,800 dances recorded in manuscript or printed sources to 1810.[5] The cotillion was based on the *contradanse française* and, although the dance utilized figures from English country dances, it was performed by four couples, facing in a closed square formation.[6] The dance consisted of two parts: the figure and ten or twelve changes. To begin the dance, couples would perform the first change; at the conclusion of the change, the figure would be performed, alternating thereafter with a different change. Reels were a staple of the Scottish dance repertory and danced in a line or circle of at least three people. The signature figure of a reel is called a "hey," wherein the dancers perform an interweaving pattern resembling a figure eight. The minuet was the most celebrated court dance of France, originating in the 1660s, and by the early 1700s performance of the minuet was the focus of numerous dance manuals, not only in France but throughout Europe as well. Although many of the dancing masters who traveled throughout colonial America certainly knew the minuet in its pure form, it is unlikely that many Americans performed the dance as it had been known in the court of Louis XIV. Dancing masters simplified the steps and altered the figures, creating a group dance that was performed in a circle or in a line, as an English country dance.

By the end of the eighteenth century, dancing schools and social balls were an established and important part of American society. Colonial Americans considered dance to be part of a genteel education, and they valued the ability to dance well. Although itinerant dancing masters moved from town to town, others in urban areas earned a relatively good living by teaching the fashionable dances, proving the value of dance as a means of educating youth in bodily exercises, of acquiring grace and manners, as well as teaching an elegant recreation. For, as one early nineteenth-century author stated, "Dancing is the most enchanting of all human amusements, it is the parent of joy, and the soul and support of cheerfulness; it banishes grief, cheers the evening hours of those who have studied or laboured in the day, and brings with it a mixture of delightful sensations which enrapture the senses."[7]

The Nineteenth Century: The Ballroom as a Mirror of Society

In 1884,[8] New York dancing master George E. Wilson declared, "in all civilized communities, dancing is considered one of the necessary accomplishments of life."[9] Indeed, the ballroom was an ideal setting to illuminate how nineteenth-century ladies and gentlemen demonstrated their understanding of polite behavior that was required for acceptance into society. (Throughout the nineteenth century, men were "gentlemen," women "ladies.") To be successful at managing the rituals of attending or hosting an evening of dancing, one was required to adhere to many rules. For example, not only was one expected to know the latest steps and figures, off the dance floor and in the supper room, ladies and gentlemen might be faced with management of napkins and deciding whether to eat celery with a fork.[10] In addition, one might even be expected to sing or play the piano during an evening's festivities. In this increasingly class-conscious society, members of the same class were presumably separated and protected from the uninitiated and vulgar through their proper demonstration and understanding of etiquette, including the rules and regulations for all aspects of an evening of dancing. Nineteenth-century men and women were preoccupied with learning the proper way of conducting themselves not only in the ballroom but also in all social interactions; explicit rules seem to dominate the era.

Nineteenth-Century Advice Books

During the nineteenth century, a rapidly expanding, highly structured, class-oriented society was hungry for knowledge through which to better themselves. As America moved from a rural-based economy to one centered in the urban environment and cities were places of strangers, society created an unyielding set of rules and regulations to govern every aspect of bodily and emotional control. Carroll Smith-Rosenberg has noted, "Rigid dress codes and rigid rules of physical deportment are often reflections of societies experiencing rapid transformation."[11] Indeed, these codes are abundantly clear in advice manuals that describe balls.

With growing ritualizations of such activities as eating and dancing, the question became: How did one learn how to behave in a society that increasing thought of itself as "polished"? Of great importance in becoming "polished" was the assumption that it was necessary to code strangers; for only through dress, attitude, manners, and demeanor could one be assured of another's character. With increased literacy, dance and etiquette manuals were circulated in great numbers by eastern, urban book publishers who were eager to meet the needs of this rapidly expanding, middle-class society. Although these manuals provide an enlightening view of nineteenth-century middle-class society, their information cannot be assumed to be the only panorama of American life. As cultural historian John Kasson notes, however, "they impart a fruitful codification of standards that governed social interaction in a powerfully influential urban bourgeois culture."[12]

Dancing and Bodily Control

"It is hardly possible to enumerate the disadvantages that arise from an awkward deportment of the person. It is therefore of the utmost consequence to commence by forming a genteel and elegant carriage or deportment of the body."[13] The importance of composure and complete control over one's body, as illustrated in this quote, is echoed throughout nineteenth-century dance and etiquette manuals. Dance and etiquette manuals from the first two decades of the nineteenth century stressed not only deportment but other topics as well, such as the employment of time, choice of companions, the manner of walking, how to bow, and how to hand fans and calling cards. (Owing to lax or nonexistent copyright laws, most of these U.S.-published manuals were, in fact, of British origin.)

Between the 1820s and the Civil War, a large number of self-help manuals were published, reflecting changes in Jacksonian America that completely dispensed with the sentimental language that characterized late-eighteenth- and early-nineteenth-century manuals. The authors and compilers of these new middle-class advice manuals helped establish new codes of civility that profoundly affected social relationships. Furthermore, these manuals provided standards that were intended to assess entire social classes. To answer the criticism of European writers such as Mrs. Trollop and Charles Dickens, as well as the growing uneasiness of the eastern establishment toward the unrefined manners of the expanding west, it became common for manuals to establish categories of precise rules that, directed at the uninitiated, left absolutely nothing to chance.[14] "Never scratch your head, pick your teeth, clean your nails, or worse than all, pick your nose in company; all these things are disgusting. Spit as little as possible, and never upon the floor."[15] (This last sin was considered "nauseous to ladies," and, along with the smacking of lips during meals, they were habits, according to many foreign travelers, notorious in America.)[16] As polite society became more introverted and private, such diatribes were no longer found in etiquette or dance manuals after the 1870s. These topics were now deemed too vulgar even for print.

Suitable attire, proper pronunciation, and acceptable topics for conversation each had specific rules. When inviting a lady to join in a quadrille, young gentlemen "were earnestly advised not to limit their remarks to the weather and the heat of the room."[17] *True Politeness, A Hand-Book of Etiquette for Gentlemen* (written by "an American Gentleman" to advertise its authenticity), published in New York in 1847, suggested, "When conversing with young women, do not discourse of metaphysics, but chat about the last fashion, the new opera or play, the last concert or novel, etc. With single ladies past twenty-five, speak of literary matters, music, etc., and silently compliment them by a proper deference to their opinions. With married ladies, inquire about the health of their children, speak of the grace and beauty, etc."[18] "When a gentleman is invited out for the evening he need be under no embarrassment as to what he shall wear. Fashion has ordained for him that he shall always be attired in a black dress suit in the evening. . . . Plain and simple as the dress is, it is a sure test of a gentlemanly appearance. The man who dines in evening dress every night looks easy and natural in it, whereas the man who takes to it late in life generally succeeds in looking like a waiter."[19]

The mockery intended by that author points to an important ongoing change in nineteenth-century urban ballrooms. As more rural people moved to the city, certain refinements of character, dress, and manners were imperative for acceptance into polite, genteel society. Thus, more books were published to assist in overcoming the objections of "looking like a waiter" in an effort to turn all Americans into "ladies" and "gentlemen." The so-called Jacksonian rudeness generated an astonishing number of books that were pushed westward by publishers who cared little that the ideals of behavior were established by white, urban males. Most of the dictates in these manuals were not appropriate or even possible to the settlers of the new territories or the new residents of America's growing cities. However, these etiquette writers expressed the perpetual desire to institute an "American" code of manners that would regulate social interchange and tone down what these arbiters of society saw as excesses of democracy. For example, English etiquette writer Charles William Day noted: "In a mercantile country like our own, people are continually rising in the world. With the possession of wealth, they acquire a taste for the luxuries of life, expensive furniture, gorgeous plate, the use of which they are only imperfectly acquainted. But, although their capacities for enjoyment increase, it rarely happens that the polish of their manners keeps pace with the rapidity of their advancement; hence, such persons are often continually reminded that wealth alone is insufficient to protect them from the mortifications which a limited acquaintance with society entails upon the ambitious."[20] Day's retitled work, *Hints on Etiquette, and the Usages of Society: With a Glance at Bad Habits Adapted to American Society*, was published in New York, Boston, and Philadelphia during the 1840s.

One of the fears played to excess by etiquette writers was to stress that public evaluation of behavior would not only come from one's neighbors or family but also from a large, fluid, and mostly anonymous urban multitude. A new kind of embarrassment and sense of shame fed upon the uncertainties of status, of belonging, of living up to admittedly ambiguous and conflicting standards of social performances. Vulgarity and rudeness in nineteenth-century society were often construed as a kind of social obscenity, a special scorn for behavior that was considered unacceptable: an insolent gesture, such as leaning back in a chair; a man's gaze toward a woman who did not want to return his glance; asking a lady to dance prior to an appropriate introduction; forgetting the latest quadrille figure—any and all of these could, and did, create humiliation and increased the sense of vulnerability.

Dance manuals also contributed to this sense of vulnerability. As a manual from 1844 noted, "There are many unacquainted with dancing, who labor under an erroneous impression that 'the steps' are all that are necessary to be learned to fit a person for the ball-room."[21] During the latter nineteenth century, when self-help manuals were all the rage, dancing masters became alarmed at their growing popularity, which encouraged the aspiring to purchase a book, practice with a chair, and, after observing a few dances, venture out onto the dance floor with a good partner at his side. "Let no one essay to teach him or herself this difficult art," warned one writer. "Let everyone, who would pass muster in the ball room, take lessons from a Professor, and then practice at home."[22] Another observed: "The notion is very generally entertained that dancing can be picked up by attending balls, and the figures from observation—a most absurd conclusion."[23]

Readership for Dance and Etiquette Manuals

Prior to the Civil War, the readers of these manuals, which ranged in price from ten cents to more than ten dollars, were mostly middle-class, urban novitiates into society. After the Civil War, readership included not only the middle class and the uninitiated but also a new class of nouveau riches who could afford to give—during the last twenty-five years of the century—the lavish parties and balls that became increasingly popular during that era of conspicuous consumption. Authors addressed their prefaces to the "young ladies in the West and East who were becoming new housekeepers"[24] or to the "young men who are rising in the world."[25] Those "whose surroundings and circumstances do not permit of the adoption of the same rules that apply to the conduct of social life in large cities" could find solace in *Good Manners,* published by the Butterick Publishing Company in 1888. Abby Longstreet directed her *Social Etiquette of New York* to the "unfortunates who have been reared at remote distances away from the centers of civilization." Dance manuals were targeted to those who had "neglected, or have not had an opportunity of attending dancing schools."[26] The primary audience for these manuals were women, however,—urban, middle-class women—who did not work outside the home and who aspired to become "ladies." Manuals on how to arrange tableaux and theatricals, song books, instructions for card games, and books on fortune-telling were available to assist a lady with the activities taking place in her parlor. Of great importance to this audience were the dance manuals intended to assist with the planning of diverting evenings of dance.

Rules of the Nineteenth-Century Ballroom

Organized dancing during the nineteenth century took two forms: public or private balls. Public balls, sometimes referred to as assemblies, were events given for specific reasons, such as a charity, military, or subscription ball. In all cases, public balls were—in spite of their name—extremely exclusive, and, through a committee, one might be "invited" to purchase a ticket.[27]

The most popular form of dance throughout the nineteenth century, however, was the private ball, given in the home. These at-home parties might be very elaborate affairs, with issued invitations, sit-down dinners, and large orchestras, or a more informal gathering of family and close friends, with the dances accompanied by a piano. No matter the form of organized dancing—public or private—nineteenth-century dance and etiquette manuals were available to assist with every aspect, from the rules for proper bodily deportment and the basic dance steps, to what to serve for supper, what kind of music to provide, lighting, preparing the dance floor, and how to dress for the occasion. Other subjects covered in great detail included the protocol of invitations, which were to be issued ten days in advance, in order "to give an opportunity to the men to clear away engagements, and to women—time to prepare the artillery of their toilet."[28] It need not be mentioned that invitations were to be answered promptly.

Balls generally consisted of twenty-one dances, with a supper break after the twelfth dance. Hostess were advised to place "large blocks of ice in every convenient spot" to help alleviate the problem of heat and poor ventilation.[29] More than one author complained that hostesses frequently invited more than a room could comfortably hold, stating that an invitation to a crowded ball was not hospitality but an infliction.

Etiquette on the ballroom floor was strict and remained virtually intact throughout the century. Once a gentleman obtained a partner, he was not to leave her side until restored to her chaperone. Married ladies were accompanied to balls by their husbands; unmarried ladies did not go to balls alone but were chaperoned by their mothers, married sisters, or elderly lady friends. Gentlemen's responsibilities included guarding ladies against collisions while dancing and returning them to their chaperones at the end of the dance. The gentleman was required to ask his partner if she wanted any refreshments, and, if she replied in the affirmative, he would see her to the refreshment room, staying with her until she was finished. This behavior was expected for each partner. Of course, gentlemen were also admonished to be on time for each dance.

It was not usual for gentlemen to ask ladies to dance, unless they were introduced by the hostess or a mutual friend. Some manuals complained that this rule was rather irrational: A hostess ought not to invite any man who would not be considered a proper partner. Thomas Hillgrove suggested, "In private parties introductions are not considered necessary. The having been invited by the host is a voucher for respectability."[30] A man was bound to hold by the rules, however, and, if he wished to dance with a young lady with whom he was not already acquainted, he was required to request an introduction from the hostess or some member of the family. Having an introduction in order to dance did not mean that a gentleman could presume the acquaintance lasted outside the ballroom. He must not, therefore, acknowledge her if he met her on the street, unless she recognized him first. Women were not to refuse one partner in order to select another. If a lady refused to accept an invitation to dance with a gentleman, she was instructed to say that she was sitting out the dance. Choice was not allowed, and a lady waited until somebody asked her to dance; yet even if he was the worst dancer in the room, accepted etiquette required she must either consent graciously or not dance at all.

Nineteenth-Century Dance Manuals

During the first third of the century, dance instructors devoted much time to the manner of walking, how to get in and out of a carriage, how to walk backward, ladies' curtsies and gentlemen's bows, and how to hand fans and calling cards. In 1802, Boston dancing master Saltatore published *A Treatise on Dancing: And on Various Other Matters, Which are Connected with That Accomplishment*, providing one of the first glimpses of the early-nineteenth-century American ballroom and the wide variety of accomplishments taught by dancing masters at that time. Fully one-third of the book is devoted to subjects such as observations on the employment of time, choice of companions, conversation, behavior and the passions, and a section on the healthful aspects of dancing. The book also includes discussion on deportment, including the attitude of the body, bows and curtsies, and the handling of a hat and, of course, a description of the popular ballroom dances and twenty steps and step combinations appropriate for the performance of English country dances and cotillions.[31]

By the late 1830s, a certain segment of the middle-class dancing population most certainly continued to demonstrate some technical ability, but most were being discouraged from such displays of agility, for the manuals warned against looking too much like a dancing master. (The social position of dancing masters declined dramatically throughout the nineteenth century.) The truth of the matter was that fewer and fewer people were able to technically grasp the steps. As more and more rural people—who had not had the advantages of dance and etiquette lessons—moved into the cities to seek work, a larger proportion of the population was resorting to dance lessons later in life. Dance and etiquette manuals published in the 1840s began to reflect the more down-to-earth necessities: "Do not amuse yourself by hacking the woodwork or in any way mar the furniture because it defaces and destroys property, increases unproductive and fatiguing labor and has a tendency to provoke ill temper."[32] New York dancing master Thomas Hillgrove admonished his students to avoid "loud conversation, profanity, stamping the feet, writing on the wall, smoking tobacco, spitting or throwing anything on the floor."[33] Manuals no longer provided detailed explanations on subjects such as the correct method of handing calling cards or elaborate steps for group dances. Now, one was merely advised to "walk or slide gracefully through the dance . . . a familiarity with the figures being all that is essential."[34]

After the Civil War, it is difficult to find dance manuals with any substantive information on etiquette or, in fact, information on giving balls. For example, *Wehman's Complete Dancing Master and Call Book* (1889) devotes less than one page to the subject of giving balls, and Allen Dodworth's *Dancing and Its Relations to Education and Social Life* (1885) contains no discussion about ballroom etiquette. In fact, etiquette books—a separate genre of self-help publications—had become compendiums of information on every ceremonial aspect of life. For example, Florence Howe Hall's *Social Customs* of 1887 contains thirty-three chapters on invitations, dinner parties and how to give them, etiquette of the table, luncheons, afternoon teas, balls and dancing parties, etiquette of the ballroom, introductions, dress, and advice on voice, language, and accent. Thus a middle-class (or nouveau riche) lady or gentleman would need to own both a dance manual to learn the fashionable dances of the day and an etiquette manual to obtain information on the ceremonial aspects of life.

Nineteenth-Century Dances

Two configurations of dances dominated the nineteenth-century middle-class ballroom: round dances that were performed in closed position by couples and identified most commonly by the waltz and group dances that included English country dances, cotillions, quadrilles, and the parlor game known as the German. As noted, for the first twenty years of the nineteenth century, complex steps and step combinations were described for country dances and quadrilles. For example, quadrille figures often consisted of solo variations, and the figures themselves were not called by a prompter until later in the century. Dancing lessons were certainly required, as well as much practice. Although it is unlikely that *everybody* was able to perform at the same level, certainly one's standing in society increased when technical feats were accomplished with skill.

English Country Dances, Cotillions, and Quadrilles

English country dances continued to be popular in rural settlements throughout the nineteenth century, and collections continued to be published in areas such as New Hampshire. "Those never-ending still beginning performances,"[35] however, were rarely performed in urban ballrooms after the 1840s. As the middle class became more and more fearful of strangers, fewer ladies and gentlemen wanted to take part in a dance that required that they dance with such a great number of people—including, perhaps, those who had not been properly introduced or were of questionable character. Instead, the cotillion and its successor, the quadrille, rose in popularity. Requiring only eight people (four couples) in a square formation, one could more selectively choose acquaintances. Emphasizing the growing concern for class consciousness, several dance and etiquette manuals suggested that, if going to a public ball, one should arrange ahead of time to have a suitable vis-à-vis, or opposite couple, while dancing the quadrille to lessen the possibility of dancing with "inferiors."

Although the eighteenth-century cotillion remained popular during the early years of the nineteenth century, eventually it was deemed too long and too difficult to remember (the figure and alternating changes were not prompted by a caller, requiring the performers to memorize not only the dance's step combinations but the figures as well). Thus, the changes were dropped and the quadrille evolved, consisting of a series of figures, usually four or five. By midcentury, however, ladies and gentlemen of the ballroom required the assistance of a prompter, who called out the figures, and numerous manuals were published that described the requirements of the caller in detail.[36] The quadrille was, undoubtedly, the most popular group dance throughout the century, and, although one walked through the figures, numerous quadrille variants were popular, including waltz, polka, mazurka, and galop quadrilles.

Couple Dances

The biggest revolution in ballroom social dancing resulted from the rising popularity of a new form of couple dance: the round dance, primarily the waltz, polka, and galop.[37] The position taken by couples meant that, though the enjoyment of dancing with a partner was very much evident, these dances were danced, not for the pleasure of a viewing audience, but because the continuous turning of the waltz and the rapid movement through space of the polka and galop were exhilarating. Unlike group dances, such as English country dances or the quadrille, in which chaperones or others who were sitting out the dance might enjoy the social intercourse of the figures, dances in round position focused only on those participating. The early-to-mid-nineteenth-century waltz, with its whirling pivots, which always traveled in one direction, created in the performer a state that best is described as delirium. Some objected to this: "Vertigo is one of the great inconveniences of the waltz; and the character of this dance, its rapid turnings, the clasping of the dancers, their exciting contact, and the too quick and too long continued succession of lively and agreeable emotions, produce sometimes, in women of a very irritable constitution, syncopes, spasms, and other accidents which should induce them to renounce it."[38]

Perhaps the most unique feature of the waltz, as practiced from the late eighteenth century to the mid-nineteenth century, was that no leading was required.[39] The five steps (in six counts) were arranged so that couples turned clockwise as partners and traveled counterclockwise around the ballroom with prescribed steps.[40] This method of never reversing and traveling in one direction became impractical, however, as ballrooms became more crowded and fewer "ladies" and "gentlemen" were acquainted with the steps. Although dance manuals throughout the century indicate that dancing masters clearly preferred the five-step waltz, midcentury manuals begin to describe a six-step waltz, which allowed performers to dance both clockwise and counterclockwise. For those who were unable to master the six steps, dance manuals offered an even simpler version called *deux temps*. Edward Ferrero's instructions simply state, "The step consists of two slides, with each foot alternately turning."[41] (Later, in 1885, dancing master Allen Dodworth provided similar instructions for the same dance, which he called the "Ignoramous Waltz.") The steps for both these variations allowed couples to dance in formations other than the large circle, which was required for the five-step waltz. In other words, couples could dance within a large circle, in place, or, in fact, anywhere within the ballroom. This added flexibility created a not inconsiderable problem, however; somebody had to decide whether to dance clockwise, counterclockwise, and along what path, to avoid collisions with other dancers. Thus, leading their partners was added to the list of ballroom tasks for gentlemen.

Perhaps it is coincidence that this midcentury change from an un-led, five-step waltz to a six-step waltz led by the gentlemen paralleled the era when America's family social structure changed dramatically. The growing industrial society found women less often working side by side with husbands or extended family members in farming or artisan endeavors. As work left the confines of home, men pursued their trades and professions in urban factories and shops; women were removed from the workplace and centered their lives on activities of the home (including evenings of ballroom dancing), church, and calling on other ladies in what has been described as the "institution of visiting."[42] Women became completely dependent on their husbands (or male relatives). Even ballroom dresses for women of this era included tightly laced corsets under bodices, which laced in the back. A midcentury lady was unable even to dress herself. Duple-meter couple dances popular throughout the nineteenth century included the polka, schottische, and galop (gallop). These steps were energetic, utilizing leaps, hops, and rapid sliding (figure 2.1).

The German

During the 1840s, a new category of group dance became increasingly popular. Called "cotillon" (sometimes spelled cotillion)—but not to be confused with the earlier dance of the same name—the dance was also known as the German. The German was a series of party game figures, led by a conductor or leader, and danced to a prescribed set of rules. Performed predominately

Figure 2.1: The starting position for a quadrille from *The Dance of Society* by William B. DeGarmo, published in New York, 1875.

to waltz music, many figures of the German were extracted from quadrilles; however, other figures fell into the category of games, as there frequently was a winner or loser.

To dance the German, "all should be seated with their partners around the room, leaving as much space in the centre as possible." The importance of the leader was strongly emphasized because the leader organized the figures, chose the couples, and maintained order. (To deal with unruly participants, *Professor Baron's Complete Instructor* recommended the leader "be firm and immovable and restore order to his ranks in a quiet but decisive manner."[43] On the other hand, William B. DeGarmo encouraged his readers to obey the leader "however stupid or unadvisable" the commands might be.[44])

The primary venue for performing the German was at private parties where "all should be upon terms of familiarity."[45] Some manuals suggested figures that would be appropriate at larger gatherings, but most authors felt that the German was "adaptable only to the performance of a limited company of intimate acquaintances, where merriment and even a little choice humor could rather advance than check the general enjoyment."[46] This "choice humor" was most often at the expense of the gentlemen players. For example, in a figure known as "The Fan," two gentlemen would be instructed to sit on chairs, with a lady seated in the middle. The lady would hand her fan to the man with whom she chose not to dance; the losing gentleman would be required to hop behind the dancing couple waving the fan.

Dance and etiquette manuals placed great emphasis on decorum and deportment in carriage as well as admonishing participants to dance with ease, no matter how complicated the steps or figures. An example of what might be considered unbecoming physical decorum can be seen in a late-nineteenth-century figure called "The Race." "Whips and reins are necessary properties for this figure. Each person is provided with whips and reins. Each couple dance. Partners are chosen and the ladies proceed to drive the gentlemen, who race from one of the room to the other, obedient to the whip and rein. All dance."[47]

The popularity of the German increased markedly by 1875, and it almost always appeared on the programs of private balls. Sometimes it was performed after midnight, when the other dances of the ball had concluded and, presumably, the very young had retired. On other occasions, it was the only "dance" on the program.

End of the Century

Carroll Smith-Rosenberg has noted the "anger of women caught between the promises of political power and social equity that Jacksonian society held out to all Americans, and the restrictions the Cult of True Womanhood placed on all women."[48] Once removed from the workplace, the Industrial Revolution produced "the dependent, isolated nineteenth-century housewife, a pale reflection of her colonial mother and grandmother."[49] An examination of the literature, including dance and etiquette manuals, recipe and home-centered advice manuals, antidance and religious tomes, medical textbooks, and school curricula, shows, beyond a doubt, that the spheres of men and women were distinctly separate. Contacts between men and women, especially as detailed in manuals describing the ballroom ritual, show a world of stiffness, formality, reserve, and ceremony.

Today's audience might consider many of the figures of the German silly or quaint. No doubt, with its props of whips and reins, "The Race" could be viewed as completely bizarre. During the closing decades of the nineteenth century, it is possible to observe a multiplication of female role alternatives: women attending college, reentering the workplace (many times as professionals), and taking to the streets with causes ranging from the right to vote to prison reform to temperance. These and other elements increasingly strained relationships. The growing popularity of these humiliating German figures that are found at the end of the nineteenth century also point to the growing rift between the genders.

Men's clubs and lodges were extremely popular during the last quarter of the century, and numerous writers commented that gentlemen became more and more isolated from society. One writer grumbled that "club life among gentlemen tends more and more to postpone marriage."[50] The rising popularity of these clubs also paralleled the steady decline of the number of men who attended dancing schools, and writers frequently complained that gentlemen were more and more out of place in many mixed social situations, including ballrooms. Etiquette writer Florence Howe Hall complained that she was tired of seeing "a black-coated and dismal group, like so many crows around the doorway" congregating at balls.[51]

At the end of the nineteenth century, women continued to attend dancing schools and to organize balls and parties. Men, for the most part, did not follow suit. Without formal study of the latest ballroom dances, a man was frequently ill equipped to dance with anyone, and as previously noted, a gentleman also faced the prospect of spending many hours performing the German, during which he could be humiliated or made the object of jokes. An Italian traveler to Saratoga, New York, in the 1880s noted: "And I could particularly note the difference in character between the two sexes, a difference so great that one might suppose them members of two different races. The men have a rigid temperament; they speak little. . . . In the salon the American male is a fish out of water; not one of them will deny that his true place is the office, the countinghouse, or the political meeting."[52] It is no wonder manuals and foreign visitors noted that the millennium closed with many men gravitating farther to the periphery of society.

Notes

1. Kate Van Winkle Keller, *"If the Company Can Do It!" Technique in Eighteenth-Century American Social Dance,* 3rd ed. (Sandy Hook, CT: Hendrickson Group, 1996), 5.

2. Ibid., 40.

3. John F. Kasson, *Rudeness and Civility: Manners in Nineteenth-Century Urban America* (New York: Noonday Press, 1991), 19–20.

4. Ibid., 13.

5. In *"If the Company Can Do It!"* Keller notes that figures for more than 2,800 country dances are recorded in American manuscript and printed sources to 1810, 10.

6. *Cotillon* was anglicized as "cotillion" in English-language dance manuals. For the purpose of this chapter, we are using the later spelling. There were two types of *contredanses* in French ballrooms: the *contredanse française,* which was performed by

couples facing in a square, and the *contredanse anglaise,* which was performed in a line, as in English country dances.

7. T[homas] Wilson, *An Analysis of Country Dancing* (London: W. Calvert, 1808), vi.

8. For an in-depth look at nineteenth-century dance practices, see Elizabeth Aldrich, *From the Ballroom to Hell: Grace and Folly in Nineteenth-Century Dance* (Evanston, IL: Northwestern University Press, 1991).

9. George E. Wilson, *Wilson's Ball-room Guide and Call Book, or, Dancing Self-Taught* (New York: Excelsior, 1884), x.

10. The proper use of eating utensils was of concern in polite society and is discussed with great frequency in late-nineteenth-century etiquette books. For example, see Florence Howe Hall, *Social Customs* (Boston: Estes and Lauriat, 1887).

11. Carroll Smith-Rosenberg, *Disorderly Conduct: Visions of Gender in Victorian America* (New York: Oxford University Press, 1985), 48.

12. Kasson, *Rudeness and Civility,* 5.

13. Alexander Strathy, *Elements of the Art of Dancing* (Edinburgh: F. Pillans, 1822), 27.

14. Mrs. [Frances] Trollop, *Domestic Manners of the Americans* (New York: Reprinted for the Booksellers, 1832); and Charles Dickens, *American Notes* (Cambridge, MA: Riverside Press, 1869).

15. *The Art of Good Behaviour* (New York: C. P. Huestis, ca. 1845), 31.

16. See, for example, Mrs. Manners [Cornelia Bradley Richards], *At Home and Abroad; or, How to Behave* (New York: Evans and Brittan, 1853), 26.

17. *Mixing in Society* (London: Routledge, 1860), 165.

18. *True Politeness, A Hand-Book of Etiquette for Gentlemen* (New York: Manhattan, 1847), 24.

19. *The Ball-Room Guide, A Handy Manual for all Classes of Society* (New York: Frederick Warne, ca. 1860), 25.

20. Charles William Day, *Hints on Etiquette and the Usages of Society* (London, 1834), 103.

21. *The New Ball-Room Guide; or, Dancing Made Easy. By a Man of Fashion, from the Fortieth London Edition* (New York: Burgess and Stringer, 1844), 12.

22. Ibid.

23. *The Illustrated Manners Book* (New York: Leland Clay, 1855), 407.

24. *American Code of Manners* (New York: W. R. Andrews, 1880), i.

25. Ibid.

26. *The Ball-Room Instructor* (New York: Huestis & Croft, 1841), 15.

27. For example, the public balls and assemblies so vividly described in Jane Austen novels were in fact highly selective affairs.

28. *The Laws of Etiquette, By a Gentleman* (Philadelphia: Carey, Lea, and Blanchard, 1836), 113.

29. *Manners and Tone of Good Society,* 3rd ed. (London: Frederick Warne, ca. 1879), 133.

30. Thomas Hillgrove, *A Complete Practical Guide to the Art of Dancing* (New York: Dick & Fitzgerald, 1863), 154.

31. Other manuals published in the United States that provide steps and step combinations for English country dances, cotillions, and quadrilles include E. H. Conway's *1820 Le Maitre de Danse; or the Art of Dancing Cotillions,* 2nd ed. (New York: C. S. Van Winkle, 1827), and *Elements and Principles of the Art of Dancing from the French of J. H. G. Professor of Dancing in Paris, by V. G. Professor of Dancing in Philadelphia* (Philadelphia: J. F. Hurtel, 1817), which was originally published in 1811 in France.

32. Miss Sedgwick, *Morals of Manners; or, Hints for Our Young People* (New York: Wiley & Putnam, 1846), 89.

33. Hillgrove, *A Complete Practical Guide*, 29.

34. Edward Ferrero, *The Art of Dancing* (New York: By the Author, 1859), 121.

35. Eliza Leslie, *The Behaviour Book* (Philadelphia: Willis P. Hazard, 1853), 321.

36. For example, William B. DeGarmo's *The Prompter*, 4th ed. (New York: Wm. A. Pond, 1868); *Dancing and Prompting, Etiquette and Deportment of Society and Ball Room. [By] Professor Bonstein* (Boston: White, Smith, ca. 1884); *Dick's Quadrille Call-Book, and Ball-Room Prompter* (Boston: Dick & Fitzgerald, 1878); and Frank Leslie Clendenen, *Fashionable Quadrille Call Book and Guide to Etiquette* (Chicago: C. Himmelman, ca. 1899).

37. For a history of the waltz, see Elizabeth Aldrich, "Waltzes, L'Allemande, and the Twelve Quadrille," in *The Extraordinary Dance Book T. B. 1826: An Anonymous Manuscript in Facsimile*, commentaries and analyses by Elizabeth Aldrich, Sandra Holl Hammond, and Armand Russell (Stuyvesant, NY: Pendragon Press, 2000), 10–26.

38. Donald Walker, *Exercises for Ladies* (London: Thomas Hurst, 1836), 148–49.

39. Leading is required, for example, in modern ballroom dance. The man guides the lady throughout the ballroom and determines when step changes or variations are introduced.

40. English dancing master and choreographer at London's King Theatre, Thomas Wilson provided the first complete English-language description of this waltz in *A Description of the Correct Method of Waltzing* (London: Sherwood, Neely, and Jones, 1816).

41. Ferrero, *The Art of Dancing*, 73–74.

42. Smith-Rosenberg, *Disorderly Conduct*, 61.

43. Samuel Baron, *Professor Baron's Complete Instructor in All the Society Dances of America* (New York: J. Young, ca. 1880), 79.

44. DeGarmo, *The Prompter*, 78.

45. William E. Greene, *The Terpsichorean Monitor* (Providence, RI: E. A. Johnson, 1889), 14.

46. C. H. Cleveland Jr., *Dancing at Home and Abroad* (Boston: Oliver Ditson, 1878), 85.

47. Baron, *Professor Baron's Complete Instructor*, 147.

48. Smith-Rosenberg, *Disorderly Conduct*, 21.

49. Ibid., 15.

50. [Abby Longstreet Buchanan], *Social Etiquette of New York* (New York: D. Appleton, 1879), 123.

51. Hall, *Social Customs*, 140.

52. Carlo Gardini, *Gli Stati Uniti: Ricordi con 76 Illustrazionie Carte*, 2nd ed. (Bologna, Italy: Nicola Zanchelli, 1891), in Oscar Handlin, *America: A History* (New York: Holt, Rinehart and Winston, 1968), 374.

3

"Just Like Being at the Zoo"

Primitivity and Ragtime Dance

Nadine George-Graves

Introduction

The period from the late nineteenth to the early twentieth century is often regarded as merely the precursor to the more exciting Jazz Age and Harlem Renaissance, particularly in terms of popular music and dance. The dance and musical forms of the ragtime era are important contributions to American popular culture in their own right. In addition, by examining the aesthetics of popular dance and music at this time, we are able to make claims about the racial social dynamics in the United States and, in turn, recognize the importance of the Gilded Age and ragtime era for social dance. During this time, one of the first uniquely American forms of social dance to gain national popularity developed out of an African American tradition and was influenced by European traditions and contemporaneous attitudes about race, sexuality, and class. In the time between the 1893 stock market crash and World War I, the rhythms of the ragtime piano and the youth culture of the post-Victorians greatly influenced the nature of social dance and vice versa.

Most of ragtime's dances were first popular in African American communities in the South and North and then moved from these jook joints and house parties to traveling shows, such as medicine shows, gillies (miniature carnivals), and black and white vaudeville to large venues like ballrooms (black and white) and Broadway musicals. The migrants of the Great Migration brought their dance styles to their new homes and greatly influenced the cultural mise-en-scène. The competitive spirit influenced much of the creativity in the steps, and dancers were constantly trying to outdo one another and come up with the next craze. The most popular dances were often the ones that displayed the most technical difficulty. Fancy stepping and syncopated rhythms led to gravity-defying aerials and comedic antics. In all of these venues, dancers of different racial backgrounds and classes borrowed, stole, and one-upped one another. The story of social dance during this era is a complex negotiation that can be read on the body. In this chapter, I attempt to untangle some of these dynamics. I focus on the so-called animal dances of the time and theorize on the social dynamics of these dance encounters. The terms "animal dance" and "ragtime dance" were, at times, conflated, but it is important to distinguish the dances that actually reference animal-like movement. The physical vocabulary of these rural Southern black dances greatly influenced the urban and Northern multiracial ragtime dances.

Before delving into these negotiations, I first offer a preliminary discussion of some of the preragtime and early ragtime dances that did not have animal names attached to them and that were not necessarily mimicking animal moves to provide context for my argument about the importance of animality and primitivity in social dance during this period.

Cakewalk

The Cakewalk was the most popular black social dance to influence the social dancing of the ragtime era. In fact, many early rags are Cakewalks, and the Cakewalk's syncopated rhythms directly led to ragtime music's style. The Cakewalk has its roots on the Southern plantation when slaves would get together and hold contests in which the winners would receive a cake often provided by the master.[1] The style of dancing has many influences, including African competitive dancing, Seminole dancing in which couples paraded solemnly, and European dancing and promenading that the slaves witnessed in the big house. The Cakewalk was a mockery of these European styles, but when the slaves performed for the whites, their masters often mistook the playful derision for quaint approximations of their dances. In this couple dance, dancers stood side by side, linked arms at the elbow, leaned back and pranced about high-stepping and putting on airs (figure 3.1).[2] The men usually wore suits with tails, top hats, canes, and bow ties. The women wore long dresses, heels, and often carried a parasol. Cakewalks were a regular feature in minstrel shows and black vaudeville, and because of the influence these traveling shows had on popular dancing, the Cakewalk quickly made its way to Northern dance halls. The Cakewalk led the way for Southern black dances to gain popularity in the North, thereby playing a seminal role in the creation of ragtime dance.[3]

Figure 3.1: The original sheet music cover for Scott Joplin's "The Ragtime Dance" is an illustration of the negotiations between race and class in social dance. Note the man's nod to the Cakewalk. In *The Collected Works of Scott Joplin,* vol. 2, Americana Collection Music Series 1, ed. Vera Brodsky Lawrence, The Music Division, The New York Public Library for the Performing Arts, Astor, Lenox and Tilden Foundations, 1971.

Texas Tommy

The Texas Tommy bridged ragtime dancing and swing dancing. Many consider it to be the first swing dance because it was the first to include a breakaway from a closed partnering position to an open position that allowed
for acrobatics, antics, improvisations, and showing off. After the couple did
the basic step of a kick and three hops on each foot, they would break away
and improvise in keeping with the timing in order to come back together
for the basic step again.

Origin myths of these dances provide dramatic lore, and stories of who
invented what continue to be disputed. Rumors and disputes abound, and the
Texas Tommy serves as a great example. Among many origin stories, the Texas
Tommy is said to have been born at the Fairmont Hotel in San Francisco, which
had a very ritzy ballroom and where the house band invented the music for
the dance. Several dancers are credited with either inventing or popularizing
the dance, including Johnny Peters and his partner Mary Dewsen (and later
Ethel Williams). Peters and Williams won many contests and performed the
Texas Tommy in the Broadway musical *The Darktown Follies. Tommy* was a
slang term for a trench soldier at the turn of the century. A "Texas Tommy"
was a female prostitute who worked the "trenches" in the early 1900s. There
are also rumors of the dance going back to the Civil War, in which a famous
black dancer named "Tom from Palestine" (Texas) put a glass of water on his
head and frenetically moved his lower half without spilling the water. Another
rumor has the dance originating in eastern Texas by a blues singer, "Ragtime
Texas Henry" Thomas, who played jook joints in the late 1800s.[4]

Truckin', the Black Bottom, Ballin' the Jack, and Slow Drag

Some dance moves had their own names, though they were most popular as
a variation or breakaway in other dances. For example, Truckin' was a variation that was a pigeon-toed rhythmic shuffle or slight, quick hopping. The
index finger pointed up and shook in double time in the direction the dancer
was moving (usually four shuffles to each diagonal), while the shoulders rose
and fell. The move was a way to break away from and return to one's partner.
The Black Bottom began as a solo challenge dance but was most popular as
a breakaway. The featured move in the dance is the slapping of the buttocks
while hopping forward and backward, stamping the feet, shaking the index
finger on the other hand, rolling the eyes, and gyrating the hips. Slow drag
was popular in Southern jook joints and occurred late at night by dancers

exhausted from hours of fast-paced dancing. Couples would hold each other tight and slow grind to the slow, erotic music. When moving in any direction, the first foot stepped and the second dragged to join it, illustrating a slow, delayed sensuality. The couple might move away from each other slightly and then come back in and grind until the end of the evening, sometimes barely moving.

Ballin' the Jack was a sensual grind similar to snake hips (the name describes much of the dance) but with more sexual connotations. Originally its own dance, it later became a popular part of the Lindy Hop. It was a serpentine, circular, shuffling dance that had its roots in the plantation ring shout. In Ballin' the Jack, the head, shoulders, and feet stay still while the rest of the body undulates and the hips rotate. A good description of the choreography comes from the lyrics to "Ballin' the Jack":

> First you put your two knees close tight
> Then you sway 'em to the left,
> Then you sway 'em to the right
> Step around the floor kind of nice and light
> Then you twis' around and twis' around with all your might
> Stretch your lovin' arms straight out in space
> Then you do the Eagle Rock with style and grace
> Swing your foot way 'round then bring it back
> Now that's what I call "Ballin' the Jack."[5]

African Roots and Animal Dances

By the 1910s, one of the most popular trends in ragtime dancing was the animal dance craze. So popular were the animal dances that at times the entire genre of ragtime dance was known as animal dance. The African roots of African American animal dances have been well established. As Katrina Hazzard-Gordon claims, "Social dancing links African Americans to their African past more strongly than any other aspect of their culture."[6] An early example of this recognition can be seen in the writings of Mura Dehn,[7] who claimed that the dances were "just like being at the zoo":

> The Africans in exile who gave the Aesop's Fables to Europe thousands of years ago, never lost their acute awareness of the animal world. Following the old tradition the American black slaves created new fables, ditties and dances about animals observed in their daily life, with a humorous point of view on motion and character. Sometimes with a moral attached to it. The animal dances of voodoo celebrations and their descendants the

animal spirits entered [sic]. The Coon Era finally were [sic] incorporated into the general social dance of black and white America. In ragtime, in jazz, and now in rock the old steps and names reappear renewed by the current styles: Horse, Pony, Fox, Raccoon, Snake, Chicken, Alligator, Dog, Rooster, Peacock, Eagle, Crow, Buzzard, Rabbit, etc. are by now imperishable incarnations of black American dance phantasy [sic].[8]

Different African traditions met on the plantation to create the first cultural blending of African American movement styles.[9] Versions of animal dances occurred throughout slavery. Some animals (like rabbit, spider, and monkey) serve as metaphors for survival.

> Rabbit in de gyordin (general's call)
> Rabbit hi oh (all hands respond)
> Dog can't ketch um
> Rabbit hi oh
> Gun can't shoot um
> Rabbit hi oh
> Mon can't skin um
> Rabbit hi oh
> Cook can't cook um
> Rabbit hi oh
> Folks can't eat um
> Rabbit hi oh[10]

The animal dance mentioned most frequently by ex-slaves, according to Lynne Fauley Emery, is the Buzzard Lope. Emery cites Emma and Mary Stevens of Sunbury, Georgia, "We do git tuh gedduh an hab dance an pahties an big suppuhs, we does duh Snake Hip and duh Buzzard Lope. An addalas dance we did duh Fish Talk an duh Fish Bone an duh Camel Walk."[11] It held a prominent place at slave festivals like the John Canoe.[12] In fact, scholars speculate that the festival received its name from the Ashanti name for buzzard, "Yankoro." In one description, a person lays on the floor representing a dead cow. Another dancer imitates the movements of a turkey buzzard with the following directions:

March aroun'!	(the cow)
Jump across!	(see if she's daid)
Get the eye!	(always go for that first)
So glad!	(cow daid)
Get the guts!	(they like 'em next best)
Go to eatin'!	(on the meat)
All right!-cow mos' gone!	

Dog comin'!
Scare the dog!
Look aroun' for mo' meat!
All right!-Belly full!
"Goin' to tell the res'"[13]

Other animal dances of the plantation included the Pigeon Wing or Chicken Wing, the Turkey Trot, the Fishtail, the Fish Bone, the Camel Walk, the Snake Hips, and the Mosquito Dance. Plantation dances were also called "coon steps," and certain plantation songs were called "coon songs." This appellation further associated blacks with animals (raccoons) in mostly derogatory ways.

Most ragtime dances of the teens had an animal name attached to them because of the popularity of animal dances. The Bunny Hug, for instance, was a simulation of rabbits fornicating, with rapid hopping, shaking, grinding, and wiggling. The Grizzly Bear was an imitation of a dancing bear, in which the dancers would take clumsy, heavy steps to the side on toes while making an ungraceful bend at the knees. The couple, facing each other, hugging so that their chests met and their arms flopped over each other's shoulders, would move forward and backward in this ungainly manner. During the dance the dancers would yell out, "It's a bear!" They might also turn back-to-back with their arms up, bent at the elbows, fingers curled like a playful attacking bear. The Turkey Trot—one of the first animal dances to gain popularity—involved the couple facing each other, the man holding the woman tightly around the waist, and the two of them moving forward and backward in a straight line, occasionally flapping their arms. The man might move behind the woman and add a little hop while flapping arms. He would then snuggle up behind her, and the two would hop, skip, and jump until they broke again and returned to the face-to-face position.[14] From these three examples, it is clear that the dancers of the time were using dance to push the boundaries of sexual politics and decorum.[15]

By analyzing the animal dances of the ragtime era, I argue that we might also gain insight into the complicated class and racial politics of the time. The animal dances performed by blacks on the plantations and later in the free rural South were closer to the African traditions than the dances popularized in the black urban and Northern cabarets. Even further removed were the animal dances marketed to the white ballroom dance community. In these settings, dancers negotiated a balance between the loose, weighted black animal dances, the desire to create freer, more carefree dance, and prevailing notions of propriety associated with notions of race, class, and gender.

White Influences

White styles also influenced the development of social dance on the plantation. As mentioned, scholars have attempted to unravel the negotiations around the Cakewalk, arguing that whites saw their slaves prancing about in high-stepping haughtiness as an amusing attempt at their social dancing. The slaves, on the other hand, used the Cakewalk to subversively mock the pretensions of white society.[16] The prominence of discussions of the Cakewalk lead to the conclusion that slaves only mocked the high ideals of their masters and mistresses. Often ignored are the dances that did physically absorb ideas about class from the white models. The slave caste system in which lighter-skinned house slaves were afforded more privileges by and lived closer to whites also deeply influenced the development of social dancing on plantations in the United States.[17] Some house slaves therefore considered themselves to be better than darker-skinned field slaves. To further distinguish themselves, many adopted the genteel manners of their owners.[18] In terms of social dancing, these slaves learned (probably mostly through observation) white pattern dances such as the English Square Dance, the French Quadrille, the Figure Dance (similar to the square dance) and the Sixteen-figure Round Dance.[19] They then brought these steps and corresponding ideas about class to the field hands, who combined the European styles with African traditions. Similarities between the call-and-response practices of African styles and the calling out of square dance instructions and the intricate patterning of quadrilles no doubt aided in a smooth blending of traditions. These slaves took pride in dancing quadrilles, reels, and cotillions. Isaac Stier described the experience of participating in these kinds of dances on a plantation in Mississippi. Note the pride with which he describes the dances and the assumptions about class and status. Also, note the use of the terms "ladies" and "gents" to direct the dancers:

> Us danced plenty, too. Some o' de men clogged an' pigeoned but when us had dances dey was real cotillion, lak de white folks had. . . . I use to call out de figgers: "Ladies, sashay, Gents to de lef, now all swing." Ever'body lak my calls an' de dancers sho' moved smooth an' pretty. Long after de war was over de white folks would 'gage me to come 'roun' wid de band an' call de figgers at all de big dances. Dey always paid me well.[20]

After slavery, blacks who stayed in the South established membership clubs and jook houses as venues for social gatherings. Other former slaves moved from rural to urban settings and brought their dances with them and continued to share movement styles at honky-tonks, after-hours clubs, and rent parties. In urban settings, African American dances met with other European styles (like the waltz). Physically, one of the most important influences was the proximity of the dancer to the floor. As recurred later with the Lindy Hop and jitterbug, the European influence served to move the body farther away from the ground in keeping with a Christian notion of uprightness (in all senses of the word) and closeness to God. On the flip side, the rigid rules for European dances gave way to more improvisational styles. The movement of the body toward a more upright stance was also influenced by the fact that more black workers were moving away from agrarian lifestyles, which shifted the importance of the earth and groundedness. Occupations like logging and railroad work would exert influence on African American social dance in rhythm and movement style. These are the circumstances out of which ragtime dance developed.[21]

At the beginning of the twentieth century, much African American leisure time was spent social dancing.[22] In the years between 1905 and 1915, more animal dances became popular, including the Kangaroo Hop, Eagle Rock, Horse Trot, Kangaroo Dip, Chicken Scratch, Crab Step, Herringbone Twist, Lame Duck, and Grizzly Bear. Nonanimal dances that gained in popularity included the Black Bottom, Ballin' the Jack, the Charleston, Truckin', the Drag, the Strut, and the Cakewalk. The African and African American elements that influenced ragtime dance include improvisation, percussive accompaniment, call-and-response, juba, the ring shout, the plantation Cakewalk, funeral dances, struts, and seasonal dances. European influences include the emphasis on couple dancing over group and solo dances, Irish step dances, Scotch-Irish jigs, German reels, Dutch chimney dances, Latin dances, and sailor hornpipes. At this point in history, these influences could have only occurred in the United States; however, the cultural interactions were not simply a pleasant exchange of steps. Speaking of this mix of cultures, Hazzard-Gordon claims, "Between 1877 and 1920, African-Americans saw their music and dance adopted (poorly) by the white theater, the recording industry, and the newly emerging popular culture industry, while they suffered systematic exclusion from those markets."[23] In this statement, Hazzard-Gordon points to the complexities of cultural appropriation. I argue that it is less the mixing of cultures that is problematic than the subsequent disenfranchisement, exploitative commercialization, and disavowal of African American culture by hegemonic forces.

Though these dances were an important part of the development of black musicals, the broadest-reaching influence for ragtime dances occurred with the incorporation of ragtime dance with white ballroom dance when black dancers gave lessons to whites. Not surprisingly, blacks were rarely credited in nonblack arenas and usually reaped very little monetary gain in comparison to white instructors. As the ballroom dance industry reached international influence, blacks were even further marginalized. Vernon and Irene Castle (white dance instructors) are credited with being the most influential teachers of ballroom styles. Even if they and other white dance teams and instructors did not set out to erase African American styles and African Americans themselves from the traditions of social dancing, their assumptions about the implications of the body moving in space had just that effect. These white dancers and instructors removed the African American influences on the movement styles that they considered lascivious because they were looser limbed. They emphasized the uprightness of the torso to be more in keeping with the European tradition. In effect, they "whitened" ragtime dance for white patrons of their dancing schools. The loaded terms of "graceful" and "dignified" were used to distinguish their style of dancing from so-called less-civilized forms. They moved the form away from the African improvisational tradition to a European codified technique.[24]

The Castles were considered exemplars of class and comportment. The titles for some of the chapters of their book *Modern Dancing* include: "Grace and Elegance," "Proper Dancing-Costumes for Women," "Modern Dances as Fashion Reformers," and "Proper Dance Music."[25] In a historical dance video recording produced by Dancetime Publications, the performers playing Vernon and Irene Castle discuss how they refined social dance: "No more twisting, shaking, wiggling, or flouncing. The key to dance now is . . . panache."[26] The unspoken sentiment is that the twisting, shaking, wiggling, and flouncing were the stuff of Negroes, and, in order for ragtime dance to be proper enough for whites, they would have to make changes. In particular, the Castles spearheaded the official elimination of many animal dances they deemed unseemly, vulgar, or too sensual, like the Bunny Hug, the Turkey Trot, and the Grizzly Bear.[27] The Castles and others whitened ragtime dance at the same time they offered their version as an escape from European constraints, decadence, and corruption. Though in one sense they succeeded in democratizing ballroom dance by moving it away from a privileged, private pastime for upper-class whites to a public, middle-class white activity, in another sense they helped ensure that this type of social dancing would not be a venue of social equality between whites and blacks.

Primitivity

The phenomenon that I will focus on for the remainder of this chapter is what I call "primitivity." It is one of the most pervasive influences of racial formation and has direct roots in ragtime dance. Using critical race theory, I build on the work of Homi Bhabha, Franz Fanon, Antonio Gramsci, Brenda Dixon-Gottschild, and others to explain the role of ragtime dance in the creation of national and racial identity and social power. In a recent *New York Times* article about an up-and-coming choreographer, a prominent artistic director called her work "rooted in classical ballet but with strong jazz overtones and also a more ethnic or primitive side."[28] I am less concerned with the choreographer (who is white) per se than with the continued association of the terms "ethnic" and "primitive." The usage here is not particularly negative. In fact, one might even say that the comment was meant to be a compliment; however, the constant association between the "ethnic" (here the author means nonwhite, despite the fact that white people have ethnicity) and the "primitive" is fraught with racial biases. The association (and the shifts in accompanying value judgments) may be traced back before ragtime dances developed; however, the prominence of the animal dances of the ragtime era and the influence of Darwin on social theory at this time led to a particular reading of the movement style and its originators that has had resonant consequences. The association between blacks and animals in these dances was seized upon as further evidence that blacks existed at an earlier stage of biological development, somewhere between apes and whites. They were therefore considered cruder, simpler, baser. The irony and complexity is evident, however, in the fact that primitivity was celebrated at the same time it was disparaged:

> This ragtime appeals to the primitive love of the dance—a special sort of dance in which the rhythm of the arms and shoulders conflicts with the rhythm of the feet, in which dozens of little needles of energy are deftly controlled in the weaving of the whole.[29]

> On occasions, I have been amazed and amused watching white people dancing to a Negro band in a Harlem cabaret; attempting to throw off the crusts and layers of inhibitions laid on by sophisticated civilization; striving to yield to the feel and experience of abandon; seeking to recapture a taste of primitive joy in life and living; trying to work their way back into that jungle which was the original Garden of Eden; in a word, doing their best to pass for colored.[30]

Interestingly, another sense of the word "primitive" did not develop such strong associations with ragtime dances. "Primitive," as in "prime" or "primary," was not embraced. Also, even though primitivism is the belief that so-called primitive cultures and ways of living are inherently better than more technologically dependent ones, this does not translate into direct social power.

From as early as the fourteenth century, the term was used in relation to the early Christian church. In the eighteenth century, however, naturalists solidified the use of the word "primate" to describe the highest order of the class Mammalia, including humans, monkeys, and apes. The resistance of the Christian church to the association of humans with monkeys and apes and the disassociation between Christianity and the term "primitivism" are probably not coincidental.[31] The connections between "primitive" and "primate" were and are too close. Also, the negative connotations of "primitive" (simple, base, vulgar, uncivil, closer to monkeys, and so forth) gained currency over the course of the nineteenth and twentieth centuries. If we take these two senses of the term (the simple/uncivil and the pure/superior) as we examine U.S. popular culture at the dawn of the twentieth century, we see that although whites loved the primitivity of ragtime, it was more for the former sense of the term than the latter. Ragtime dance allowed them to be tourists in a less formal culture. It allowed them to relax the rigidity of Victorian culture along with some of the rules and patterns of social dance.

Though rarely used to discuss dance, the political theories of Antonio Gramsci are useful here.[32] The language around primitivity and ragtime dance feeds directly into the formation and organization of consent and power relations. A prominent definition of Gramsci's concept of hegemony is the means by which dominant social and political systems exercise coercion and bring about acquiescence of subjects without resorting to overt force. Language is a vital tool of hegemony. The language around ragtime dance demonstrates an important mechanism in this structure. Language is strategic, and the language of primitivity around discourses of ragtime dance reinforced the so-called othering of blacks for whites and vice versa. Even though descriptions of ragtime dance and music that used the rhetoric of primitivity were hegemonic tools by the dominant structures, they also served blacks by giving them a sense of ownership over important cultural forms—the first uniquely American music and dance contributions. Blacks also championed the values of the so-called freeing dance style. In the end, though, there were limits to how far blacks could maneuver within this system.

For blacks at this time, there existed an ideological debate around popular social dance. Using W. E. B. DuBois's articulation of a double consciousness, many blacks saw ragtime dance from a black consciousness as the outgrowth of a rich slave tradition of syncopation and complexity. Ever mindful of how black culture was received by whites and the implications for social justice, however, many blacks saw ragtime dance from a second consciousness (through the eyes of whites) and denounced the genre for fear of judgments made about the entire race based on one aesthetic genre. The influence of religion also must not be ignored. Because of the mores and moral dictates of the time, the movement styles of ragtime to some were lascivious and debauched. For some blacks, spiritual conservatism was part and parcel of respectability and social uplift. Before jazz became known as the devil's music, ragtime held the honor of being viewed as the torch on the path toward iniquity.[33]

One might well imagine a different phenomenology of ragtime dance and music if the second sense of the term primitive had more influence. A rare, but not quite obsolete, definition of the term primate is "one who is first in rank or importance; a chief, head, superior, leader."[34] How might the reception of ragtime dance and music have been different if it were considered primitive in this sense? Undoubtedly, the association of black bodies dancing and animalism would have meant something other than the vulgar. In many African belief systems, animals are worshipped as the earthly representatives of the gods. The United States in the early twentieth century might have seen the connection between African religiosities that venerate animals and other parts of the natural world with Christianity, all around the concept of primitivity. Had these ideas about the animal incarnation of divinity held sway over ragtimers (black and white), the phenomenology of ragtime dance would have been a much different experience. But that connection was not made. Instead, an incipient racial negotiation that seemingly championed a freer dance aesthetic but surreptitiously perpetuated injurious labels prevailed.

Erasing Race

This racial negotiation is further complicated by the long-term disassociation of ragtime dance from its roots in black culture. Deplorably, many contemporary accounts of ragtime dance try to erase race from the history of this era in social dance.[35] Most of the Web sites I came across in conducting my research provided only a cursory mention of the black performers of ragtime dance or the influence of black musicians like Scott Joplin; many others failed to mention African Americans at all.[36] The pictures on these sites are almost exclusively of white dancers. If one ignorant of black social dance history were to turn to the Internet, he or she would come away thinking that African Americans had nothing or little to do with the genre. This is how history is altered and important figures are lost. Ignoring or erasing race from the history of ragtime dance creates an inaccurate history of social dance in the United States. Consider the fact that ragtime dance was not just a form of expression of the body through space but was also the embodiment of contemporaneous negotiations regarding race, gender, sexuality, religion, morality, generation, and class as I argue in this chapter. Beliefs about the races were part and parcel of the scandalous, liberating, exciting verve of the dances.

Revisionist history places ragtime dance's roots in the waltz and Victorian ideology instead of the jook joints and dance halls of the black South and North. For example, at the 1997 Conference on American Band History, Frank Cipolla, SUNY Buffalo professor emeritus, claimed ragtime as a reflection of Theodore Roosevelt and the freedom of the American spirit, yet he does not mention ragtime as a reflection of the condition of the first generations of free African Americans. Without looking at the African American spirit of freedom, an incomplete picture is painted. In the same vein, the Dance-time Publication video *How to Dance through Time,* volume 2, *The Ragtime Era 1910–1920,* pictures a white couple on the front cover and features only white dancers.[37] Again, in another video series by the company, *Dancetime: 500 Years of Social Dance,* volume 2 (which features ragtime dance), not a single black dancer is present.[38] Also, they cite Irving Berlin as the creator of the ragtime sound, completely ignoring Scott Joplin and other black musicians.[39]

By reclaiming the African American roots of ragtime dance in this chapter, I do not mean to make an essentialist argument about authority, ownership, and the body. Physical culture is in constant flux, and African Americans have always been adept at the reinvention of cultural identity. Bhabha agrees with Fanon when he warns against the "dangers of the fixity and fetishism of identities within the calcification of colonial cultures" and recommends against "roots" being "stuck in the celebratory romance of the past."[40] Of course, ragtime dance was, and is, important to cultures other than African American and is a part of American culture as a whole. Ragtime dance, like most cultural production, is a blend, as I have shown here. Some see this encounter as the Africanization of European dances.[41] Others see it as the Europeanization of African dances. Because black pioneers of dance forms are often not given due credit or cited as influential, these cultural negotiations are relegated solely to general aesthetic influence or ignored altogether.

Others respond by condemning the negotiation as cultural theft.[42] Unfortunately, some make the argument that only when an African American form becomes popular with a broader audience does it become important. This chapter attempts to counter such fallacies and address a wider spectrum of the dialectic. I hope it will spark further research and dialogue.

Notes

1. Incidentally, we get our phrases *take the cake* and *piece of cake* from this practice.

2. For more discussion of the racial and political implications of Joplin's sheet music covers, see Susan Curtis, *Dancing to a Black Man's Tune: A Life of Scott Joplin* (Columbia: University of Missouri Press, 1994).

3. The high stepping of the Cakewalk also influenced marching bands and New Orleans balls.

4. Sonny Watson's StreetSwing, available at http://www.streetswing.com, is a good source for origin myths. The site provides rumors and sources without too much speculation about the veracity. It is important not to devalue rumors and oral accounts when studying this era, particularly when definitive documentary evidence is not extant. The accuracy of these descriptions is suspect, however.

5. Jean Stearns and Marshall Stearns, *Jazz Dance: The Story of American Vernacular Dance* (New York: Da Capo Press, 1994), 99.

6. Katrina Hazzard-Gordon, *Jookin': The Rise of Social Dance Formations in African American Culture* (Philadelphia: Temple University Press, 1990), 3.

7. Mura Dehn was a Russian émigré who was a dancer at the Savoy and a devotee of jazz dance. She documented many dance styles on film and theorized about the importance of social dancing.

8. Mura Dehn Collection (box 3, folder 64), The Jerome Robbins Dance Division, The New York Public Library for the Performing Arts.

9. Dancing, other than animal dances, also existed on the plantation. Some of these include the breakdown, set de flo', Charleston, shouting, and dances that imitated daily work (pitchin' hay, corn shuckin', and cuttin' wheat). Also, I do not mean to suggest that the slave experience was monolithic. Certainly, the experience of slaves dancing in New Orleans, with its intricate caste system, was much different from the slave dancing in Charleston. Unfortunately, space permits me to speak in only general terms about the types of dancing that existed on plantations. For a more detailed explanation, see Hazzard-Gordon, *Jookin'*.

10. Hazzard-Gordon, *Jookin'*, 45–46.

11. Quoted in Lynne Fauley Emery, *Black Dance: From 1916 to Today* (Princeton, NJ: Dance Horizons, 1988), 94.

12. Evidence of John Canoe celebrations can be found throughout the African diaspora. For more, see ibid., 30–34.

13. Lydia Parrish, *Slave Songs of the Georgia Sea Islands* (New York: Creative Age Press, 1942), 111.

14. For a more detailed description of the Turkey Trot, see Julie Malnig, *Dancing Till Dawn: A Century of Exhibition Ballroom Dance* (New York: New York University Press, 1992), 6.

15. For more descriptions and discussions of ragtime dances, see Thomas L. Riis,

Just before Jazz: Black Musical Theater in New York, 1890 to 1915 (Washington, DC: Smithsonian Institution Press, 1989); Jacqui Malone, *Steppin' on the Blues: The Visible Rhythms of African American Dance* (Chicago: University of Illinois Press, 1996); Edward A. Berlin, *King of Ragtime: Scott Joplin and His Era* (New York: Oxford University Press, 1994); Edward A. Berlin, *Ragtime: A Musical and Cultural History* (Los Angeles: University of California Press, 1980); Tera Hunter, *To 'Joy My Freedom: Southern Black Women's Lives and Labors after the Civil War* (Cambridge, MA: Harvard University Press, 1997); Sally Banes and John F. Szwed, "From 'Messin' Around' to 'Funky Western Civilization': The Rise and Fall of Dance Instruction Songs," in *Dancing Many Drums: Excavations in African American Dance*, ed. Thomas F. DeFrantz (Madison: University of Wisconsin Press, 2002); Susan Curtis, *Dancing to a Black Man's Tune: A Life of Scott Joplin* (Columbia: University of Missouri Press, 1994); William J. Shafer and Johannes Riedel, *The Art of Ragtime: Form and Meaning of an Original Black American Art* (Baton Rouge: Louisiana State University Press, 1973); Lewis A. Erenberg, *Steppin' Out: New York Nightlife and the Transformation of American Culture, 1890–1930* (Chicago: University of Chicago Press, 1981); as well as Stearns, *Jazz Dance;* Hazzard-Gordon, *Jookin';* and Emery, *Black Dance.*

16. The Cakewalk also exerted much influence on black musical theater and performers like Bert Williams. Ada and George Walker cakewalked their way to renown on the vaudeville and early musical stages. Dora Dean and Charles Johnson created high-class cakewalking as part of their ballroom dancing. Later, Margot Webb and Harold Norton would also create an elegant ballroom dance team.

17. The politics of this caste system were also quite pronounced in the West Indies.

18. It is beyond the scope of this essay to detail the reasons why different types of caste systems developed among slave societies. Too simple is the explanation that masters tried to exert more control over their slaves by allowing some to think themselves superior to others. Undoubtedly, there also existed an independent need for slaves to feel good about themselves. Unfortunately, this often came about by disparaging other slaves.

19. The quadrille was an extremely important dance in West Indian slave societies. Excellence in dancing quadrilles meant the acquisition of class, respectability, and European social mores. The Mura Dehn Collection in The Jerome Robbins Dance Division at The New York Public Library for the Performing Arts contains collections of interviews between Dehn and West Indians about the importance of dancing quadrilles to their lives.

20. Quoted in Emery, *Black Dance,* 100.

21. For more, see Hazzard-Gordon, *Jookin'.*

22. Again, it is important to note that not all African Americans were going to these venues for social dancing. These were primarily working-class establishments. Many in the upper classes, as well as many very religious African Americans, looked down on the atmosphere of these places and the looseness of the dancing.

23. Hazzard-Gordon, *Jookin',* 93.

24. Though beyond the scope of this work, it is important to note that negotiations were played out in ragtime music as well as dance. For a discussion of the "whitening" of ragtime music, see Berlin, *Ragtime: A Musical and Cultural History,* 102.

25. Vernon and Irene Castle, *Modern Dancing* (New York: World Syndicate, by arrangement with Harper and Brothers, 1914). Banes and Szwed point out that *Modern Dancing's* wording for instruction echoes African American processes of learning, suggesting that the Castles absorbed the "pedagogical rhetoric" of African American

culture; Banes and Szwed, "From 'Messin' Around' to 'Funky Western Civilization,'" 183.

26. Carol Teten, *Dancetime DVD: 500 Years of Social Dance*, vol. 2, *The 20th Century* (Kentfield, CA: Dancetime, 1998).

27. No doubt, these dances continued in unofficial social settings.

28. Claudia La Rocco, "Choreographing a Toothlock on a Dancer's Tongue," *The New York Times*, July 24, 2005.

29. Hiram K. Moderwell, "Ragtime," *The New Republic*, October 16, 1915, 285.

30. James Weldon Johnson, *Along This Way* (New York: Viking Press, 1933), 328.

31. As early as the mid-seventeenth century, the animal was separated from the divine, and humans were considered to have both in the forms of flesh and spirit. The goal, then, was to move the self as much away from the animal and as much toward the divine as possible. The moral and the spiritual were removed from the inferior animals and all things associated with animality.

32. Gramsci argued for the inclusion of a wide range of seemingly nonpolitical human activity for the understanding of politics, society, and culture. So, using hegemony to discuss dance is not inconsistent with his ideas.

33. For more on the politics of respectability, uplift, and black spirituality, see Evelyn Brooks Higginbotham, *Righteous Discontents: The Women's Movement in the Black Baptist Church, 1880–1920* (Cambridge, MA: Harvard University Press, 2006); Kevin Kelly Gaines, *Uplifting the Race: Black Leadership, Politics, and Culture in the Twentieth Century* (Chapel Hill: University of North Carolina Press, 1996); and Hunter, *To 'Joy My Freedom*.

34. *Oxford English Dictionary Online*, http://dictionaryoed.com/cgi/entry/50188568, accessed August 1, 2005.

35. This phenomenon occurs with the cultural roots of the tango, rumba, and other Latin dances in this era as well. Unfortunately, space prevents me from discussing the nuances of these other negotiations here.

36. For example, see the Library of Congress Web site on dance instruction manuals, available at http://lcweb2.loc.gov/ammem/dihtml/diessay7.html, and the vintage dance time line Web site, available at http://www.mixedpickles.org/20cdance.html.

37. Carol Teten, *How to Dance through Time*, vol. 2, *The Ragtime Era 1910–1920* (Kentfield, CA: Dancetime, 2003).

38. Teten, *Dancetime DVD*.

39. Outrageously, even when demonstrating the Black Bottom, the Charleston, swing, the Twist, disco, break dancing, the Moonwalk, voguing, and hip-hop, the videos feature no black dancers and make very little reference to black culture. These claims and omissions are not innocuous. This is irresponsible and dangerous revisionist dance history.

40. Homi K. Bhabha, *The Location of Culture* (New York: Routledge, 1994), 9.

41. See Eric Foner and John A. Garraty, eds., *The Reader's Companion to American History* (Boston: Houghton-Mifflin, 1991).

42. For interesting discussions of these complex negotiations, see Eric Lott, *Love and Theft: Blackface Minstrelsy and the American Working Class* (New York: Oxford University Press, 1995); Brenda Dixon Gottschild, *Digging the Africanist Presence in American Performance: Dance and Other Contexts* (Westport, CT: Praeger, 1998); and Langston Hughes's poem "Note on Commercial Theatre," in *Hughes: Poems* (New York: Everyman's Library, 1999).

4

Apaches, Tangos, and Other Indecencies

Women, Dance, and New York Nightlife of the 1910s

Julie Malnig

In January 2006, Santa Rosa, California's Montgomery High School, moved to ban from its school dances an explicit form of social dancing. Freaking, which had been sweeping the nation's schools, has been described as a dance involving two or more couples "thrusting their hips in close proximity," in acts that administrators describe as demonstrably and overtly sexual.[1] Sometimes referred to as "vertical sex," freaking involves couples or small groups of dancers thrusting and grinding their hips and pelvises against one another, usually to hip-hop and rap music. Many of the motions, in fact, are derivative of what many a high school student might see on MTV these days, or in the movie *Dirty Dancing*, for that matter. Although the freak dance phenomenon itself was not new (it had been making headlines in local newspapers for at least several years prior and causing consternation among school boards and parents), what differentiated the Santa Rosa case was that the school elected to impose written rules prohibiting drinking and limiting dance behavior.[2] The stipulation: Students and parents must sign a form promising to heed the guidelines before students could attend the next weekend's school dance. As one anxious, forty-three-year-old mother said of her sixteen-year-old daughter's participation in the dances (which she has now forbidden): "It's encouraging sexual promiscuity; it has to be. Those kids are getting turned on."[3] The new rules were apparently put in place, reported the Santa Rosa *Press Democrat*, after an incident at one dance involving drunken students and behavior that, according to the school principal, "went beyond the bounds of propriety."[4]

Both this language and the sensibility behind it are the very same that might have been uttered by an early-twentieth-century moral reformer when the Turkey Trot, Grizzly Bear, and other prototypes of the so-called rag dances or modern dances first made their appearance in ballrooms around the country. Propriety, refinement, grace—these were the watchwords used by anxious moralists of the time to attempt to quell the outbreak of dancing of the Progressive Era, a period that saw major shifts in the substance, style, and context of social dance in the United States. Gone was the second-position ballet stance and with it much of the cordiality and restraint of the nineteenth-century ballroom as dancers prized a greater sense of individuality and spontaneity. African American– and Latin-inspired styles now permeated the ballroom, and the ballrooms themselves moved out of the rarefied atmosphere of exclusive clubs and private homes and into the more unscripted world of the cabaret and public dance hall.[5] Swaying hips, flexible torsos, and, yes, more mobilized pelvises were put on display as social dancers tested the "bounds of propriety."

Moral and religious injunctions have gone hand in hand with social dance for eons. We know, for instance, that when first introduced in the early nineteenth century, the waltz caused a furor among moralists and clergy because of its closed-couple position and the way it sent dancers whirling around the dance floor. The historical reasons for the protests against social dance have typically focused on apprehensions of sexual promiscuity and lower-class rebellion, as well as long-standing Protestant taboos against the body.[6] Invariably, the arguments always come back to fears of (and for) the feminine: that the dancing would wreak havoc on the morals and sexual development of women and girls, threaten their roles as keepers of the domestic sanctity of home and hearth, or tempt their susceptible sexual natures. Their arguments and the *way* they were cast interest me most here: a time of intense cultural change, when ideas about women's behavior and suitable demeanor were actively and openly debated and gender relations literally played out on the dance floor.

What I illustrate in this chapter are the ways women—primarily white, middle-class, and working-class women—performed in dialogue with these cultural prohibitions and injunctions and in so doing attempted to reconcile nineteenth-century social and moral values with the expectations of the current age.[7] In one sense, the social dance phenomenon of the period was a rhetorical one as a variety of pundits, preachers, teachers, and reformers used the so-called dance craze as a way to assert or preserve conservative social values. But of course, it was a deeply *kinesthetic* phenomenon, a bodily practice born of the visceral combination of movement and music that women of different classes and ethnic backgrounds might use as a means of enhancing, exploring, and solidifying identity in a time of deliberation over their status as so-called New Women. I attempt here to encapsulate some of the major ideas and arguments of contemporary dance scholars regarding the way dance, culture, and ideology came together to shape changing concepts of femininity in the early twentieth century.

Social Dance Background

Some context helps place this social dance phenomenon into perspective. During the Progressive Era, from about 1890 to 1920, the country reoriented itself to major cultural and technological developments in the wake of industrialization, among them an emerging consumer culture; huge urban growth; greater job opportunities; massive immigration, including black immigration from the South; the rise of a new middle-class leisure culture; and the greater emergence of women in public life. The social adjustments to be made were many, as Americans adapted to a new consumer-based culture in which the primary modes of production were no longer centered in the home but in large and impersonal businesses and institutions. Alongside the expansion of business and commerce was a strong progressive reform movement that monitored the various injustices arising from corporate capitalism and spreading urbanism. Middle-class women reformers, in fact, were some of the most vociferous advocates for the eradication of social ills and active in causes ranging from child labor laws to prostitution to temperance. Dance halls and cabarets, too—along with other public amusements, such as theaters, movies, and amusement parks—would eventually become lightning rods for the reformers.

The cause of the consternation had to do largely with the marked difference in the look of the dance from the nineteenth to the twentieth century. The typical nineteenth-century ball in both middle- and upper-class contexts tended to be a highly organized affair, held either in the drawing rooms of private homes or specially rented spaces in clubs and restaurants. By the 1910s, social dance moved into more publicly oriented institutions—cabarets, dance halls, restaurants, hotels—that altered patterns of dancing and socializing. In the cabarets (precursors to the popular nightclubs of the 1920s and 1930s), the dimly lit chandeliers, postage-stamp-size dance floors, and closely moving bodies (necessitated in part by the small dancing areas) encouraged greater mingling and sociality between the sexes.[8] Although the round dances of the nineteenth century (the waltz, polka, and galop, for instance) did allow for a greater closeness between couples—part of the reason for the controversy surrounding the waltz—couples still performed in counterclockwise position around the floor in patterned steps, attuned to the movements of their fellow dancers. (Elizabeth Aldrich's chapter in this collection discusses the role that nineteenth-century dance played generally in social life.) Early-twentieth-century dances, on the contrary, allowed couples to improvise steps and become virtually oblivious to the movements of their fellow dancers.

Changes in musical style, most notably ragtime music, greatly affected the look and shape of social dancing as well, spurring the rag dance phenomenon that swept the country from 1908 through the early 1910s (see Nadine George-Graves's chapter in this collection). Although eventually transformed, subdued, and formalized by the dance-teaching establishment, the rag dances were emblematic of the changed configuration of the body in social dance generally of the early twentieth century. The rag dances evolved from both black and white working-class dance halls and clubs in urban areas across the country, where they were then picked up by professional performers as stage dances. As ragtime music itself evolved in the United States and merged with the popular tunes of Tin Pan Alley, it became something of a hybrid, an amalgam of African American–inspired and European-derived musical forms that took the country by storm.[9]

The rag dances, as developed in primarily white middle- and working-class communities, represented a basic spatial reorientation of the ballroom-dance body, in which the torso, shoulders, and hips were more fully engaged and partners assumed close, often gripping holds. As one observer noted of the Turkey Trot as performed in ballrooms in the 1910s, "In the first place you don't take your partner's hand and you don't confine yourself to encircling her waist with only one arm. You encircle with both arms and she puts her hands behind your collar at the back."[10] In the ragged quality of the irregular, syncopated rhythms, social dancers might experiment with elongated bends, body holds, dips, or other improvised steps.[11] Although the animal dances, such as the Turkey Trot, Grizzly Bear, and Chicken Reel (so named, then, for the excitable pumping of the arms and erratic hip movements), were somewhat interchangeable and often indistinguishable from one another, what united them was their rhythmic sense and improvisatory nature, in which couples might spontaneously break from a formal hold. When dancers improvised and broke from their partner, as dance historian Danielle Robinson vividly notes, "they *divided* their torsos into discrete parts, such as shoulders, waist, and hips . . . angular body lines proliferated as limbs *jabbed* into space."[12] The syncopated inflections of ragtime music also affected the look of the more traditional social dances. The Hesitation Waltz, for instance, incorporated syncopation into a basic three-step waltz, allowing the dancing couple to literally hesitate or sway on the second and third counts. At the same time, Latin dance styles, such as the tango and an incarnation of the Brazilian tango called the maxixe, also found favor as ballroom style generally began to loosen up. These dances, too, were more rhythmic and made more dramatic use of the body in their use of alternating rest and action steps and varied tempos.

Women and the Sexual Double Standard

The nature of the dances, the dance contexts, and their enormous proliferation only further fueled the "rhetoric of moral panic" of the period, as dance historian Ann Wagner notes, which made synonymous women's greater participation in public life with a perceived erosion of morals, breakdown of family life, and a fear of sexual permissiveness. Women and men were now participating in a culture that licensed public commingling and sociality in a way not seen in the previous century. The corollary idea was that as women ventured out of the home, they were also "out of control."[13] Part of the distress over the dance "epidemic" stemmed from the greater visibility and exhibition of the female body, demonstrated not only in public amusements and entertainments but also in the physical culture movement, which had set the stage for a new female athleticism.[14] Not to be underestimated, too, was the emergence of birth control during this time, which also lent itself to cultural debates about the female body. Mass marketing and advertising were powerful tools in conveying the idea that women had within them the power to shape and mold their own bodies. The multitude of mass-produced representations of women, circulating in a variety of contexts, such as billboards, posters, department store windows, and magazine covers, became part of the iconography by which women would come to see and know themselves.[15] Women's clothing, for instance—in particular dance clothing—came to emphasize the idea of the natural body, one unencumbered by wires, slips, and other paraphernalia, so that women might now take pleasure in the experience of their own bodies. The professional women exhibition ballroom dancers, in fact, were prominently featured in all the popular magazines of the day modeling new, freer, and more movement-oriented fashions and extolling the physical and psychological benefits of dance. As fashion historian Anne Hollander notes of this period, "The change in the sexual agreement between men and women was mainly enabled by changes in female image and self image."[16] The dance floor licensed such experimentation with presentation of self, and *this*, of course, was one of the moralists' greatest concerns.

Although the term "New Woman" was bandied about freely and in many ways became a convenient marketing tool for ambitious advertisers, as historian Susan Glenn notes, it *was* a concept used "to portray the continuous, dramatic renegotiation of gender concepts as women experimented with new kinds of public behavior."[17] The New Woman actually encompassed several different groups of women. At the turn of the century, it referred to middle-class, career-oriented, college-educated women interested in suffrage and social reform; later in the 1910s, it came to represent women who rejected bourgeois social conventions, pursued artistic and creative lives, and supported the idea of the then popular concept of companionate marriage. But other New Women, still, were working-class women, those either living with their parents or independently, partaking of the new leisure culture and in the process breaking down stereotyped ideas about women's relationship to family, marriage, and home.[18] Although middle-class women's economic situation enabled them to partake more readily of many of the new urban leisure activities, all still labored under the increasingly weighty mantle of the "cult of true womanhood," an ideological holdover from the nineteenth century that, as historian Carroll Smith-Rosenberg notes, "prescribed a female role bounded by kitchen and nursery, overlaid with piety and purity, and crowned with subservience."[19] In this view, women were presumed to possess an "instinctive modesty," and the new urban amusements represented deleterious influences that might cause women to deviate from what was considered their essentially pure state.[20] Old ideals died hard, as the New Women attending college, entering the workplace, organizing around suffrage, or attending nightclubs (minus a male companion) were still subject to the belief systems of a previous era.

Women and Social Dance Culture

By 1912, public dance halls and cabarets became a rallying point around which ideas about women's place in society were debated, in large part because of the immensity of the popularity of social dance and the numbers of women these institutions attracted to their doors. Reformers as well as educators, social workers, religious pundits, and social commentators joined in the chorus debating women's sexuality and moral disposition. The idea that women themselves might be instigators of their own pleasures seemed anathema to many; women's essential nature was not the problem, they argued, but the circumstances in which women found themselves—unlicensed clubs (often run by unscrupulous operators) with close dances, rhythmic music, available men, and sometimes liquor. As historian Elizabeth Perry has noted, many of the reformers, like the temperance and antiprostitution activists, believed that alcohol "weakened a girl's ability to resist sexual temptation." Grounded in what Perry calls a "post-Victorian but pre-modern concept of sexuality," the reformers acknowledged women's sex drives but certainly viewed the dances and the clubs as potentially perilous diversions from women's *true* path of purity and virtue.[21]

The commentators could be fierce in their condemnations: "The evil influence is inevitable," lamented columnist Ethel Watts Mumford. "The very air of these places is heavy with unleashed passions." Prominent muckraking journalist Rheta Childe Dorr (also a member of the National Woman Suffrage Association) was unstinting in her estimation of the dance halls on young girls. It was, according to her, "a straight chute down which, every year, thousands of girls descend to the way of the prodigal."[22] Even though the critics advocated reform, not abolishment, of the dance clubs (dance, after all, might provide necessary recreation and cultural uplift, particularly for the working classes), theirs was a protectionist outlook nonetheless, which at its core urged maintenance of "social purity."[23]

The distrust of these institutions stemmed in part from the perception that they promoted a "lessened self-possession, a surrender of intellect and emotions" that was beyond the control of authorities.[24] And, of course, in many respects, this was true. As Belle Lindner Israels, a former settlement house worker, noted of practices at Bowery dance halls, "the fact remains that the average girl has small powers of discrimination." She goes on: "The girl whose temperament and disposition crave unnatural forms of excitement is nearly beyond the bounds of salvation; but ninety out of one hundred girls want only what they are entitled to—innocent relaxation."[25] But in such seemingly "unnatural forms of excitement" many women found a welcomed release from more formal nineteenth-century social conventions. We can see how many of women's dance practices, as carriers of coded gender expression, enabled them to assert their sexual identity and in ways that were not always so easily policed.

In the middle-class cabarets, a unique pattern of dancing developed: professional, exhibition ballroom teams, hired by the clubs, would rise from their tables and glide to the dance floor, after which the public followed suit. Although they did not slavishly copy the professionals—that was not the point—social dancers took their cues from the teams who wordlessly gave them license for experimentation: to linger over the dances, and each other, in improvised steps and patterns of their own devising. This democratization of the ballroom refers not only to these newly sanctioned spaces for social dancing but also to an atmosphere that promoted the idea of the *availability* of dance to amateur social dancers no matter their level of experience or expertise. With their plush, romantic interiors—the Leon Bakst screens and murals and dimly lit chandeliers—the cabarets promoted a sense of heterosexual coupling, but one within which women social dancers were encouraged to become active agents in the quest for pleasure.[26]

A particularly salient example of a changed ethos of social intermingling and one in which women were prominently engaged was the afternoon tango tea or *thés dansant,* held at clubs, restaurants, even department stores.[27] Ostensibly opportunities for young women and men to learn dancing from professional ballroom teams, these social gatherings were places for unescorted women to meet the opposite sex. The reformers, of course, found these situations a direct affront to the traditional cult of women's sexuality; Ethel Watts Mumford remarked in *Harper's Weekly,* "Just what is an afternoon tea? Do you picture it, oh, New York Mother, as a peaceful gathering over a silver pot and a steaming cup?" She, and others, feared that the unprecedented numbers of women drawn to the tea dances might succumb to the wiles of the so-called tango pirates, the young male dancers who presumably preyed on innocent wives and daughters. For critics, the tango teas were one more "trap" laid by city life for "young unwary feet"[28] (and other body parts). For the women attendees, most of them of the middle class, partaking of the tea dance was indeed a kind of surreptitious pleasure afforded to them as they temporarily operated outside the bounds of the conventional heterosexual coupling of ballroom dance. These revised social conventions represented by the tango tea, enabled women, for a time, to choose their own partners and thus, as dance scholar Linda Tomko suggests, become "the consumers of dance services supplied by men."[29]

Similar patterns of socializing held true for the working-class dance halls, which were generally of three types, the latter two causing the most consternation: those linked to fraternal organizations and voluntary organizations; social clubs run by entrepreneurs in basements of saloons and tenement house; and saloon dance halls, often annexed to drinking establishments. Although in the commercial dance hall, as in the cabaret, the emphasis was on male-female pairing, women often came and mingled in same-sex groups and then "coupled off" later during the evening.[30] The dances themselves tended to be brief (about five minutes each) and thus created more unstructured time for socializing with the opposite sex.[31] Although a so-called trickle-down theory of culture is often assumed during this period—in which the middle and upper classes set patterns of cultural norms that were then copied by the lower classes—it was equally the case that immigrant and working-class women initiated cultural forms that some reformers attempted to stifle before they might penetrate to other classes.[32] One dance, referred to frequently in investigative reports compiled on the dance halls, was known as spieling, a very fast waltz in which couples "hung" from one another with outstretched arms while whirling each other around at great speeds. (Rheta Childe Dorr surmised that the excessive spinning created a euphoria that only heightened the young girls' desire to drink.[33]) Another variant was something called the Half-time Waltz, most likely a type of Hesitation Waltz, which, according to Dorr, contained "a swaying, and contorting of the hips, most indecent in its suggestion."[34] In these athletic and energetic variations, one could argue that young women and men were essentially parodying the more traditional male-female ballroom dances of the time; moral reformers and critics interpreted these as a rebuke to standard gender conventions, too, as traditional notions of "leading" and "following" also broke down.[35]

The practice of breaking was also common: Male dancers might approach a group of women dancing together, then select one, and remain with her for the duration of the dance. This fed fears about the so-called spieler, a young male dance assistant hired to pair female wallflowers with willing male partners (the working-class version of the tango pirates), whom Rheta Childe Dorr colorfully described as "a sinister creature, who lives on the earnings of unfortunate girls."[36] (Equally scorned were the so-called pace makers, men hired to rouse the reluctant into dancing.) As historian Kathy Peiss and others have pointed out, such practices often had the effect of undermining women's interests, as they were temporarily placed in debt to men (as in the practice of treating, in which would-be male suitors bought their dates drinks, dinner, or gifts in exchange for their company or sometimes sex).[37] Nonetheless, the clubs, like the tango teas, afforded women the possibility of exercising choice regarding their male partners and the ability to "express a range of personal desires" unhindered by parental supervision or guardianship.[38]

Not the least of the concerns of these and other rag dances was their association with black culture, which factored into the "moral panic" of the period. Racist attitudes were characteristic of the nation as a whole during this time, which witnessed an exodus of African Americans to the North and a mixing of races in public establishments.[39] The enormous popularity of ragtime in many quarters was feared as it might inevitably lead to "adoption of other African American traits," as ragtime historian Edward Berlin explains; racial and sexual overtones got inextricably linked as the dances came to represent a kind of "cultural miscegenation."[40] Indeed, these attitudes were evident in the language used to describe the more sexually connotative ragtime dances. Said one Miss Mae Helstead, inspector for public school recreation centers, "You know perfectly well that these dances came to us from the Barbary Coast, the Apaches of Paris and similar untutored sources. The movements of the various steps, assisted by the music to which they are danced, stimulate too much abandon, too much swaggering, too much freedom." Helstead cites one recreation center (like the Santa Rosa high school decades later) that attempted to impose an edict on all new dancing (of the type that was deliberately coarse) and stick instead "to the two-step, the waltz and the quadrille as formerly we've danced them. . . . There is a floor committee and if they attempt the new dances they are stopped."[41] The language of "abandon," "animalistic," and "primitive" all bespoke the deep-seated anxieties of black-derived forms in that they might arouse women's susceptible natures and lead to her moral downfall.[42]

The popular exhibition ballroom teams in many ways helped quell the ballroom dance craze's more excessive characteristics. The women exhibition ballroom dancers, in particular, maintained a curiously dual status. On the one hand, they were clearly role models for New Women; not only did their form of dance encourage women to participate more freely on the dance floor, but in their demeanor and public presentations, they also bespoke a new sense of female independence. Some, like Joan Sawyer, were outspoken suffragists and also represented a new brand of entrepreneurial businesswomen, many of whom owned their own cabarets and clubs.[43] And although they became darlings of the advertising industry and were used to endorse everything from corsetry to footwear, they served as models, nonetheless, for less inhibiting styles of dress and more flexible forms of social decorum.

On the other hand, in their task of transforming what were considered the rough-and-tumble rag dances into elegant exemplars of "refined" couple dancing, they actually became aligned in some ways with the goals of the reformers. With the help of their shrewd promoter, socialite Elizabeth Marbury, famed ballroom dancers Irene and Vernon Castle published a dance and etiquette book, *Modern Dancing,* that advocated "correct" ballroom stance and posture; established a dance school, Castle House (for "refined" ballroom dancing); and sponsored events similar to the subscription dances of the late nineteenth century. As the accompanying photograph of Irene Castle with her chiffon Corticelli dress, neat bobbed hair, and glamorous good looks reveals, how could anxious moralists complain (figure 4.1)?

The calls to refine the dances were also a way to standardize and make them teachable and came not only from the exhibition ballroom dancers but also from dance teachers and studio owners eager to capitalize on the public's appetite for social dancing. (The Fred Astaire and Arthur Murray franchises that blossomed in the 1920s are prime examples of the merchandising of social dance practices.) Part of this codifying effort, too, reflected a deep, cultural distrust of the *potential* of the body in unchecked rhythmic improvisation. Despite all such attempts to harness both the dance craze and women's impulses on the dance floor, one could not always account for what bodies were doing *in the moment* of dance. As dance scholar Carol Martin notes in her chapter in this collection, although social dance is typically "regulated largely by moral, legal, and social codes" it is also "unregulated in the informal ways it can pass from body to body."[44] Cabaret and dance hall culture of the early twentieth century in essence fostered a community of women who, through a type of wordless, kinesthetic connection—whether by modeling the professional teams or copying each other—were learning about their bodies and gaining acceptance and validation in those efforts by their peers. Even the exhibition ballroom dancers, the apparent standard bearers of "correct" ballroom style and form, could communicate to social dancers types of movements still unauthorized by the critics. For instance, in his 1914 manual, *Dance Mad, or Dances of the Day,* dance teacher Leslie F. Clendenen denounced what he considered improperly executed dance movements, but these positions were almost identical to those performed by some of the professional teams (figures 4.2 and 4.3). In fact, many of the exhibition teams also performed for late-night-only patrons at the cabarets where their suggestive versions of the Apache and other sinuous couple dances were typically on display for public consumption and thus available to be copied and learned.

Figure 4.1: Exhibition ballroom dance star Irene Castle models fashionable dance dress of the era. Circa 1913. Billy Rose Theatre Division, The New York Public Library for the Performing Arts, Astor, Lenox and Tilden Foundations.

Inevitably, women social dancers, emboldened by the new dance climate, either defied the restrictions or found alternative means and sources of dancing. In an example from the middle- and upper-middle-class context, the New York society pages reported on a shocking breach of social propriety when three young couples "invaded" the Plaza Hotel ballroom and persisted in performing the Turkey Trot. As *The New York Evening Sun* reported, "At the strains of the second two-step, the couples, separate, as they remained all evening, picked out their corners, and swayed, swayed, swayed." Although one of the matrons made a special appeal to the "handsomely" dressed women, "each

Figure 4.2: An illustration of the kinds of dips and bends
social dancers should avoid, in Leslie F. Clendenen's *Dance
Mad*. Jerome Robbins Dance Division, The New York Public
Library for the Performing Arts, Astor, Lenox and Tilden
Foundations.

girl, in each couple, went right on swaying."[45] The hotel manager made some
vague gestures toward barring the dance in the future, but for that evening,
the dancers remained.

Similarly, in the working-class dance halls and clubs, many of the propri-
etors and managers, eager to capitalize on the new leisure entertainments,
simply ignored any injunctions against so-called indecent or otherwise in-
decorous forms of social dancing and let their clientele do as they pleased.
As Kathy Peiss notes, "In the anonymous spaces of the commercial dance
halls neither floor managers nor social conventions restrained the sexual
implications of the dance movement."[46] Reformers found limited success by
promoting local ordinances against drinking or fining clubs for code infringe-
ments, but it proved much more difficult to legislate *social* controls, rather
than legal ones. Although antivice organizations, such as the Committee on
Amusements and Vacation Resources of Working Girls, regularly made site
visits to rout out questionable dance establishments, there were simply too
many of these clubs to oversee.[47] Many dance halls proliferated through a
kind of underground network beyond the purview of investigators.[48]

Figure 4.3: Famed exhibition ballroom team Maurice and Walton in a sensuous dip position generally disapproved of by dance teachers. Circa 1914. Billy Rose Theatre Division, The New York Public Library for the Performing Arts, Astor, Lenox and Tilden Foundations.

At times, social dance may reinforce social codes and societal behaviors; at others it may subvert them. During the early years of the twentieth century, the dance floor became a kind of rehearsal ground where new modes of conduct and behaviors were, if not always undermined, certainly tested and tried. With new generations of women moving increasingly into the public sphere, large immigrant populations dominating work places and leisure establishments, and a growing commercial culture that catered to citizens' physical desires and wants, gender relationships came under renewed scrutiny. As women began to assume greater prominence and independence, their efforts were challenged on moral, religious, and cultural grounds to quell what to many seemed like a rising insubordination. Albeit in different fashions and forms, both middle- and working-class women, whether single or married, were united in what historian Lois Banner has suggested was their response to "a new self-assertion and vigor and a new sensual behavior, a desire for pleasure that flew in the face of Victorian canons of duty and submissiveness."[49] Not to be underestimated in this new dance context was precisely the power of pleasure whereby women might feel liberated to imagine and reinvent themselves in new ways beyond confining societal dictates. In the moment of dancing, of responding directly and viscerally to the movement and the music, gendered patterns of identity might be abandoned, altered, or challenged.[50] In a 1912 essay in *Harper's Bazaar,* writer, poet, and suffrage supporter Alice Duer Miller gestures toward a rapprochement between the moralists and the "younger generation," arguing that the new dances have not destroyed romance, only the "romance based on false mystery and artificial barriers." In describing what women have gained in occupation, education, and social life, she refers to their new "liberty of enjoyment,"[51] an apt phrase, I believe, for the experiences of women foraying into the modern age.

Notes

1. Catherine Gewertz, "Freak Dancing Craze Generates Friction, Fears," *Education Week,* February 28, 2001.
2. Martin Espinoza, "Montgomery High Bans Sexually Explicit Freak Dancing: Sr. School Requires Random Breath Tests to Fight Alcohol at Dances," *The Press Democrat* [Santa Rosa, CA], January 28, 2006. See also Melanie Asmar, "High School Dances Grind to a Halt," *Concord* [NH] *Online Monitor,* September 21, 2006.
3. Olivia Barker, "Teen Craze Bumps Up against Morality," *USA Today,* reprinted in the *Indianapolis Star,* June 4, 2001, City Final Edition, E01. See also my interview with sex educator Deborah Hoffman, in which I discuss the freak dance phenomenon, "Talk of the Nation," National Public Radio, June 21, 2001, http://www.npr.org/templates/story/story.php?storyid=1124678.
4. Espinoza, "Montgomery High Bans." In her fascinating book *Adversaries of Dance: From the Puritans to the Present* (Urbana: University of Illinois Press, 1997), Ann Wagner discusses how opposition to dance continues to this day, especially in small evangelical and fundamentalist towns and cities across the country.
5. For further history on nineteenth and early-twentieth-century social dances, see Julie Malnig, *Dancing Till Dawn: A Century of Exhibition Ballroom Dance* (New York: New York University Press, 1994).
6. Again, see Wagner, *Adversaries of Dance,* who offers one of the most comprehensive discussions of the reasons for these attitudes historically. See also Elizabeth Aldrich, *From the Ballroom to Hell: Grace and Folly in Nineteenth-Century Dance* (Evanston, IL: Northwestern University Press, 1991); and Susan C. Cook, "Watching Our Step: Embodying Research, Telling Stories," in *Audible Traces: Gender, Identity, and Music,* ed. Elaine Barkin and Lydia Hamessley (Zurich, Switzerland: Carciofoli, 1999), 192.

7. Considerably more research needs to be conducted on the role of black women and social dance during this period, particularly in the New York City region. The majority of the white middle- and working-class dance halls in the New York City area, with some exceptions, did not allow blacks. For more on black social dance arenas, see Katrina Hazzard-Gordon, *Jookin': The Rise of Social Dance Formations in African-American Culture* (Philadelphia: Temple University Press, 1990), 124, 128. For one of the best discussions of black women and public dance-hall culture in the Atlanta area in the 1910s, see Tera Hunter, "Dancing and Carousing the Night Away," in *To 'Joy My Freedom': Southern Black Women's Lives and Labors after the Civil War* (Cambridge, MA: Harvard University Press, 1997), 169–86. For an informative discussion of social dancing in the 1930s and 1940s, see also Marya Annette McQuirter, "Awkward Moves: Dance Lessons from the 1940s," in *Dancing Many Drums: Excavations in African American Dance,* ed. Thomas F. De Frantz (Madison: University of Wisconsin Press, 2002), 81–103.

8. See Malnig, *Dancing Till Dawn.*

9. See Edward A. Berlin's *Ragtime: A Musical and Cultural History* (Berkeley and Los Angeles: University of California Press, 1980); and Edward A. Berlin, *King of Ragtime: Scott Joplin and His Era* (New York: Oxford University Press, 1994). For an insightful discussion and history of ragtime dance, see also Danielle Robinson, "Race in Motion: Reconstructing the Practice, Profession, and Politics of Social Dancing, New York City 1900–1930" (PhD diss., University of California, Riverside, 2004). Robinson defines ragtime dancing "as the dancing practiced to the music that was called ragtime" (55) and contends that it was a melding of African American and European American dance forms (60). Her main thesis, and a compelling one, is how the rag dances become coded as black and became a way for European immigrants to establish a sense of American identity (62–63, 99–126).

10. "They Will Try Out the Turkey Trot (Dancing Standardizers May Then Decide to Bar It if It Seems Bad)," *New York Sun,* January 9, 1912, 7, col. 3.

11. Berlin, *Ragtime,* 20, 29.

12. Robinson, "Race in Motion," 111. Robinson makes a case for the inherent modernism of the newly fashioned rag dances, which she characterizes as celebrating "change, difference, discontinuity, and disruption" (111). She also notes how the rag dances, and other dances such as waltzes set to ragtime music, represented a "style of movement" more so than a set format of steps (57).

13. Wagner, *Adversaries of Dance,* 394. Such so-called sex panics, as historians Kathy Peiss and Christina Simmons note, generally "represent efforts to interpret and control changes in sexual behavior, but they also speak metaphorically to the dangers nonconformity of any sort presents to the social order"; Kathy Peiss and Christina Simmons, "Passion and Power: An Introduction," in *Passion and Power: Sexuality in History,* ed. Kathy Peiss and Christina Simmons (Philadelphia: Temple University Press, 1989), 10.

14. For a discussion of how the mass media of the day promoted images of the female body, see Julie Malnig, "Athena Meets Venus: Visions of Women in Social Dance in the Teens and Early 1920s," *Dance Research Journal* 31, no. 2 (Fall 1999): 34–62. For an interesting analysis of the dance craze and its association with sexuality and the irrational, see also Cook, "Watching Our Step," 186.

15. Stuart Ewen and Elizabeth Ewen, *Channels of Desire: Mass Images and the Shaping of American Consciousness,* new ed. (Minneapolis: University of Minnesota Press, 1992), 53.

16. Anne Hollander, *Sex and Suits: The Evolution of Modern Dress* (New York: Kodansha International, 1995), 137.

17. Susan Glenn, *Daughters of the Shtetl: Life and Labor in the Immigrant Generation* (Ithaca, NY: Cornell University Press, 1990), 209.

18. For a discussion of the history and concept of the New Woman, see Carroll Smith-Rosenberg, *Disorderly Conduct: Visions of Gender in Victorian America* (New York: Oxford University Press, 1985), 177; Lois Rudnick, "The New Woman," in *1915, the Cultural Moment,* ed. Adele Heller and Lois Rudnick (New Brunswick, NJ: Rutgers University Press, 1991); and Sara Evans, *Born for Liberty: A History of Women in America* (New York: Free Press, 1989). See also Glenn, *Daughters of the Shtetl,* who notes that "for women, in particular, modernity meant breaking down traditional negative female stereotypes and expanding the feminine presence and voice beyond the customary spheres of home and marketplace" (3).

19. Smith-Rosenberg, *Disorderly Conduct,* 13. Joanne J. Meyerowitz, *Women Adrift: Independent Wage Earners in Chicago, 1880–1930* (Chicago: University of Chicago Press, 1988), explains what "emancipated" really meant in the working-class context: "The subcultures they formed failed to remedy low wages, promoted female economic dependence, and encouraged women to value themselves as sexual objects. Still, as they knew, their challenge had genuine, though limited, meaning. They defied the sexual double standard, explored sexual desire, and established independence from supervision, at least in their leisure hours" (141).

20. Barbara Welter, "The Cult of True Womanhood: 1820–1860," *American Quarterly* 18, no. 2 (Summer 1966): 158; Lewis A. Erenberg, *Steppin' Out: New York Nightlife and the Transformation of American Culture, 1890–1930* (Chicago: University of Chicago Press, 1981), 81.

21. Elisabeth I. Perry, "'The General Motherhood of the Commonwealth': Dance Hall Reform in the Progressive Era," *American Quarterly* 37, no. 5 (Winter 1985): 720, 724.

22. Ethel Watts Mumford, "Where Is Your Daughter This Afternoon?" *Harper's Weekly,* January 17, 1914, 28; Rheta Louise Childe Dorr, *What Eight Million Women Want* (Boston: Small, Maynard, 1910; New York: Kraus Reprint, 1971), 209–10.

23. Perry, "'The General Motherhood of the Commonwealth,'" 721.

24. John F. Kasson, *Amusing the Millions: Coney Island at the Turn of the Century* (New York: Hill & Wang, 1978), 101.

25. Belle Lindner Israels, "Way of the Girl," *The Survey* 22 (July 3, 1909): 488, 496. Israels chaired the Committee of Amusements and Vacation Resources of Working Girls in New York City. Prior to that, she had been an assistant to the Committee on Entertainment and Exhibitions of the Educational Alliance in New York City, where she studied the amusement activities of young women. See also Belle Lindner Israels, "Diverting a Pastime: Are We to Protect the City's Youth and Yet Provide for the Natural Demand for Entertainment?" *Leslie's Weekly,* July 27, 1911, 94, 100. For further demonstration of this protectionist attitude of the reformers, see also Perry, "'The General Motherhood of the Commonwealth,'" 721–22.

26. Linda Tomko, *Dancing Class: Gender, Ethnicity, and Social Divides in American Dance, 1890–1920* (Bloomington: Indiana University Press, 1999), uses the phrase the *spectacularization of social dancing* to refer to the way in which the cabaret experience made social dancers themselves the focus of attention, enabling them, in essence, to become the performers. She notes how patrons "thus became the subject for examination, evaluation, and possibly emulation by other observing diners" (27). For women social dancers, the context was important in helping them perceive themselves as subjects of their own experience.

27. For an interesting essay on the role of the department store in relationship to

consumer culture and appeals to women customers, see William R. Leach, "Transformations in a Culture of Consumption: Women and Department Stores, 1890–1925," *Journal of American History* 71, no. 2 (September 1984): 319–42. For more on early-twentieth-century consumer culture generally, see William Leach, *Land of Desire: Merchants, Power, and the Rise of a New American Culture* (New York: Pantheon Books, 1993); and T. J. Jackson Lears, "From Salvation to Self-Realization: Advertising and the Therapeutic Roots of the Consumer Culture, 1880–1930," in *The Culture of Consumption: Critical Essays in American History, 1880–1980,* ed. Richard Wrightman Fox and T. J. Jackson Lears (New York: Pantheon Books, 1983), 3–38.

28. Mumford, "Where Is Your Daughter," 28.

29. Tomko, *Dancing Class,* 23.

30. Kathy Lee Peiss, *Cheap Amusements: Working Women and Leisure in Turn-of-the-Century New York* (Philadelphia: Temple University Press, 1986), 105.

31. In addition to chapter 4, "Dance Madness," in Peiss's *Cheap Amusements,* which documents the social mores and dance habits of women in working-class dance halls and clubs, see Israels, "Way of the Girl"; Louise de Koven Bowen, "Dance Halls," *The Survey* 26 (July 3, 1911): 383–87; John M. Oskison, *Public Halls of the East Side* (New York: University Settlement Society of NY, 1899), 38–40, The Humanities Collection of The New York Public Library. Other extensive descriptions of dance-hall culture and the ragtime dances may be found in the Committee of Fourteen manuscript papers (a citizen's advocacy group active from 1905 to 1927), housed at the Manuscripts Division of The New York Public Library for the Humanities and Social Sciences. Danielle Robinson has worked closely with these materials in her dissertation, "Race in Motion."

32. Peiss makes a case for this argument in her book *Cheap Amusements,* but see p. 8 in particular for her views on the way culture worked in two directions here. For further discussion of how working-class women set standards of style emulated by the middle classes, see Glenn, *Daughters of the Shtetl,* 209, who argues that in their leisure patterns, young immigrant women were defying the traditions of the shtetl and presaged habits and patterns seen later in the flappers of the 1920s. Glenn, citing Meyerowitz, notes how "middle-class 'bohemians' in America in the 1920s learned about new sexual possibilities not only from 'highbrow' sexologists but also from 'lowbrow' sexual exploits of working-class women" (296).

33. Dorr, *What Eight Million Women Want,* 208. This sentiment, of course, echoes that of nineteenth-century critics of the waltz documented by Elizabeth Aldrich in her chapter in this collection. On the "loss of control" characteristic of the spieling dances, see also Tomko, *Dancing Class,* 24.

34. Dorr, *What Eight Million Women Want,* 208.

35. Robinson, "Race in Motion," 106; Tomko, *Dancing Class,* 25.

36. Dorr, *What Eight Million Women Want,* 214.

37. Peiss, *Cheap Amusements,* 106–7; Tomko, *Dancing Class,* 26–27. See also Andrew R. Heinze, *Adapting to Abundance: Jewish Immigrants, Mass Consumption, and the Search for American Identity* (New York: Columbia University Press, 1990), 123. Heinze also explores the concept of treating, along with dating patterns, whereby "young people gained new opportunities to regulate their social life" (123).

38. Peiss, *Cheap Amusements,* 106. Another way in which young working-class women might express their personal desires and preferences at the clubs was through their choice of clothing. For a discussion of how working-class women used dress and physical adornment as important elements in imaginatively reconceiving themselves in new ways, see Nan Endstadt, *Ladies of Labor, Girls of Adventure: Working Women, Popu-*

lar Culture, and Labor Politics at the Turn of the Twentieth Century (New York: Columbia University Press, 1999), 52–53.

39. See, for example, Wagner, *Adversaries of Dance*, 255.

40. Berlin, *King of Ragtime*, 88.

41. Jean Hamilton, "At the Public School Recreations Centres They Put a Ban on Everything but Old Fashioned Dances," *New York Evening Sun*, January, 13, 1911; Social Dance Clipping Files (1919–1920), The Jerome Robbins Dance Division, The New York Public Library for the Performing Arts.

42. In her chapter in this book, "'Just Like Being at the Zoo': Primitivity and Ragtime Dance," Nadine George-Graves offers a compelling reading of the concept of primitivity and speculates as to why the understanding of primitivity by white culture, as that having to do with coarseness or vulgarity, took precedence over the notion of primitive as connoting "first" or "original." She also points out how whites latched onto ragtime during this time as a way of unlocking or discovering parts of themselves hitherto repressed and that enabled them to "be tourists in a less formal culture."

43. See Malnig, "Cabaret Dancing," in *Dancing Till Dawn*.

44. See Carol Martin's chapter in this book, "Reality Dance: American Dance Marathons."

45. "Turkey Trot Seen at a Plaza Dance (Southern Society Didn't Want It and Was Somewhat Shocked)," *New York Evening Sun*, January 14, 1912.

46. Peiss, *Cheap Amusements*, 104.

47. Ibid., 105.

48. Dorr, *What Eight Million Women Want*, describes what were known as throwaways, cheap, printed cards "scattered broadcast over chairs and benches, on the floors," which notified the clientele of other dance halls situated around the city (206).

49. Lois Banner, *American Beauty* (New York: Alfred A. Knopf, 1983), 187.

50. For an interesting discussion of the nature of the relationship between dance music and the body and the potential subversiveness of "interior" experience, see Jeremy Gilbert and Ewan Pearson, *Discographies: Dance Music, Culture and the Politics of Sound* (London: Routledge, 1999), 48. For a discussion of the way that social dancing (in contemporary clubs and dance halls) is related to a "temporary blotting out of the self" that is not only pleasurable but also potentially beyond the means of social control, see Angela McRobbie, "Dance and Social Fantasy," in *Gender and Generation*, ed. Angela McRobbie and Mica Nava (London: Macmillan, 1984), 144.

51. Alice Duer Miller, "The New Dances and the Younger Generation," *Harper's Bazaar*, May 1912, 250.

Section 11

Evolving
Styles

5

Reality Dance

American Dance Marathons

Carol Martin

From their start as hourly dance contests in the 1920s through their development as infamous Depression-era entertainment, dance marathons troubled the murky line between the real and the theatrical well before the culture of video, film, and virtual reality started featuring either documentaries or reality shows. The shows featured hometown "girls" and "boys," amateur dancers seeking the immediate material reward of prize money, food, and gifts from spectators in mostly run-down, grumbling dance halls. If there was fifteen minutes of fame, that was good, too. No one was sure where real life left off and theater began. Dance marathons were real and not real, theatrical but not theater. In their strange blend of fiction and nonfiction, dance marathons anticipated the blurring of representation, simulation, and real life that we now experience as ordinary reality. In what ways were the performative circumstances of dance marathons a particular confluence of economics, social dance, regulation, and the particular skills of a generation of performers who knew the social dances of the day? How did this confluence help formulate the performative circumstances of American life as we know it?

Initially, dance marathons were hourly contests paradigmatic of the hedonism of the 1920s and then, after the stock market crash, the Great Depression. In the 1920s and the 1930s, contestants brought the dance language of heterosexual love and companionship to working-class venues, changing the context for the social dances of the day from the harmony of the dancing couple to the rivalry of singular accomplishment. The very first dance marathon—not yet called that—occurred on March 31, 1923, when in the process of establishing the first American record for nonstop dancing, Alma Cummings wore out six partners, one after another, as she kept dancing for twenty-seven hours at the Audubon Ballroom at 168th Street and Broadway in New York City from March 30, 1923, at 6:57 P.M. to March 31, 1923, at 9:57 P.M.[1] Cummings drew an enormous amount of publicity in the form of praise and speculation for the record she achieved; her diet, her shoes, her religion, her sex, and the six male partners she wore out were all reported in newspapers. At the finale of her dancing, the room was strewn with cigarette butts and perfumed with the odors of sweat and stale coffee, but this did not prevent the occasion from being celebrated as something uniquely American. The moment Cummings broke the record that was previously set in Sunderland, England, by two dance teachers, the band played "The Star Spangled Banner" to make it clear that this was not only a personal best but also a national triumph.[2] Cummings's victory was marked by the 1920s cultural discourse about record breaking—human agency in the face of mass mechanization—that became, in the Great Depression of the 1930s, a Darwinian discourse of survival of the fittest. Industrial notions of setting records shifted to enacting Darwin's world of evolutionary competition.

Several other American challengers—the first one, Helen Mayer in Cleveland, with a record of fifty-two hours and sixteen minutes—surpassed Cummings. Youth culture, the 1920s sense of freedom of expression, and the newly felt position of women who had at long last won the vote provided the cultural engine for the competitions. Leisure provided the realm. Neighborhood dance halls, ballrooms, and saloons equipped with dance floors provided the ready-made venues for the new bodily rhythms emerging from black culture.[3] Initially, the dancing was mainly the fox trot and improvisations based on what fatigue necessitated. Exhaustion was counterbalanced by a record-setting frenzy that made the dancing take backseat to the contests, which took several months to develop. Edna Smith remembers joining a marathon in 1928 at the Manhattan Casino dance hall in Harlem:

> In those days when they held dances they would have box seats all around.
> Clubs [social clubs] would rent the place and people would go and carry
> drinks and dinners and so forth, just like they were going to a picnic. . . .
> The funny part of it was when I went into it I was about three-months
> pregnant. I lived in Pittsburgh, Pennsylvania and I was visiting New York. I
> heard about the contest while I was there and I decided to join it. It didn't

take much to be accepted. They took your blood pressure and listened to your heart.[4]

The $1,000 prize money attracted Smith, especially because she already had three children. It all seemed simple enough. Dance and win. Even though he was out of work, when Smith's husband heard that she had joined a dance marathon, he came to the Casino to try to convince her to quit. Instead, he joined the operation as a cook. Edna danced all day long to Victrola music and at night to a live band. After 11:00 P.M., things changed. Late night was when "all the big stage people and the wealthy people would come to see us. I guess they came to view us acting like fools. They would offer extra money for the couple that could do the best waltz. We would come to life then, 'cause after a while we were just barely standin' on our feet. Whoever would do the best waltz or the best two-step would get $10 or $15. The audience, people who also went to cabarets and places like the Cotton Club, would applaud for the couple they liked and the couple that got the most applause would win."[5]

Smith remembers the contest as racially mixed, although not without race politics. The tension, Smith recalls, was the ways in which some contestants were favored over others. "The only tension was about the Puerto Rican couple. The little Puerto Rican girl was very beautiful and down the line somewhere the manager decided the couple would get married on the floor. The idea was we would keep dancing. It would be a dancing wedding. When the deal went down it came out that they were already married. They were getting extra money for the wedding. They were going to have a private tent to stay in together after they were married. That's when some of the contestants got upset. Someone said they were already married and they were just out to get more money and it wasn't fair. Whatever it was it was soon squashed out."[6]

The promoter was a man Smith remembers as Lazaro, an Italian man who also ran a boat from Pittsburgh to New Orleans for Mardi Gras. Lazaro may have wanted to cheat on the wedding for the sake of entertainment, but he could not cheat on the food or the actual dancing, both of which were constantly on view. "In the morning you had a choice of bacon, ham, sausage, hot cakes, eggs, grits, cream of wheat, any kind of cereal. In between meals we always had snacks. If you had people there that you knew, they could always bring stuff to you, but you had to keep dancing while you ate. You wouldn't think about eating during the rest period, you just wanted to sleep.[7] Early on there was not a precise method for record keeping. Eventually, the time danced was offset by time taken to use the toilet, to change clothes, to shower, to eat, and even to take a rest. Once these possibilities were established, it was a short distance to dance marathons that could last days, weeks, and even months at a time.

Knowing that drama sells, marathon publicists often featured one contestant over the others or honed in on a particular conflict of a hero/heroine versus a villain. From the early 1920s to the early 1930s, as the contests got longer and longer, the dancers kept adding the popular dances of the moment. The Great Depression cemented a form of contest that was typically forty-five minutes of dancing and fifteen minutes of rest every hour around the clock. Richard Elliott, the publicist and advance man who worked with Hal J. Ross, recounted his account of marathon time in an interview:

> You started out in motion, not dancing, in motion, forty-five minutes an hour day and night. Then there were fifteen minutes of rest. Now there was a little out on that one because for one hour, we said so in public, like 6:00 or 7:00 in the morning, why they [the contestants] could stay off the floor, and take baths or whatever. Most of them slept, but that's okay, they had an hour. When you only have fifteen minutes off the floor you lose some of those minutes going to your bed. And you've got to wash your face once in a while and you've got to do something about your clothes. So fifteen minutes an hour for twenty-four hours add up to six hours, and then with the extra hour we gave them, seven hours was the very maximum amount of sleep they could get. But when you start figuring time to change clothes, go to the toilet, get to and from the rest quarters, wash etc., you'd have to cut that time to four hours at the most. So four hours was the most amount of sleep any contestant could get. The rest of the sleeping they did while they were on their feet.[8]

By the 1930s, the nightlife and leisure culture of the 1920s was a faded dream that the patriotic bunting of most dance marathons could recall but not re-create. For the working class, the Depression indicated that modernization had failed to bring the promised release from labor and economic insecurity. Unemployed or underemployed, desperate with time on their hands, men and women turned to performance both to reenact and forget the world in which they were living. Marathons turned social dance—the Charleston, fox trot, waltz, two-step, jitterbug, and Lindy—into working-class spectacles of disinherited workers. The setting, however, was not the machine landscape of industrial capitalism made famous by Charlie Chaplin, but the saga of personal relationships lived in publicly simulated artificial soap-opera-like versions of daily life. Dancers fell in and out of love, ate their meals, shaved, did their hair, read letters from families and friends, and generally took care of all but their most private basic needs in public. Spectators ranged from members of the working class who empathized with the dancers to the rich on slumming expeditions and everyone in between. Social dancing has long been subject to the rapid appearance of new forms followed equally swiftly by their replacement. From the waltz to square dancing, the Charleston to jitterbug, dances come and go even as the physical memory of individual dances persists in individual bodies long beyond their moment of popularity. As a repertoire of embodied practice, social dance is both regulated largely by moral, legal, and social codes and unregulated in the informal ways it can pass from body to body. Social dance's physical transmission from body to body means that it can be about both forgetting and remembering, making it an ideal vehicle for the transformation of meaning over time. Much of the legislation of the period marks the change from the celebration of pro-American record setting to a suspect illegal activity punishable by fine or a jail term. New York State prohibited dance marathons with the following ordinance:

> The people of the state of New York, represented in Senate and Assembly, do enact as follows:
>
> Section 1. The penal law is hereby amended by inserting therein a new section, to be section 833 to read as follows:
>
> Section 833. *Marathon dance contest and participation therein prohibited.* Any person, firm, association, or corporation promoting, conducting, or advertising and each person participating in a marathon dance context or performance continuing or intended to continue for a period of more than eight consecutive hours, whether or not an admission fee is charged and/or is not to be awarded to one or more participants for participation therein, is guilty of a misdemeanor.[9]

Although dancing does not have the same real/performed binary as theater, it does create its own performative reality. The dance marathon version of this reality was threatening enough to warrant legislation against them all over the country.[10] Dancing directly engages the body by employing weight, volume, force, rhythm, and velocity, without having to use either text or character. It is experienced immediately in real time and place without the necessity of referring to other times and places. This is especially true of social dance, which uses social occasions as its existential rationale and draws from immediate social, cultural, and political contexts. At these events, the dancer is herself, albeit often an enhanced self in special clothing, performing extraordinary movement in spaces specifically marked, even if only temporarily, for the dance. A dancer need not be a character; her performance persona need not be created outside the demands of the dancing. She can be, for all intents and purposes, only herself in her actions. But a performer of social dance does not have the filter of playing a character in her public performances. Persona, yes, but character, no. Dancing is a nondaily way of conducting one's self in complex configurations of the body, time, and space. Grace, effort, decorum, attitude, and élan all matter in ways that are exceptional but not fictional in relation to the conduct of daily life. An actor in a play is almost always something or someone other than herself. Acquiring this other self is a process that the actor creates anew each time she prepares a role. She is not herself, but someone else, when she performs.

Different schools of acting theorize the distance between the self and character in different ways that have historically supported specific kinds of dramatic literature. The task of the actor is to realize a relationship between self and character that successfully conveys the content of the play that is always larger than any individual role. At dance marathons, the dancers were themselves, but the narratives promoters created about them were fictional, allowing spectators to project identities and desires onto the contestants. Spectators learned the dancers' biographies by reading the dope sheets (a daily bulletin issued by the promoters in order to keep interest in the marathon), talking directly to contestants over the rail, or by listening to the promoters and emcees attempting to link the contestants' performance personae to their private selves. Dance marathons were a place where promoters and spectators created fictional dramas out of contestants' lives. Straight from popular culture, typical dramas revolved around the innocent blond ingenue (well before blonds became associated with licentiousness), the dark-haired female villain, the sadistic male floor judge, the young couple in love, and the beneficent patriarchal promoter:

> The never-smiling [contestant Chad] Alviso worked with the floor judges to rile spectators to fiery indignation. Her victim more often than not was the feminine "fairhair," a vulnerable ingénue always about to drop from exhaustion. In a typical scenario Alviso would elbow blond Norma Jasper in the ribs at a moment when the floor judge just happened to be looking the other way. Jasper would feign collapse. Spectators tried to intervene by yelling frantically to the judge to disqualify Alviso for foul play. The closer Jasper's knees came to the floor, the more enraged the audience became over Alviso's attack on the seemingly innocent dancer.[11]

Spectators were caught up in an allegiance to one or more of these widely dissimilar types. The range of types and their myriad interactions, of course, were what created the hullabaloo, excitement, drama, and controversy. The blood, sweat, and tears of dancing whatever dance was most popular at the moment were woven into a contest embroidered with dramatic and gendered narratives embedded and enacted in the dancing, in the music, in the contest, and in the stands. Time was real time, space was real space, the band was really playing, and contestants were actually dancing, eating, falling down, and getting into fights.

The struggle lasting endless hours, days, and weeks of dancing was real enough, but the theater made of the struggle was factual nonsense. Dance marathons were fixed, staged, and arranged to facilitate excessive dramatization. If a contestant was a good performer, he or she could turn any actual occurrence into a fictional narrative with a life of its own. A hurt foot, for example, could be played as a life-threatening injury, perhaps forcing a contestant out of the contest. Promoters exploited such events by creating dance marathon "hospitals" equipped with glass walls so that spectators could watch their heroes (or villains) get treated. Staff costumed in white played the parts of doctors and nurses. At times, it was difficult to know what was the main attraction and what was the sideshow. Everything had the possibility of becoming spectacle: eating, sleeping, shaving, jealousy, love, temptation, falling out of the contest, getting injured, and recovering. Life on display, no matter how staged, always broke the frame of theater. Promoters staged weddings during the marathon for couples who fell in love; they added a "cot night" for contestants to sleep in public, and they set up meals on sawhorses so spectators could see the contestants eat while dancing.

In this and other ways, dance marathons prefigured today's television reality shows that are the direct inheritors of the marathon format: compete, suffer, endure, eliminate, and fail or triumph. In many ways, dance marathons were equally theater and dance. The excitement of witnessing celebrity being created and the spectacle of the ignoble trying to change their status all while dancing was a very engaging spectacle. The patina of glamour and fun was highly polished at the beginning of the contests, but the polish soon wore off. This was all to the good from the promoters' point of view because what people really came to see were spectacles of suffering. The losers were always more interesting than the winners. The drama was theirs. They cried and struggled as they carried the literal and metaphoric hope of winning. They were feted with elimination ceremonies in which their failed efforts became performances within the overall performance of the marathon. The winners typified the American dream, whereas the losers lived the American real life (figure 5.1). And contradictions proliferated.

Figure 5.1: A floor judge makes sure that contestants follow the rules of the contest. Circa 1930s. Courtesy, collection of Carol Martin.

Dance marathons invited spectators to watch them as real contests but to judge them as theatrical entertainments. Special features were added every day to the shows. Over time, the contests evolved into more and more difficult trials. In order to keep the public coming, the marathons needed to keep adding extra attractions and push the contestants to greater extremes. The marathon halls were a modern version of the ancient Roman Colosseum, whose entertainments also grew increasingly violent in order to please an increasingly jaded public.

The possibility of local and national celebrity that 1920s nonstop dance contests held out got inverted during the Depression into spectacles of the impossibility of being able to dance long enough to survive. "Consciousness itself was altered; the very perception of time and space was radically changed," notes historian Warren Susman of the period.[12] Coupled with this shift in perception of space and time came the conflation of real life with staged real life. Although only a very few could actually become celebrities, everyone could behave and dress like them. Success hard won with moral integrity was no longer a value. Dance Marathons presented the private individual as a public commodity even as they staged the transformation of the industrial optimism of measured time into a brutal division of life into ever smaller temporal units of productivity. Success accompanied with personality, no matter the ethics, was what counted in the world of dance marathons, where somehow, under the dingy lights of a low-down dance hall, promoters, performers, and spectators collaborated in creating the illusion that something spectacular was happening, that there was still something worth dancing for, worth struggling for, worth winning—with a smile—despite spiritual and physical exhaustion and pain.[13]

Promoters invented narratives about couples falling in love, couples falling out of love, while sleep-deprived marathoners acted out hallucinations (known as going "squirrelly") as they were prodded to ever more extreme actions by sadistic floor judges. Fabricated from the promoters' conscious exploitation of the desperation of the Depression, these narratives were untrue and true at the same time. They were someone's story, but not necessarily the story of the contestants. As in theater, the narratives became real for the spectators and often enough for the dancers, too. The conditions, needs, and desires that punctured the theatricality of dance marathons were rapidly incorporated into the contest, making the division between the real and the staged a meaningless separation. The tawdry spectacle of dance marathons fashioned drama by creating confusion about the very nature of the spectacle. Were they really contests? Yes. Were they fixed shows parading as contests? Yes. Were the contestants really contestants? Yes. Were the contestants professional entertainers? Yes. Were the promoters legitimate showmen? Yes. Were the promoters flimflam artists? Yes.

Social dance in the context of dance marathon contests was situated in the material changes during the first half of the twentieth century. It was "a change from a producer to a consumer society, an order of economic accumulation to one of disaccumulation, industrial capitalism to finance capitalism, scarcity to abundance, disorganization to high organization."[14] Twentieth-century social dance, when it broke from the rigorous demands of set movement patterns requiring instead individual expression, became the vehicle for enunciating a new emphasis on personality, self-realization, and competitiveness. Personality was what film stars had and what everyone wanted; it was "the quality of being somebody."[15] It was as cost effective then as it is now to make celebrities from real life.[16] Character no longer counted; personality and drama were what sold. So that is what promoters set out to create. As traveling shows, dance marathons did not so much import celebrity as make celebrities out of local "boys" and "girls." Just as reality television or *American Idol* transforms previous unknowns into stars, dance marathons created their own stars. Celebrity was publicly proclaimed but not officially sanctioned. From a bourgeois point of view, low-culture notoriety based on physical labor was a degraded status. This was constantly negotiated by the dance marathon dope sheets that featured gossip about the show and its contestants. Dope sheets, when they worked well, added a glossy melodramatic patina to the mat surface of real life during the Depression.

The drone of marathons, however, was more quotidian than glossy, as the contests morphed from hourly dance contests into events of weeks and sometimes months in duration, at the same time that many entertainers, ballroom dancers, vaudevillians, and comedians were forced out of work first by the rise of the film industry and the transformation of theaters into movie houses and then by the Depression. Marathoners, according to publicist Richard Elliott, "were mainly young people who had nothing else to do or young people who couldn't find a job, and want to win the prize money and while they were doing it get fed. They got fed for a month or two, which is quite a while. They had their doctor bills paid. Sometimes they'd even give them clothes."[17]

The only auspices controlling marathons were promoters and the emerging religion of commodity capitalism. During the Depression, dance marathons became big business but never a legitimate business. Even though promoters created the National Endurance Amusement Association (NEAA), the crooks in the business made the headlines, giving all the shows a bad name. Small-time promoters would go into "virgin towns," open a show, rake in cash, and leave before paying any of their bills or awarding prize money. These were gruesome shows of unregulated exploitation.[18] An account in the entertainment magazine *Billboard* characterized the shows this way:

> Looking in on a going show or two, observing an enthusiastic audience and a line at the box office, with seats sold and, when vacated, resold, Mr. Green promoter is all set to reap a harvest—of headaches! Lacking even a fraction of the knowledge and experience along with financial backing of the successful producer in the field, he rents a hall and induces a group of boys and girls—mostly inexperienced and unprepared—to enter. Because of a small bankroll he engages a staff, from emcee all down the line, with lowest salary as the principal qualification. Inefficiency causes trouble to start probably with the first of seven or eight daily meals. Before long the kids on the floor, sensing that all is not kosher, become unmanageable. Patrons lose interest in the thing, if it attracted any in the first place. Result: No prize money and kids stranded, help unpaid, causing agitation toward unfavorable legislation. The story of the "Flopathon" is all too familiar to some of us. Reputable producers have had flops too. But invariably they

have paid prize money, salaries to help and all other obligations, thereby promoting confidence in their future shows.[19]

Some of what went on in marathons was scam, often enough scam with a sense of humor and enhanced by expert showmanship. Certainly the profits were real enough. When the contest would end, no one knew. If attendance began dropping, the promoters added new gimmicks. Sometimes promoters chained contestants together, made them run backward, do duck waddles, and run special elimination features in which the last contestant or couple to finish was automatically eliminated from the contest. If these did not work, they found a way to swiftly end the contest, pay off the surviving contestants, and move on to the next city. Or they simply skipped town, leaving their bills unpaid and the contestants stranded.

The circumstances of the marathon created the next scene. "Round and round we go and where we stop nobody knows" was the metaphor of life that emcees and promoters narrated. Marathon enthusiast George Eells recalled, "As a kid, even though I didn't know rationally what was going on, I knew intuitively that these were lives in turmoil. It was a heightening of what you find in ordinary society because it was all enclosed in one room."[20] Characteristic of the genre is a dope sheet from a 1933 dance marathon in Tulsa, Oklahoma, that one day reported that nearly all the contestants were in need of medical attention: "Jimmy Parker and Helen Leonard, one of the crowd's favorite couples, were having an especially tough time. Jimmy's feet were said to be a solid mass of blisters, and Helen's ankles were on the verge of collapse. When a grueling grind [a strenuous contest within the contest] failed to eliminate anyone, Allen 'Frankenstein' Franklin, the floor judge, turned up the heat with a special announcement about the next evening's entertainment."[21]

Marathon promoters also stole ideas from the circus sideshow. In the sideshow, we are promised the world's strongest man, tallest man, man with the smallest head, most tattooed private parts, the world's tiniest man, hairiest woman, fattest woman—histrionic jaw-dropping types that invite us to suspend our disbelief. If this were theater, we would be agreeing to believe in what we know is not real. In the context of circus, it is real. That woman really does have a beard and that man is actually very small. What we make of these factoids is at least partially dependent upon what we think of the circus. These are freaks, real but abnormal; real but not usual within the sideshow. These freaks also reassure the ordinary spectator that he or she is normal. So also with dance marathons, but with a difference. In the marathons, spectators could believe both that these contestants were just like them and unlike anyone they knew. If the circus sideshow posits absolute difference, dance marathons posited a difference that existed only due to circumstances.

The membrane separating spectators from performers at dance marathons was very thin. As part of a culture of poverty relying on an audience out of work and on performers working for very little, the psychic distance between spectatorship and spectacle was short.[22] Survival, or failing to survive, was the looming subject that everyone understood. The struggle for survival was performed as something that could be demonstrated in a theatrical event and, even more, actually achieved through theater.[23] The primal scene of dance marathons' theatricality was raw industrial capitalism operating in the midst of nostalgia for agrarian self-determination and control. Promoters, who were in fact bosses operating from a superior economic position, took on the role of the good guys who gave contestants a chance to win a lot of money and fame even as they provided the public with entertainment. The producers provided the capital while the dancers supplied the muscle and sweat. The dancers were antiheroes who lost the battle even if they won the contest. Most of them, winners and losers alike, were discarded after the show was over. Some went from marathon to marathon, eking out a marginal living. A very few became marathon stars. And fewer still, such as Red Skelton, June Havoc, and Anita O'Day, went from dance marathons to bigger things in the entertainment world. The labor of the dancers was mostly not rewarded. Contestants were pitted against one another, and in order to win most were willing to do anything: lie on ice, sleep in front of spectators, dine on display, get married, perform daily grooming rituals, and, of course, dance, dance, dance.

Dance marathons often displayed an ebullient promise of American capitalism by draping their arenas in red, white, and blue. How ironic that this celebration of America was offered to the disinherited, jobless, and sometimes homeless people dancing and watching. It was an America they believed in but could not participate in no matter how hard they tried or how long they danced. As in the marathons, millions of Americans during the Depression were losing, were being forced out of the race. Weirdly, people heard the call: "If you can't work, then dance." The marathon offered a form of wage labor governed by the clock (as in industry) but without regular wages. What could be more paradigmatic of the Depression? Dance marathons staged the ways in which the family was no longer the core of production and therefore no longer the basis of social relations. As Stuart Ewen notes, "The connection between work and survival still existed, but it was socialized so as to pull the rug of necessity out from under the family as an organization."[24] The patriotic bunting signaled fealty for a future no one could see. Entrepreneurial venture was in the domain of a rising business class that created a state of confusion in interpersonal relations. The family was no longer a coherent unit of production but a unit of consumption. The plot, if there was one, was to make even the grimiest contest appear like legitimate American entertainment. "Wage slavery" isolated people in their struggle for survival.[25] The contestants danced, spectators danced during contestants' rest breaks, and the whirling mirror ball forever reflected the tiny shapes of couples in its fractured, shimmering surfaces.

There were no labor strikes—that other important form of pageantry—at dance marathons, as there were no marathon unions, no unity gluing the contestants together. Most participated as entrepreneurs or individuals; a few teamed up as couples. Political resistance was the antithesis of these big-boss-managed, homegrown events. To participate was to dance, that was the alpha and omega of it. Dance or die. To enter a dance marathon was to place oneself in a public spectacle as a unit of consumption: consumption of space, time, food, and attention. The reward lay beyond the horizon in another place. There was no other recourse. This was the without-rights bottom of the food chain.

This kind of situation—not only what marathons were, but also what they symbolized—aroused much criticism. Reformers were the natural middle-class enemy of dance marathons. They wanted to protect women and minors from coming into sensual or sexual contact with strangers. To many, the reformers were so-called church ladies who wanted to keep others from having fun. In reality, they represented a challenge to the culture of exploitation. The strange twist is that the reformers were maligned as bad guys, depicted as middle-aged women devoid of sexuality, whereas promoters were promoted as fun-loving "big daddies" acting in the interest of contestants while making bundles of cash: a not so opaque form of discrimination against women that still exists today but is not fashionable to mention. At dance marathons, management was the winner. But, as I hope I have shown, no matter their reputation for being easy, fun-loving, and socially radical places, dance marathons were inherently conservative contests staged wholly for the financial benefit of unregulated management. Under this veil, anything could happen. And it did. Reformers sought regulation and protection, especially for young women who were the most vulnerable to exploitation.

At the same time, a burgeoning, progressive middle class had been making cultural and economic investments in leisure activity since the beginning of the twentieth century. "The boy without a playground is the father to the man without a job" became the famous slogan of the playground movement that emerged at the end of the nineteenth century.[26] Active recreation enhanced public socializing, morals, positive competitiveness, and even work ethics, the sentiment went.[27] For some, recreation also created the opportunity for social control. The middle and upper classes believed that "proper" play created proper behavior.[28] Advocates of this point of view envisioned supervised leisure as finally breaking out of the puritan cage, although they sought to impose new "constraints of their own devising."[29] Dance marathon promoters followed in the creation of a form of entertainment of their own devising. Promoters were the controlling bosses who fought lawmakers for the right to stage contests while devising universes that ideally could be independent of outside regulation and legislation. By the time of dance marathons, working-class ethnic populations had already left their mark on WASP leisure. They enjoyed themselves in action rather than contemplation in ways that some found revelatory. In *The Damnation of Theron Ware*, a best-selling novel of the 1890s, the Methodist minister protagonist finds himself at an Irish-Catholic picnic where he sees "in mingled amazement and exhilaration" the "universal merriment" of football, horseshoe tossing, swimming, swinging, dancing, and especially beer drinking. "It is a revelation to me," he tells the Catholic priest with excitement and envy, "to see these thousands of good, decent, ordinary people, just frankly enjoying themselves like human beings. I suppose that in this whole huge crowd there isn't a single person who will mention the subject of his soul to any other person all day long."[30] Whether this vision of leisure indicated absence of spiritual life, introspection, morality, or the need for wage earners, whether working or middle class, to have a separate place for free time is not clear.

Legal obstacles eventually held sway over the contests. Many cities and states began to pass ordinances banning dance marathons on the grounds that they threatened the lives of contestants, were unregulated, attracted undesirable elements, and the promoters often were con men. Added to this, the nation's appetite for live performance of the kind the marathons offered was declining. Across the country, vaudeville houses and legitimate theaters were being converted into movie theaters and "palaces" that offered spectators a relatively opulent environment in which to enjoy the desirable or detestable lives of others: their manners, their clothes, their homes and apartments, their predicaments, and of course, in many of the movies of the 1930s and 1940s, their elegant or fanciful dancing. All this dancing was projected on screen much, much larger than life. World War II created an enormous job market. People could no longer hang around marathons for days or weeks on end. War propaganda presented a new vision of America as a progressive, moral, and freedom-loving nation rescuing the world from the Nazis and the Japanese imperialists. After the end of the war, the American home became the focus of the "greatest generation." America no longer lived on top of the flagpole but on top of the world. The seedy, gritty marathons no longer told the story Americans wanted to hear about themselves. And so, they vanished. But not quite. Roller Derbies and other marathon-like entertainments continued on television throughout the 1950s. And even in the twenty-first century, the enormous popularity of reality television programs such as *American Idol*—with its combination of highly skilled and clunky contestants and the thrill of winning or being eliminated—displays the ways in which the underlying narrative of dance marathons continues to live.

Notes

1. Carol Martin, *Dance Marathons: Performing American Culture of the 1920s and 1930s* (Jackson: University of Mississippi Press, 1994), 4.

2. Ibid.

3. Ibid., 11.

4. Carol Martin, "Interview with Edna Smith," *New Observations: Life on the Floor—Art, Sport, and Scam* (1986): 19.

5. Ibid.

6. Ibid., 21.

7. Ibid., 22.

8. Carol Martin, "Interview with Richard Elliot," *New Observations: Life on the Floor—Art, Sport, and Scam* (1986): 7.

9. Martin, *Dance Marathons*, 149.

10. Ibid., appendix.

11. Ibid., 51.

12. See Warren I. Susman, *Culture as History* (New York: Pantheon Books, 1984), xx.

13. Ibid., 273.

14. Ibid., 275.

15. Ibid., 277.

16. See Neal Gabler, "Our Celebrities, Ourselves," *Chronicle of Higher Education* 49, no. 27 (2003): B.7.

17. Martin, "Interview with Richard Elliot," 7.

18. See Martin, *Dance Marathons*.

19. Jimmy Scott, "Is the Endurance Show Durable?" *Billboard*, April 14, 1934, 43.

20. Carol Martin, "Interview with George Eells," *New Observations: Life on the Floor—Art, Sport, and Scam* (1986): 17.

21. Martin, *Dance Marathons*, 56.

22. Ibid., 41.

23. Ibid., 43.

24. Stuart Ewen, *Captains of Consciousness: Advertising and the Social Roots of the Consumer Culture* (New York: McGraw Hill, 1976), 116.

25. Ibid., 117.

26. Roy Rosenzweig, "Reforming Working-Class Play: Workers, Parks, and Playgrounds in an Industrial City, 1870–1920," in *Life and Labor: Dimensions of American Working-Class History,* ed. Charles Stephenson and Robert Asher (Albany: State University of New York, 1986), 172.

27. Ibid., 166.

28. Ibid.

29. Ibid., 167.

30. Ibid., 164.

6

The Trianon and On

Reading Mass Social Dancing in the 1930s and 1940s in Alberta, Canada

Lisa Doolittle

Every Friday and Saturday night during the 1930s and 1940s in southern Alberta, everybody danced, or so the story goes. And that is about as far as "the story" goes. Serious considerations of popular dancing are largely absent from existing historical records of this time and place, despite the apparent omnipresence of dancing in so many people's lives. Social dancing happened on a large scale at a pivotal time for community formation in Canada's West, when profound social changes occurred as the Great Depression gave way to World War II. What was going on besides and through and because of all that dancing? And how to investigate such an ephemeral phenomenon? My project is to use the written, spoken, and dancing texts together to illuminate a particular geographical-historical moment and in the juxtaposition of diverse sources reflect on how dancing participates in the process of creating and remembering history.

Dancing is a kind of history written on the body. This corporeal history is elusive; its study requires new approaches. The field of dance studies has adopted intertextuality as one useful tool for expanding the perspectives from which we can consider both artistic and vernacular dance forms. My study draws inspiration from the intertextual, historiographic approach of dance historian Lena Hammergren, who states that all sources can be considered texts and that what emerges are "patterns of meaning laid down at an earlier time."[1] Social dance presents particular kinds of challenges; popular dancing, especially in regions far from cultural centers, leaves only fragmentary traces. Although intertextual theorists normally work with completed texts, Hammergren emphasizes that fragmentary or embodied texts come to us "loaded with traces of codes that form a kind of text from which the historian can proceed with a search for intertexts." The codes imbedded in fragmentary texts—in personal memoirs, in remembered dances, or in cross-generational interviews—create a kind of "a grid or a texture of significations" rather than a linear story.[2] Unraveling strands of this rich texture reveals contradictions; although many histories seek to conflate such "inconsistencies," in an intertextual reading this richness may instead be expressed. Documents on this dance moment are scarce, yet along with local, personal, oral, and embodied sources we can reread a historically marginal story, posing the massive phenomenon of social dancing in southern Alberta dance halls during the 1930s and 1940s as a distinctive and crucial part of a pervasive and shifting cultural ethos.[3]

Today, I can still stand in the Trianon Ballroom in Lethbridge, Alberta's third largest city and the center of the region I will discuss here.[4] The Trianon first opened its doors as a dance hall in 1931 and ceased operating in 1966.[5] In the 1930s and 1940s literally hundreds of little Trianon-like halls graced small Canadian prairie towns, although most of these dance halls have since disappeared. In Lethbridge alone, four major dancing establishments were packed with patrons dancing to live bands on as many as three nights a week—the YMCA offered hostess dances for military personnel, the Kiwanis club gave teen dances every Friday night, and one could dance at the Masonic Hall and in local hotels.[6] Other magnets for dance activities in southern Alberta included the dances in community halls and outdoor pavilions in Burdett, Champion, Enchant, Maple Grove, Willow Creek, Whitla, Retlaw, Picture Butte, Iron Springs—and these are just a few from the southern Alberta region.[7] By my calculations, there was a dance hall for at least every four thousand inhabitants in the towns, and the proportion was even higher in rural areas. These staggering statistics, combined with an indelible and widespread collective memory of dancing in the good old days, suggest that mass social dancing was indeed a crucial territory for the staging of choreographies of community cultural values.

Although the phenomenon was widespread, the dancing, the venues, the participants, and the meanings attached to the activity vary through time and from place to place. From photographs and oral accounts, we know that the interior decoration of the dance halls expressed a range of regional identities. In the National Parks town of Waterton in the nearby Rocky Mountains, tourists joined masses of locals to dance in a huge lakeside pavilion for several decades. The international crowd enjoyed allusions to Canada's rugged wilderness in a decor comprised of hundreds of stuffed samples of wild animals (eagles, hawks, bears and bear cubs, wolverines, and mountain goats) mounted on every beam and column. For dancers at the Lethbridge Trianon, cardboard palm trees and ceiling stars alluded to the tropics, a differently exotic natural locale. Seemingly superficial differences of decor signal differences in the way people danced and the way they understood the significance of that dancing. Some striking local deviations from the received myths about the "good old dancing days" emerged in the research, suggesting that a unified account would be inadequate and, worse, misleading.

This material first drew my attention as I began a choreographic project exploring local dance cultures.[8] As I researched this deeply nostalgic moment for my theatrical evocation and as audiences reacted to the performance's re-presentation of the past, I became acutely aware of how we weave past realities into the present. The strands that make up the fabric of this region and this time, embedded in documentary, oral, embodied, and artistically transformed versions of the social dance story, include rural/urban dichotomies, invisible yet deep racial divides, and fluctuating gender identities.

Documents

Histories and archived documents traditionally privilege the grand and public. Unsurprisingly, dancing, because conceived as frivolous and private, does not tend to get detailed or coherent consideration in traditional histories. Yet the vast public choreographies these sources reveal are important to any understanding of the dancing itself. Over the two decades of my research, studies of Western population migration reveal the massive exodus from farms to towns, a group choreography with enormous public and private consequences. In 1931, two-thirds of Alberta's population lived in rural areas, a proportion that remained stable for more than a decade. By the end of the war, in 1946, 44 percent lived in cities, and this proportion reached 50 percent by the 1950s. By 1946, around seventeen thousand people lived in Lethbridge. The population migration figures suggest a shift in cultural values parallel to the demographic shift.[9] The vast distances between communities in 1930s southern Alberta meant that a rural culture had emerged here that did not occur to the same extent in the more populated regions in the United States, where easier travel and migration leveled distinctions between rural and urban traditions.[10] The experience of dancing followed this pattern, from dancing in homes and small community halls to more professional, urban dance halls. Likewise, the forms of social dance that were prevalent in urban centers supplanted the more locally meaningful dance forms.

People think of Alberta as an agricultural region with the requisite rural conservative mindset. But, in fact, the cultural values of the city and its dominant cultural group (Anglo-American) always shaped patterns of leisure and work in the region. The views of this dominant group prevail despite huge variations in the existing ethnic composition of the community and ongoing immigration. Lethbridge was, and still is, the closest urban center to two enormous Blackfoot reservations (Kainai and Pi'ikani). Since the early part of the twentieth century, the region has hosted Hutterite colonies, Chinese coal mine and railroad workers, and diverse European immigrant populations attracted by agricultural work and settlement prospects. During World War II, the city of Lethbridge was home to a British Commonwealth Air Training Plan base (1,500 personnel, mostly British ethnicity, and trainees from New Zealand, Australia, and Great Britain). The largest POW camp in Canada (with a capacity for 12,500 internees, mostly Germans captured in African battles) was established here, and 370 Japanese families, mostly from British Columbia's west coast, were resettled nearby and forced to perform hard labor in sugar-beet fields. This cosmopolitan demography was reflected neither in public leisure activities nor in attendance at the dance halls. Rigid racial boundaries were occasionally legislated but were more consistently maintained by an ethos of European colonial superiority.[11]

Social dancing appears in the public record most often subsumed under the category of leisure and is further buried under the headings of music and musical entertainment. In such discussions, photographs and detailed descriptions of male-dominated orchestras and bands are common. Dancing, an everyday activity carried out by ordinary people, remains an embodied memory, rarely captured for posterity in image or text. Histories of leisure that do discuss social dance fit it unproblematically into utilitarian notions about mid-twentieth-century leisure, reflecting the Protestant, Anglo ideas about hard work as the purpose of existence.[12] In this code, dancing provides either the recuperation needed to produce more hard work or light relief from the seriousness and tragedy of the distant war. Documents marginalize dancing and minimize its meanings; however, oral accounts can dialogue with documents to reveal not only nuances missed in documents but also some central historical issues.

Voices

Firsthand intergenerational encounters—like the oral history type of interviews in this project—participate in different codes of cultural transmission than do documentary records. Some historians regard oral histories as unreliable, inevitably contaminated by the vagaries of human memory and by the subjectivities of both interviewer and interviewee. Oral historians, however, value the rich, messy embodied information that unfolds in an interview. Further, the discrepancy between fact and memory ultimately enhances the value of oral sources as historical documents because consistencies among "inaccurate memories" of the same event in oral accounts often indicate deeply held collective beliefs, at least as important for the historian to analyze as "mere facts."[13] One documentary history concludes that women had limited access to leisure outside the home, because documentary evidence shows that they did not have equal access to male activities such as hunting, sports, bars, and clubs, thus representing women's lives as oppressively confined and overworked.[14] Yet frequent dancing at community events and at home significantly diminished the feelings of isolation for many prairie women. Although in traditional histories the dancing disappears, oral histories, as we shall see, recount a liberatory impact of dancing in women's lives. An analysis of alcohol laws, for instance, juxtaposed with seniors' descriptions of drinking at dance halls, uncovers cultural obsessions with the gendered (and also classed and ethnically specific) identity of the "respectable" citizen and social dance's liminal position on the scale of "respectable" activities.[15]

Most glaring in the documents I examined was the lack of information and analysis about how dance activity was actually regulated (unlike the contemporary environment of nightclub fire and occupancy regulations associated with alcohol consumption, drugs, and violence). By contrast, elaborate regulations (provincial and federal) existed for controlling public and private sale and consumption of alcohol in Alberta before, throughout, and after the period I am discussing here.[16] Although alcohol was not officially available at most dance halls, public social dancing seems to have held a strategic position in negotiating social tensions around alcohol consumption and, more broadly, what constituted appropriate pleasures and for whom. Public dance halls avoided the age restrictions (during the 1930s and 1940s, a person had to be twenty-one to drink alcohol legally in Alberta) and expense of purchasing licenses to sell alcohol. The majority of dance hall patrons were under drinking age, and no other mixed-gender leisure activity was provided for this socially mobile mating-age group.[17] In contrast with dance halls, bars were to be quiet and orderly places; for decades Alberta was graced with beer parlors with funereal atmospheres. Regulations about alcohol consumption in bars were gender-specific. Sometimes women were not allowed in bars at all, some communities mandated separate rooms for men and women, and still others required a separate entrance for "ladies and escorts."[18] Mixed-gender alcohol consumption apparently represented a threat to social order. Meanwhile, as long as the dancing was separate from drinking, it did not require regulatory control.

Oral sources, however, repeatedly link alcohol, violence, and prostitution with dancing.[19] Many informants told me that clandestine drinking always did occur at dances—mickeys were stashed in toilet tanks, in the parking lots, behind the billboards. Although respectable women did not drink, respectable women went to dances.[20] The public fiction that no one drank at dance halls allowed women to participate in public fun. The conflict between actual behavior and ideal behavior locates an area of rapid social change, in which ideas about gender-appropriate "respectability" were evolving. Personal accounts about flamboyant female behavior on the dance floor suggest that dancing was for many women at this time a place where they could experiment with, or fantasize about, new-found empowerment and liberation.

Liquor regulations also manifested attitudes about class and race segregation. Many local citizens of aboriginal, eastern European, or Asian origin were excluded by class and ethnicity from formal leisure institutions. Having nowhere else to go, they showed up in the less respectable bars, poolrooms, and cafés, further reinforcing stereotypes about their lack of respectability.[21] Dance halls did not expressly forbid admission to racial minorities, yet few non-Anglo-Americans attended. So how was it that few "Orientals" and even fewer "Indians" appeared in dance halls? Do tacit racial exclusions represent only a benign if neglectful attitude toward minorities? After all, when documents account for dance only as a frivolous leisure activity, participation or nonparticipation would be inconsequential. Or do these gaps point to more ugly truths about how dancing participated in the creation and regulation of a nonegalitarian social order at this time?

The repertory of dances described by informants reiterates racial exclusion, consistently including waltzes and fox trots—iconic dances of Anglo-

American, white-bourgeois culture. The regular evening dance programs at the Trianon showed little variation in ethnic origins, with the waltz and the fox trot seemingly globalized at this time through migration, tourism, mail-order instruction manuals, and eventually even radio dance lessons (figure 6.1). Many of the dancers interviewed also mention dances not related to British colonial conditions, particularly Germanic, folk forms—the schottische, the seven step, or the polka—or alternatively the rural western dance forms like the square dance. Most thought of these dances as novelties in a regular evening of dancing, however, and many were relegated to Thursday evenings when the focus was on so-called old-time dancing.[22] Len Isaacson remembers early country dances of the 1930s in the tiny rural communities "where they danced the kind of dances we've just been talking about (fox trot, waltz, and quickstep), but they also did old time dancing, the schottishe, which I never cared for much, and square dances . . . the French minuet, . . . polka." In the city—at the Trianon—he does not remember ever seeing a square dance or a schottische. "It was just straight fox trot, waltz, jive. And man did they jive in those days."[23] "Everyone" danced the "standard" dances, although it seems that as time passed, the regional or ethnic specialties were increasingly set apart on separate evenings or dropped from the repertoire.

The often-repeated phrase "everyone danced" needs redefinition: "Everyone" in the code of these oral histories meant white people of Euro-American extraction. When asked, my respondents did not seem to find the exclusion of visible minorities problematic. Martha O'Brien imagined the local Chinese dancing "in their own little homes" because "they didn't dance like we did." She acknowledged that Indians were by far the biggest problem for local acceptance, lamenting that the natives did not "seem to know how to behave."[24] Thus, the identity of the dancers also expressed the larger social structure of only apparent unity, a unity that was achieved through selective racist exclusion. My informants did not consider this exclusion a problem, an example of how, even in the absence of regulatory measures, minority experience is embodied out of the historical record.

In the documentary record, social reformers and clergy repeatedly attacked social dance during this period as a time-waster and an immoral surrogate for sex.[25] But personal stories tell a different tale. The danger in the implied sexuality in social dancing does not seem to have been a big concern for any of my interviewees. Passing and laughing reference was made to the colloquial name of the slow waltz: a "buckle shiner." One informant said he met his wife at a dance hall. But most interviewees surprisingly talked little about romance and a lot about community related to dancing, especially

Figure 6.1: Alberta Ranch Boys play the Trianon Ballroom. Circa 1945–55.
Courtesy of the Galt Museum and Archives, Lethbridge, Alberta, Canada.

in reference to the 1930s. "I have wonderful memories of those days, the good clean fun, and attended a dance once or twice a week. It was common to dance with around thirty guys in one night. I have often thought that I was born at a good time; there couldn't have been a more sociable time in history than what I experienced."[26] "When we were younger, they [parents] used to take us with them, and we'd go to these dance halls. We'd dance and throw the coats on a big table and half the kids are sleeping in that."[27] The danced image of the couple as an enduring unit was not "the point" of an evening of dancing. Although couples left with the partner they came with, everyone changed dance partners all night long. Typically, the whole family came along. The dance floor was then a socializing space, not just the courting space.

Memories of the Depression years express ideas about community identity different from these of the later wartime. The stories of early country dances uniformly reflect a community focus that was age-inclusive and homemade.

"At home when I was still young, we used to dance, we used to . . . roll up the rug in the front room and we'd dance at home. And that's where I learned to dance. I'm surprised our front room floor didn't wear out."[28] And if they wanted to dance longer than the dance was supposed to, they'd take up a collection to pay the orchestras to stay longer . . . so we'd get home at three o'clock in the morning and get up at seven to milk the cow. . . . [P]eople made their own fun."[29]

Interviewees, although nostalgic about the good old days, simultaneously say they could not wait to get away from failing farms. Some women were eager to leave behind the backbreaking double day of farm and family labor for employment and more modern conveniences in the city. The women's 1940s stories hinted at how dancing contributed to the empowerment experienced by women on the home front. Vi Watson, who continued to go dancing with her sister and girlfriends while her husband was on active duty, claimed increasing agency, not just waiting to be asked to dance. Elaine Sander corroborates: "During the war, when there was a shortage of men, women danced together . . . and then the men would cut in we'd dance with them."[30]

The end of the war seemed to destroy the imagined unity of the community. Watson noticed at dance halls in the city an escalation of the problems with alcohol and violence "connected to the war when guys would come home on leave. . . . I guess they were single, but I guess it didn't really matter if they were single or not. They used to go outside and drink and then there'd be fights. My husband never was much of a dancer, and I always was. I used to tell him you spend more time fighting than you do dancing, and that's why he couldn't dance."[31] The colloquial names of the local dance halls at this time tell it all: The Trianon was alternatively known as the Bucket of Blood or the Gonorrhea Racetrack. O'Brien complained about the snobbery of returning active servicemen, who danced only within their own crowd. As class structure shifted after the war, she saw in the dancing an increasing tendency for society to become "clique-y."[32]

The codes of oral history include subjects' editing out the negative and retaining the positive aspects of the past that preserve a preferred picture of community and individual identity. The older people we interviewed constantly contrast the past (good) values of dancing (and society) to the present (poor) values they see embodied in contemporary social dance. O'Brien disapproved of both the open sexuality she observed in the extremes of hypercloseness and the asocial behavior expressed in the hyperdisconnection between current youth dancers and contrasted this with the more appropriate distance (to her mind) between dance partners of her own generation.[33]

These metanarratives, points at which the subjects reflect on their reflections to get at the notion of passing history, let us see the role of generational memory in creating the accepted story of "history." Further, the individuals' experiences of their own life stories color the picture we receive of the times. Thus, the early 1930s (when my informants were teenagers) were innocent, rural, and family oriented. The late 1930s and early 1940s were tough but exciting and romantic; they were young unmarried adults. The late 1940s were about self-sacrifice and pulling together for a larger community as they took on the full responsibilities of adulthood and family life. Other generations might look on these same decades with very different eyes. The similarities between the oral histories reveal a shared cultural mythology in which past social dancing is conflated with positive memories of youthful energy and wartime togetherness, and dancing comes to embody an exhilarating time of change and youthful power.

Moving Bodies: Dancing Here and There

How did this region's dancing relate to the social dancing in other North American locations during this time period? Trends are not easily deduced from a small sample of oral or documentary sources. Yet by partnering these various fragments with dancing bodies, we glimpse new facets of the cultural choreography that social dancing displays in its global circulation and local reinterpretation. The repertoire and performance of dancing in this region underline tensions—as rural to urban migration accelerated—around the cultural trope of the cut-off, backward, or innocent rural region that emphasizes, by contrast, the sophistication or perhaps the sinful nature of contemporary urban life. Even in the 1930s, this seemingly remote region was hardly hermetically sealed from outside influences. Individuals recount moves from country to city or migrations to and from centers like Los Angeles; London, England; Toronto; Vancouver; and Victoria and comment comparatively on the way people danced in a variety of settings.

As local dancers and musicians themselves astutely assess the nature of their dancing community in comparison with larger trends, they alternately claim the Lethbridge region had plenty in common with dancing elsewhere and that regional and individual differences existed. Musician Joe Horhozer toured throughout Alberta and into British Columbia and as far east as Toronto. When asked to compare the dancing he observed, he claimed that a Lethbridge dancer would not stand out like a sore thumb in any of the venues he played. Martha O'Brien spent time in the small community of Burdett with a family who visited relatives in Los Angeles every summer. They would come back with new dances, and she remembers learning the Varsity Drag and the Big Apple from them. Vi Watson knew about "risqué" dances like the Black Bottom and called dances like the Big Apple and the Charleston, already passé in the 1930s, the "silly dances."

The dislocations of the war heated up the pace and extent of dance knowledge exchange. Ralphine Locke registered as a hostess (a volunteer dance partner) at dance halls in Calgary. She met a U.S. serviceman who was a native of Mexico and learned tango and rumba from him.[34] Other interviewees encountered dances like the Lindy Hop, Lambeth Walk, and conga line at air force bases outside Alberta and air force training centers inside the province that were populated by temporary immigrant air force recruits from the white British Commonwealth nations. Isaacson danced in London while posted there as part of the Royal Canadian Air Force, where he remembered some contrasts to his own experiences as a dancer: "The English were good dancers. They took long gliding steps . . . they danced different, they were good dancers. The ones I saw anyway."[35] Isaacson's experience of dancing in Lethbridge was thus more bounce than glide and more spatially contained.[36] City-dwelling, middle-class O'Brien very much admired the Quebec Fusiliers and their wives' jitterbugging at servicemen dances she attended at the elegant Empress Hotel in Victoria, but she said emphatically that dancing in Lethbridge was not like that. Her community is and was envisioned in a dignified smooth dance, not a jive. On the other hand, Grant Strate, a native of small-town Cardston, remembers wild dancing and that the skills of the dancers he knew were highly developed.[37] In that "dry" Mormon town, spectacular display of physical mastery in dance was the only permitted way for young people to move on the edge of accepted mores. Dancers in crowded prairie dance halls—sedately cheek to cheek or wildly jiving—enacted the evolving tensions in broadly accepted cultural identity tropes for this place: about hick/hip (region), his/hers (gender), and home/alien (race).

Memories: Dancing Then and Now

To examine evidence carried in the moving bodies of dancers alive then and still dancing now, my students and I participated in Friday night seniors' dances. If we grant that bodies make history, we can put past and present bodies together to construct a collective narrative of meaning that allows for a continual exchange between past and present.[38] One of my students described the current seniors dance scene beautifully: "The dancers glide across the floor, never bopping or bumping. The swishing noises made by the feet wiping the floor was almost hypnotic, and made more music than the band did. . . . While the older couples were contained in nice little spheres moving gracefully around the room, we were all elbows and knees, and jerky moves trying to get out of the way. . . . They moved like silk, there's no other way to describe it."[39] The older dancers used a language of etiquette and a repertory of dance steps whose meanings we youngsters attributed to an elegant and polite past we could barely imagine. The subtle qualities of movement this group of seniors displays include a held, almost immobile, torso on top of which heads gaze over shoulders or tilt to make pleasant conversation. The higher the level of experience, the more flexible this stance appears, even though uprightness remains the main motif. Rigidity in the pelvis is not admired, but hips rarely sway or rotate. A close and regular rhythmic relationship between footfall and beat of the music is essential, but heavily accented rhythm never occurs. Steps do not travel far, feet barely leave the ground. Arms perform slight variations on the standard social dance positions, and the open-held hands do not pump up and down. Easy collaboration, with the man controlling the type, size, and direction of the steps, makes for good partnering; women commented that trying to dance with an inexperienced male dancer was like a battle. The marked lightness and delicacy of the movement—so different from the horizontal gliding quality of globalized competition ballroom dance—can be partly attributed to the frailty of age, but it is also an authentically embodied sense of sprightly grace and likely the definitive "groove" that drove the dancing in the past. I could conjecture that the movement on the dance floors back then was also rhythmically uniform and bouncy, energetic with a light touch.

The dancing I felt on the floor of the seniors' center generally participates in an ideology of an unchanging hierarchy of social relationships. It demands coordination between two moving bodies improvising with set dance steps and figures according to a set of rules. The dancers are couples with clearly differentiated gender-specific roles to perform. The more experienced one is, the more one gets to improvise, but innovation is not prized. The dyads are integrated into a larger mass, in which couples move in their own multidirectional way but use harmoniously coordinated steps to a single beat. The early-to-mid-century ideal picture of frontier western Canadian society was that many individual impulses synthesized into a single purposeful and dynamic enterprise. The cheek-to-cheek couple image (which stretches from the nineteenth-century introduction of the waltz through to the present day) is as long lived as it is far flung. Of course, new meanings for this image evolve over time and in different contexts. Its endurance may have to do with the success with which it holds a huge variety of values in dynamic tension. Although the consistent qualities of danced movement may incorporate ideas about regional identity, it is inaccurate to generalize that these qualities of the dancing equate to a single "identity." Dancing here in the past mobilized community cohesion and embodied coercively conservative forces that sought to maintain the status quo. At the same time, and in the same place, for some dancers participation in dances connected to nascent forces of female liberation or release from religious strictures. The older people may resurrect or restore past values by performing them weekly in the protected environment of the dance space, even as they make new relationships and create a new and different community. Repeat performances of embodied experiences glue the past to the present.

Interpretations

A few moments in the creation and audience reception of my choreographed version of the Trianon's past further highlight some of the powerful forces that shape the retelling and reperformance of histories. None of the racist elements I encountered in my research ended up in the choreography.[40] My student dancers resisted the inclusion of choreography performed to Perry Como's racist 1945 song "Dig You Later (A Hubba-hubba-hubba)," which makes light of Japanese suffering from American nuclear bombs that ended the war in Asia, despite the historical fact that this song was widely popular in North America at the end of the war. They were sensitive to the fact that many of our stories came from people who fought against the Japanese and felt that without further contextualization such images would offend war veterans and their families. As non-Asians, they also felt that it was not their role to stir up old guilt in this community where the Japanese Canadians, who had been forced to move here by wartime internment measures, are now quietly integrated into the community. I agreed and minimized potentially upsetting references, but we see in the present as in the past how, when it comes to racial tensions, gaps and silences persist.

Many audience members in my age group said the piece really captured the period. In contrast, one of the older people remarked that "of course they didn't dance like that!" Another did not know what the story was supposed to mean, confused perhaps by the codes of the contemporary dance theater genre. Another was inspired to tell me an even more off-color story than the one we performed—offered by Elaine Sanders, about losing a shoe on the dance floor. Vi Watson recounted how women on occasion would lose their buttoned panties owing to the exertions of dancing and how one could become deft at kicking the dropped clothing under nearby chairs. Len Isaacson congratulated me on a worthwhile project and sent me a clipping about the role of social dancing in upholding the values of the LDS (Mormon) church. Competing versions of history emerge in the creative process, and responses to the artistic product illustrate tensions around what performance is for and who gets to make and tell history.

In southern Alberta, dancing bodies participated in the creation of, re-wrote, or refused to participate in the canon of "the good old days when ev-erybody danced." My intertextual staging of the choreography of the times, in dance scholar Naomi Jackson's words, "conceives of dance as inherently and necessarily a cultural discourse, inseparable from society, and dance as specific textual arrangements which can only be analyzed in relation to the general cultural fabric of which it is part, and which, in turn, is part of them. . . . What appears natural is shown to be a cultural construct of a particular group of people at a particular time and place in history."[41] As I juxtapose various texts, "master narratives" about this place and that time can be seen as simply the culturally dominant view, only one of many pos-sible standpoints. Examining the systems inherent in a variety of culturally coded genres (documents, interviews, old dances, new choreographies of old dances) allows us to consider contradictory viewpoints without having to resolve or erase them. Simple concepts about what constitutes a histori-cal record and how dance encodes identity are challenged when documents have to waltz with reminiscences and when artists and academic writers find themselves fox-trotting into real people's lives.

Acknowledgments

Special thanks to all the seniors who contributed reminiscences to the pro-duction and to this chapter, including Svend Andersen, Hazel Berke (Ding-man), Ralphine Locke; to students Meg O'Shea, Erin Sander, Corey Makolo-ski, Robin Weiland, Chris Godziuk, Brad Rosgen; to Bernice Hartley and the Fritz Sick Seniors Centre, John Savill at the Trianon, and the Galt Museum and Archives, Lethbridge. I am indebted to Pam Schweitzer at Age Exchange, London, England, for her mentorship in my reminiscence theater work; to the Department of Theatre Arts, University of Lethbridge, for its support of the *Trianon and On* production; and to Iro Tembeck for her visionary in-clusiveness of all kinds of dance scholarship at the Estivale Symposium in Montreal and beyond.

Notes

1. Lena Hammergren, "Intertextuality and Historiography: Reading a Dancer's Ca-reer" (paper presented at the Society of Dance History Scholars Conference, Albuquer-que, NM, 1999), 118.

2. John Frow, "Intertextuality and Ontology," in *Intertextuality: Theories and Prac-tices*, ed. M. Worton and J. Still (Manchester, U.K.: Manchester University Press, 1993), 45–55, as quoted in Hammergren, "Intertextuality and Historiography," 118.

3. Few Canadian historical writings notice dance. The following, however, con-tain important discussions about recreational dance and related issues: Aimée Viel, *Lethbridge on the Homefront 1939–1945*, Occasional Paper No. 32 (Lethbridge Histori-cal Society, 1998); Donald J. Wetherell and Irene Kmet, *Useful Pleasures: The Shaping of Leisure in Alberta 1896–1945* (Regina, SK: Alberta Culture and Multiculturalism/ Canadian Plains Research Centre, 1990); Elaine Leslau Silverman, *The Last Best West: Women on the Alberta Frontier 1880–1930* (Montreal: Eden Press, 1984), 154–56; and James Gray, *Red Light on the Prairies* (Toronto: Macmillan, 1971), 155–77.

4. The Trianon Ballroom in Chicago was one of the Midwest's grandest dance estab-lishments. Trianon is also the name of a village razed by King Louis XIV of France in order to build himself a casual amusement spot (Le Grand Trianon) on the grounds of highly formal Versailles. Although few who danced in southern Alberta knew or cared about this derivation, this name grafted onto prairie dance halls succinctly en-capsulates the region's colonization by New World American and Old World Euro-pean culture.

5. *The Lethbridge Herald,* May 28, 1966. Information found in an unattributed pho-tograph caption, which noted that "Freddy Weiterman, who has operated the Trianon for weekly Saturday night dances since last November, is seeen unlocking the door for the old ballroom's last dance."

6. Viel, *Lethbridge on the Homefront,* 24.

7. For northern Alberta (Edmonton), see Wetherell and Kmet, *Useful Pleasures,* 234.

8. Student performers collected stories about the dance hall days from elderly rela-tives. Over a seven-month period, we combined family stories with local seniors' remi-niscences to create a twenty-minute choreographed work, *Trianon and On,* performed in February and March 2000 at the University of Lethbridge and in Calgary.

9. Peter Smith, "Urban Development Trends in the Prairie Provinces," in *The Making of the Modern West: Western Canada since 1945,* ed. A. W. Rasporich (Calgary: University of Calgary Press, 1984), 134.

10. Wetherell and Kmet, *Useful Pleasures,* 10, 13.

11. Laws that targeted leisure activities of ethnic minorities included bills excluding Japanese Canadians from public bars during World War II and earlier federal Indian Act laws banning the performance of First Nations' traditional ceremonies at their dance gatherings. After the war, Germans were easily accepted into the community, whereas Japanese Canadians, Chinese Canadians, Hutterites, and aboriginals were not. As Aimée Viel notes, "Pre- and post-war developments with regards to these par-ticular communities would suggest that rather than being based solely on perceived threats to security or on wartime hysteria, much of this (discriminatory) treatment

was related to widespread nativist sentiments already present before the war"; Viel, *Lethbridge on the Homefront*, 40.

12. Wetherell and Kmet, *Useful Pleasures*, 361.

13. For an important analysis of how and why inaccurate memories are important to history, see Alessandro Portelli, *The Death of Luigi Trastulli and Other Stories: Form and Meaning in Oral History* (Albany, NY: State University of New York Press, 1990).

14. Wetherell and Kmet, *Useful Pleasures*, 381.

15. Two local judges, one the son of the original proprietor of the Waterton dance hall, provided insights into the regulatory environment of the times.

16. Prohibition existed in Alberta only between 1915 and 1923 by referendum.

17. Interviewee Judge MacLean maintained that liberalizing drinking laws was a major factor in the decline of the dance hall. When the drinking age was lowered to eighteen and cocktail lounges began permitting mixed-gender drinking in the 1960s and 1970s, dance halls lost their clientele.

18. Wetherell and Kmet, *Useful Pleasures*, 351–70.

19. A letter to the Lethbridge Historical Society (June 22, 1984) closes with a disparaging description of how the dance hall came to be known as the "gonorrhea racetrack," a place where "chippies" hung out and infected soldiers on leave.

20. Provincial movie censors believed that all films showing scenes in which women were intoxicated should be banned or have the offending scenes removed; Wetherell and Kmet, *Useful Pleasures*, 352.

21. Intense regulation aimed at reducing and containing drinking behavior contrasted with more permissive regulatory legislation that provided a segregated area for prostitution in Lethbridge until 1942; Gray, *Red Light on the Prairies*, 155–77. Prostitution became a problem only when associated with alcohol; Wetherell and Kmet, *Useful Pleasures*, 354.

22. Joe Horhozer states that only a certain crowd liked the old-time dancing. None of those dances were played on the Wednesday, Friday, or Saturday night programs when everyone was either smooth dancing or doing the jive.

23. Len Isaacson, interview with the author, February 1, 2000.

24. Martha O'Brien, interview with the author, January 20, 2000.

25. For a discussion of the evolution of antidance attitudes in the United States, see Ann Wagner, *Adversaries of Dance: From the Puritans to the Present* (Urbana: University of Illinois Press, 1997), 292–315. In Alberta, the United Farm Women, a powerful lobby group, lodged a formal complaint in 1931 requesting regulations stipulating that dances end at midnight because late-night dancing was "detrimental to health and sometimes to morals"; Wetherell and Kmet, *Useful Pleasures*, 234.

26. Hazel Berke, interview with the author, October 1999.

27. Vi Watson, interview with the author, January 25, 2000.

28. O'Brien, interview with the author, January 20, 2000.

29. Isaacson, interview with the author, February 1, 2000.

30. Elaine Sander, interview with the author, October 15, 1999.

31. Watson, interview with the author, January 25, 2000.

32. O'Brien, interview with the author, January 20, 2000.

33. Ibid.

34. Ralphine Locke, interview by her granddaughter Robin Weiland, October 17, 2000.

35. Isaacson, interview with the author, February 1, 2000.

36. Marshall Stearns and Jean Stearns, *Jazz Dance: The Story of American Vernacular Dance* (New York: Macmillan, 1979), describe the bounce/smooth evolution of the

Lindy: "[U]nlike earlier Dixieland Jazz and the Toddle which was danced to it—a bouncy, up-and-down style of dancing—swing music and the Lindy flowed more horizontally and smoothly. There was more rhythmic continuity" (325).

37. I thank Grant Strate for his comments on this aspect of my paper at the Estivale Symposium, University of Quebec at Montreal, in May 2000.

38. Susan Leigh Foster, *Choreographing History* (Bloomington: Indiana University Press, 1995), 10.

39. Meg O'Shea, notes to the author, February 2000.

40. See Michael Frisch, *A Shared Authority: Essays on the Craft and Meaning of Oral and Public History* (New York: State University of New York Press, 1990). "We rarely acknowledge how profoundly power, privilege, and freedom from historical constraint have conditioned our basic relationship to the past" (20).

41. Naomi Jackson, "Intertextuality and Dance: Some Theoretical Reflections," in *Dancing Bodies, Living Histories: New Writings about Dance and Culture,* ed. Lisa Doolittle and Anne Flynn (Banff, AB: Banff Centre Press, 2000), 229.

7

Negotiating Compromise on a Burnished Wood Floor

Social Dancing at the Savoy

Karen Hubbard
and Terry Monaghan

The Savoy began and remained a highly contested social space where popular creativity confronted "social control." The ballroom opened and closed in the midst of citywide controversies arising from changing trends in popular dance that were perceived as threats to dominant racial, class, and gender values. The 1951 *Savoy Story* anniversary program described Harlem's premiere dance space as "A luxury ballroom to accommodate the many thousands who wished to dance in an atmosphere of tasteful refinement, rather than in the small and stuffy halls and foul-smelling, smoke-laden cellar night clubs which were the illegal, but prosperous upholstered sewers of the prohibition era." Journalistic hyperbole ran riot when the Savoy opened in 1926, claiming that entrants would be greeted by "a dazzling spacious lobby framing a huge, cut-glass chandelier and marble staircase, an orange-and-blue dance hall with a soda fountain, tables, and heavy carpeting covering half its area; the remainder a burnished dance floor, 250 feet by 50 feet, with two bandstands and a disappearing stage at the end."[1] For a while, when openly hosting white customers, the management described the ballroom in the relevant publicity as the "home of happy feet" where "social, racial and economic problems fade away to nothingness."[2] After World War II, that welcome was withdrawn, but the original promise of bombardment "with a barrage of the most electrifying spasm of entertainment ever assembled under one roof"[3] remained good for the population of Harlem, who continued to call it "The Track."[4]

Many writers have tended to dwell on the seemingly positive "smiley" aspect of the ballroom's dancing in the New York press.[5] Prevailing images of "happy" African Americans remorselessly dancing the night away, although true on many occasions, still tells only part of the story. A vindictive six-month police closure of the Savoy in 1943 brought into the open a range of hostile attitudes toward the ballroom that its management had to deal with on a daily basis. In 1936, for example, management attempted to replace the Thursday "kitchen mechanics" evening, usually the raunchiest night of the week, with "old-style" entertainment. Instead of the usual packed ballroom of live-in maids and their male partners "letting off steam" before the former had to work all weekend as domestics, it was proposed that communally sung minstrel songs and dances such as the Cakewalk, quadrille, and waltz should be the replacement. The "kitchen mechanics" apparently thought otherwise, and "their" Thursday soon reverted to its usual format.[6] Grasping the management's role in facilitating its customers in the face of adversity is key to understanding the Savoy's social dancing during its thirty-two-year span of operation. Responding to pressures to "control" and at times "reshape" dance-floor creativity, management both devised positive marketing spin to deflect criticism and selectively promoted dance-floor-inspired practices that boosted the financial well-being of the ballroom.

There are thus two broad narratives of the Savoy's social dancing. One comprises a range of "hostile" or "dismissive" viewpoints, which have tended to work together in varying ways, whereas the "supportive" ones, both old and new, have been largely self-serving in their respective "defenses" of the ballroom's dancing. Both perspectives played and play varying roles in shaping the perception of the Savoy's pattern of social dancing. The two white businessmen—Moe Gale and Jay Faggen—who came uptown in 1925 to open a "luxurious ballroom" where Harlemites would want to dance were mindful of the critical views of the socially influential lobbies that disapproved of such activities.[7] Despite the early limitations placed on boisterous dancing, the huge success of the Savoy's opening year led its owners to attempt to provide a similar dancing program for the Chicago Savoy Ballroom that opened on Thanksgiving 1927. Subsequent accounts, though, have tended to pay more attention to celebrated, "iconic" nights when major non-Savoy swing bands were present rather than to its initial purpose of providing an outlet for the mass social dance aspirations of the predominantly black local community.

Drawn from the largest and one of the most diverse urban concentrations of people of African descent anywhere, the Savoy's audience acquired a unique composition. The advance guard of native New Yorkers who established the African American settlement in Harlem in the early twentieth century were soon heavily diluted by new arrivals from the South, the Caribbean, and other overseas locations. Zealously guarding its special niche of providing seven-nights-a-week dancing for them in Harlem, the Savoy capitalized on the special qualities of this mixed community. Attempts at launching rival ballrooms intended to operate all week did not survive for long. As the dominant provider of the key leisure activity of social dancing, the Savoy not only articulated the cultural aspirations of the local black communities but also developed a broader relationship with other black communities of the greater New York area. Through the black press and the dancers' grapevine, the Savoy became an entertainment destination for the black communities of Brooklyn, New Jersey, the Bronx, and Connecticut, in particular.

The twenty-five million pairs of social dancing feet that moved across the Savoy's burnished dance floor between 1926 and 1958 told their own diverse but nevertheless significant stories. Their many cultural identities enriched the dancing and enhanced the sense of community through sustaining individual group identities, thus enabling new arrivals to locate their compatriots as the wider diasporic mix grew. The actual variety of styles popular at the Savoy reflected this broad inclusive ethos. Enthusiastic remembrances of old dance forms alternated with the development of new ones and even the celebration of other communities' dance fads in a way that would now be considered quite odd in a venue that soon came to be considered the epitome of the latest dances.

Designed as a "ballroom palace," the Savoy provided a more dignified environment for social dancing than the usual jook joints, nightclubs, and dance halls open to black Americans. There remained many, though, not willing to acknowledge this distinction. African American jazz dance of the 1920s received few accolades from the leading dance modernists, such as Isadora

Duncan, Ruth St. Denis, Ted Shawn, and Rudolph Laban, as compared with those received by its jazz music first cousins from notable composers and orchestra leaders of the day. The quality of the Savoy's decor and its insistence on polite and considerate etiquette, along with the best music of the day, enabled many others to see such dancing in a new light. The dance floor was treated with special reverence. The bouncers made sure that no one smoked or drank there, and it was stripped and polished every night so that the manager, Charles Buchanan, could see his reflection in it each morning.[8]

Interest in the Savoy's actual social dancing has invariably been diverted by the spectacular achievement of the ballroom's elite dancers who were usually referred to as Savoy Lindy Hoppers. The second generation of these dancers, Whitey's Lindy Hoppers (WLH), became especially prominent during the height of the swing era from 1935 to 1943. While sustaining the reputation of the Savoy by their dominance of New York City's major dance contest—the Harvest Moon Ball—and through their resultant performances in newsreels, feature films, stage shows, and touring productions throughout the United States, they still masqueraded as social dancers at the Savoy in front of visiting celebrities and bussed-in tourists. Despite this apparent ambiguity, each major mode of the Lindy Hop—social dance, competition, and performance—developed further in separate realms of major business activity inside and outside of the Savoy (figure 7.1). However far apart these activities appeared to be outside the ballroom, the essence of each artistic achievement was infused back into the general mix when the core Savoy Lindy Hoppers returned to the Savoy. Thus even while establishing their worldwide performance reputation, WLH still significantly contributed to the development of social dancing at the Savoy.

The Early Years

The Savoy's first years of operation emphasized cabaret-type entertainment and fancy-dress theme nights that probably imitated the Roseland Ballroom's format in midtown Manhattan, which the Savoy's physical layout had replicated.[9] Evidently finding it difficult to keep up this pace of intensive programming, the management initially closed the ballroom on Mondays. Finally, though, the management was able to keep the ballroom open for a full week by resorting to its first specific dance promotion by making Mondays "Waltz Night." Although Mondays eventually acquired a different character, a waltz, "Home Sweet Home," remained the last dance played at the Savoy every night for its thirty-two years of operation. Early observers noted the fox trot

Figure 7.1: Members of Whitey's Lindy Hoppers dance at the Savoy among other purely social dancers. Circa 1936. Courtesy of TL Images.

and one-step and dancing to "the blues."[10] This latter type of dancing would have been the marginally acceptable Slow Drag. Based on a very close-hold technique and writhing hip movements, in a private party setting it tended to be stationary with the girl's arms around the boy's neck and the boy's arms placed around her waist, sometimes sliding onto her buttocks. The dance was otherwise known as Dancing-on-a-Dime, or more recently as the Grind, and the Savoy bouncers insisted that the couples keep moving.

Although the Charleston was still the "latest dance" in the months following the Savoy's opening, it was sparingly mentioned in early reporting or Savoy advertisements. In an obvious sense, the management did not need to market dancing, as that is what the audiences did on entering the ballroom. No doubt, though, they were also wary of possible racially based accusations of unleashing "ungovernable passions" by encouraging the rhythms of the "tom-tom."[11] The bouncers were directed to quietly curb vigorous expressions of the dance, such as the Charleston or the exuberant collegiate versions of the many varieties of up-tempo close-hold styles of dance that usually were called the Shag. The basic format of the latter varied according to whether the dancers started with one or two hops followed by a series of kicks in between their partner's legs and whether the dance had a six- or eight-beat pattern. One variation of this dance, the breakaway, consisted of a pivotal move away and back by two dancers on one side who thus alternated between an open and closed hold.

In addition to curbing the more expressive forms of street-level Harlem creativity, the Savoy advertised how the ballroom's defining "quality" had been introduced by downtown white folks. Thus Moe Gale and Jay Faggen reportedly arrived in Harlem with a special expertise in running major ballrooms, along with the cash necessary for its implementation. Few aspects of these stories stand up to close inspection, however. Despite various claims, Gale and Faggen had little experience in ballroom management, and obviously inflated figures were cited as to what it cost to open the Savoy. Far from actually building the Savoy, they moved into an existing building. Impossibly exaggerated figures were given as to the size of its dance floor.[12] As the initially impressive ballroom facility began to be taken for granted and focus shifted to the new dances, the subsequently often repeated story emerged that the Lindy Hop was merely an appreciative response to Charles Lindbergh's first solo flight across the Atlantic in 1927.[13] In other words, Harlem was supposedly imitating rather than originating.

Although downtown Manhattan was decked out with bunting for Lindbergh's grand ticker-tape homecoming after his heroic flight, Harlem, and especially the Savoy, was adorned with decorations for the first major convention to be held in New York of the black nonprofit charitable fraternal organization the Elks—Improved Benevolent and Protective Order of Elks of the World. (The IBPOEW, as it was known, was founded in 1899 after two men were denied membership in the white Elks, or BPOE.) The impromptu dancing that occurred outside the Savoy during the associated main parade on Lenox Avenue consisted entirely of Cakewalking and the Charleston. Not too long after the Savoy closed, Dr. Conrad Gale, a brother of Moe Gale and the only member of the owning group to take an analytical interest in ballroom dancing, alluded to "the often-looked-for connection between Lindbergh's flight and the appearance of the Lindy Hop" that had not been found.[14] Presenting the Lindy Hop as an anonymous, novelty response to Lindbergh's flight, rather than an aesthetic expression of evolving African American consciousness in Harlem, in effect obscured its true identity. Any real appreciation of the epic character of the movement imagery of this dance that rhythmically harmonized the improvisational creativity of two people in a dancing partnership with the social mass of other people with whom they responsively shared the dance floor was blocked. After this "Nordic hero" thoroughly disgraced himself in the lead-up to World War II by his involvement with the Nazis, the Savoy management abandoned the Atlantic flight association for a while. When peace came, though, they returned to the alleged Lindbergh connection tale.

George "Shorty" Snowden, who actually created the Lindy Hop in 1928 with his partner Mattie Purnell, recalled the tight control exercised over the permitted styles of dancing in the ballroom during its early days that precluded exuberant dance innovation.[15] His versatile fellow dancers had to calm down their exertions to an acceptable form of Shag or other medium-speed dance while under the bouncer's scrutiny. Or they preempted them by taking fast traveling steps to different parts of the dance floor, where, out of sight, they returned to more expressive modes. Lifting and acrobatic techniques, such as in adagio, the apache, and possibly the Texas Tommy, were largely confined to cabaret slots or special exhibitions in society bookings. The Savoy's young dancers no doubt keenly looked on in their search for more adventurous forms. The Lindy Hop, though, had to originate outside the Savoy because of continuing management hostility but surreptitiously made its way onto the ballroom floor toward the end of 1928. Confusion surrounds this point, however, because another dance *did* emerge at the Savoy, which specifically referenced Lindbergh's flight. Charles Buchanan claimed to have unwittingly named it the Lindbergh Hop when sarcastically asking some dancers at the Savoy "if they were trying to hop like Lindbergh." Buchanan's subsequent, dismissive attitude toward even the elite Savoy Lindy Hoppers makes this believable. In a 1980 interview with Jervis Anderson, he was still describing these expert dancers as "raggedy kids" for whom buying new shoes was pointless. According to Buchanan, they were so used to dancing in shoes with holes in them that they would not be able to perform in good ones.[16]

The Lindbergh Hop, though, did not create any great stir in Harlem let alone turn social dancing upside down around the world as the Lindy subsequently did. Both Leonard Reed, the producer and choreographer, and Alfred Leagins, one of Snowden's original performers who continued social dancing at the Savoy until it closed, affirmed that the Lindbergh Hop was a different dance. Specific references to the Lindbergh Hop were still made in mid-1929, although by then it could have begun to merge with the increasingly triumphal Lindy Hop. Snowden, who innovated the Lindy in another Harlem dance hall, the Rockland Palace, gave a confusing account, however, of the relationship of these two dances for the Stearns book, *Jazz Dance.*[17] Based on a late-1950s interview, it reads as if Snowden was trying to salvage the memory of the critical role he played in creating this dance without challenging the popular, if far from accurate, claims about Lindbergh's involvement.

Snowden's claim to have originated the dance form is supported by the observation that the Lindy Hop was the first noteworthy African American dance to be created in the North as opposed to being brought from the South as part of the turn-of-the-century Great Migration.[18] In effect, it was a major reordering of almost the entire African American social dance experience. The Lindy Hop also involved a redefinition of gender relations that struck at the core of prevailing derogatory and demeaning racial characterizations of African Americans. Developing into a comprehensive and rhythmically charged critique of the European partner-dancing tradition, it articulated a new aesthetic of cultural equality. Dominated by continuous rhythmic play in its defining swing-outs, the two partners rhythmically improvised while separating apart and drawing back together. The driving reciprocal dynamic of both partners characterized the essential vitality of the dance that paid minimal deference to the ballroom conventions of leaders and followers. Through such mutually assertive roles of independently and jointly sustaining a combined interactive rhythmic response to swing music, the new Lindy Hoppers made a major contribution to transforming the way these dancing African Americans not only saw each other but also how other blacks and whites perceived them. Defining individual expression in the context of working closely with another person (i.e., thus revealing its true jazz character) enabled the Lindy Hop to make such a dramatic impact. Black dancing bodies became "hep" and respectfully imitated.

Despite the management's continuing hostility, the new Lindy enthusiasts inevitably gravitated to the Savoy because of its unique seven-nights-a-week operation. As the Lindy Hop's popularity grew in and outside of the Savoy, a vacuum developed arising from the management's reluctance even to mention the name of the dance. Popular conjecture was probably responsible for filling this gap. Despite the fifteen-month time lag between Lindbergh's initial solo flight across the Atlantic and the actual naming of the Lindy Hop in September 1928, it came to be believed that these two events had coincided.

Furthermore, the management's attitude itself backfired. Keeping quiet about its newly emerging Lindy Hop scene turned the Savoy into a chic must-see in the late 1920s and early 1930s for the white carriage trade who visited Harlem each night after the theaters closed. Rumors of this new dance had spread abroad before the Savoy management finally came around to acknowledging its existence. Diaghilev, who could not have visited the Savoy in person, was reported as singing its praises while sitting in the London Savoy shortly before his death. He even bemoaned the possibility that it was probably no longer "fashionable."[19] The Savoy's new dance scene had become a well-kept but open secret in which downtown enthusiasts reveled. Early writings describing the Savoy, thus, were usually fictional or did not specifically mention the ballroom, although everyone who knew was able to recognize the location.[20]

Saturday night in the early days of the Savoy was "squares night," when ordinary black and white folks flocked to the ballroom and, in the opinion of the Savoy Lindy Hoppers, unduly constrained their dancing. On Sunday nights the celebrities came, but Snowden and the other leading dancers would wait outside until Buchanan begged them to come in and display their prowess. The management's resolve was fading. Reinforcements joined Snowden in the shape of George "Twist Mouth" Ganaway, a supple and gymnastic dancer who appeared on the scene in early 1929. Together they designated the northeast corner of the ballroom—the left side of the bandstand when faced—as the location for leading dancers to meet. Subsequently romanticized by Jean and Marshall Stearns as the so-called Cat's Corner—a phrase never used in the lifetime of the Savoy—it was probably more the result of a compromise between management and dancers.[21] Being a space the elite dancers could occupy without disrupting the circular flow of the dancing traffic, it also became a location where visitors could stand and watch.

In reality, the selection of The Corner, as it actually became known to the Savoy Lindy Hoppers, followed a common ballroom practice of more skilled dancers congregating on the left side of the bandstand and, depending on the shape of the ballroom, positioning themselves farther away according to decreasing levels of skill. Possibly owing to the Savoy's shallow configuration, the less-skilled enthusiasts would meet up in the right-hand corner to work at improving their skills until they felt competent enough to cross over. Concessions were made to the Savoy's dedicated enthusiasts in fall 1929 when the Tuesday night 400 Club promotion was given over to the enhancement of Lindy Hopping skills. Possibly these two innovations were linked in that the management was beginning to see the benefits that could accrue from working with these dancers rather than against them.

The Effects of the Crash

The 1929 stock market crash dealt a pulverizing economic blow that left the Savoy teetering on the edge of bankruptcy, during which Charles Buchanan resigned for a brief period over a punitive salary cut. The popularity of the Lindy Hop itself receded, and there were widespread expectations that Latin dances would be the "next thing." The Savoy claimed to stage the first rumba competition in the United States and advertised in Spanish-language newspapers.[22] Although jazz music and dance bounced back as swing, Latin music and dance remained regular features of Savoy programming. As such, the latter probably marked a significant separation between the tastes of the Savoy Lindy Hoppers and the ballroom's general social dancing audience. The former tended to avoid Latin dances, with some surviving members even denying their regular inclusion. The Savoy's social dancers, on the other hand, not only grew increasingly inclusive in their tastes but also came to expect the ballroom's programming of the "latest dances."

The Great Depression saw new white and black generations, with a pronounced interest in integration, taking to the Savoy's floor. Increasingly replacing the rich, white carriage trade, penurious and even radical white dancers began attending the Savoy to learn from and dance with the ballroom's regulars. The emergent second generation of Savoy Lindy Hoppers similarly became integrated more into the ballroom's operation. As opposed to the standoffish attitude of Snowden's dancers, for example, they began organizing the Saturday night competitions for the "squares," suggesting perhaps that the Savoy as a whole was becoming more "hep." Led by local community initiatives to recover from the devastating impact of the stock market crash and then Franklin D. Roosevelt's presidential victory of 1932 and the New Deal, a broader inclusive ethos emerged, with which swing in general and the Savoy in particular were already practicing.

During the early 1930s, however, the Savoy management appeared to remain uncertain over what direction to move. They continued experimenting with Latin but in 1933 returned to cabaret with a bigger and more lavish production than attempted before, called the "Savoy Vanities." Following gangster warnings arising from an unexpected resultant loss of white trade in their clubs, the Savoy abruptly switched its attention to the "latest dance sensation"—the shim-sham-shimmy—and organized demonstrations and competitions.[23] Consisting of four eight-bar phrases of well-known steps danced in a line, the Shim Sham had actually been popular in Harlem for a few years already. Leonard Reed and Willie Bryant initially devised this easy-to-learn chorus line routine for the stage. Unexpectedly, it attracted social participation with audiences enthusiastically joining in with demonstrations of this new dance in clubs and ballrooms.

The Savoy began vigorously promoting new steps—Truckin' in 1935, the Suzie-Q in 1936, and Peckin' in 1937. The latter had a rival when the Big Apple suddenly swept the United States after being introduced to New York by a group of white college students during their summer vacation.[24] Having observed the locally originated version at the Big Apple Club, a black night spot in Columbia, South Carolina, they devised their own called challenge dance largely based on the Shag. Subsequently, Herbert White, founder of WLH, directed Frankie Manning to choreograph a Lindy Hop performance version.[25] A social version was contrived for the Tuesday 400 Club functions. Although a circular pattern remained the basis for all versions, the social dance forms featured a caller who announced the steps to be collectively danced or challenged individuals or partners to enter the ring to "shine."

Curiously enough, least remembered are the dances actually created at the Savoy.[26] Most notable was the Ballroom, an adagio type of slow Lindy Hop, often danced gracefully in a triplet time. Leading exponents were Austin and Austin of WLH, and "Shoebrush," one of the Savoy's best-known social dancers. Possibly inspired by close observation of expert adagio cabaret performances at the Harvest Moon Ball, it satisfied a Harlem need for slower and more fluid, although still highly rhythmic, expressive body movements than the upright stance of conventional European ballroom dances could facilitate. The other popular Savoy creation was the Tranky Doo, sometimes known as the Savoy Routine, which was usually danced to the original Erskine Hawkins version of "Tuxedo Junction." Comprising a sequence of basic Lindy steps, it was regularly danced in the ballroom in the 1940s.[27] The failure of Savoy promotional material to make reference to these otherwise highly popular forms probably stemmed from the dances not being included in the Harvest Moon Ball. In part, at least their noninclusion reflected the emergence of a new strand of independent dance tastes among the ballroom's social dancers that did not blend with the kind of dance values the Savoy management were interested in promoting.

The Savoy's dancers during this period left little out of their dance referencing. Although not especially popular, the tango was danced and often featured the Rudolph Valentino–styled "Sheik" and his sister, one of the Savoy's notable eccentric couples.[28] The main 1930s rival to the Lindy, the Shag—of which youthful white Lindy Hoppers were especially scornful—was nevertheless danced at the Savoy. Rather than stemming from any direct continuity with the past, it had been reintroduced by college boys from Yale, Harvard, and other elite universities who came to the Savoy for Sunday afternoon matinees. They taught local female partners or the Savoy hostesses, who passed it on. Similarly, the Peabody—a kind of very quick two-step that was said to derive from the paso doble—sped around the ballroom especially to the Jimmy Lunceford number "White Heat," thus giving rise to one suggestion of how the Savoy's most popular nickname of "The Track" originated. Although the dance was especially popular in Queens, the fastest Peabody dancer at the Savoy was Charlie Milo, who came from Brooklyn, according to Jimmy Valentine, one of the few white members of WLH and certainly the only one-legged one.[29]

Special events by Afro-Caribbean community associations and the booking of Latin bands sustained the variety of the ballroom's dances. Fancy-dress events were the one enduring feature of the original cabaret-styled entertainment that remained popular enough to survive, other than the special events organized by private clubs. Perhaps the reason for this popularity was the opportunity that fancy dress provided Harlemites to indulge a sense of what seemed to be the "exotic," such as Arabian, Russian, and Chinese nights or the annual Barn Dance on Labor Day. The women were invited to dress in their "gingham gowns" and the men in their "best overalls" to do "folk dances." Authenticity was not a great concern when attempting square dancing, but complaints were voiced on occasions if real bales of straw were not used to decorate the ballroom!

The longer the Savoy survived, the more it came to embrace the different socioeconomic strata of Harlem society, and thus the "formals," in other words the club and special social event bookings that took place on most Wednesdays and Fridays, created a more genteel atmosphere. In general, the Wednesday functions were more for the less elite social club's private bookings with the preferred attire being black tie, whereas the Friday black "elite" society functions went for white tie. Lindy Hopping took place on such nights, but few Savoy Lindy Hoppers attended. On the regular open nights—Thursdays and Saturdays to Mondays—the dancing audience would consist, apart from the visitors, largely of groups of young people from the Savoy's regular hinterland. Unless driven by a desire to master Lindy technique that impelled them to transgress the boundaries of the social groups they arrived with, these groups of young people took little interest in anyone else, including visiting celebrities and even the Savoy's own elite dancers. Nevertheless, the latter's steady enhancement of the Savoy's reputation quite likely was at least an indirect influence on them choosing to dance at this ballroom rather than the many alternative venues open at the same time on weekends.

The Lindy Hop at the Savoy, however, was not just another social dance form. In effect, the ballroom was the end of the line for an ascending network (in skill terms) of local so-called cellar clubs, neighborhood dance halls and church socials that covered the entire city and beyond. Most of these venues had one or more accomplished Lindy couples. Although some were happy to stay put, others went in search of more challenging Lindy Hopping with or against the skilled dancers encountered when ascending the chain of venues. Even dancers who virtually began at the Savoy faced challenges. Thus, eminent Lindy Hoppers such as George Snowden, Alfred Leagins, Frankie Manning, and George Sullivan all recall dismissive confrontations with prospective female partners arising from their allegedly inadequate dance skills.[30] The general tenor was "go home and learn, and don't come back until you know how." Instead of classes in those days, you had to work out for yourself where you had gone wrong, and with a mixture of advice, experimentation, and close observation of current leading exponents discover your own way forward. Even among its social dancers, the Savoy had an unusually high preponderance of skilled exponents, and new ones arrived all the time. The diversity of expression in their dancing set the tone for an infinite variety of interpretations at all levels of social dancing. As Frankie Manning puts it, "Everybody at the Savoy had their [own] style."[31] Contrary to recent assertions, there was no specific "Savoy style" of Lindy Hopping.

Post–World War II Dance Styles

After World War II and an uncertain transitory period when the leading dancers experimented with the new bebop in such dances as the Bop-Lindy, the Bop-hop, the Jersey Bounce, and the Applejack, the 1930s spirit got renewed; there was an inclusivity of dance forms, and many new ones were devised.[32] Although a black couple scored a surprise win in the new polka category at the Harvest Moon in 1948, there was little enthusiasm for it at the social level at the Savoy. If anything, the dancers were more interested in both slower and faster modes. A new variant of an older dance called The Walk, which itself derived from the one-step, came to be known as Walking-the-Floor. A so-called story dance, in which a couple portrayed a three-minute affair through a sequence of physical dance expressions of romantic attraction and rejection, it had a kind of tango feel to it, although danced in swing time. The new up-tempo dance was the Stew, as devised by three of the leading third-generation dancers, Lee Moates, George Sullivan, and "Big Nick" Nicholson, that put emphasis back on the original floor routine aspect of the Lindy. Its name referred to the wide range of Lindy floor and air steps it incorporated but was danced in a line formation when performed onstage by a group or by one couple when danced socially. In a similar fashion, these same dancers developed the Stops routine of WLH into a more generally practiced first and second Stops, which could be incorporated into social Lindy or used as a kind of practice dance to gauge the levels of new aspirants.

The major new dance of the 1950s to hit the Savoy was the mambo, which was closely followed by its slower relation, the cha-cha-cha. Incorporating a great deal of Lindy partnering technique, this midtown version of the dance centered on the Palladium Ballroom scene that was distinct from the more "authentic" Cuban ethos of the El Barrio scene in East Harlem and the South Bronx.[33] The generous acknowledgments of the swing techniques incorporated into both the music and the dance of midtown mambo attracted the interest of the Savoy dancers (figure 7.2). Lindy and mambo dancers attended one another's ballrooms, with some like Teddy Brown and Vicky Gadson becoming notable in both, without losing their original styles. The mambo also became the new interracial scene, whereas the Savoy largely reverted to its original character of being primarily for African Americans. There was still a regular white attendance, but this replicated early patterns in consisting largely of people in the know who gained admission through personal connections. In the postwar period, yellow taxicabs began the practice, which remained common until comparatively recently, of refusing to drive to Harlem; policemen stood by key subway stations in Harlem and advised emerging white visitors intent on visiting the Savoy to return home.[34] Buchanan told the press that there was no reason anyway for white people to come to the ballroom.

Nevertheless, the Savoy recovered from the lost years and began to flourish again. Some of its more lavish events such as the Beaux Arts Ball, organized by the National Urban League Guild each February, became major New York social events and received wide coverage. Epic band battles continued to be staged as the dedicated 400 Club dancing continued on Tuesday nights and the riotous "kitchen mechanics" on Thursdays. Black sororities and fraternities took the place of the white college boys who no longer came on Sunday afternoons. Virtually every dance form hitherto mentioned continued to be danced, from square dancing to the Charleston.

Figure 7.2: Jackie "Dee" Danois, one of the leading mambo dancers from the Palladium Ballroom, dances The Ballroom with Lee Moates, one of the Savoy's leading Lindy Hoppers. Danois, who taught at the Dunham school for a while, utilized Dunham technique in this pose. Circa 1953. Courtesy of Jackie Danois.

The Waning Years

Despite the Savoy's revival from the negative impact of the 1943 closure, or possibly because of it, planning began to close the ballroom for good. In 1953, an initial agreement was announced between the Savoy owners and the city to sell the land the ballroom stood on for a new housing development. At almost the same time, the so-called threat of interracial dancing suddenly reemerged with a new generation of white youth buying and dancing to rhythm-and-blues records, as the original "black" version of rock 'n' roll was known. Combined with the Savoy's renewed Lindy enthusiasm, the specter of a new white influx into Harlem arose again.

Complications arising from the redevelopment plans for the site delayed the Savoy's closure. This time lag enabled the Savoy to "dangerously" overlap with the new rock 'n' roll scene that had already begun sweeping the country and the world. Hollywood had inadvertently sparked off a new international interest in the jitterbug through making the cheapest of exploitation movies.[35] Attempting to cash in on the huge response to the Bill Haley record of the same name, the 1956 *Rock Around the Clock* featured on-screen surviving Hollywood swing-era jitterbugs, most of whom had been trained, or strongly influenced, by Dean Collins, an ex-Savoy Lindy Hopper. Despite the popularity of new, mostly line-dancing responses to this music, Hollywood led the rest of the world to believe that the new excitement centered on the jitterbug, or jive as it largely became known outside of the United States.

Thus, the new, third-generation Savoy Lindy Hoppers began investing the same intensity of time and energy into their dancing as WLH had previously done and began moving at incredible speeds. At the same time, the new rock 'n' roll enthusiasts were coming to the ballroom to dance the Madison, the Stroll, and the Continental. This duality increasingly alarmed the Savoy management. Charles Buchanan announced in the Harlem press that he would not allow such "dangerous . . . rock 'n' roll" dancing in the Savoy after the downtown press chided new young, white enthusiasts for their inept attempts at Lindy-style dancing.[36] The correspondent urged them to look to the Savoy, where "the real thing" could still be seen.

Until the end, which came in July 1958, the Savoy thrived on a potent concoction of African American dances that were comprehensively remembered and reenacted in the ballroom's complex dancing program. Harlem's especially favorable conditions and the unspoken role of the Savoy, when it opened in 1926, to "control" controversial dance forms unwittingly led to the creation and development of the Lindy Hop. The management and owners found it to be in their best financial interests to facilitate three extraordinary decades of an unusual mass aptitude for social dancing. It was thus ironic in the extreme that the Savoy apparently closed largely to forestall the later versions of the Lindy from becoming an even greater dancing "threat." As a result, one of the most sophisticated social dancing audiences in the world dispersed between a variety of smaller uptown and larger downtown venues, none of which could adequately replicate the Savoy's unique vision of what such dancing was really about.

Acknowledgments

Various discussions with our interviewees (see notes) and the following individuals have been of great assistance: Earl Barton, Lance Beneshik, Gill Brady, Eunice Callan, David Carp, Elnora Dyson, Chad Fasca, Panama Francis, Pat Jenkins, Joe Lanza, Alfred Leagins, Larry Shultz, Dickie Harris, Leonard Reed, Ruthie Rhinegold, Sally R. Sommer, George Sullivan, Robert Farris Thompson, George Valerio, Coley Wallace, Eleanor Watson, and Eva Zirker.

Notes

1. Dan Burley, Ben Murray, and David Watkins, "Script and Continuity," in *The Savoy Story* (1951).

2. Stevens Watson, *The Harlem Renaissance* (New York: Pantheon Books, 1995), 4.

3. David L. Lewis, "Harlem My Home," in *Harlem Renaissance: Art of Black America* (New York: Studio Museum in Harlem, 1994), 77.

4. The Savoy management almost always called it the "Finest Ballroom in the World" while it was open and in 1936 inscribed that subtitle on the front of its entrance marquee.

5. For a detailed literature review of the Savoy, see Terry Monaghan, "'Stompin' at the Savoy': Remembering, Researching and Re-enacting the Lindy Hop's Relationship to Harlem's Savoy Ballroom" (paper presented at "Dancing at the Crossroads: African Diasporic Dances in Britain," Royal Festival Hall, London, August 1–2, 2002), 31–83.

6. This attempted program change could well have risen from the Savoy management's mid-1930s fears that moves were about to be made to close the ballroom for allowing interracial dancing, as described in Norma Miller's *Swingin' at the Savoy: The Memoir of a Jazz Dancer* (Philadelphia: Temple University Press, 1996), 83–86.

7. Their respective roles were expediently rewritten as time passed. An early *New York Age* news report, "Savoy Ballroom, in Less than 2 Years Has Become Most Famous Institution in Harlem—A Rendezvous for Visitors," attributes the origination and establishment entirely to Faggen (August 27, 1927, 60). *The Savoy Story*, the Savoy's 1951 anniversary publication, described Gale and Buchanan as the "founders," whereas *The New York Times* obituary for Gale restored the role of Faggen ("Moe Gale Dies," September 3, 1929).

8. Bill London (former cleaner at the Savoy), interview by Terry Monaghan, April 4, 1999, New York City.

9. The physical layout of the Savoy was almost identical to the pre-1956 Roseland Ballroom, apart from being slightly larger and not having pillars in the middle of its dance floor as the latter did.

10. Rudolph Fisher, *Common Meter* (London: X-Press, 1996; originally published in February 1930 in *The Baltimore Afro-American*), 143.

11. The racial myth that the rhythms of the "tom-tom" were essential for people of African descent and could attract the unwary white person, especially if played at a faster tempo than the standard pulse rate, was still prevalent. *The New York Age* (April 9, 1932, 4), for example, took issue in an editorial with Ed Sullivan, who, although noted for his sympathetic attitude to "Negroes," had written in *The Evening Graphic*, "Sometimes, when the traffic noises [in Harlem] are stilled you can almost hear tom-toms in the air." *The New York Age* wondered, "How many residents of Harlem would recognize tom-toms were they to hear them beaten?" Even the otherwise eminent and perceptive dance critic John Martin alleged in his early writings that the effect of jazz dance rhythm was, "Hypnotic in a marked degree, and psychological in that it tends to increase the blood pulse and it produces thereby a fast stimulation. This hypnotic effect of elementary rhythm persisted in over a period of time was well known to primitive man and was used deliberately by him in the production of frenzy and licentiousness"; John Martin, *The Modern Dance* (New York: Dance Horizon, 1933/1965), 40. Martin's later writings suggest that he considerably modified this viewpoint.

12. The size of the ballroom's dance floor (200 feet by 50 feet) has been repeated many times since then despite the impossible limitation of the standard 199–foot block width of buildings in Manhattan. (The figures, though, have varied at times as the opening quotation in this chapter demonstrates.) See a report in *The New York Age*, March 6, 1926, as cited in Samuel B. Charters and Leonard Kunstadt's *Jazz: A History of the New York Scene* (New York: Da Capo Press, 1981), 186. More plausible estimates of the dance floor's size, of 80 feet by 30 feet, were noted by Buchanan in private interviews.

13. The first known specific link of Lindbergh's flight to the inception of the Lindy Hop came in a speech by Savoy representative George Ganaway in February 1934 that featured an outline "history of the Lindy Hop" as recollected by Carl Johnson; Carl Johnson, interview by Terry Monaghan, February 29, 2000, Columbia, SC.) The occasion was the Savoy's 4th National Lindy Hop Competition that took place on President's Day from 1931 to 1935.

14. John A. Lucchese, *Joey Dee and the Story of the Twist* (New York: Macfadden, 1962), 62.

15. Jean Stearns and Marshall Stearns, *Jazz Dance: The Story of American Vernacular Dance* (New York: Schirmer, 1968), 316.

16. Jervis Anderson, *This Was Harlem* (New York: Farrar, Straus, Giroux, 1981), 312–13.

17. Stearns and Stearns, *Jazz Dance*, 323.

18. Mura Dehn discusses the creation of the Lindy Hop in Harlem, in particular, in the draft of her study "Jazz Dance"; see file 5 "Jazz Dance," Mura Dehn Collection, Jerome Robbins Dance Collection, The New York Public Library for the Performing Arts. See also Joel Dinerstein, *Swinging the Machine: Modernity, Technology, and African American Culture between the World Wars* (Amherst: University Press of Massachusetts, 2002), 254.

19. Harold Acton, *Memoirs of an Aesthete* (London: Methuen, 1948), 240.

20. Most notably, Carl Van Vechten, *PARTIES: Scenes from Contemporary New York Life* (New York: Knopf, 1930), 183–90; and Fisher, Common Meter, 136–47.

21. Historian Robert Crease did not find any former Savoy dancers from the 1930s period who recalled ever using the term "Cat's Corner" to describe the location where they used to meet up and rehearse; Robert P. Crease, "The Lindy Hop," *Research Forum Papers* (Baltimore: Goucher College, The 1988 International Early Dance Institute), 9.

22. The claim for the first U.S. Rumba competition is made in *The Savoy Story*. The Savoy also advertised in *La Prensa* in 1930 and 1931.

23. "Harper Revue Out of Savoy: Local Dance Hall Returns to Policy of Presenting Leading Bands," *New York Amsterdam News*, April 26, 1933, 8; Charles Buchanan, interview by Peter Bailey and Lloyd Williams, 1980, New York City.

24. Kyle Chrichton, "Peel That Apple! The Story of the Big Apple, Which Started Out to Be a Dance and Became an Epidemic," *Collier's*, December 4, 1937, 22, 48.

25. This routine as danced by Whitey's Lindy Hoppers can be seen in the film *Keep Punching*, dir. John Clein, 81 min., Sack Amusement Enterprises, 1939.

26. These provisional observations are based on discussions with "Sugar" Sullivan, Ruby Reeves, Vicky Gadson, Martha Hickson, Sylvan Charles, and other former Savoy dancers from the period 1994–2004 to distinguish the different types of slow dancing at the Savoy that recently have been arbitrarily merged as one dance (the blues) by current so-called swing dancers. The latter have possibly been misled by Mura Dehn's use of the term *The Blues* in *The Spirit Moves* (Mura Dehn, 1951), by which she specifically meant the dance called the ballroom but which the swing dancers seem to assume refers to all slow dancing to blues music. These details will be extensively footnoted in Monaghan's forthcoming dissertation on the Savoy.

27. The Tranky Doo is danced in *The Spirit Moves* by Esther Washington, Al Minns, and Leon James, although Mura Dehn misspelled its name as "The Trunky Doo" in the titles.

28. Miller, *Swingin' at the Savoy*, 107–8.

29. I obtained this information in an e-mail of August 15, 2005, from Peter Loggins, who had previously interviewed Jimmy Valentine.

30. See Marshall Stearns's interview notes with George Snowden, December 17, 1959 (in artist files in the collection of The Institute of Jazz Studies, Rutgers University, Newark, NJ), and the obituary for Alfred Leagins by Terry Monaghan, *Dancing Times*, January 2000, 349. For an expanded profile of Leagins, see the "Social Dance" section, *Savoy Ballroom News*, available at http://www.savoyballroom.com. Frankie Manning's case was slightly different in that he was challenged in this manner by his mother; see interview with Frankie Manning by Robert Crease, "Jazz History Oral History Project, The Swing Era," July 22–23, 1992, 25, Smithsonian Institution; and interview with George Sullivan by Terry Monaghan on April 20, 1996, Miami, FL.

31. Frankie Manning, "Get That Swing, Live," interview for *The Washington Post*, January 26, 1999, available at http://discuss.washingtonpost.com/wp-srv/zforum/99/music990126.htm (accessed May 24, 2005).

32. The Bop-hop was the first African American dance that had to be described to the New York community in how-to-do-it diagrams. See "How to Do the Bop Hop: Bop-Converted Benny Goodman Band Introduces New Dance Step on Tour," *Ebony* 4, no. 9 (July 1949): 23–25.

33. See chapters 4 and 5 of John Storm Roberts, *Latin Jazz: The First of the Fusions 1880's–Today* (New York: Schirmer Books, 1999).

34. Ernie Smith, interview by Terry Monaghan, July 7, 1998, New York City; James Maher, interview by Terry Monaghan, June 22, 1999, New York City.

35. In the greater New York area before 1940, the term Lindy Hop referred to the dance of that name, as danced by Lindy Hoppers. The term jitterbugs, on the other hand, referred to especially raucous swing music fans, who typically danced the Shag, if they danced at all. The term the jitterbug only began to denote an actual dance form (in effect a modified version of the Lindy Hop) in the early 1940s. The 1942 Harvest Moon Ball Association renamed its Lindy Hop category as the Jitterbug-Jive without explanation, but it seemed to presage a general name change for the dance form. Increasingly, the two words were conflated to mean the same actual dance, with the previous meanings of jitterbug being forgotten. The same dance was renamed rock 'n' roll between 1956 and 1959 in the Harvest Moon Ball Competition, but it then reverted back to jitterbug in 1959 and continued in use until the last major Harvest Moon Ball in 1974.

36. "No Rock 'n' Roll at Savoy Ballroom," *New York Amsterdam News*, July 27, 1957, 14.

8

Rumba Then and Now: Quindembo

Yvonne Daniel

Rumba then was something to look forward to! A hot Sunday afternoon in 1987 in the placita near the marina—that would be the time for and the site of the neighborhood gathering in Matanzas. A few guys—some old and some very young—would be playing checkers on a bench in the one corner of the square that was shaded by a small, thin tree. Other people crowded against the walls of the buildings on the shady side of the street, smoking cigarettes profusely, exchanging casual greetings, and passing on hot rumors. Several sizes and shapes of drums were being carried out from a large rickety bus and placed on the sidewalk; it appeared that each set of two drums had one straight-backed chair assigned to them.

Rumba then was a time of relief: a time for a walk down to the water on the marina, a time to let go of the six-day work week, a time to rustle and shift the hot Cuban air, a time to notice the jacaranda tree's vibrant orange-red blossoms or the wild-growing poinsettias amid the dusty parched earth. Every once in a while a blast from the speakers would sound out a huge screeching whistle as technicians connected cables and adjusted microphones. The air was still, hot, with aromas of chicken, pork, and beef, congri, and fried plantains, coming from two-burner stoves in tiny, dark kitchens that were deep within each home in the city.

Rumba then was a time of hope. The gathered people expected a small spectacle, a memorable music and dance event. Everyone had on her/his cool outfit. Members of Afro-Cuba had on white tee shirts with logos, over burgundy red skirts and jeans. Los Munequitos had on blue shirts and pants and Ana (the first and only woman in the group then) had on a navy blue summer dress with slender shoulder straps and teeny pink roses painted across its flowing length. Everyone hoped for a lively Rumba, even though their shoes were worn around the edges and there were no handkerchiefs to wipe their sweat. Each performer and each viewer wished to witness the Rumba that everyone seemed to talk about or to remember—one of those fantastic happenings—then!

This was one of those fantastic Rumbas that everyone talked about. Not only was the entire battery of drummers from the main rumbero families of Matanzas there, but also, Jesus Alfonso had just returned to the creative leadership of Munequitos; Titi and Gollo were still alive and drumming; and Pedro, el negro, had just disbanded his Obatola group and had joined up with Afro-Cuba. To top it off Saldiaguera, from the original Munequitos group, who had retired long before, attended and sang with all the others. Vertier and Carnet keep the vocals, the harmonies, and the rhythms perfectly in sync—coño. Even Los Compadres from Havana could not resist the challenges in the Matanzas calls.

The Rumba songs multiplied; the gallos roared alternately, but over-all, they elaborated melodies and improvised lyrics until the burning sun softened. The small crowds had swollen to packs of neighboring districts and covered the entire placita. Ana had danced yambu with little (then) Bárbaro, and Teresita had danced guaguancó with Danilo. Each couple was happy and playful, Ana with her ever-ready grace and Teresita with her spinal fluidity; both matched Bárbaro's youthful bravura and Danilo's sinewy seduction. Viewers marveled at how low they danced while still keeping the clave foot pattern and no one could understand how the men never succeeded to "possess" the women in their numerous vacunao attempts.

Yes, Rumba then was a lived fantasy of fun, food, cool casual outfits, rum and often cold, quenching beer. People remembered the atrocious so-cial conditions before and just after the Revolution, but they also remem-bered the steady improvements by 1987. There was a perceived and lived experience of shared access to growing social justice (since no system is perfect) for most of the population and in terms of health and education, there was booming evidence of a healthy, informed, and educated Cuba. Life had been exceedingly hard with war and rebuilding, but life had been filled with hope and ideals to work toward. The rhythm of Rumba was consonant with that time, with those ideals and objectives, consonant even with the shortcomings and outright failures of post-revolutionary practices. These errors were consumed as a passing tone is consumed in a melody's contour, or as in the circular path of a figure eight shape of a trill's ending. These errors were submerged under the blocking gesture of a rumbera's skirt, warding off the vacunao. Rumba then was beautiful, even though it too had its problems that resulted in unlovely actions, angry outbursts, and sometimes in physical fights.

Brief Overview of Rumba in Cuban History

Rumba originated in Cuba in the mid- to late-nineteenth century.[1] Its music eventually traveled to Spain, parts of Africa, Mexico, across the Caribbean, and to the United States, but its original dancing stayed planted for the most part in the urban and rural homes, communal patios, and public squares of mainly black Cuban neighborhoods. By the end of the twentieth century, its pretenders had traveled from Cuba to flashy cabarets, intimate theaters, and other performance settings of international display, and, in the process, rumba accumulated significantly varied dance patterns and numerous stylizations.[2]

Early rumba was mimetic, often telling stories about rag dolls, flying kites, harvesting and preparing rice, and wayward boys and their grandmothers who caught them *rumbancheando*. That rumba was graceful, delicately alluring, and included the Kongo-Angola approach and retreat pattern of a dancing partnered male and female (e.g., from *yuka* and *makuta*, lingering Central African dances in Cuba). Additionally, traditional rumba made use of ample hip isolation and rhythmic improvisation. These three elements were at creative variance with layered, syncopated percussion: three drums, a stick-beating bamboo box, a shaker—all in sync with the claves of satirical and/or romantic songs.

These graceful mimetic rumbas, called *rumba yambú* or *rumba de cajón* (box rumba—because they played rhythms on codfish and candle boxes instead of the outlawed drums), were identified with the older generation and *el tiempo de España*, the colonial and enslavement period. They were among the first transforming and creolizing dances of the new environment, which took form and structure from Central and West African dances and layered these with fresh European and American stylistic content. Rumba form came forth with the customs, mannerisms, gestures, clothing, new language, and new understandings of the Americas. In its urban beginnings, rumba was performed near the ports, in common patio areas of tenement neighboring homes called *solares,* and among a variety of peoples—granted, mostly among freed blacks, the enslaved, and indentured others—but it claimed a resistant motif on the Cuban soul, despite the prestige, popularity, and simultaneous development of *son,* another popular Cuban dance form.[3]

Cuban *son* predates rumba.[4] *Son* began among Spanish immigrants who came in the sixteenth century, albeit already enculturated with Afro-Spanish, *ladino,* or Moorish bloodlines and customs from African-influenced Spain of the eighth to fifteenth century. Cuban *rumba* had to wait for its African creators who also came to the island in the sixteenth century but who accumulated significant numbers by the end of the nineteenth century. The isolated Spaniards of early Cuba settled the new ranch lands and waited for limited, occasional sociability. They had their guitar-like instruments (*guitarras, laúdes, tiples,* and *bandurrias*) and their *decima*-stanza songs to keep themselves entertained. They looked forward to intermittent parties and dancing, which came with sparse local visiting, the religious celebrations of the Roman Catholic church, and the arrival of ships with new supplies of people, instruments, trends, and fashions. As time went on with more colonial settlement and the trappings of European court values, the ranch farm solo performance accumulated a salon development and the European *contredanse* became the American *contradanza.* As soon as these set dances shifted and permitted the dancing couples to face one another—as in what historian John Chasteen calls "the dance of two"—the *danzón* became the staple dance of late-nineteenth-century Cuban society, followed by the *son.*[5]

The rumba developed "on the other side of the tracks" primarily among Africans and their descendents and away from the European colonial class. The dance/music form utilized a full range of percussion, human voices in responsorial patterns laced with comedic and provocative subjects, and a wide spectrum of playful, sensual, and suspenseful dance movement.[6] Types of rumba must have differentiated by the end of the nineteenth century because in part they depended on specific social conditions. A critical indicator for dance type differentiation was the African male to female ratio.

Both *rumba yambú* and *rumba guaguancó* (still the most popular type of rumba) required the *pareja,* the male and female dancer, and a resulting, sensuous double entendre in lyrics, dance movements, and dance climax/apex/raison d'être. It was in the urban areas where a close ratio of males and females prevailed that the earlier graceful and slow *rumba yambú* began to alternate with this other rumba. Eventually *rumba* acquired a quicker tempo and a chase rather than polite flirtation. It also acquired specific gestures:

for the male, a pelvic thrust (his gesture of possessing the female), called *vacunao,* and for the female, an obscuring and deflecting gesture, the *botao.* When the dance form accentuated or added this fast chase and suggestive gestures, it acquired the name *rumba guaguancó.*

Another kind of gender ratio produced yet another rumba type. The huge imbalance in the male to female ratio within the black population was predicated on sugar refinery development and not just sugar cultivation. Refineries came to Cuba later than elsewhere in the Americas, and in the 1880s even more enslaved Africans were needed to keep up with Cuba's sugar industry and more African men were used and were settled away from urban ports. In rural areas of Matanzas province near the refineries (people say in Cárdenas), huge numbers of laboring males were placed together in anticipation of the *zafra,* or sugar harvest. When not working, men danced together in challenge performance, and the third classic type of rumba emerged, *rumba columbia.*

Rumba carried a misleading reputation, as did many trendy dances of the times (like the English country dance and the minuet earlier, as well as *danzón*). They were all trashed by gossip and newspapers but enjoyed by many. Rumba also shared in the estimation of African dances as "lewd and lascivious." Dance chronicler Médéric Louis Elie Moreau de St. Méry relates colonial attitudes about African dances in 1796, saying in essence that they were risqué.[7] As we read Moreau de St. Méry with twenty-first-century eyes, however, we see a sense of freedom that characterized the African manner in dancing any dance, theirs or those of their colonial masters. Their movements were considered improper because the African or African American dancer would divide the torso while dancing, accent hip action, and sometimes lower toward the floor, all of which was considered very "uncivilized" and "barbaric" for those who loved to dance elongated at the back and elevated on the ball of their foot and toes. Ultimately, despite its magnetism and admirable force, African dance was rejected because of the way in which the torso displayed utter flexibility. Torso division allowed the lower pelvis area and the upper abdomen and chest areas to move forward and backward, side to side, and around in clockwise or counterclockwise directions. The dancing torso could be smooth and sensuous in sustained energy force or erratic and aggressive in percussive bursts of energy. It could swing, vibrate, and nuance a myriad range of expressiveness, and rumba utilized all of the dancing torso's potential.

Watching rumba performance or watching Africans dance together stimulated interest and often tremendous fascination.[8] Even in the twenty-first century, we can imagine watching two African-descended performers display playful flirtation without any touching, in a world of rhythmic diversity! The male's bravado and personal sense of invitation and pleasure are most obvious; the woman's mixture of demureness and knowingness, her occasional tempting presentations, and her lingering sensuality augment the sense of aesthetic and sexual tension. Despite nineteenth-century outcries against racial mixing as well as against specific dances, the sensuality and sexuality of African-descended performance, in both music and dance, pushed European men to dance with African-descended women.[9] Their hopes surrounded fantasies of seduction and rape and permitted physical contact with the socioreligiously forbidden black or brown woman. Through her dance, they experienced the exotic world of the African dancing body, African torso flexibility, and Creole rhythmic hypnosis. Over time, the entire European-descended population measured portions of African performance style within their "cups of tea"—their dance preferences.

There were two tracks of rumba development, one inside and the other outside of Cuba. In Cuba, Fernando Ortiz commented on how rumba had "degenerated" by the mid-twentieth century.[10] For example, he referred to traditional *guaguanco* performance that then contained some risqué material as a mimetic story line (reminding me of mimetic *rumba del tiempo de España*). Two popular scenarios placed the woman on her hands and knees (on "all fours")—in one, washing the floor and in the other, supposedly shoeing a mule (*herrar la mula*). In the now infamous rumba song "Lola [or "Lala"] no sabe na" for example, a *rumbera* mimes washing clothes—hanging them out to dry, ironing, sweeping and mopping the floors, washing dishes, and sewing—in front of her dancing male partner, all in the midst of her traditional rumba step. She responds to the instructive lyrics of the lead singer. She wiggles and gyrates within her partner's stealthy gaze, and he waits for her complete array of sensual gesturing before he attempts his *vacunao*.

For Ortiz and other Cubans in the 1920s to 1950s mainstream society, this rumba was too suggestive, too sensual, too explicit. Historian Louis Pérez explains: "For respectable Cuban society, bourgeois and middle class alike, the notion that the *son* or the rumba symbolized Cuba was as inconceivable as it was inadmissible."[11] With its risqué scenarios, rumba continued to be "lewd and lascivious" or *"baja cultura"* (low culture) for a society that (officially) preferred nineteenth-century movement—the ballroom *danzón*. Despite this perspective, twentieth-century Cuban society eventually offered rumba performance to both a domestic commercial market as well as an international tourist market.[12]

In aesthetically rendering a playful dance of flirtation, the rumba couple reinforced the seductive *mulata* and the cool *macho* as a profound etching on the Cuban mind—at once an etching of Cubanness and dance but also an etching of racism and sexism.[13] For performance, light-skinned or white performers were first preferred over dark-skinned Cuban performers. The suggestion of possessing the *mulata,* the "easily laid" black or tawny-skinned female, was almost always highlighted in theaters and cabarets. Rumba began a metamorphosis, a journey toward commercialism and appropriation inside Cuba.

Original rumba continued in yet another form of "black" social life: the rumba gathering, a festive affair in which elaborate attire, sumptuous foods and drinks, and all sorts of current dance fads, as well as skilled and virtuoso rumba performance, were included. The rumba gathering was always *quindembo*—a huge mixture—in this case, of dances.[14] Dark- and light-skinned Cubans continuously secured the rumba types and their virtuoso performance level over decades. They taught it to the younger generation and fostered the care and expertise of rumba drummers, singers, and dancers within their communities.

Although some Cubans might say that rumba "died out" by the middle of the twentieth century, other observers of daily life among "black" Cubans point to the two- and three-year-olds who can still differentiate between rumba rhythms and *oricha* rhythms, little four-year-old girls who know how to demonstrate a *botao* or the protective gesture in response to a *vacunao* before they can read or write, and numerous precocious drummers of five- to eight-year-olds, who today in twenty-first-century Cuba still display their genius through improvisational rumba drumming. The insistent desire for "home" (Africa or Cuba) and "home-style" performance (deep communal social interaction) in communal gatherings have kept a constant *rumba clave* rhythm and a sufficient communal sense so that traditional rumba has thrived along with its variants inside Cuba for more than a century and a half. Since the Revolution of 1959, domestic support of the three classic types of rumba established traditional rumba performance inside Cuba through the organization of the Cuban National Folkloric Dance Companies in Havana and Santiago de Cuba (both ends of the island). A by-product of these institutions was the identification of Rumba Saturdays and Sundays.[15]

Rumba in the Mix

Rumba then became flashy, slick, packaged seamlessly for international consumption; she was wizard virtuosity. She was sequined and layered with gold chains. Rumba then had a "PR" man and a woman agent, who both needed their cut off the top and Rumba often played in a Son key.

Overview of Rhumba Outside of Cuba

Rhumba, as rumba was most often called in its 1930s international heyday, was also *quindembo*—not simply a mixture of feasting, dancing, singing, and music making, but also a mixture of dances with the same name.[16] Outside of Cuba, rhumba became a dance of what I call the "amorous two," the touching partnered couple. This powerfully suggestive name—rhumba or rumba—was applied in many ways.[17] From its first international trips to Paris in 1927, Berlin in 1931, and Chicago in 1933,[18] rhumba performance mixed traditional rumba elements with its lighter-skinned "sister," the Cuban *son*, making *son* rumba's dance "pretender." This was not particularly hard to do because they both had the same mother and father: African and European music/dance heritages. Cuban musicologists Argeliers León, Olavo Alén, and María Teresa Linares note *son's* African elements: the manner of playing the guitar and *tres* in the *son*, deriving from the eastern (historically more African) side of the island and the alternation of chorus and soloist as an African element (although Spanish also) that continues in Cuban musical forms, including *son* and rumba.[19] Music historian John Storm Roberts describes the *son* as "certainly the classic Afro-Cuban form, an almost perfect balance of African and Hispanic elements."[20] And nineteenth-century understanding held that *son* was basically a black style of dancing.[21] Thus, the facile *quindembo* of sister dances (cousins, if you like), one *mulata*/rumba and the other *trigueña/son*, assisted the public craze for the enticing but "lewd, crude, and forbidden" rumba in a segregated and elitist domestic society as well as in the racist international environment.[22]

Around the turn of the twentieth century, *rumba* was fully developed, taking references from daily life, political situations, rumor, and gossip and weaving them as musical bits and danced segments within three main types of rumba form. From the 1920s to the 1940s, industrialization and an increasingly organized labor force along with many new ideas and currents had augmented the agricultural island of sugar and tobacco with an additional social environment, a new layer of island paradise for tourists, especially from the United States and Europe.[23] At this point, rumba joined other Cuban dance forms in nightclub spectacles, Hollywood movies, and presentations of "the exotic other," albeit doctored up for international consumption.

Just as the stage magically transforms everything, rumba was transformed gradually during the first two decades of the twentieth century. At the 1932 World's Fair in Chicago, Cuban performers danced an altered version of rumba that was more upright than in classic, traditional Cuban rumba; their clothes were elaborated and theatrical with endless rows of ruffles, like a rooster's feathers standing on edge and like a peacock's elongated plumed tail, accentuating a Spanish rather than an African flare. Performers danced to rumba rhythms with extensive instrumentation beyond percussion and voice; elaborate orchestrations of brass and reeds meshed with a *son*-like visual image and spatial configuration for the movement. This was not genuine rumba but a commercial version for both the Cuban and international tourist markets (see illustration 8.1 of staged *rumba* that went outside of Cuba).[24]

Other means of *quindembo* ensured the pretender's success. Music publishing companies produced a medley of rhumbas on sheet music, much of which was simply categorized as rhumbas because of its "Latin" or rhythmic feel. Even some Cuban compositions, such as Emilio Grenet's tango-conga "Ay Mama Inés," Moisés Simons' *son* "Con picante y sin picante," and the Chiquita Banana jingle, were lumped into the rhumba category. French musicologist Isabelle Leymarie reports: "From 1913 to 1915, the American record companies Victor and then Columbia . . . spread the *danzón*, the *son*, the *guaracha*, and the bolero abroad, labeling almost everything 'Rumba'."[25] Additionally, the movie industry did not attend to the distinctions of Cuban dance creations but indiscriminately named movies and played music in movies that had little or no relationship to real rumba, let alone to classic rumba types (e.g., George Raft's movies *Rumba* and *Bolero* in 1934).[26]

More so than conga, bolero, the U.S. fox trot, or other Latin American dances that were also called rhumbas outside of Cuba, *son* body orientation matched the image that stage, movie, and theatrical performers thought was appropriate for public rhumba performance away from its native *solar* ambiance. For example, in traditional rumba (*rumba del campo*), both males and females dance with flexed knees and tilted backs at the forward diagonal as they circle each other in small steps with an abundance of hip swaying, chest shifting, and shoulder shimmying. Rumba's distinct foot steps, whether actualized exactly or syncopated and varied, are flat-footed, gentle stamps (RRLL, RRLL, etc.). In *son*, males hold females upright, face to face, and above a repetitive and alternating right and left three-step foot pattern (RLR-hold, LRL-hold, etc.), they gently accentuate the hips. The dancing couple travels through space with rhythmic elegance and sensuality. Thus, in body orientation, foot alternation and placement patterns, and proxemics, the dance called international rhumba or commercial rhumba eventually became closer to Cuban *son* performance than it was to its namesake, despite the inclusion of risqué theatrics described earlier in "Lola no sabe na" and "Herrar la mula."

From the beginning, in attempts to make Afro-Cuban rumba less "crude" and more acceptable to both domestic upper-class Cubans and international audiences, rumba was robbed of much of its essence in the name of supposed sophistication. Performers and producers tried to make rumba more proper or fit for the public. Cuban dancer and dance educator Alfredo O'Farril states: "What happened to the Rumba when it began to be called 'cabaret' was fundamentally the result of advertising the Cuban woman's body as cheap merchandise, just like toasting sex and liquor. This is what was sold to outsiders. The majority of European and North American countries consider the underdeveloped countries as cities or municipal districts—*aldeas*. So they created a type of ballroom dance in their own (European) image: the Tango, Merengue, Son, and Rumba, which were sold as an elaborate product, one that was cleansed of its black element."[27]

In reality, the performers who spread rhumba outside its original *solar* ambiance to the theater and outside of Cuba to the international stage did so often without real expertise in traditional rumba.[28] The first of these performers were light-skinned or "white" Cubans from the middle and upper classes with conservatory training and concert aspirations before they became involved with popular theater and dance, such as Carmita Ortiz and Julio (Pons) Richards. They drew their stylization from cultural values of the time that degraded things African and yet peppered their execution with what the audience wanted, including *mulata* sensuality and *macho* bravura. Their references were from blackface musical theater of the day and from vague and imagined notions of the rumba. It was in this vein that the renowned *mulata* entertainer Rita Moliner began to emphasize Afro-Cuban elements in her performances.[29]

Slowly, rumba moved toward Santiago and the *son* moved toward Havana, as musicians crossed both ends of the island.[30] Many Cubans who had difficulties finding jobs in rural areas moved to urban centers and became part of the *septeto* musical development of the 1930s. Cubans outside of the western provinces of Havana and Matanzas were less familiar with traditional rumba, such as its *rumba tajona* form that was played on bread crates in and around Havana in western Cuba. Some were familiar with *rumba chancleta*, a Santiago/eastern form that featured clicking sandals within rumba performance. Dark-skinned workers found employment in theaters as *rumberos*, even though some of them were just as ignorant of traditional rumba as the first light-skinned Cuban performers had been. With light- and dark-skinned performers featured as *rumberos*, the Cuban theater scene modeled a staged rumba for the international tourist scene. As dark-skinned Cubans became more involved in the tourist trade inside Cuba and as the cabaret format of rumba was featured outside Cuba, traditional rumba became "staged rumba" inside Cuba and "rhumba" outside of Cuba. The rhumba craze of the 1930s was in full force. The dance team that has been documented repeatedly and that caused quite a stir in their demonstration of rumba and other Cuban dances at the Chicago World's Fair in 1933 was Afro-Cuban: René Rivero Guillén and Ramona Ajón (la pareja de baile René and Estela).[31] They were from Matanzas in western Cuba, an origin site of rumba, and perhaps danced close to a traditional rumba style (figure 8.1).[32] Their performance at the World's Fair, however, was supposedly the first time rumba was danced "without embarrassment."[33]

The need to bring rumba up from baja cultura still permeates the issue of the rhumba craze. For such cases, quindembo seems like the most likely solution. Rhumba outside of Cuba was mixed just as its promoters inside Cuba had mixed it earlier. Rhumba on stage had some traditional rumba elements, such as the chase of the female, the sensuous and accentuated hip movements, fancy footwork of the male in pursuit, and body part isolation (like vibrating shoulders), but these rhumbas were danced in a son key with more upright posture, gentle hip accents, and son's patterned foot alternations, not rumba's.[34]

> An Informed View of a "First World" View of the Aldea Cubana
> Rumba played in a son key, a bolero key, a guaracha key, a conga key and none of these had anything to do with Rumba. They were all Cuban creations and were put into the mixture, called Rhumba. In the world flurry of excitement over Cuban rhythms and Cuban melodies by Cuban composers and played by Cuban ensembles, Cubans were witnesses to their dance and music's bastardization.
>
> Rumba, herself, could adapt to a Son pretense. After all, she wanted to confront the U.S. and Europe in their attempts to show off the lindy and the two-step. Rumba wanted at least to lend a Cuban sense to the big band scene; so she yielded to Son and let Son dance in her place.

Mambo, Son, and Rumba-like Projections

The same sort of conflicting forms (e.g., Cuban versus other, domestic versus international) occurred in the 1950s with the popularization of Cuban mambo, a descendent of son. In this case, mambo became son's pretender and quindembo reigned again. Inside Cuba, the mambo arrived and sported fresh energy. Taking its name and essence from the repeated riff section of the son musical form over which improvisation takes place, a modernized

Figure 8.1: Noted *rumbero matancero* René (Rivero) and *rumbera* Estela (Ramona Ajón), who brought staged rumba to the Chicago World's Fair in 1933. Photo courtesy of Robin D. Moore and the Lázaro Herrera Collection, Museo Nacional, Havana, Cuba.

version of *son* appeared called mambo. For the dance movement in Cuban stylization, however, a series of coordinated movements that were influenced by jazz music and Lindy Hopping of the 1940s were featured.

Cuban mambo featured a bouncy toe-step pattern on alternating feet that combined hip flexion from front to back in double time. This pattern was followed by another, also rather bouncy in feeling and form. In tropical Cuba, there were few occasions for acrobatics; rather, this mambo variation had little jumps that shoved parallel knees two times on either side of a dancing partner. The next repetitive pattern was a step, step, step, kick-R, step, step, step, kick-L, which had a variation with couples changing sides in three counts and making the big kick facing each other on count four.[35] In Cuba, a series of "cutesy" steps typified the mambo dance pattern, and the dance did not enjoy much popularity as it gained elsewhere in the 1950s. Most of the creative juice that made the dance a craze elsewhere (as opposed to the music) was because of what Puerto Rican musicians and Puerto Rican, African American, Italian, and Jewish dancers added to Cuban creativity outside of Cuba.[36]

Outside of Cuba, when mambo recordings of Arsenio Rodriguez, Machito's Afro-Cubans, Perez Prado, or Puerto Rican Tito Puente sounded in the 1950s, the dancing *pareja* moved in *son's* familiar, alternating footsteps: RLR hold, LRL hold; however, the partners did not hold each other in the closed partner position of *son* for the 1950s mambo outside of Cuba. The dance-of-two or "amorous two" had become boring and constricting and needed to liberate its partners.

The *mambo pareja* chose its antecedent Kongo-Angola approach-and-retreat pattern—a rumba style and manner. Without touching between the dancing-two, there was room and need for play, flirtation, and competition. The partners left the upright *son* position and assumed a slight forward tilt over bent knees, also reminiscent of traditional rumba body orientation. Then the proxemics of rumba style separated the dancing couple. The male and female dancers improvised over the repetitive rhythm: sometimes turning, sometimes in opposition, sometimes complementary to one another. Thus, mambo, the daughter of *son*, drew upon her "Aunt Rumba's" characteristics. She set these not to rumba percussion alone but to *son's* orchestrated brass trumpets and trombones, contrasted with saxophone, piano, bass, and full percussion variety—bongos, congas, timbals, guiro, and of course the inescapable claves of all Cuban music. Among social and particularly competitive ballroom dancers, this mambo dance description would not be familiar; for them, rather a *son*-like foot pattern, *son*-like proxemics, and certainly *son*-like body orientation are more in keeping with their competition mambo. *Quindembo* yet again![37]

More of Contemporary Quindembo
Rumba then became pregnant with twins in the late-twentieth century. Their fathers were Salsa and Santería. She had never been exclusive, taking the bits and pieces of ordinary and extraordinary life and creating her patchwork quilt, her obra, as antidote for nineteenth- and early twentieth-century social situations. Rumba loved these two, Salsa and

Santería, and married them both separately, since both gave her so much of what she needed.

She needed expanded rhythms and thicker textures, so she broke into Salsa's song, stopped the brass mambo and sounded out her familiar percussion conversations. And the dancers adjusted accordingly. Their uplifted, passing, circling Salsa dropped a little lower, that is, the body shifted gears, lowered if you will, for supportive strength. The Salsa feet that pivoted and turned on toes now touched the floor fully, and pointedly stamped Rumba's simple, indelible pattern. She added her rhythms within his Salsa: her recurring image, hint, and smells and, quickly, joined his dance with expert facility.

Then, Santería took her away from Salsa. He washed her face with rose water and brushed her from head to toe with cooling leaves. Santería turned Rumba around three times counterclockwise and layered her with multiple petticoats. Her Rumba skirt acted as fundamento or founding principle color beneath the mounting colors of her new overskirts: white for Obatalá, golden yellow for Ochún, red for Changó and Oyá, blue for Yemayá, green and purple for Ogún, and red and black for Elegua. He then wrapped her head in white cloth and called for the batá drums to enter the salon. They, singing with Rumba's tumba drums, caused Rumba to dance differently. She alternated: first as she unfolded her original Rumba, then she superimposed a fitting farewell to Salsa, and finally, sensing and connecting with the spiritual resources of Santería—refreshing in and around her head—bata Rumbasón was visible, audible, and felt.

Conclusion

There should be little surprise regarding the substitution of *son*-like perfor-mance for genuine rumba in the 1930s and 1940s, the substitution of rumba-like performance for *son*-derived mambo in the 1950s, and the substitution of *son*-like performance for both rumba and mambo at least since the 1950s in American and British ballroom dancing. This is the course of popular dance. It is always borrowing, returning, imitating, shifting, reversing, in-verting, improvising, and in the process shaping and polishing yet another named creation of the current day. And that creation is then susceptible to other manipulations of old and new gestures as well as different ordering of emphases and standardizations. Sometimes, the original "comes back," meaning, it comes into public popularity and in full force on its own but in a new era.

Rumba has not become a museum piece. So far, there have always been pockets of traditional *rumberos* refining performance style and, most important, teaching proper form to their children, neighbors, and international friends (figure 8.2). Witness the recent film on traditional rumba enthusiastically documented in New Jersey.[38] What may be helpful to observers and interested researchers is more clarity within the naming of certain related dances; but then, it is not we—the researchers—but (all of) us—the community—who names the dances.

There is always *quindembo*—a mixture of dance movement vocabulary—which keeps building and refreshing itself with every new movement trend. Dance *quindembo* is influenced by every linguistic, technical, and cultural change that comes into the social environment. Popular dance takes from all the bits and pieces of social life (political, religious, economic, and social) and weaves a kaleidoscope of movement patterns and sequences that thrill, energize, and ultimately refresh and relax performers. Popular dance is *quindembo*.

Figure 8.2: Noted *rumberos matanceros* Ana Perez and Diosdado Ramos of Los Muñequitos, who brought traditional rumba to the United States for the Colorado Dance Festival in 1993. Photo by Yvonne Daniel, in Cuba, 1987.

Rumba for the Ages
Rumba had such a love-life—and, for a very long time! She gloried in her fame and gave to orchestras, bands, and her drum battery too. But Timba entered the solar of life and boasted of golden teeth, diamond piercings, caps and sneakers, mid-drift blouses and mini skirts, and of course sexy, new, interests. Timba was rougher than Salsa had ever been: more wild and street and brusque. And he was not half as soothing as Santería had been, despite his multiple gestures of coolness. Still Timba sought her too and, at intervals, even made all the music stop just to see her do her "vintage thing." She had soul and so did he, and while he did not wish her constantly, he knew he needed her essence to brighten and top off, as well as meaningfully deepen his array. She was still "dope," and she knew it and she showered it at just the right time.

Now, Rumba elegantly waits her turn. When the full-out music cuts out, stops all electronics for human inspiration only, she gracefully enters—with skin on skin drums, human lead voice and coro, and in ever-hot body-rhythms and suspenseful vacunaos and botaos. Her body soars across space and time from core stylizations of Nieves Fresneda, Librada Quesada to Ana Perez and Teresa Perez-Domé. Coño—can she dance! She fits into Santería, Salsa, Timba, as well as son—engaging everyone in hearty fun and healthy desire. Then she takes her seat with freshened dignity to wait for her next dance partner and the decorative pleasures he will supply. She remains in down-to-earth elegance, incredible rhythmic splendor, alert to her eternal clave!

Notes

1. Researchers rarely designate a specific date for the origin of a dance, but musicologist Isabelle Leymarie links the song "El Yambú," which surfaced around 1850, to the beginnings of rumba; Isabelle Leymarie, *Cuban Fire* (London: Continuum, 2004), 29. Cuban musicologist Olavo Alén, *Géneros Musicales de Cuba: De lo Afrocubano a la Salsa* (San Juan: Editorial Cubanacán, 1994), 47–48, states that the beginnings of rumba follow the abolition of slavery in 1886 when formerly enslaved peoples clustered in peripheral urban spaces. The dance data suggest that enslaved Africans were part of the formation process of rumba, especially *rumba columbia,* and we know that prior to the full blossoming of any aesthetic creation, there are traces and precursors that come to solidify the form. Thus from midcentury through the end of the nineteenth century, rumba was probably percolating and forming among both the enslaved and free dark-skinned Cubans.

2. In this chapter, I refer to traditional rumba's displacement over decades in terms of a so-called pretender called rhumba, which I will explain further later.

3. Alén, *Géneros Musicales de Cuba,* 47–54.

4. *Son* developed throughout the Hispanic Americas and took on different characteristics. For Cuban *son*, see Yvonne Daniel, "Cuban Dance: An Orchard of Caribbean Creativity," in *Caribbean Dance from Abakuá to Zouk,* ed. Suzanna Sloat (Gainesville: University Press of Florida, 2002), 41–46; for Mexican *son,* see Susan Cashion, "Dance Ritual and Cultural Values in a Mexican Village: Festival of Santo Santiago" (PhD diss., University of Michigan at Ann Arbor, 1984), 131–33.

5. John Chasteen, *National Rhythms, African Roots: The Deep History of Latin American Popular Dance* (Albuquerque: University of New Mexico Press, 2004), 115–16.

6. Cf. liner notes in *Cuba, I Am Time,* ed. Al Pryor, Jack O'Neil, and Nina Gomes (Bethpage, NY: BlueJacket Entertainment, 1997), 19–22.

7. Médéric Louis Elie Moreau de Saint Méry, *Dance: An Article Drawn from the Work by M. L. E. Moreau de St.-Méry, Entitled Repertory of Colonial Information,* trans. Lily Hastings and Baird Hastings (Brooklyn, NY: Dance Horizons, 1976 [1796]).

8. Beyond Moreau de St. Méry, see Fredrika Bremer, *Cartas Desde Cuba* (Havana: Editorial Arte y Literatura, 1980 [1851]); Père Jean Baptiste Labat, *Nouveau Voyage au Isles de l'Amérique,* trans. Anthony Bliss (La Hague, 1724); Alejo Carpentier, *La Música en Cuba* (Havana: Editorial Letras Cubanas, 1979 [1946]); cf. the drawings of Miguel Covarrubias and the poetry of Nicolas Guillén and Langston Hughes.

9. Chasteen, *National Rhythms, African Roots,* 199–203.

10. Fernando Ortiz, *Los Bailes y el Teatro de los Negros en el Folklore de Cuba* (Havana: Editorial Letras Cubanas, 1951), 329–30.

11. Louis Pérez, *On Becoming Cuban: Identity, Nationality and Culture* (Chapel Hill: University of North Carolina Press, 1999), 202.

12. For a full discussion of this complex national position and historical process, see Pérez, *On Becoming Cuban,* 198–218.

13. See also Robin Moore, *Nationalizing Blackness: Afrocubanismo and Artistic Revolution, 1920–1940* (Pittsburg: University of Pittsburg Press, 1997).

14. *Quindembo* is of Bantu linguistic origins, *ki n'dembo,* and means "mixture."

15. Yvonne Daniel, *Rumba: Dance and Social Change in Contemporary Cuba* (Bloomington: Indiana University Press, 1995).

16. John Storm Roberts, *The Latin Tinge: The Impact of Latin American Music on the United Status* (Tivoli, NY: Original Music, 1979), 76–99; Moore, *Nationalizing Blackness,* 166–91; Pérez, *On Becoming Cuban,* 165–218; Leymarie, *Cuban Fire,* 44–107; Ned Sublette, *Cuba and Its Music: From the First Drums to the Mambo* (Chicago: Chicago Review Press, 2004), 362–91.

17. A big reason to keep the spelling of rhumba is that it contrasts with original, traditional rumba, and the differentiation in spelling points out two rumba types. Unfortunately, the ballroom dance community has dropped the *h* in rhumba and now uses rumba quite often for its performance name. This misleads students and the public in thinking that rumba is more similar among all its variants than it is. In Spanish, there are many terms to specify which rumba is being performed or discussed (e.g., *rumba traditional, rumba de cajón, rumba del campo, rumba de salon, rumba commercial, rumba internacional, rumba brava, rumba chancleta, rumba tajona, or yambú, guaguancó, columbia, bata rumba, mañunga,* etc.).

18. See Moore, *Nationalizing Blackness,* 158 and 160 (photographs), 11–12, 173, 180. See also Janheintz Jahn, *Muntu: The New African Culture,* trans. Marjorie Grene (New York: Grove Press, 1961), 84.

19. Argeliers León, *Del Canto y el Tiempo* (Havana: Editorial Letras Cubanas, 1984); personal communication with Argeliers León at the Casa de las Américas, Havana, Cuba, August 1986; Alén, *Géneros Musicales de Cuba,* 28; María Teresa Linares, *La Música y el Pueblo* (Havana: Editorial Pueblo y Educación, 1984 [1979]), 14.

20. Roberts, *The Latin Tinge*, 231.

21. Leymarie, *Cuban Fire*, 31.

22. The place of Cuba in the international community, during the 1920s to 1950s particularly, was centered in adventure, gambling, and sexual fantasy, with music and dance steering the activity among North American and European tourists and Cuban society; for example, Pérez, *On Becoming Cuban*, 187–98).

23. In this chapter, I am focused on the structural elements of Cuban rumba movement. Elsewhere, I have critically and cross-culturally analyzed the content of dance in tourist settings, including those of Cuba; see Yvonne Daniel, "Dance in Tourist Settings: Authenticity and Creativity," *Annals of Tourism Research* 23, no. 4 (1996): 780–97.

24. Moore, *Nationalizing Blackness*, 171–82.

25. Leymarie, *Cuban Fire*, 49.

26. Daniel, *Rumba*, 20, cf. 7, 168f.

27. E-mail communication with Alfredo O'Farril, February 11, 2007, translated and edited by the author.

28. Moore, *Nationalizing Blackness*, 173–82.

29. Ibid, 174.

30. Although Leymarie cites a switch of armies that brought musicians to opposite ends of the island in 1906 (*Cuban Fire*, 33), historian Louis A. Pérez contends that this line of thinking stems from conventional thought regarding the spread of musical culture. Rather, he suggests the spread of *son* occurred during the actual presidency of José Miguel Gomez around 1911 or 1912. Then Pérez corrected President Gomez's association with the given year in Leymarie, 1906; Gomez did not become president in the 1905 elections, only later. Last, Pérez could not account for a recorded move of the army from either side of the island to the other at that time or any other in Cuban history (personal communication with Louis A. Pérez, summer 2003).

31. See Moore, *Nationalizing Blackness*, 186; Leymarie, *Cuban Fire*, 61.

32. I agree with Robin Moore that the data on dancers who brought rumba outside Cuba are exceedingly limited, and I am not privy to Cuban archives for research on this chapter. Moore gives good biographical summaries of a few who popularized it in Cuba, such as Carmita Ortiz, Rita Montaner, and Alicia Perlá, and he underscores the importance of René Ribero and Ramona Ajón; Moore, *Nationalizing Blackness*, 173–75, 186, 264–65. I have gathered other names and partial names in the process of this short, primarily library and informant, research: Pepe (José Benito), Garabato, Evaristo Benda, Juan Olimpo Lastre, Carmen Cuerbelo, Yolanda and Pablito, Delita, Killer Joe Piro, El Pidio and Margot, Paulito and Lilón, Rodney (Roderico Neyra), Rolando Espinosa and Anisia, Rolando Lima and Estela, and Carlos Yera and Pascualino; see Leymarie, *Cuban Fire*, especially. None of my Cuban informants could name the Cuban dancers with whom either U.S. Americans or Britons took classes in the 1930s to 1950s.

33. Jahn, *Muntu*, 84.

34. For a full discussion of Cuban music and dance within the grip of North American tourist and market forces, see Pérez, "Representation of Rhythm," in *On Becoming Cuban*, 198–218, which includes rumba, *son*, and mambo. For more on Cuban dance, see Roberts, *The Latin Tinge*, 127–59; Moore, *Nationalizing Blackness*, 223–25; Yvonne Daniel, "Cuban Dance: An Orchard of Caribbean Creativity," in *Caribbean Dance from Abakuá to Zouk*, 23–55; and Leymarie, *Cuban Fire*, 157–65.

35. Popular dance teachers from Conjunto Folklorico Nacional in Cuba (e.g., Lourdes Tamayo in 1986, Moraima in 1998, and Ivan in 2001) teach these as standard dance movements from the past. Also, teachers from Danza Nacional (e.g., Margarita Criegh

and Manolo Vasquez Robaina taught the same mambo step series to students in the Stanford University Cuban workshop, summer 1990. Although these may be formalized patterns that Cuban dance teachers or governmental officials want in terms of demonstrating mambo, they would still be close, if not genuine, representations of what the dance looked like when it was popularized in Cuba.

36. See *Machito, A Latin Jazz Legacy,* prod. and dir. Carlos Ortiz, 57 min., First Run/ Icarus Films, 1987, for this dance and ethnic history within the New York scene and in relation to Cuba; cf. Katherine Dunham's choreographies for "Mambo" (1954). For a thorough examination, see Angel Quintero-Rivera, *Salsa, Sabor y Control: Sociología de la Música "Tropical"* (Mexico City: Siglo Veintiuno Editores, 1998); cf. Pryor, O'Neil, and Gomes, including an overview of Cuban dance by María Teresa Linares, in *Cuba, I Am Time,* 59–70.

37. In elite ballroom society of the United States and Britain, this was modified into an alternating step repetition: quick, quick, slow, or slow, quick, quick in a varied rhythmic and directional pattern. Their rhumba was danced to a variety of music, some modernized *son,* but also to music unrelated to Cuban rumba or *son.* Juliet McMains, a ballroom dance specialist (see her chapter in this collection) states: "About ballroom Rumba styles: There are two main styles of ballroom Rumba—American and International—which are basically two different dances and have little in common except the name Rumba. . . . One is the American, box, or square Rumba. The basic step for this competition dance is taught in two different rhythms: QQS or SQQ. The International style Rumba . . . uses a rhythm of hold 1 and then step on beats 2, 3, 4 of each measure"; personal communication, August 31, 2005.

38. For traditional rumba's public resurfacing amid the height of hip-hop/rap/house dance popularity in 2003, see *Dame la Mano,* dir. Heddy Honnigmann, 112 min., Pieter Van Huystee Film and Television, 2004.

9

Embodying Music / Disciplining Dance

The Mambo Body in Havana and New York City

David F. García

Throughout the 1950s, the mambo predominated in the popular culture landscapes of North America, Latin America, Europe, and even parts of Asia and Africa. More than just a musical and dance style, mambo became a spectacle for audiences as well as a way of life for dancers and musicians. Mambo attracted the attention of novelist Jack Kerouac, filmmakers Robert Rossen and Emilio "El Indio" Fernández, dance choreographer Katherine Dunham, and even symphonic composer Rolf Liebermann. And it still remains active in the Latin imaginary of novelists, filmmakers, and musicians as represented by Oscar Hijuelos's 1990 Pulitzer Prize winning *Mambo Kings Sing Songs of Love*, its 1992 film adaptation *Mambo Kings* directed by Arne Glimcher, and Lou Bega's 1999 international pop hit "Mambo No. 5." But despite its deep entrenchment in the culture and consciousness of the Americas and beyond, mambo has not been the focus of extended scholarly research or critical analysis. Because of its popularization globally, mambo is especially primed for research and analysis from a transnational and critical perspective.[1]

Like other transnational musical and dance phenomena, the mambo defies a simple definition. In the late 1930s and early 1940s, prior to its commercialization by the popular culture industry, mambo involved new ways
of playing and dancing to what was otherwise established Cuban dance
music. Its musical characteristics included the use of short and syncopated
rhythmic patterns at specific sections of an arrangement. Different types of
ensembles with distinct instrumentation including *charangas, conjuntos,* and
big bands participated in these new developments.[2] The musical repertories
of these ensembles were diverse, including *danzón,* guaracha, bolero, and *son
montuno.* By 1950 though, important early figures and groups in the music—
Arcaño y sus Maravillas, Arsenio Rodríguez y su Conjunto, Julio Cueva y
su Orquesta, Machito and His Afro-Cubans, and Dámaso Pérez Prado—had
popularized their own idiosyncratic style, and mambo had also become an
international phenomenon, transcending any one particular individual or
regional style. Mambo dance is also difficult to define for similar reasons.
Mambo dancers in New York City, the United States in general, and continental Latin America were more accustomed to the music as performed
by big bands, whereas dancers in Cuba and the Caribbean in general were
attracted to *charangas* and *conjuntos.* Dance styles that were identified with
particular regions, musical genres, and ensembles further complicate a simple
definition of mambo dance.

Despite mambo's rich and complex history, historians have been mostly
concerned with defining the origins of mambo music, debating its musical
essence, and identifying the musician who invented that essence.[3] Art and
dance historian Robert Farris Thompson has provided a somewhat alternative
approach to the study of mambo in positing the Kongo spiritual and aesthetic
essence in the music and dance.[4] Though there is much to be documented
on the mambo's development and learned from its resonance with African
aesthetics, these questions only begin to address its cultural, social, and
historical significance. Studying the music and dance from transnational,
postcolonial, and psychoanalytic perspectives will offer new insights into
the mambo's engagements with dominant discourses and processes of commodification, national identity, and race.

In this chapter, I begin to engage these approaches in studying the early
reception of mambo music and dance in the United States and Latin America. I focus on the "mambo body" conceived of not only as dance but as a
nexus of dominant power relations and discourses, histories of social agency
and identity formations, and individual experiences. I draw from Veit Erl-

mann's theorization of dance in his study on *isicathamiya* in which he states that "dancing can reproduce the givenness of the dominant order, but it can also provide the models for its transformation. To dance is to produce not only signs but also social experience itself."[5] This perspective on dance focuses our attention on the *meanings* (not origins) of mambo dance as these were performed, constructed, and reclaimed by dancers, musicians, and writers.

I also draw from Patria Román-Velázquez's work on salsa music and dance in which she reminds us that because salsa is performed in different parts of the world, identities and experiences are uniquely linked to the times and places in which these performances occur.[6] Yet Román-Velázquez also demonstrates that the dominant cultural constructions of the body and ethnicity foster the perception of salsa as a homogenous "Latin" genre that transcends time and place. Similarly, the places in which musicians, dancers, and observers experienced mambo constituted a constellation of social clubs, nightclubs, movie theaters, homes, and dance halls located throughout the Americas. Still, critics of the mambo, whether writing from Havana, New York City, or elsewhere in Latin America, perceived the music and dance as a product of a foreign source or different race and thus a threat to the racial and cultural patrimony of the nation.

In short, the mambo body constitutes an interpretive framework through which I focus on shared, competing, and contradictory meanings and experiences of mambo dancing and music as these were embodied, imagined, and articulated in Havana and New York City in the 1940s. In the first section, I outline the early history of mambo music and dance, briefly tracing its trajectories through the social and popular cultural landscapes of these two cities. I focus the remaining chapter on addressing how the mambo body simultaneously promoted empowering modes of expression and incited perceptions of U.S. cultural imperialism and African primitiveness among musicians, dancers, and writers. It is particularly revealing that dance teachers and critics articulated these perceptions in the dominant discourses of racial inferiority, national identity, and sexual impropriety. Ultimately, my aim is to understand the embodied experience and reception of the dance. It is especially important to emphasize that although I focus on its history and reception in Havana and New York City, I also draw on reports on mambo music and dance in Mexico City to stress the mambo's transnational history and contemporaneity throughout the Americas, thereby writing against the conventional linear narrative of the existing literature on mambo.

The Emergence of the Mambo Body

"Strange territory" is how mambo dancer Pedro Aguilar, better known as Cuban Pete, described the Palladium upon his first visit to this midtown Manhattan dance hall around 1949.[7] The Palladium would soon become internationally known as New York's most popular place for mambo music and dance. It featured social as well as professional and exhibition dancers such as Cuban Pete and his partner Millie Donay. Before his arrival at the Palladium, however, Cuban Pete had already begun to dance in places located in East Harlem and the South Bronx, garnering the recognition and praise of these locales' predominately local Puerto Rican audiences. His impression of the Palladium is particularly significant because it suggests that places in which mambo was featured were quite distinct in terms of musical and dance styles, audiences, and physical surroundings, no matter whether these locales were located in the same city or in different countries. His characterization of the Palladium as "strange territory" also suggests that Cuban Pete and other Latino dancers might have experienced a heightened sense of self-consciousness as they became the objects of desire and anxiety of professional dance teachers and critics who flocked to the Palladium and other settings to observe this newest dance craze. It is this objectification of mambo dancers in particular that calls for a critical conception of the mambo's meanings as these were performed and constructed in Havana and New York City.

From the late 1930s and early 1940s, the term *mambo* as it was applied to popular music and dance resisted a uniform designation. Nevertheless, it is generally accepted that mambo initially referred to the syncopated rhythms or patterns in *contratiempo* (against time) that musicians played during a certain section, usually the finale, of an arrangement. This section constituted the liveliest part of the arrangement in which dancers executed their most animated movements. Most historians agree that Orestes López of the Cuban *charanga* Arcaño y sus Maravillas composed the first mambo, appropriately titled "Mambo," in Havana in the mid- to late 1930s.[8] The first mambo that Arcaño's *charanga* actually recorded, however, was Israel "Cachao" López's "Rarezas" in 1940. This new style of music and dance consisted of the *danzón's* conventional ABACA arrangement scheme and choreography but with an added finale. Director Antonio Arcaño explained that this newly added final section featured the *nuevo ritmo* (new rhythm) that members Orestes López, Israel "Cachao" López, and others innovated for Cuban dancers who reciprocated with inventive dance steps.[9] By 1943, *conjunto* leader Arsenio

Rodríguez began to record *son* music that featured similar structural and rhythmic innovations. Rodríguez named his new final section "diablo" and similarly explained that this section was added to give dancers "a kick in the ass."[10] By 1944, Cuban musicians and arrangers René Hernández, Bebo Valdés, and Dámaso Pérez Prado began to implement rhythmic figures in *contratiempo,* usually in specific sections, in their arrangements for the big bands of Julio Cueva, Casino de la Playa, and Hermanos Palau.

The social and racial makeup of the audiences of these ensembles (*charangas, conjuntos,* and big bands) is important to note because it largely determined how musicians and dancers in Havana characterized these new styles of dance music. As I discuss elsewhere, Arcaño's and Rodríguez's musical innovations were made in collaboration and dialogue with their dancing audience, which consisted mostly of the black working class of Havana.[11] This integrative interrelationship between these musicians and dancers translated into the accentuation of the dancers' movements in the musical textures of Arcaño's and Rodríguez's styles; *contratiempo* or offbeat accentuation and movement was the predominant element of these new musical textures and dance styles. Moreover, Arcaño's and Rodríguez's audiences tended to describe their styles not as mambo but rather as *negro* (black). *Contratiempo* would also become the defining principle of mambo music as performed by big bands in Havana and throughout the Americas. These big bands, however, whose instrumental configurations were modeled on American swing bands, performed primarily for the Cuban white upper classes. Because of the racial and class makeup of big band musicians and their audiences, the styles of most big bands were characterized as *blanco* (white).

As in the music, the name *mambo* was not attributed to any one particular dance style at this time. Rather, it was used to identify a new trend in the existing *danzón* dance choreography, whereas the dance styles associated with Arsenio Rodríguez's *conjunto* and the big bands mentioned previously were also known by the music's existing names *son montuno* and *guaracha,* respectively. Similarly, the recording industry did not use the term "*mambo*" in its marketing or labeling of records until 1946. For example, RCA Victor labeled Arcaño's "Rarezas" (recorded on April 29, 1940) a *danzón,* Rodríguez's "Pilla con pilla" (recorded on November 16, 1943) a *guaracha rumba,* and René Hernández's arrangement of "Figurina del solar" (recorded on February 24, 1944) a *guaracha.* All of these recordings feature the mambo's defining patterns in *contratiempo,* but as Cuban pianist and director René Touzet confirmed, musicians were playing the music "with a mambo flavor, but we didn't call it mambo."[12]

The appellation of the term *mambo* to music and dance took a similar trajectory in New York City. In 1946, as Cuban Pete notes, Latino dancers were dancing *danzón, son montuno,* guaracha, bolero, and rumba in dance halls such as the Grand Plaza and Tropicana in the South Bronx and the Park Plaza in East Harlem.[13] Nevertheless, guaracha and rumba music as performed by Latin big bands began to include the new mambo section, which attracted the attention and excitement of Latino dancers. Cuban vocalist Miguelito Valdés sang about this new development in Cuban and Latin dance music in his recording of "Algo nuevo" (Something New), which he made in 1946. Then, by 1947 and 1948 the popular press in Havana and New York City began to publish articles on an emerging "mambo revolution" in music and dance, band leaders began to name themselves the "king of the mambo," and record companies began to label their music "mambo."[14] Also, dance teachers began to advertise mambo dance lessons, such as Jack Stone, who printed an ad in *La Prensa,* a Spanish-language newspaper in New York City, offering dance lessons in rumba, tango, fox trot, samba, *vals,* Lindy, mambo, and bolero.[15] New York's other Spanish-language newspaper, *El Diario de Nueva York,* began to print ads referring to the Palladium as the *cuna,* or cradle, of mambo music and dance.

This coalescence of music and dance with the recording and print media industries marked a significant stage in the history of mambo. Although it had emerged as a stylistic innovation in the performance of existing forms of Cuban music and dance, now it had become an object of reification, fascination, and anxiety among ethnically diverse observers and audiences. Musically, this meant that some arrangements were written to consist entirely of what had been the syncopated sections of the *danzón, son montuno,* and guaracha. But while dancers began to adjust their dancing to these new mambo arrangements, they and Latin big bands continued to perform rumba, guaracha, and *son.* Dance teachers and critics, however, had difficulty managing this diversity of musical and dance genres particularly because they perceived mambo as a homogenous dance style. Writing in *Dance Magazine* in 1951, Don Byrnes and Alice Swanson, who claimed to have begun teaching "ballroom mambo" in 1948, stated that mambo dance "defies a one-shot analysis. . . . [T]here are innumerable interpretations and methods of presentation."[16] They added that mambo "is an innovation by a group of very real 'Latins from Manhattan'—Puerto Rican boys and girls who frequent the Palladium Ballroom on Broadway. Many of these youngsters had learned Cuban bolero and Cuban rumba step patterns in a dance hall known as the Park Palace, in Harlem, a favorite rendezvous of Cuban dancers."[17]

It is passages such as these in which we can read two common strategies in dance teachers' and writers' discourse on mambo dancing. The first was to posit a lack of organization and discipline in the dance. In fact, Latino dancers executed various dance steps and privileged individual styles in their dancing. This seemed to frustrate professional dance teachers wanting to teach (read codify) the next big dance fad. The second strategy was to racialize and geographically spatialize the mambo's "unwieldy" and "foreign" origins. In New York City, this strategy buttressed the desire to discipline and familiarize mambo dancing for a broader non-Latino audience, whereas in Havana and other parts of Latin America critics' "othering" of mambo dancing as "North American" buttressed their similar desire for a racially homogenized nation. As both strategies employed racist stereotypes, mambo dancing afforded dancers a powerful means by which to recast these dominant stereotypes.

Commodifying, Racializing, and Experiencing Mambo Dance

"It is now the responsibility of the teacher to standardize, discipline and properly present this thrilling dance to make it acceptable."[18] The authors of this statement, Don Byrnes and Alice Swanson, followed it with a description of what they claimed to be the mambo's four "step patterns to be in general use."[19] *Life* magazine's 1954 article on the mambo's popularity in the United States made a similar presentation, identifying, however, only one basic step pattern.[20] As these and other sources suggested, one had to learn the basic foot pattern to dance mambo. Yet, as late as 1958, dance teachers and critics such as Robert Luis and Dorothea Ohl could still not agree on what constituted the mambo's basic dance step.[21]

As dance teachers struggled to identify the mambo's basic step pattern, many Palladium dancers distinguished two groups of mambo dancers. The following insightful explanation made by Palladium dancer Luís "Maquina" Flores is worth quoting at length:

> When you walked in the Palladium . . . the people that frequented the right side of the dance hall were us people. . . . On the left side of the Palladium, [where] the tables [were located], . . . you had a lot of dancers that were from the tables. They used to dance as professionals. The people on the right side were the trendsetters, OK? . . . We did not care to be a so-called professional from the left side, OK? Now every time that the story is told, it's told from the left side. But what they don't say is that the left side learned from the right side. We were the ones to make up the steps. We were the trendsetters in dressing, OK?[22]

As Flores suggests, "right-side" dancers, or "real Latins from Manhattan" as Don Byrnes and Alice Swanson described them, resisted identifying with "so-called professional" or "left-side" dancers, both in spatial terms (i.e., not sitting at the "left side" of the Palladium) and in terms of how they danced. As trendsetters, "right-side" dancers developed their individual style of dancing mambo by incorporating their entire body in interpreting the music rather than relying solely on any one particular foot pattern. As former Palladium dancer Barbara Craddock emphasized, mambo or "right-side" dancers "*felt* the music from the inside. They moved to the sound of the music."[23] Another "right-side" Palladium dancer, Tony "Peanuts" Aubert, added that mambo dancers "danced based on the music." Referring to the body's interpretations of specific arrangements and musical events such as breaks and brass punches, he said that "we interpreted the music."[24] Cuban Pete made a similar observation, alluding perhaps to the "left side's" preoccupation with using the so-called "correct" foot patterns: "People weren't dancing with their hands or their whole body at that time. And to me, I always felt that even part of your body if you're a dancer . . . comes into great play. It's necessary. And the different stories that Millie and I thought of to tell on the floor, my hands—and, hey, I talk with my hands as it is."[25] Social dancers in Havana were also not concerned with following prescribed foot patterns consistently. In commenting on Arcaño's dancers, writer Cuellar Vizcaíno noted: "The dancer doesn't even mark [the beat] with the foot but rather with the shudder of the body (figure 9.1)."[26]

This disjuncture in apprehending mambo dance—quantifying and standardizing steps versus embodying sound—provides us with two distinct, yet equally significant, understandings of mambo dancing. For the "right-side" dancers quoted previously, their descriptions of dancing mambo emanated from an embodied experience in which sound and movement were merged through the body. Many other dancers that I have interviewed have consistently used the term *feeling,* as in "feeling the music," in describing not only the inner emotions involved in dancing but also their actual embodiment of the musical sound or rhythmic texture.[27] In addition to such synesthetic descriptions of the interrelationship of sound and movement, dancers and musicians have also emphasized the individualized, extemporaneous, as well as communal aspects of dancing mambo. In addressing how dancers interpreted breaks in the music, Cuban Pete has remarked: "You [had] so many numbers that had different types of beats [that] might have called for me to drop. Where somebody else couldn't do my drops they would find

Figure 9.1: Cuban Pete "dancing with his hands" at the Palladium. Circa 1953. Cuban Pete, like many other "right-side" Palladium dancers, was keen on synchronizing his bodily movements with the dynamic events of a particular musical arrangement. Courtesy of Cuban Pete and Barbara Craddock.

Figure 9.2: *Life* (December 20, 1954) photo of Cuban Pete and Millie "telling stories" on the dance floor of the Palladium. Cuban Pete and Millie were the featured mambo dance couple at the Palladium through the first half of the 1950s. Many Mambo dance enthusiasts, like those seated on the floor as well as at the tables behind, modeled their dancing on the steps and moves that Cuban Pete and Millie developed and made popular. Yale Joel/Time & Life Pictures/Getty Images.

something to do or don't do anything. Each music has its own feel, and each one digests according to how he feels."[28] In Cuba, Antonio Arcaño noted that during the *danzón's* mambo section, "the dancer yells, *creates* steps and contorts his body *in plain communion with us* [the musicians of his *charanga*] in the *ritmo Nuevo*" (figure 9.2).[29]

Many dance teachers, however, interpreted such variables (extemporaneous step patterns, drops, and breaks) in their dancing as "extreme" and requiring standardization in order to present the dance as a sellable commodity for the social or ballroom dance market. "The potential dance market is enormous. If *Mambo* is *intelligently* demonstrated without that 'extreme effect,' [then] it will intrigue students of social dancing anywhere."[30]

Teachers and critics also racialized the dancers and dance. In an article titled "Touch of Jungle Madness: Denizens of Broadway Go Slightly Primitive under Spell of the Wild Sweaty Mambo" published in the *New York Daily News,* Jess Stearn employs numerous racist stereotypes from the discourse of African primitivism in his descriptions of mambo music and dance as he observed these at the Palladium: "It [mambo] may turn the Great White Way into a veritable Congoland before it is through. . . . It is wild. It is grotesque. It is sexy. It is the Mambo. . . . The Mambo, danced to a tom-tom beat, is as primitive as any African war dance—without paint, feathers or hors d'oeuvres prepared from white explorers."[31] Others drew from social Darwinian evolutionist discourse to the same effect. The mainstream pop singer Percy Faith, who had become popular in part because of his Latin novelty recordings, attempted to explain the mambo's popularity: "I think people like to hear this music because it takes them back to the primitive—back to the very beginning when there was just drums. If you throw four or five Latin drummers into a piece, it's an exciting splash of primitive color."[32]

As was the case with early jazz, mambo music and dancing evoked similar racist stereotypes from the discourses of social evolutionism and African primitivism in the language of writers and musicians alike.[33] Here, I draw from Homi Bhabha's use of both postcolonial and psychoanalytic theory in his theorization of the stereotype.[34] As Bhabha explains, the stereotype has been the major discursive strategy of colonial discourse, and it is ambivalence that gives the stereotype its currency.[35] By ambivalence, Bhabha means the vacillation between the stereotype's perceived fixity of meaning and the need for it to be anxiously repeated and attributed to different objects for the sake of maintaining its currency and original significance. Stereotypes are thus repeated to make familiar what is otherwise encountered as foreign, novel, or different. As we can see in the previous examples as well as in *Life's* title "Uncle Sambo, Mad for Mambo," critics and others employed many stereotypes from the interrelated colonial discourses of African primitivism (jungle madness, Congoland, wild, grotesque, tom-tom beat, African war dance, face paint, feathers, cannibalism) and social Darwinian evolutionism (primitive stage, drums) to convey this otherwise novel dance and musical form in terms familiar to their readers and audience. But why the need to employ stereotypes from these particular discourses to convey a Cuban and Latin dance form as "African" and "primitive"?

To answer this question, I turn to Bhabha's application of Freud's theory of fetishism to further read the function of racist stereotypes.[36] For stereotypes function not merely as modes of making familiar peoples and cultures that are otherwise different, but as mechanisms to cope with this difference, the recognition of which, Bhabha argues, produces anxiety in the "colonist" (i.e., the colonizer and colonized). Underlying this anxiety is desire (from Jacques Lacan) for a (mythical) racial and cultural purity and superiority. We might suggest, therefore, that the sound of mambo music and the ways in which mambo dancers used and moved their bodies to that sound reminded Stearn as well as Don Byrnes, Alice Swanson, Robert Luis, Dorothea Ohl, the editors of *Life*, Percy Faith, and many others of racial and cultural differences that in turn threatened their primal fantasy of a white racial origin. As such, skin color, the body, and sound—the very agents of their anxiety and pleasure of racial and cultural difference—became the fetish objects of their desires and anxieties, which they articulated most effectively in the discourse of African primitivism. Furthermore, professional dance teachers needed to deem mambo dancing, as performed by "real Latins from Manhattan" or "right-side" dancers, as disorganized, undisciplined, wild, sweaty, grotesque, and sexually uninhibited in order to keep intact their desire for a white ra-cial origin and superior Western civilization. It is especially revealing that Stearn focused his observations on non-Latino female teenagers, housewives, and grandmothers and attributed their enjoyment in dancing mambo to its "feverish intensity" and "contagiousness." It is easy to sense the anxiety in Stearn's passages in which he cautions the loss of the "Great White Way" (read the white race as well as Broadway) to "Congoland" (nonwhite races) at the hands of the "wild," "grotesque," and "sexy" mambo.

One can apply the same concepts of stereotypes, desire, and anxiety to read Cuban and Mexican critics' observations on mambo dancing in Ha-vana and Mexico City, though here the primal fantasy involves national integrity as well as racial homogeneity. Cuellar Vizcaíno reported the fol-lowing from Havana: "The enemies of the Mambo allege that with it the *danzón's* elegance and grace disappears. . . . They claim that [mambo] came from the [North] Americans like an aggression on our *pure* national dance [*danzón*], introducing in it dull movements and gestures that have nothing to do with our customs."[37] One such enemy of mambo as danced by the Cuban youth was Cuban composer and music historian Odilio Urfé, who, writing in 1948, attributed the dance's vulgarity and crudeness to North American models: "The danzón's contemporary choreography is a crude copy . . . of the dances of the North Americans. They have completely erased the elegance and comportment that Cuban dancers in other epochs made popular, like unequivocal signs of good morals. The youth of today will say that it is what is popular today, what is modern, but they will never cease to be vulgar."[38]

Mexican critic Federico Ortiz Jr., writing in 1951, expressed similar sentiments within the discourse of African primitivism: "The Mambo . . . according to the opinions of some academics . . . is nothing more than a classic deformation of the songs of the old African tribes, which still exist, foreign melodies that originated in North American jazz. . . . It is hoped that the entire Americas react against this particular [music and dance] and support the popular music of their own people, thereby displacing the music that comes to us from outside."[39] The North or African American models that Urfé, Ortiz, and others were referring to were swing music and dance. Robert Farris Thompson suggests that these influences were introduced to black Cuban dancers through African American films such as *Cabin in the Sky* and *Stormy Weather* in the early 1940s.[40] Jazz and Lindy Hop dance also had a significant impact on mambo music and dancing in New York City. Millie Donay, for instance, actively incorporated features such as the shimmy into her dancing.

Critics of the mambo in Latin America and the United States seemingly diverged in their critiques of the dance. For North American critics, mambo dancing embodied the wild and sexually uninhibited essence of primitive Africa, an essence that could nevertheless be disciplined into a socially acceptable and thus marketable product. For Latin American critics, mambo music and dance embodied U.S. cultural imperialism and a "deformation" of an atavistic African essence, both of which posed an insidious threat to the perceived cultural and racial integrity of, in this case, the Cuban and Mexican nations. But, though their othering of the mambo—"Latin American" and "African" by North American critics and "African" and "North American" by Latin American critics—constituted an obvious contradiction, they articulated their critiques from a shared fantasy of a white racial origin and national identity based on a white, Eurocentric essence. In Cuba, for instance, the fact that youth who drew from African American dance forms (swing and Lindy) were black themselves threatened the myth of a Cuban "race" supposedly borne of the process of *mestizaje* (racial miscegenation). Any signs that reminded Cuban nationalist critics of the nation's racially diverse population and particularly its black population clearly incited its desire for a racially undifferentiated (i.e., white) Cuban nation.[41] Ultimately, whether from the United States or Latin America, critics and others resorted to nationalist and moralistic rhetoric ("pure," "vulgar," and "sexy") as well as racist stereotypes ("wild," "African tribes," cannibalism) to perpetuate the currency of the superiority of the white race and Eurocentric culture.

For many dancers throughout the Americas, however, dancing to mambo music encompassed not only entertainment but an empowered mode of social experience that enabled them to reappropriate, resist, and contend with these discourses and stereotypes. For example, black intellectuals and political leaders in Cuba and the United States had already established and fostered mutually influential dialogues in shaping their respective identity formations as expressed through their respective *Afrocubanismo* and Harlem Renaissance movements in the 1920s and 1930s.[42] Black Cuban dancers' incorporation of African American dance styles into their so-called national dances signified not only a continuation of this African diasporic dialogue but also their critique of the discrepancies of the official Cuban ideology of *mestizaje* and their lived experience in a racist society. As I have argued elsewhere, the Cuban institution of black working-class social clubs, in which Arcaño y sus Maravillas and Arsenio Rodríguez y su Conjunto developed the earliest styles of mambo music, afforded black dancers and musicians a crucial artistic autonomy in a larger social milieu in which dancing was one of the most segregated cultural activities in Havana.[43]

In addition to their resistance to sharing the same space with "left-side" or professional ballroom dance teachers, many Palladium dancers, particularly non-Latino female dancers like Millie Donay and Barbara Craddock, challenged the dominant social norms structuring sexual comportment and interracial relations. Donay's partnership with and eventual marriage to Cuban Pete in the early 1950s is especially revealing. As one of the most innovative mambo dance couples, Cuban Pete, a Puerto Rican of color, and Donay, an Italian American, reappropriated aspects of Cuban and African American dance that for many critics signified the "wild," "primitive," and "undisciplined" legacy of Africa and combined them into a highly unique and influential style of mambo dancing. In addition, as surviving film footage suggests, Donay's individual dance style thrived on incorporating sexually suggestive moves, which we can read as her simultaneously reversing the gaze of male critics and flaunting the accepted comportment of ballroom dancing upon which professional teachers wanted to discipline mambo dancing. For his part, Cuban Pete, who briefly taught Arthur Murray's dancers aspects of his style, emphasized that he "felt good" knowing that dance critics and professional ballroom dance teachers, including those hired by Murray, were closely observing him as he danced despite their motivation to codify mambo dancing for the social dance market. Cuban Pete has remarked that "left-side" dancers learned from "right-side" dancers not only from observing them on the floor of the Palladium, as Luis Flores claimed, but also by directly employing them at their dance studios.[44]

In this chapter, I have aimed to understand the mambo as a socially and historically contingent as well as a transnational phenomenon. Writings on mambo by dance teachers and critics are especially useful sources in interpreting its reception in Havana and New York City. As with its predecessors—the tango, samba, and *danzón* of the nineteenth and early twentieth centuries— mambo incited pleasure and anxieties over questions of proper comportment as well as racial and national integrity.[45] More research into its local reception in Mexico City, Lima, and other cities will further the critical appreciation of mambo as a transnational music and dance genre linked by questions of race, national identity, sexuality, gender, and commodity culture.

Notes

1. My current research involves the critical examination of mambo music, dance, and culture in Havana, Mexico City, the United States, and South America. I am particularly interested in mambo as a transnational phenomenon disseminated through the recording, film, and print media industries.

2. The typical instrumentation of a *charanga* includes flute, violins, piano, bass, timbales, congas, and guiro. That for a *conjunto* includes trumpets, piano, tres, bass, bongo, and congas. And that for a big band includes trumpets, saxophones, piano, bass, timbales, bongos, and congas.

3. See Leonardo Acosta, "¿Quién inventó el Mambo?" in *El Mambo,* ed. Radamés Giro (Havana: Editorial Letras Cubanas, 1993); Leonardo Acosta, "Reajustes, Aclaraciones y Criterios Sobre Dámaso Pérez Prado," in *El Mambo,* ed. Radamés Giro (Havana: Editorial Letras Cubanas, 1993); Cristobal Díaz Ayala, *Música Cubana del Areyto a la Nueva Trova,* 3rd ed. (San Juan: Editorial Cubanacan, 1993); Natalio Galán, *Cuba y Sus Sones* (Valencia: Artes Gráficos Soler, 1983); Radamés Giro, "Todo lo Que Usted Quiso Saber Sobre el Mambo," in *El Mambo,* ed. Radamés Giro (Havana: Editorial Letras Cubanas, 1993); Gustavo Pérez Firmat, *Life on the Hyphen: The Cuban-American Way* (Austin: University of Texas Press, 1994); Max Salazar, "Who Invented the Mambo?" *Latin Beat Magazine* 2, no. 8 (1992): 9–14; Odilio Urfé, "La verdad sobre el Mambo," in *El Mambo,* ed. Radamés Giro (Havana: Editorial Letras Cubanas, 1993).

4. Robert Farris Thompson, "Teaching the People to Triumph Over Time: Notes from the World of Mambo," in *Caribbean Dance from Abakuá to Zouk,* ed. Susanna Sloat (Gainesville: University Press of Florida, 2002), 336–44.

5. Veit Erlmann, *Nightsong: Performance, Power, and Practice in South Africa* (Chicago: University of Chicago Press, 1996), 183.

6. Patria Román-Velázquez, "The Embodiment of Salsa: Musicians, Instruments, and the Performance of a Latin Identity," in *Ethnomusicology: A Contemporary Reader,* ed. Jennifer C. Post (New York: Routledge, 2005), 295–310.

7. Pedro Aguilar, interview by Henry Medina, 1983, Miami, FL.

8. In fact, historians have given various dates for the composition of "Mambo." Urfé, for example, claimed that it was composed as early as 1935; see Odilio Urfé, "Danzón, Mambo, y chachachá," *Revolución y Cultura* 1 (1979): 54–57. To complicate things more, Arcaño y sus Maravillas did not record "Mambo" until 1951. To my knowledge, this recording of "Mambo" is the earliest documented (either recorded or notated) source.

9. Ileana Boudet, "Arcaño y sus Maravillas," *Revolución y cultura* 25 (1974): 35.

10. David García, *Arsenio Rodríguez and the Transnational Flows of Latin Popular Music* (Philadelphia: Temple University Press, 2006), 50.

11. Ibid.

12. Touzet left Havana for New York City in 1944; René Touzet, telephone interview with the author, 2000.

13. Pedro Aguilar, interview by Henry Medina, 1983, Miami, FL.

14. Manuel Cuellar Vizcaíno, "La revolución del Mambo," *Bohemia* 40, no. 22 (May 30, 1948): 20–21, 97–99.

15. *La Prensa* printed this ad on November 4, 1949.

16. Don Byrnes and Alice Swanson, "Mambo: A Vest Pocket Analysis," *Dance Magazine* 25, no. 10 (October 1951): 36.

17. Ibid., 29.

18. Ibid., 36.

19. Ibid.

20. "Uncle Sambo, Mad for Mambo," *Life* 37, no. 25 (1954): 16.

21. Their debate centered on the use of the American box, Cuban box, and off-beat rumba as the basic dance step for mambo; see Robert Luis, "Rumba's Anniversary," *Dance Magazine* 32, no. 6 (June 1958): 66–67; Dorothea Ohl, "Mambo Not a Dance?" *Dance Magazine* 32, no. 6 (June 1958): 67–68.

22. Luís "Maquina" Flores, interview with David Carp, 1993, Riverdale, NY.

23. Barbara Craddock, interview with the author, 2002, New York City.

24. Tony "Peanuts" Aubert, interview with the author, 2002, New York City.

25. Pedro Aguilar, interview by Henry Medina, 1983, Miami, FL.

26. Cuellar Vizcaíno, "La revolución del Mambo," 21.

27. Elsewhere, I discuss the role of *son* dancers in the formation and embodiment of Arsenio Rodríguez's *son montuno* style; see García, *Arsenio Rodríguez*, 41–47.

28. Pedro Aguilar, transcribed interview by David Carp, 1993, Miami, FL.

29. Cuellar Vizcaíno, "La revolución del Mambo," 97, emphasis mine.

30. Byrnes and Swanson, "Mambo," 29.

31. Jess Stearn, "Touch of Jungle Madness: Denizens of Broadway Go Slightly Primitive under Spell of the Wild Sweaty Mambo," *New York Daily News*, May 6, 1951.

32. Leonard Feather, "Percy: No Faith in Phony Latins!" *Down Beat*, November 19, 1952, 12.

33. For examples of racist stereotypes in early jazz poetry, see Sascha Feinstein, *Jazz Poetry: From the 1920s to the Present* (Westport, CT: Greenwood Press, 1997), 15–22.

34. Homi K. Bhabha, "The Other Question: Stereotype, Discrimination and the Discourse of Colonialism," in *The Location of Culture* (London: Routledge, 1994).

35. Ibid., 94–95.

36. Ibid., 106–8, in which Bhabha explains his application of Freud's theory of fetishism to read the use of racist stereotypes in colonial discourse as driven by the anxiety and desire experienced in the recognition/disavowal of sexual/racial difference.

37. Cuellar Vizcaíno, "La revolución del Mambo," 21, emphasis mine.

38. Urfé, "La verdad sobre el Mambo," 34–35.

39. Federico Ortiz Jr., "El Mambo y su infuencia malsana," *La opinion*, July 8, 1951, 7.

40. Thompson, "Teaching the People to Triumph Over Time," 338.

41. For critiques of Cuba's racial and national ideology, see Aline Helg, *Our Rightful Share: The Afro-Cuban Struggle for Equality, 1886–1912* (Chapel Hill: University of North Carolina Press, 1995); Katherine Hagedorn, *Divine Utterances: The Performance of Afro-Cuban Santería* (Washington, DC: Smithsonian Institution Press, 2001); and García, *Arsenio Rodríguez*, 12–31.

42. On the history of Afro-Cuban and African American dialogues, see the essays in Lisa Brock and Digna Castañeda Fuertes, eds., *Between Race and Empire: African-Americans and Cubans before the Cuban Revolution* (Philadelphia: Temple University Press, 1998).

43. García, *Arsenio Rodríguez*, 55–60.

44. Pedro Aguilar, recorded telephone interview with the author, 2006.

45. John Charles Chasteen, *National Rhythms, African Roots: The Deep History of Latin American Popular Dance* (Albuquerque: University of New Mexico Press, 2004).

10

Rocking Around the Clock

Teenage Dance Fads from 1955 to 1965

Tim Wall

The year 2005 marked the fiftieth anniversary of the chart success of Bill Haley and the Comet's "Rock Around the Clock"[1] and the fifty-first anniversary of the United States Supreme Court's landmark declaration that segregated schooling for black and white pupils was inherently unequal. The media featured prominent commemorations of 1955 as the start of rock 'n' roll, the "birth of the teenager," and the rebirth of popular dance. Far less attention was given to the milestone in civil rights, yet both the musical recording and the legal decision were intertwined.

Haley's recording reached a wider audience as the soundtrack to the opening and closing credits of the 1955 film *Blackboard Jungle,* an exploration of juvenile delinquency and race in U.S. urban high schools. In Britain, the film's screening was linked in newspapers to stories about riots in cinemas and of young people "jiving" in the aisles.[2] The following year, the record's title was recycled as the title for a film starring Bill Haley, in which his fusion of white country and black R & B works as a metonym of an integrated world of teenage culture. By juxtaposing music, dancing, and the politics of race, these films tied together youthful rebellion with dreams of racial integration. The commercial success of the films and the record demonstrated that the new prosperity of young people could be exploited if only one understood the meanings of this teenage culture.[3]

Dancing was a central form of music consumption in this new teenage culture, thus it is no coincidence that dancers and dances are featured prominently in the films and television programs aimed at the new teen market. Dancing came to dominate post–rock 'n' roll music, both records and radio broadcasts, over the next ten years. During this period, there were hundreds of dances, each strongly related to one or two recordings, and most only securing popularity for a few months at best. It is possible to piece together a basic cultural history of rock 'n' roll, beginning with its roots in black R & B and white country music, its dissemination through radio (and subsequent simplification of the dance forms), and its representation in film. Of course a comprehensive study of all the dances, music, venues, and media of popular culture of the 1950s and 1960s would demand a volume of its own. Here, then, I attempt to elicit a few of the most telling threads from the more complex history, drawing on secondary accounts, an analysis of dance as represented in contemporary media sources, as well as film and fan Web sites that help re-create the time. In addition, I will discuss the related issues of the growth of black teenage dances (like the Slop, the Walk, and the Bop) in the late 1950s in tandem with the development of a new black pop, the wider media profiles of dance and black pop in youth TV shows, and the dispersal of black dances and records to white culture (focusing on the Madison and Twist fads in 1960). I conclude with some thoughts about the decline of dance in white culture and its renaissance in black communities in the late 1960s.

All too often, the significance of teenage dance culture—the dances and their relationship to music, youth culture, and the politics of race—is most often reduced to an indicator of the perceived triviality of the moment. Almost all histories see this period as an interregnum between the excitement of early rock 'n' roll and more sophisticated rock music that would form in the late 1960s. As I will show, these accounts tend to emphasize the music as watered-down pop, the media and record industry as manipulators of naive teenagers, exploiting the power of good-looking teen idols over musical originality, and fad dances as ephemera. Even those celebrations of the period—like John Waters's film *Hairspray* or dance-fan Web sites—present dance culture through the restricted lens of postmodern kitsch.

If we replace these subjective aesthetic judgments with the view of a cooler eye, we can see that music and dance were profoundly linked in new forms of social organization that transformed the key assumptions of the music industry about popular music culture. The earlier record industry rule of thumb that different communities purchased different types of music became an increasingly poor guide to recording and selling music. "Rock Around the Clock" sold strongly among white and black Americans and Europeans,[4] and by 1963 the long-running chart for sales among black consumers had been discontinued.[5] Mid-1950s rock 'n' roll records like Haley's dispensed with the entire major record company infrastructure of A & R (artists & repertoire) departments, songwriters, arrangers, and trained musicians. Sheet music publishing became incidental as record sales became the primary source of revenue; radio, film, and then television became the key means through which records were promoted. Musically, the genre categories of white mainstream pop, white country, and black R & B became blurred as songs were covered by artists from other traditions or crossed over from one market to another.

Historian Brian Ward sees this biracial youth market—in which black artists accounted for an unprecedented proportion of pop hits among white record buyers and the young black audience bought white pop—as a profoundly different expression of mass black consciousness from the R & B music that preceded it and soul music that followed. He explicitly links this new consciousness, and its musical expression, to the campaigns against racial segregation. Ward documents the widely held view among African Americans in this period that the success of black artists with white audiences heralded a significant shift in attitudes to race, that the popularity of white rock 'n' roll stars with black teenagers represented an important interracial sensibility (Haley's enthusiasm for black R & B was welcomed in black journals like the *Birmingham World* and *Chicago Defender*), and that black artists saw the new black pop as a realization of their cultural and commercial ambitions.[6] As I will show, dancing was far more than a simple way to consume this new biracial pop but held a central place in the way that this music became meaningful to its young audiences. Teenagers from various communities related to dance and music in different ways and for different cultural ends, even when they danced to the same music with the same moves. As symbolic of an aspiration for integration as the new black pop was, however, it did not represent actual integration, nor did ideas of "youthfulness" overcome racial inequalities.

Popular Dance and the Birth of Rock 'n' Roll

The story of the birth of rock 'n' roll is so well known that it is worth starting by making it strange, by exploring how it developed within British popular culture. The music was first taken up by a small but culturally significant group of mainly working-class youth, known as the Teddy Boys, whose name referred to their adoption of men's Edwardian dress styles. They expressed their position as an underclass by combining a European sartorial statement with the music and dance of American youth culture and a stance and attitude picked up in the slew of U.S. youth-oriented high school films like *Blackboard Jungle* and *Rock Around the Clock*. In 1955, films like these were important to young Europeans because rock 'n' roll could not be heard or seen through the BBC-monopolized broadcast media (there would be no domestic music radio in Britain until 1967, and television made almost no provision for young people). These imported films gave access to the new music and, as important, ways of dancing. Watching documentary footage of young Britons jiving in the mid-1950s reveals the dances to be British variations on the Lindy Hop dance associated with the popularity of prewar swing, combined with moves copied from the imported high school films.

Cultural theorist Dick Hebdige has suggested that for the Teds, "rock seemed to be spontaneously generated, an immediate expression of youthful energies which was entirely self-explanatory."[7] This coding of rock 'n' roll primarily as "youthful" and "exciting" obscures a set of paradoxical attitudes toward racial politics that contextualized the music in the United States. On the one hand, there is an undoubted debt to African American culture, signaled in the widespread use of terms from black vernacular speech—for instance, the use of the verb "to jive" and the adjective "jiving" as terms used to talk about dance—among British rock 'n' roll fans. On the other hand, Teddy Boy subculture was strongly associated with racial conflict among black Caribbean migrants. By contrast, for young black Americans, rock 'n' roll was differently coded. The music's strong R & B origins connected it to the small-scale neighborhood bars or jook joints of black urban communities and back farther again to the Southern rural entertainment spots of African American communities to produce what Katrina Hazzard-Gordon has called the "jook continuum."[8] This connection is reflected in the way that the key black dances of the early and mid-1950s—the Bop and the Stroll—draw on a lineage of posture, body movement, and proxemics developed within a segregated African American culture.

However, as Ward has demonstrated, the idea of rock 'n' roll simultaneously offered teenage African Americans a symbol of an integrated, modern, young America. As the music began to be associated with a biracial youth culture by both consumers and industry in the late 1950s, a new hybrid black pop developed in conjunction with new forms of dance expression. As we will see, these new dances were created in different spaces (high school rather than jook joint) and performed new cultural functions (the possibility of integration rather than links to the past) for baby-boomer black Americans. Nevertheless, it is instructive to note the many practices the jook joints contributed to the wider youth dance culture that developed in both black and white communities from the mid-1950s.

Most emblematic was the jukebox: the relatively cheap, coin-operated, mechanized record player, sounding out R & B music released by small, regional record labels.[9] The idea of the jukebox was also the model for the increasingly large number of radio stations that now switched the orientation of their programming to the black community, as their former audience of affluent white Americans and their more costly general programming had been lured away by television. In turn, the playlists of these jukeboxes and radio stations gave white American youth access to musical forms that race politics, culture, and geography usually kept segregated. It was no coincidence that Elvis Presley belonged to the first generation of white Americans who could access African American music on Memphis's WDIA radio without leaving their own cultural sphere.[10]

However integrated the market for rock 'n' roll music in the United States was, it was consumed in segregated cultural institutions. By adopting black musical forms initially through the radio, teenage white Americans culturally severed the music from the dance practices of the "jook continuum" in which it had developed. This was further reinforced by the way black pop records were used in the so-called disc hops that developed as the central institution of the teenage dance fads that followed. These events were most often organized in school halls or recreational facilities and based upon dancing to records rather than live bands, which had been predominant for earlier generations. Increasingly, they became commercialized and then incorporated into the promotional strategies of radio DJs or record companies. In this context of white American teenage culture, rock 'n' roll—just as in Europe—connoted "excitement," "newness," and "youthfulness." White and black American teenagers may have shared a continent, but for most the gulf of cultural segregation was as wide as an ocean. So, though radio and disc hops allowed a sonic cultural exchange, the physicality of dance remained initially separate. White dance forms in the mid-1950s continued to draw on the staples of the big-band dance culture of the swing era rather than the black R & B dances, like the Bop and Stroll, that dominated black teenage dance culture.

The key antecedent of white rock 'n' roll dance, therefore, could be traced back to the ballrooms of Harlem in the 1930s and the partner dance, the Lindy Hop. The dance's name—allegedly drawing on Lindberg's successful transatlantic air flight in 1927—came into widespread American usage to describe the offbeat hop, which formed the basic step.[11] Using a swinging body motion and the distinctive hop or skip-based step, couples moved within a bounded floor space. In black dance halls, it developed into a competitive culture featuring breakaways in which the dancing partners demonstrated complex footwork and choreographed proxemics and acrobatic twists, partner balances, "air steps," and throws.[12] By the end of the 1940s, the dance was known as the jitterbug, and in Europe as the jive. Its characteristic moves can still be seen in the practices of those dancing in *Blackboard Jungle*. Thus, though young white dancers of the mid-1950s were dancing to a new music (rock 'n' roll), their dance moves represented a continuation of movement with origins in black popular dance of the twentieth century, via 1930s Harlem.

As I will show, by 1960 this was to change, and the dance moves of black youth were to become the most significant influence on white teenage dance. In fact, it is possible to identify a transitional popular dance—the mambo—that grew out of swing that also had many of the characteristics of the youth dance culture that was to follow. The mambo developed in the early 1940s in U.S. Latin American communities and was then copied first by black, and then white, Americans. On the one hand, like the Lindy, it was a couple dance and danced to big-band jazz. On the other, it turned the usual step-beat relationship of earlier social dance on its head by using pauses where there would formerly have been steps. Latin rhythms, or often just the word "mambo," were inserted in a range of songs, recordings, and other ephemera, even when they held little resemblance to the dance or the music performed in Spanish Harlem or the south side of Chicago.

The progress of the mambo from ethnic dance culture to the nightclubs of New York and later the dance halls of small towns also reminds us that innovations are always unevenly distributed across different social groups and residual elements are retained just as emerging practices are incorporated. In segregated America, these dance halls created distinct dance cultures, each with their own practices, which sound recordings could not share. It would not be an overgeneralization to argue that these dimensions—whites separated from blacks, urban dance halls adopting the novelties of metropolitan nightclubs—were characteristic of the first half of twentieth century of popular dance.

This was not to remain so for long, though. Just as rock 'n' roll shifted the assumptions and meaning of popular music, the developments in teenage culture a few years later were to transform the meanings of popular dance. And just as radio played a significant part in allowing the transmission of black music to white communities in the development of rock 'n' roll, television was to have a significant role in the transmission of black moves to white youth a few years later. As I will show, however, our grasp of these innovations is too often lost in the totalizing histories that construct the musical revolutions of rock 'n' roll as significant but the revolutions of dance fads of the late 1950s and 1960s as simply a conformist, novelty-driven, mainstream television conspiracy to exploit youth.

1960s Dance Fads: The Madison and the Twist

A fuller understanding of the cultural dynamics of the dance fads of the early 1960s can be gained through an examination of the dances most associated with these fads: the Madison (the first nationwide fad) and the Twist (the most widespread and prominent).[13] They provide a revealing case study of the way that the disparate elements of 1960s dance culture—as mediation, music, and movement—came together as a meaningful cultural experience.

Like most fad dances of the 1960s, both the Madison and the Twist have a distinctive set of codified dance moves (often like the Twist signified in the dance's name). They are linked strongly to a particular recording, and they were featured prominently on teen television programs. The Madison is what we would now call a line dance, which originated on the Baltimore broadcast *The Buddy Deane Show* and was performed primarily to Ray Bryant's 1959 recording "Madison Time." The Twist was a noncontact couples' dance, popularized on Philadelphia-based and nationally syndicated Dick Clark's *American Bandstand,* and danced at this point to Chubby Checker's recording of the same name.[14]

There is a tendency to explain these dances as pure media creations, replaced at an increasing rate by the next new thing, limited in form compared with the popular dances that preceded them, and so requiring little dancer competence. This is revealed in the "here today, gone tomorrow" sense of the term "fad dance" itself. It is also reflected in Charlie Gillett's contention that "locally differentiated dancing styles were replaced by a nationally homogeneous set of styles derived from the programs . . . and the increase in turnover of styles modified the meaning of change . . . to mean a relatively minor modification"[15] and in the Stearns's view that "as the dances multiplied the quality deteriorated. Many new dances were simply charades . . . pantomimes with hand-and-arm gestures and little body or footwork."[16]

This is an overly simplistic conclusion, however. By reinserting the dance moves into their cultural and historical location, we can more clearly understand their importance and meanings and, in particular, their relationship to changes in black and white American youth cultures that took place after (but not necessarily because of) the United States Supreme Court's declaration on educational segregation.

As case studies, the Madison and the Twist also allow us to rethink exactly what we mean by competence in dancing. Here I draw on work developed by dance scholar Ben Malbon in exploring more recent dance practice. For Malbon, competence in dance is not an absolute concept, but a relative one. He formulates dancing as "a conceptual language with intrinsic and extrinsic meanings, premised upon physical movement, and with interrelated rules and notions of technique and competency guiding performance across and within different situations."[17] For Malbon, the "meaning" of particular dances can be understood in their specific historical and cultural context. In particular, he is interested in how dancing produces a construction of self around the oppositions of in-crowd/out-crowd, in the relationships of the individual to the dance space and to other dancers, and to the performance of the dance itself. To understand how the Madison and the Twist "crossed over" from African American to white American youth culture, I explore the role of television in teaching white teenagers how to perform African American–based dances, how the recordings were perceived and promoted by the record industry, and (drawing on Malbon) how the sense of competence gained on the dance floor became important as a form of modernism.

Learning the Madison and the Twist

Robert Pruter has argued that both the Madison and the Twist, and those fad dances that followed, had their origins in the African American communities. In this he sees popular dance as exhibiting the same notion of crossover that others have dealt with in relation to music. He explicitly rejects the other, more widely expressed view that the dances were media concoctions linked to trite music conceived only for commercial reasons. "Before any records were made," he argues, "[the dances] were the spontaneous outcome of the dance experience of black high-school youth."[18] He echoes Carl Belz's notion that dance was an unconscious exploration of popular music's meanings and an expression of up-to-date-ness that constituted the essence of youthful modernism. Nevertheless, Pruter himself identifies an important role for key dance party television shows, such as *American Bandstand* and *The Buddy Deane Show*, that are prominent in other historical accounts. Following Pruter then, our examination needs to relate the spontaneous popular culture of dance to its televised mediation.

The shows cohered around a simulacrum of a teen disc hop, hosted by a clean-cut, older-brother figure, that featured lip-synching appearances of the musical artists and the dancing of "ordinary" teenagers. The earliest shows were highly segregated, most offering separate days for blacks and whites; however, broadcasts must have had biracial domestic audiences as they occasionally featured both black and white social dancers (though never integrated couples),[19] and the teen dance show became a key means for artists and dances from African American culture to cross over to white dance culture. There is certainly evidence that the Philadelphia-based *Mitch Thomas Show,* targeted to a black audience, exposed white teenagers to the Bop and associated dances that gradually replaced the jitterbug in the early 1950s.[20] Robert Pruter has traced the genesis of the Twist from black culture through *The Buddy Deane Show* and *American Bandstand* to the wider white audience.[21]

This evidence also shows that before their televised appearances these highly codified dances were passed from city to city through locally organized dances. Through this process, copying became a powerful means of transmitting dance moves. Innovation, then, was a product of the culture itself—and not a simple effect of the television programs—and the search for novelty was an expression of a sense of modernity. These dance innovations needed to involve prominent display and be both quickly mastered and discarded, because they served this modernist sensibility that the new should be embraced and the old cast out.

Dance historian Julie Malnig observes that the teen dance party programs exhibit the same sense of communality—both in their construction and consumption—that was characteristic of the teenage culture itself. She concludes that these shows were a primary way in which young Americans learned to be teenagers.[22] The lesson of the shows, of course, was that a key competence of youthful modernity was the ability to dance the latest dances. This very communality, along with the fact that television gave youngsters access to the physical as well as musical aspects of popular dance, extended the possibilities for cultural exchange and did create a form of youth culture that at some level cut across racial lines. However, dancing to black music was not the same as acting to create an equal society. The black music and dances within the white teen culture may have meant "modern innovation" but not "social transformation." And the teen dance programs used already-established familial and high school models of social relationships—the older brother, the record hop—to create "a sense of community, security and familiarity."[23] These distinctions were certainly apparent to music industry entrepreneurs. As they increasingly focused their attention on the new youth audience, they attempted to assist and exploit this ability of black music and dance to cross over, and television teen dance shows became an important part of record promotion.

How the Madison and the Twist Crossed Over

The concept of crossover describes the economic exploitation of a cultural phenomenon and describes the sales success of a product aimed at one market being reproduced in another.[24] The stories of the Madison and the Twist offer telling insights into the way that these cultural and economic processes relate. The records associated with both dances reveal the cultural crossover from black, adult jook joint, via black teenage disc hops, to white high schools. Ray Bryant's "Madison Time" was an unlikely teen dance record. Bryant led a jazz piano trio playing hard bop, a music with a strong blues and gospel styling that was then a staple of the black community bar jukeboxes and radio playlists.[25] Checker's "The Twist," by contrast, is a sweetened cover of an earlier dance R & B song, recorded and promoted with white teenagers centrally in mind.

The origins of the Madison in black culture, though, go back well before the recording of Bryant's record in March 1959 in New York.[26] Dance historian Lance Benishek suggests that the Madison started in Chicago in the late 1950s;[27] Pruter indicates the dance was associated in the Midwest with a completely different recording.[28] Benishek also claims that it surfaced in Cleveland after the Baltimore Colts brought it to Baltimore in 1959. Bryant's record was clearly adopted for a preexisting dance within black youth culture and then picked up within the black entertainment world. This also explains how a hard bop instrumental became a black teen dance record with a vocal and the reasons it gained novelty status in white teenage culture. Sometime between Bryant's recording and its play on *The Buddy Deane Show,* a spoken narration was overdubbed. This narration was provided by radio DJ Eddie Morrison, whose early 1960s afternoon show on WEBB in Baltimore mixed jazz and R & B records with slick raps.

Like most radio DJs of the time, Morrison most likely hosted record hops at which he would have picked up on the popularity of Bryant's record and seen how young dancers developed dance moves to fit. He could have easily started calling some of the dance actions executed at these hops on his show.[29] The pace and funk swing of "Madison Time" is certainly ideal for Morrison's DJ style, which was characteristic of black radio talk of the

1960s.[30] For black dancers, it asserted a common culture; to white teenagers, his adjectives "wild," "crazy," "looking good," and the abstract verb "hit it" would be as exotic as the musical sounds. Morrison's lyrics also refer to contemporary television Westerns, variety shows, and spectator sports, which were common cultural references for both black and white teenagers. These cultural resonances were clearly understood in the wider entertainment world because sometime in 1960 Bryant's recording was licensed by Columbia and, with added talk-over, released as a single aimed at white teenagers. The novelty of the dance and the record, and its local popularity, brought it to the attention of the producers of *The Buddy Deane Show* and then to other such dance shows across the country. Thus, it reached a broader range of local white dancers.

The crossover of the Twist follows a similar path from black dance culture, but the details of its progress reveal other interesting aspects. Most accounts emphasize the manipulations of *American Bandstand* host Dick Clark, who supposedly picked up on the popularity of the dance, and its associated record by Hank Ballard and the Moonlighters, from Philadelphia youth. He worked with the Cameo Parkway record label (responsible for helping promote some of the key teen idols of late 1950s) to create a watered-down cover record by Chubby Checker, which Clark then hyped into national and international success.[31] The Twist was certainly one of the few fad dances that was taken up beyond teen pop in the United States and Europe, and its presentation reflected the novelty status of the mambo a decade before. The central historical implication, however, is probably to be found in the difference between two independent record companies trying to exploit the new biracial pop.

The original version of "The Twist" was released by King Records using its well-tried strategy for success in the R & B market: Combine a dance B-side with a ballad A-side. The record charted in the R & B listings in 1958, and the dance B-side was extremely popular at black record hops during the late 1950s. It did not come to the attention of Dick Clark until early 1960. Chubby Checker's recording is plainly built on crude, commercial opportunism to sell to white youngsters. The artist's stage name was an adaptation of Fats Domino, and the cover smoothed the gospel vocal recasting the R & B track as a classic piece of biracial pop. At the time, Cameo Parkway staff understood the importance of dance culture and television to the youth market in the way King promotion teams, with their roots in an earlier generation of R & B, did not. Cameo, and its more black-orientated Parkway subsidiary, released a whole slew of dance records after 1960, including variations on

"The Twist" by Checker and, more notably, Dee Dee Sharp's "Mashed Potato" and The Orlons's "Wah Watusi," which would become the staple of black dance in the early 1960s.

White youngsters were clearly attracted to the music and dance of African American culture, and black radio and record companies were adapting to a new youth audience. Television, in its pursuit of a white, middle-class audience, continued the processes of cultural dissemination that radio had begun. But now, white youngsters could both hear black music and see the associated dances. However important though, the meanings of these dances are not to be found primarily in this economic and cultural context but in the movements of the dances, in the new senses of dance competence they worked with, and in their status as fads.

Dancing the Madison and Twist

The basics of the Madison are easy to explain.[32] The dancers stand in parallel lines facing outward, their movement limited to forward and backward steps. A basic shuffle and a step-clap combination are broken up by a series of movements—tracing out letters with the foot or stylized choreographed actions like throwing an imaginary basketball—responding to a spoken narration on the record. However, the execution requires more skill and cultural competence than this description suggests. For instance, although Bryant's record is an R & B midpaced boogie shuffle in 4/4 time, the main Madison step is based on a six-beat pattern, and the shifting weight, sweeping feet, and controlled trunk feel counterintuitive to the propulsion of the music without the reinforcing communal experience of the line. Each chorus figure is built around very different movements combining steps derived from the Stroll, turns, and upper body mimes, which produce pleasurable senses of symmetry and contrast. These pleasures are reinforced by the music's "behind the beat" time, echoed in the improvised timing of the spoken narration, and its direction of the dance moves triggered by a repeated verbal motif of "hit it."

Contrary to an often-expressed view, the narration does not instruct dancers how to do the Madison[33] or describe the basic Madison figure; the other figures are merely suggested. Although the technical mastery required to perform the dance is somewhat less than that required in earlier popular dance forms, competence in the 1960s dance crazes means something different to that of the Savoy Lindy dancer. Rather than individual display and partner interaction, the Madison is built on a communal activity in which the group shaping across the entire floor produces a sense of participation and belonging. Yet the dancers are more than "rhythmically obedient"[34] music consumers. The dance is a communal and individual display of cultural competence achieved, in part, through a mastery of the figures, the unconventional timing, the knowledge of the cultural references in the narration, and their interpretation as stylized movement imbued with the insolence and understated swagger of youth.

The Twist, by contrast, is more obviously a partner dance with no real steps.[35] As the name suggests, its basic form is focused on a twisting of the body created by swinging the knees in parallel in one direction around the pivot of the ball of the foot, while swinging the upper body through the arms in the counter direction. It is performed with a strong sense of swing to a mainly up-tempo, syncopated beat. The dancers often execute shifts of balance that undermine the symmetry of the Twist in three main figure categories: lowering the body gradually through the bending of the knees; transferring weight to one leg, and then the other, often accompanied by the raising of the unweighted leg from the knee; and incorporating elements of other dances such as steps, partner turns, or upper body moves (figure 10.1).

In the historical development of social dance, the Twist seems to be a move toward the individualistic dancing of the later 1960s and the first move from couple-based dances.[36] This is largely because the coupling of the dancers is based on an orientation, rather than physical contact or holding. The moves of individual dancers are performed with reference to other couples, however, either in mirrored solidarity or dexterous competition. This creates some of the same communality produced in the Madison, underscored by a similar performance of "attitude," but with a greater emphasis on command of swing and balance as a key element of competence.

Both the Madison and the Twist, then, mark a significant break from the social etiquette that had governed social dance up until the 1950s, and we can speculate that these changes represented shifts in cultural attitudes and identity associated with postwar youth culture. Although the dancing couple had been the center of the social organization of popular dance, and remained the structure in which the individualism of the Lindy Hopper played out, the Madison and the Twist placed a heavier emphasis on the social group and on processes of shadowing and mimicking one's peers. Although both created the possibility for the more individualized dancing that was to be characteristic of the dances of the later 1960s, they were themselves strongly orientated toward group solidarity, even when they contained elements of individual display or competitive competence.

Figure 10.1: Rock 'n' Roll dancing on Dick Clark's *American Bandstand*, 1961.
Courtesy of New York World-Telegram & Sun Newspaper Photograph Collection, Library of Congress.

The early 1960s dances were swiftly superseded by a series of other dance
fads. In the five years after the Twist and Madison, scores of new dances—
including the Horse, the Pony, the Continental, the Watusi, the Hully Gully,
the Popeye, the Roach, and the Mashed Potato—cropped up across major
urban centers. All these dances shared an emphasis on prominent body
movements and on communalism, and most represented the same cultural
trajectory of black-to-white dissemination that was a key feature of the Madison and the Twist. This transmission did create a biracial pop and possibly a
new regard among young whites for black culture, but it did not, of course,
deliver the dream of integration. The speed with which they were taken up
and discarded was not a characteristic of the involvement of television or
manipulative record companies (although they were very important) but of
the modernist cultural drive among American teenagers for the "new thing"
and of the desire to be one of "the in-crowd."

The decade from 1955 to 1965 saw some significant changes in social dance. Over the twentieth century, the relationships between individual social dancers, the couple, and the community of the dance floor has shifted a number of times. The dance fads of the 1950s and 1960s did herald a greater emphasis on the individual that was to come to fruition later in the 1960s and into the 1970s. Perhaps more significantly, they shifted emphasis back to an earlier sense of group dance and away from the couple orientations of most of twentieth-century dance up to that point. The meanings of the dance articulated in a significant, but sadly not a profound, way a sense of optimism, both for a culture of youth and for the meanings of ethnic identity. In Europe, black music and forms were to take on significance for working-class youth, and the British mod subculture, with its adoration of American jazz and soul, reinterpreted modernism for another society.[37] This passion for black dance music of the 1960s survives to this day in Northern Soul.[38] Record collectors in this peculiarly British scene have a particular veneration for the dance records of Cameo-Parkway. You will not hear "The Twist," or even the "Mashed Potato," on these dance floors, however, but instead all those records that fell into obscurity or did not sell first time around.

In these lost records, as in the chart hits, are the dreams of a modern America. Built on ideas of youth and excitement, for a generation of African Americans they were also expressive of the possibility of an integrated society. That moment did not last, however, and the growth of rock music in the mid-1960s with its free-form individualistic dance styles and shift to nondance forms of practice were to take white American music away from African American texts. Black Americans, frustrated with the failure of the civil rights movement to live up to their dreams, shifted their tastes to soul and funk with their articulations of an Afrocentric identity and a whole new set of dance floor, community-bound dances.

Music, dance, and the media remain central to issues of the politics of identity. We just need to keep making the connections as we move.

Notes

1. Although the song was actually recorded in New York City in 1954, its "birth" is often noted as March 1955, when the song was featured in the MGM-produced film *Blackboard Jungle*, rereleased as an A-side single, and reached the number one spot on the *Billboard* chart (on July 5, 1955). For more on the complex history of the song, see Jim Dawson, *Rock Around the Clock: The Record that Started the Rock Revolution!* (San Francisco: Backbeat Books, 2005), 127–43; Bill Haley and His Comets, "(We're Gonna) Rock Around the Clock," in *What Was the First Rock 'n' Roll Record?*, ed. Jim Dawson and Steve Propes (Boston: Faber and Faber, 1992), 142–47. See also Rockabilly Hall of

Fame, "Rock Around the Clock Tribute," http://www.rockabillyhall.com/RockClock-Tribute.html (accessed January 2006).

2. See Iain Chambers, *Urban Rhythms: Pop Music and Popular Culture* (Houndmills, U.K.: Macmillan, 1985), 42.

3. Mark Abrams, *The Teenage Consumer* (London: London Press Exchange, Incorporated Practitioners in Advertising, 1959).

4. It was ranked at number one or two on the *Billboard* pop and R & B charts and on the *New Musical Express* chart in 1955.

5. Tim Wall, *Studying Popular Music Culture* (London: Arnold, 2003), 61.

6. Brian Ward, *Just My Soul Responding: Rhythm and Blues, Black Consciousness and Race Relations* (London: University College London Press, 1998), 123–59.

7. Dick Hebdige, *Subculture: The Meaning of Style* (London: Routledge, 1991), 51.

8. Katrina Hazzard-Gordon, *Jookin': The Rise of Social Dance Formations in African-American Culture* (Philadelphia: Temple University Press, 1990), x.

9. Such as Atlantic, Chess, Duke/Peacock, Imperial, King, Savoy, Modern, and Speciality.

10. Louis Cantor, *Wheelin' on Beale: How WDIA Memphis Became the Nation's First All-Black Radio Station and Created the Sound that Changed America* (New York: Pharos Books, 1992).

11. For a full discussion of the conflicting claims regarding the derivation of the Lindy and Lindy Hop, see the chapter in this collection, "Negotiating Compromise on a Burnished Wood Floor: Social Dancing at the Savoy," by Karen Hubbard and Terry Monaghan.

12. Christian Batchelor, *This Thing Called Swing: A Study of Swing Music and the Lindy Hop, the Original Swing Dance* (London: Original Lindy Hop Collection, 1997), 86–87, 189–91.

13. These dances are widely referenced in books and Web sites dedicated to 1960s dance and received coverage in contemporary national U.S. news magazines.

14. Although the Twist became very popular on *American Bandstand,* particularly after Chubby Checker's appearance on the show, there is some conjecture concerning where the dance first took hold. In 1959, Hank Ballard and the Midnighters introduced Ballard's "The Twist" (which Ballard had composed) at the Royal Theatre in Baltimore. Some contend that the dance then surfaced on Baltimore's teen dance program *The Buddy Deane Show.* For more on this history, see John A. Jackson, *American Bandstand: Dick Clark and the Making of a Rock 'n' Roll Empire* (New York: Oxford University Press, 1997), 213–14; Jim Dawson's *The Twist: The Story of the Song That Changed the World* (Boston: Faber and Faber, 1995), 27–28; *Dancing:* part 3, "New Worlds" (video), Rhoda Grauer, exec prod., WNET (in association with BBC-TV), 1993, which contains an interview with Buddy Deane. For a conversation with Hank Ballard, who describes how the dance moves of the Midnighters would have been too suggestive for TV, see Ron Mann's 1993 documentary *Twist* (DVD, Home Vision Entertainment, 2005).

15. Charlie Gillett, *The Sound of the City: The Rise of Rock and Roll* (London: Souvenir Press, 1988), 208.

16. Marshall Stearns and Jean Stearns, *Jazz Dance: The Story of American Vernacular Dance* (New York: Schirmer Books, 1968), 5.

17. Ben Malbon, *Clubbing: Dancing, Ecstasy and Vitality* (London: Routledge, 1999), 86.

18. Robert Pruter, *Chicago Soul* (Urbana: University of Illinois Press, 1991), 191.

19. Julie Malnig, "Let's Go to the Hop: Community Values in Televised Teen Dance Programs of the 1950s and Early 1960s" (paper presented at the Congress on Research in Dance Annual Conference, Tallahassee, FL, November 2005), 6.

20. John W. Roberts, *From Hucklebuck to Hip Hop: Social Dance in the African American Community in Philadelphia* (Philadelphia: Odunde, 1995), 35–37.

21. Pruter, *Chicago Soul*, 192.

22. Malnig, "Let's Go to the Hop."

23. Ibid., 2.

24. Steve Perry, "Ain't No Mountain High Enough: The Politics of Crossover," in *Facing the Music: A Pantheon Guide to Popular Culture*, ed. Simon Frith (New York: Pantheon Books, 1988), 51, 87.

25. Richard Cook, *Blue Note Records: The Biography* (London: Secker & Warburg, 2001), 194.

26. Jazz Discography Project, "Ray Bryant Discography," http://www.jazzdisco.org/bryant/dis/c/ (accessed January 2006).

27. Cited in Savoy Central, "Class Overview," http://www.savoycentral.org/class-overview.html (accessed February 2007).

28. Al Brown's Tunetoppers' "The Madison" (probably recorded in 1960); Pruter, *Chicago Soul*, 50.

29. Savoy Central, "Class Overview," http://www.savoycentral.org/classoverview.html (accessed January 2006); Jitterbuzz.com, Lindy Week Review, "Group Dances of the 1950s," http://www.jitterbuzz.com/dance50.html (accessed January 2006).

30. William Barlow, *Voice Over: The Making of Black Radio* (Philadelphia: Temple University Press, 1999), 134–53.

31. Tony Cummings, *The Sound of Philadelphia* (London: Methuen, 1975), 55–60; Jackson, *American Bandstand*, 213–19.

32. The analysis is based on the Edward Love–choreographed version featured in John Waters's film *Hairspray* (1988); on Bob Barrett's analysis at Friday Folk, St. Albans, "Madison—The Figures," http://www.fridayfolk.org.uk/madi40.htm (accessed January 2006); and on some personal experimentation.

33. Pruter, *Chicago Soul*, 191. He makes special note that, "of all the dance records of the 1960s the lyrics of the Madison records were the most specific as to how to do the dance."

34. Theodor W. Adorno, "On Popular Music," in *On Record: Rock, Pop and the Written Word*, ed. Simon Frith and Andrew Goodwin (London: Routledge, 1990), 312.

35. The analysis is based on the Edward Love–choreographed version featured in John Waters's film *Hairspray* (1988); contemporary footage compiled in Ron Mann's documentary *Twist;* interviews with respondents who danced in the 1960s; and some personal experimentation.

36. Gerald Jonas, *Dancing: The Pleasure, Power, and Art of Movement* (New York: Harry N. Abrams in association with Thirteen/WNET, 1998), 181–82; Cynthia Novack, *Sharing the Dance: Contact Improvisation and American Culture* (Madison: University of Wisconsin Press, 1990), 35–37.

37. Hebdige, *Subculture*, 52.

38. Tim Wall, "Out on the Floor: The Politics of Dancing on the Northern Soul Scene," *Popular Music* 25, no. 3 (2006): 431–45.

11

Beyond the Hustle

1970s Social Dancing, Discotheque Culture, and the Emergence of the Contemporary Club Dancer

Tim Lawrence

The *Saturday Night Fever* publicity shot of a white-suited John Travolta, right hand pointing up and left hand, twisting along the same axis, aiming down, quickly became (and continues to be) the consciousness-invading icon of 1970s disco culture. The image evokes a strutting, straight masculinity. Tony Manero, played by Travolta, is a Hustle expert and a straight man on the prowl; in the photo, he is pictured alone, but his look and posture reveal that he is searching for a female partner, both on and off the dance floor. Released in November 1977, *Saturday Night Fever* ushered disco into the American mainstream, where it remained for a relatively short eighteen months. Travolta and 2001 Odyssey, the discotheque featured in the film, became the key reference points for dancers and club owners during disco's commercial peak.

Beyond the celluloid sheen and marketing paraphernalia of the post–*Saturday Night Fever* disco boom, however, the 1970s dance floor functioned as a threshold space in which dancers broke with the tradition of couples dancing and forged a new practice of solo club dancing. Although the shift in style suggested that individuality and loneliness came to dominate the floor, participants in fact discovered a new partner in the form of the dancing crowd. The Travolta types may have subsequently gained a Gucci-shoed or stiletto-heeled foothold on the dance floor toward the end of the so-called disco decade, but their grip proved to be ephemeral in the postdisco era. From 1980 onward, the solo dancer, moving to the collective rhythms of the room, formed the enduring model for contemporary club culture.

The sexual and bodily politics of *Saturday Night Fever* did not appear out of thin air, of course. If dancing is an articulation of the wider world, reflecting dominant forces while providing a space for difference and resistance, the history of social dance in the United States has been intertwined with the shifting yet resilient practice of patriarchal heterosexuality. On the dance floor, this has become manifest through the partnered couple, in which the man, assuming the role of gatekeeper, both invited his female partner onto the floor and then assumed the role of dance leader. Although the position of the male lead did not go unchallenged—the twentieth century is replete with examples of social dances in which the couple would break for periods on the floor or the woman would be granted periods of relative control within the couple—the framing role of the leading man remained in place.

Dances such as the waltz and the fox trot, which allowed for minimal individual movement, were the most rigorously partnered of all, at least from the middle of the nineteenth century onward, and when couples in modern ballroom dancing developed their independence from the wider floor by developing their own individuality, this served to entrench the heterosexual couple—now unique in their relationship—still further.[1] The rise of black social dance such as the Lindy Hop (often referred to as the jitterbug) and the Texas Tommy chipped away at these practices inasmuch as they allowed partners to break away from each other and intersperse moves with individual improvisation. As Marshall and Jean Stearns, writing in 1968, noted, "[B]oth dances constitute a frame into which almost any movement can be inserted before the dancers return to each other."[2] The Stearns added that, "while a Lindy team often danced together during the opening ensembles of a big band, they tended to go into a breakaway and improvise individual steps when the band arrangement led into a solo."[3] These and other dances, such as the Charleston and the Black Bottom, integrated breakaway practices that enabled dancers (including, of course, female followers) to discover a new form of expressive freedom. The mutating tensions between the couple and the individual were, however, regularly resolved in favor of the former.

The unit of the couple faced its most sustained challenge when the Twist emerged along with the first discotheques in New York City at the beginning of the 1960s.[4] Allowing their bodies to respond to the affective space of the club, in which dancers encountered a combination of amplified sound and lighting effects, partners were couples only in name. Marshall and Jean Stearns acknowledged that the Twist and related dances had produced a "new and rhythmically sophisticated generation," but remained pessimistic about the environment in which the dancing occurred.[5] "No one could dance with finesse in such crowded darkness, even if he wished. . . . The only way to attract attention was to go ape with more energy than skill, achieving a very disordered effect."[6] Couples dancing (alternatively known as hand dancing) all but imploded, yet the individual free-form style of the Twist appeared to be an inadequate replacement when, toward the end of the 1960s, the dance went out of fashion, the music industry stopped pushing the music, and beacon discotheques such as Arthur began to close.

Contemporary disco dancing emerged out of the dual context of African American social dance and the rise of the discotheque and was propelled forward by the sudden influx of gay men into these social dance spaces at the beginning of the 1970s.[7] Up until this moment, gay men were marginal within social dance, for though they were free to go out and dance, they were not free to choose their partner. Although the door staff at flashbulb discotheques such as Arthur waived gay men to the front of the queue because of their ability to energize the dance floor, these men were still required by New York State law to take to the floor with female partners. The Stonewall Inn was one of the few venues in Manhattan where men could dance with other men, but patrons had to make do with the stuttering rhythms of a jukebox as well as regular police raids. By the time the owner of the Electric Circus, responding to the Stonewall rebellion of June 1969, invited gay men to share the dance floor with straights, the institution of the discotheque was in nosedive decline.[8] Because the Electric Circus was still marked as a straight (if tolerant) venue, the influx of gay men into the venue was minimal.

The key turning point in the culture of individual free-form dance arrived when, more or less simultaneously, David Mancuso began to put on regular parties in his Broadway loft apartment (which became known as the Loft) on Valentine's Day 1970, and two entrepreneurs known as Seymour and Shelley, who owned a series of gay bars in the West Village took over a struggling straight discotheque called the Sanctuary and encouraged their clientele to give it a go. Both venues were unique in that gay men—who required special protection until Mayor John Lindsay repealed New York

City's laws governing the admission of gay men to cabarets, dance halls, and restaurants in October 1971—were dominant on the floor (even if straights were present), and the energy and expressivity of these dancers, many of whom faced the double marginalization of being black as well as gay, kick-started 1970s dance culture.[9] A series of legendary private parties (including Flamingo, the Gallery, the Paradise Garage, Reade Street, the SoHo Place, and the Tenth Floor) emerged out of this moment, and the public institution of the discotheque also received a second lease on life that culminated in the opening of Studio 54 in 1977.

According to eyewitnesses such as spinner Francis Grasso, who surveyed the metamorphosis of the crowd at the Sanctuary from the vantage point of his DJ booth, the difference in dance styles was radical. "[Seymour and Shelley's] opening night was a bang," he told me. "I'd never seen a crowd party like that before. . . . When the Sanctuary went gay I didn't play that many slow records because they were drinkers and they knew how to party. Just the sheer heat and numbers made them drink. The energy level was *phenomenal.*"[10] That energy was founded on the newness of the experience (this was the first time that gay men had been able to dance together in a dedicated dance venue) and the wider social context (the celebratory momentum of gay liberation).

Whereas couples had dominated the straight Sanctuary, the gay reincarnation was organized around individual dancers who took to the floor by themselves. The break with partnered dancing was not total—men would sometimes grab each other before dancing or sidle up to each other on the floor—but the established matrix of social dance was nevertheless loosened to the point where it was no longer recognizable. Yet the shift toward individual free-form dancing, which was mirrored at the Loft, did not result in participants experiencing the floor as space of isolation. Instead, by moving around on a single spot, dancers would effectively groove with multiple partners. "You could be on the dance floor and the most beautiful woman that you had ever seen in your life would come and dance right on top of you," Frankie Knuckles, a regular at the Loft, told me. "Then the minute you turned around a man that looked just as good would do the same thing. Or you would be sandwiched between the two of them, or between two women, or between two men, and you would feel completely comfortable."[11] The experience of dancing with scores of other dancers helped generate the notion of the dancing crowd as a unified and powerful organism. By moving to the rhythm of the DJ and the gyrating bodies that surrounded them, gay men realized they were part of a collective movement. The idea of dancing with a partner did not so much implode as expand.

Early discotheque dancers, according to participants such as Frank Cra-panzano and Jorge La Torre (two regulars at Manhattan's best known gay venues), did not develop a defined style, such as the Twist, but instead im-provised their steps (moving backward and forward, then side to side, etc.) and, in line with black jazz dance and the Twist, generated movement from their hips. Combining grace and stamina, the dancers broke with the domi-nant practices of the late 1960s. "The dancing was very jazz-spirited," Danny Krivit, an early downtown dance aficionado whose father ran a popular gay bar in the Village called the Ninth Circle, told me. "It was just free. Before the Loft people thought they were free but they were just jerking around and jumping up and down."[12]

Dance floors were usually crowded, often to sardinelike proportions at hipper-than-thou venues such as the Loft, the Tenth Floor, and the Gallery, so there was little room to show off special steps or form circles around espe-cially skilled dancers. Some dancers would seek out unpopulated areas; Archie Burnett, a "Loft baby" from the late 1970s onward, told me how he would gravitate toward the cloak room, away from the main floor, in order to find space to work on (and show off) his steps. But the lack of space was of little concern to most protagonists, whose aim was to participate in a musical-kinetic form of individual dissolution and collective bliss.[13] Although the exhibition (or novelty) practices of the swing era involved, in the words of Jonathan David Jackson, "asserting such a pronounced sense of personal style that the black vernacular dancer's actions invite a charged, voyeuristic attention from the community at the ritual event," the partygoers of the early 1970s expressed their individuality within a more overtly participatory, less visible framework.[14]

Drugs—in particular LSD and marijuana, although Quaaludes, poppers, and speed also became popular as the decade progressed—contributed to the hedonistic quality of the dance floor experience, although New York's downtown venues were ultimately grounded in a collective rather than in-dividualistic notion of pleasure. As La Torre told me, the consumption of drugs was an enabling add-on part of the dance experience, which was ulti-mately focused on tribal transcendence rather than a narrower, individualistic high.[15] Describing the experience in similar terms, Jim Feldman, a dancer at the Paradise Garage (an expanded version of the Loft that opened in 1977), noted, "There was a sexual undercurrent at the Garage but no one was pick-ing up. Sex was subsumed to the music and was worked out in the dancing. It was like having sex with everyone. It was very unifying."[16] As Maria Pini, in an analysis of club and rave culture in the 1990s that speaks to the 1970s, comments: "This is not about a sexual longing directed towards a specific or individual 'target,' but about a far more dispersed and fragmented set of erotic energies which appear to be generated within the dance event."[17]

Contrary to some accounts of the early disco scene, out of which certain mythologies continue to circulate, sex rarely, if ever, took place on the dance floors of New York's downtown discotheques.[18] Although the evocation of sex is not altogether ridiculous—a sexual energy undoubtedly permeated the early gay discotheques, and erotic glances would regularly be exchanged—dancing at the Sanctuary, the Loft, and scores of other venues was not the first stage in the process of seduction. Revelers refigured the dance floor not as a site of foreplay—the contention of David Walsh in "'Saturday Night Fever': An Ethnography of Disco Dancing"—but of spiritual communion where sensation was not confined to the genitals but materialized in every new touch, sound, sight, and smell.[19] "The Loft chipped away at the ritual of sex as the driving force behind parties," Mark Riley, a confidante of Mancuso, explained. "Dance was not a means to sex but drove the space."[20] The ethos continues to this day, even if the club scene is now dominated by house rather than disco music. As Sally R. Sommer comments in "C'mon to My House: Underground House Dancing" (in this collection), "the redemption of total body sensuality without rampant sexuality fostered by hard dancing that engages the body and mind" remains central to the paradigm of the contemporary underground dance network in New York and beyond.[21]

The technologies of amplified sound and lighting developed at an exponential pace during the 1970s and, combining with rhythm-driven dance music and perception-enhancing drugs, established a hyperaffective environment that prioritized alternative forms of bodily sensation. Mancuso introduced the technologies of tweeter arrays (clusters of small loudspeakers, which emit high-end frequencies, positioned above the floor) and bass reinforcements (additional sets of subwoofers positioned at ground level) at the start of the 1970s in order to boost the treble and bass at opportune moments, and by the end of the decade sound engineers such as Richard Long had multiplied the effects of these innovations in venues such as the Garage. "Bass-heavy dance music provokes the recognition that we do not just 'hear' with our ears, but with our entire body," write Jeremy Gilbert and Ewan Pearson, in *Discographies*. "This embodiment is achieved through the experiential characteristics, the kinesthetic effects of the disco, the club, the dance floor, and the performative and reproductive technologies employed within them."[22]

The spread of the marathon dance session in the 1970s discotheque heightened this affective experience and was particularly pronounced at private venues such as the Loft, the Tenth Floor, the Gallery, Flamingo, 12 West, and the Garage, where the owners bypassed cabaret licensing laws by offering only nonalcoholic drinks and running a private membership system. That meant that they could stay open as long as they liked, in contrast to public venues that operated under New York's cabaret licensing laws. Mancuso started off with the seemingly audacious decision to open until 6:00 A.M.; by the early 1980s, he was holding parties that would begin at midnight and carry on until 8:00 P.M. the following evening. The substitution of alcohol with energy-enhancing drugs enabled dancers to stay on the floor for longer and longer periods of time, and this in turn encouraged them to "lose themselves" in the dance experience. Although the idea of engaging in a trance-inducing workout might not have been new—shamanistic ceremonies and drag balls functioned according to similar principles—it was a novel experience within the context of late 1960s to early 1970s North American society, and it was novel in terms of its deployment of amplified sound and disorienting light.

The sheer length of these marathon dance sessions, the reduced consumption of alcohol, and the relatively abrupt end to the practice of partnered dancing combined to create the conditions for the emergence of a new narrative of dance. Instead of regarding the night as a series of ventures onto the floor that would be interspersed by visits to the bar or leaving the floor to find a new partner, dancers started to stay on the floor for hours on end, and DJs started to sculpt a soundtrack to respond to these new conditions. Whereas 1960s discotheque DJs would build to a quick peak and then introduce a slow record to "work the bar" or "move the floor around," spinners such as Grasso and, above all, Mancuso began to build sets that would tell a story over an entire night, beginning gently before climaxing with a series of peaks, after which the spinner would bring the dancers down.

The DJ was central to the ritual of 1970s dance culture, but the dancing crowd was no less important, and it was the combination of these two elements that created the conditions for the dance floor dynamic. A good DJ did not only lead dancers along his or her (male spinners far outnumbered their female counterparts) preferred musical path but would also feel the mood of the dance floor and select records according to this energy (which could be communicated by the vigor of the dancing, level of the crowd's screams, or sign language of dancers directed toward the booth). This communication—described by Sarah Thornton, in her early analysis of late 1980s and 1990s dance culture, as "the vibe"—amounted to a form of synergistic music-making in which separate elements combined to create a mutually beneficial and greater whole.[23]

Continuous with the practice of antiphony, or the call-and-response of African American gospel, the DJ-crowd exchange can be traced to the 1960s discotheque, but the best-known spinner of that era, Terry Noël, nevertheless preferred to view himself as a puppeteer who asserted his will over an obedient, passive floor.[24] The tempo of Twist music, which was significantly more uniform than the so-called party music selected by DJs in the early 1970s, would have dampened dancer expectations of influencing a spinner's selections, and couples' dancing, inasmuch as it was still in play in the 1960s, would have further discouraged dancers from making the DJ their primary focus for communication. It was only when the unit of the couple was further weakened in the early 1970s that the wider crowd, conceived of as a communicative force, discovered its power to influence the course of a night.

The popularization of this call-and-response pattern, so familiar within gospel, on the dance floor points to the way in which the dance experience of the 1970s was experienced as a spiritual affair, albeit within a secular-to-the-point-of-sacrilegious context. This quality was apparent at the Sanctuary, which was situated in a converted church in which the DJ booth was housed in the pulpit. La Torre argues that the spiritual dimension of the dance floor experience became particularly pronounced in the second half of the 1970s when the music became less vocally driven and more instrumental, thereby allowing the mind to wander more freely. All of this anticipates Kai Fikentscher's description of the nightclub's parallels with the African American church: Both the African American church and the nightclub "feature ritualized activities centered around music, dance, and worship, in which there are no set boundaries between secular and sacred domains," and this tradition cultivated a mood of group ecstasy and catharsis on the dance floors of the Loft, the Gallery, the SoHo Place, Reade Street, the Warehouse, and the early incarnation of the Paradise Garage.[25]

The nature of the ecstatic-cathartic experience of the 1970s discotheque can be theorized in various ways. Freud's discussion of pre-Oedipal sexuality—which he characterizes as the polymorphous perverse, whereby the child experiences sexual drives that are organized around not the genitals but the entire body—is appealing when analyzing the Loft, which evoked a series of child-oriented themes in its mass deployment of party balloons and, thanks to its "safe" private party status, encouraged dancers to "regress" into a series of prelinguistic yelps, gasps, and screeches. These themes were played out in the 1970s and beyond: Baggy, sexless T-shirts were symbolic of late-1980s club culture in the United Kingdom; dummies and other kids' accessories, as well as intentionally inane kid-style melodic riffs, were ubiquitous within the Anglo-American rave scene of the 1990s.[26] Of course, these parties did not enable a literal return to a pre-Oedipal childhood, but they did establish the conditions for the rediscovery of something that is experienced (if temporarily forgotten) in childhood. Dancing in a constricted space in which the boundaried body was lost in a prelinguistic sea of touch and sensation, participants experienced subjectivity in a nonegotistic mode, which suggests that the theory of the polymorphous perverse might be more than an evocative metaphor.

Describing one of his trips to Flamingo, author Edmund White evokes the process of abandoning his cherished ego. "I am ordinarily squeamish about touching an alien body," he wrote in *States of Desire: Travels in Gay America*. "I loathe crowds. But tonight the drugs and the music and the exhilaration had stripped me of all such scruples. We were packed in so tightly we were forced to slither across each other's wet bodies and arms; I felt my arm moving like a piston in synchrony against a stranger's—and I did not pull away. Freed of my shirt and my touchiness, I surrendered myself to the idea that I was just like everyone else. A body among bodies."[27] Unable to avoid physical contact on all sides, dancers had little choice but to dissolve into the amorphous whole and, as the distinctions between self and other collapsed, relinquished their socialized desire for independence and separation.

Developing a related argument, cultural critic Walter Hughes describes the way in which the boundaried masculine body, having been penetrated sonically on the dance floor, loses its autonomy and, in turn, establishes an empathetic alliance with the repressed-yet-resistant figure of the black female diva. Disciplined by the relentless disco beat, which compels him to move, the gay male dancer embraces the traditional role of slave while experimenting with a cyborglike refusal of the "natural," his body no longer being an autonomous entity but instead a mixture of tissue, bone, and reverberating sound.[28] The emergence of Euro-disco, which isolated and reinforced the four-on-the-floor bass beat of disco and combined this rigid rhythm with the nascent synthesizer technology of the 1970s, accentuated the experience of the dance floor as a realm in which technology went hand in hand with disciplinary compulsion.

At the same time, dancers also experienced disco as polyrhythmic, especially in contrast to the thudding pulse of contemporary rock, which had long since departed from the rhythmic interplay of rock 'n' roll, and this quality underpinned Richard Dyer's compelling defense of disco, published in 1979.[29] Whereas rock, according to Dyer, confined "sexuality to the cock" and was thus "indelibly phallo-centric music," disco "restores eroticism to the whole body" thanks to its "willingness to play with rhythm," and it does this "for both sexes."[30] Gilbert and Pearson, drawing on Dyer's argument, add: "If the body in its very materiality is an effect of repeated practices of which the experience of music is one, then we can say that what a music like disco can offer is a mode of actually rematerializing the body in terms which confound the gender binary."[31]

The centrality of this experiential process—of abandoning the ego and giving oneself up to the undulating rhythms and affective sensations of the dance floor—helps explain why gay men, along with people of color and women, were so central to disco's earliest formation. Having been historically excluded from the Enlightenment project, these groups were less attached to the project of bourgeois individualism and rational advancement than their straight white male counterparts and were accordingly more open to the disturbing forces of sonic-dance rapture. Riding on the back of gay liberation, feminism, and civil rights, the core dancers of the disco era were also engaging in the development of new social forms and cultural expressions, and the floor provided them with a relatively safe space in which they could work out their concerns and articulate their emotions and desires.

The discotheque, however, did not function only as a meeting space for the outcasts of the rainbow coalition. Straight men were involved in discotheque culture from the outset, both in its 1960s (predominantly straight commercial) and 1970s (predominantly gay subterranean) guises. Although straights were relatively marginal in spaces such as the Loft and the Sanctuary, they became more prominent after club culture became more visible (especially through the commercial success of venues such as Le Jardin, which was situated in Times Square) and the media began to report on the phenomenon. Their participation became even more pronounced when the mid-1970s recession provided straight white men with one of disco's most important pretexts: the need for release. "Straight, middle-class people never learned how to party," a gay Puerto Rican partygoer told the *New York Sunday News* in 1975. "To them, a party is where you get all dressed up just to stand around with a drink in your hand, talking business. But for us, partying is release, celebration. The more hostile the vibes in your life, the better you learn how to party, 'cause that's your salvation. Now that things aren't going so well for the stockbroker in Westchester and his wife, they come down here, where it doesn't matter how much money you make, or what the label in your coat says."[32]

The broad characteristics of the early 1970s dance floor—a crowd largely composed of outsider groups that would dance as individuals-in-the-crowd in a highly affective environment for an extended period of time—could be found not only at private venues such as the Loft, the Tenth Floor, the Gallery, and so on, but also at public venues such as the Limelight (the Greenwich Village version), the Haven, Le Jardin, and Galaxy 21 (figure 11.1). Whereas the private parties were normally considered underground and the public venues commercial, the key difference between the two was social rather than aesthetic. Hard-core dancers would frequent both, but whereas their position would be protected in the private parties, which were not advertised and were not open to members of the public, they were vulnerable to "unknowing outsiders" in public venues. As such, the dance ritual practiced at the Sanctuary, the Limelight, Le Jardin, and other public venues would be every bit as purist as that practiced in counterpart private parties at the beginning of their run, but their purism was invariably short-lived, at least in comparison to the private venues.

Even so, the private party network, which referred to itself as "the un-

Figure 11.1: Despite its highly visible midtown location, Le Jardin established itself as a cutting-edge venue following its June 1973 opening, as pictured here. By summer 1975, its predominantly gay crowd had moved onto private venues such as Flamingo, and Le Jardin began to attract a more overtly suburban crowd. Photo by Waring Abbott.

derground," could hardly be described as constituting a hermetically sealed entity. These private parties influenced the mainstream by generating chart hits, and underground DJs were insistent that they received gold records, or at least free records (via the first record pools), in return for their service to the music industry. In addition, DJs were largely committed to spreading their music beyond their core dance crowd, with figures such as Nicky Siano playing at his own private party, the Gallery, as well as at highly visible venues such as Studio 54.

The precariousness of the private party network's model of dancing was illustrated in the second half of the decade when it was twisted to the point of nonrecognition. As discotheque culture entered the commercial mainstream, DJs started to push primarily chart-based music, and on the dance floor the Hustle (as well as various line dances) came to dominate. Critics such as William Safire, the conservative *New York Times* op-ed columnist, were delighted and praised the routine for marking a conservative return to self-discipline, responsibility, and communication after a fifteen-year period of "frantic self-expression" and "personal isolationism" on the dance floor. "The political fact is that the absolute-freedom days of the dance are over," added Safire. "When you are committed to considering what your partner will do next, and must signal your own intentions so that the 'team' of which you are a part can stay in step, then you have embraced not only a dance partner, but responsibility."[33]

Drawn from the mambo, the Hustle required partners to hold hands while one led the other in a series of learned step and spin sequences, and, popularized by Van McCoy's hit single, the practice subsequently emerged as a conspicuous ingredient of the discotheque revival to the extent that it was the featured dance of *Saturday Night Fever,* the film that became the key catalyst within disco's belated and, ultimately, short-lived explosion. That film, in which there is no discernable dynamic between the selections of the DJ or the movements of Manero and his codancers, became the takeoff point for the mass crossover in disco during 1978 and the template for the disco boom.

Music writer Peter Shapiro confirms that the "Hustle marked the return of dancing as a surrogate for, or prelude to, sex," yet he also maintains that "as long as you strutted your stuff on the floor, disco was essentially democratic."[34] It is difficult, however, to see how the Hustle could have maintained the individual-within-the-crowd dynamic that was so central to the early (and, ultimately, enduring) formation of disco. For sure, Hustle dancers could be expressive, but the mambo-derived move disrupted the synergistic line of communication that was so central to the dance dynamic established in the early 1970s. Significantly, the move was not practiced in any of New York's hard-core venues.

Following the release of *Saturday Night Fever*, some thirty instruction books were published on disco dancing, and their focus on the Hustle, combined with the rapid growth of Hustle classes, is indicative of the way in which the priorities of New York's downtown dancers were lost in the second half of the 1970s. It is no coincidence that the DJ in *Saturday Night Fever*, Monty Rock, is an almost wholly absent figure. Spinners such as Paul Casella, who played in a variety of venues during the 1970s, testify that it was far easier to establish a flow in a hard-core urban setting than any commercial (urban or suburban) equivalent.

Dancing, of course, could be enjoyed outside of the esoteric ambience of the private party network, and, for the most part, suburban clubbers, gravitating to local and urban venues, would not have even been aware of what they were missing. In some instances, they might not have missed much: Strong DJs were in operation outside of New York's hallowed downtown scene, and the Hustle was, ultimately, just one of a number of dance styles that were popularized in the 1970s (even if a number of the other routines also disrupted the line of communication between the floor and the booth). Of course, there is no reason to think that Hustle dancers were having a bad time, and though dance floor aficionados might have maintained that transcendence could be attained only through other moves, the producers of *Saturday Night Fever* were clever enough to capitalize on the potential pleasure of this particular dance practice. In the process, they generated a new vehicle for the popularization of social dance in the United States.

Saturday Night Fever was initially welcomed by a number of disco purists, but the excitement soon waned. The extraordinary commercial success of the film might have encouraged the rapid expansion of the discotheque sector, but the new strata of club owners tended to create third-rate venues in their rush to capitalize on the boom. Inadequate sound systems broke up when pumped hard, illuminated floors flashed out their distracting sequences, and a new generation of know-nothing DJ automatons spurred an aural diet of prescribed, shrill, white pop. Meanwhile, male dancers took to dressing, dancing, and generally behaving like John Travolta, and their come-and-get-me gestures soon began to look ridiculous to even the least discerning dancer.

The rapid dilution of the downtown dance dynamic during the course of 1978, with the glut of bad disco music that was released in the slipstream of *Saturday Night Fever*, and the fatigue that inevitably followed the film's marathon stint at the top established the conditions for national backlash against disco. The culture's demise was accelerated by the combination of a deep recession in 1979 and the gathering momentum of the "disco sucks movement," a coalition of predominantly straight white men who felt dispossessed by disco and vented their anger and revenge in frequently homophobic and, to a lesser extent, racist publicity stunts. Although hard-core DJs and dance aficionados blanched at the discourse of "disco sucks," they passively agreed with the premise that disco productions in the post–*Saturday Night Fever* climate had become, for the most part, aesthetically banal and tiresomely commercial.

The Hustle did not survive the so-called death of disco, at least not as the standard routine on club dance floors of the United States during the 1980s and beyond, but the dance practices of the downtown party did. The outward signs suggested a culture in terminal decline—thousands of clubs, many of them in suburban centers, closed in the second half of 1979, and at the beginning of 1980 the music majors ditched the word *disco* and replaced it with *dance*—but parties such as the Loft, the Garage, and the Warehouse in Chicago, as well as a host of new, groundbreaking venues such as Danceteria, the Saint, Bond's, and the Funhouse went from strength to strength. Dance floor practices in the key urban venues of the 1980s and beyond were largely continuous with those of the early 1970s, and, as described by Fikentscher and Sommer, this template has survived into contemporary North American club culture, which largely revolves around the more electronically driven genres of house, techno, and garage. As such, the dance formations of the New York downtown party network of the early 1970s have proved to be significantly more enduring than the Hustle, even though disco culture will, it seems, forever be associated with this altogether safer routine.

Notes

Many thanks to Julie Malnig for the astute comments she offered throughout the writing of this chapter.

1. Elsewhere in this collection, Elizabeth Aldrich points out that from the middle of the eighteenth century to the middle of the nineteenth century the waltz revolved around "whirling pivots" and, as such, could be practiced without a leader.

2. Marshall Stearns and Jean Stearns, *Jazz Dance: The Story of American Vernacular Dance* (New York: Da Capo Press, 1994), 323.

3. Ibid., 325.

4. Ibid., 361.

5. Ibid., 7.

6. Ibid., 5.

7. My book, *Love Saves the Day: A History of American Dance Music Culture, 1970–79* (Durham, NC: Duke University Press, 2004), opens at the start of the 1970s and investigates, among other things, the precise chronology of the evolution of 1970s club culture. A number of points that I make in this article are drawn from the book.

8. Charles Kaiser, *The Gay Metropolis 1940–1996* (London: Phoenix, 1999), 201–2.

9. For a more detailed discussion of the relationship between the Stonewall rebellion, gay liberation, and the rise of gay discotheque culture, see Lawrence, *Love Saves the Day*, 28–30. In contrast to a number of authors, I argue that disco did not so much grow out of the Stonewall rebellion as run parallel to it as part of a wider movement of gay activism, consciousness, and culture.

10. Lawrence, *Love Saves the Day*, 21, 37–38.

11. Ibid., 25.

12. Ibid., 26.

13. Ibid., 25; Archie Burnett, interview with the author, September 19, 1997.

14. Jonathan David Jackson, "Improvisation in African-American Vernacular Dancing," *Dance Research Journal* 33 (2001/2002): 45–46.

15. Lawrence, *Love Saves the Day*, 288–89.

16. Ibid., 353.

17. Maria Pini, *Club Cultures and Female Subjectivity: The Move from Home to House* (Basingstoke, U.K.: Palgrave, 2001), 165.

18. For example, Albert Goldman's *Disco* (London: Hawthorn Books, 1978), 118–119, for long the most authoritative account of 1970s American discotheque culture, describes orgiastic scenes taking place at the Sanctuary. This claim, for which (after interviewing several regulars at the venue) I have found no supporting evidence, is regularly repeated in books on club culture, including, most recently, Peter Shapiro, *Turn the Beat Around: The Secret History of Disco* (London: Faber and Faber, 2005), 15.

19. David Walsh, "'Saturday Night Fever': An Ethnography of Disco Dancing," in *Dance, Gender and Culture*, ed. Helen Thomas (London: Macmillan, 1993), 116.

20. Lawrence, *Love Saves the Day*, 25.

21. Sally R. Sommer, "C'mon to My House: Underground-House Dancing," *Dance Research Journal* 33, no. 2 (Winter 2001): 74, a version of which appears in this collection. House music dates back to 1980 or 1981, when dancers at the Warehouse in Chicago started to describe the DJ's selections—disco, boogie, and some early Italo disco—as "house music," "house" in this instance being an abbreviation of the Warehouse; Lawrence, *Love Saves the Day*, 409–10. In late 1983, young Chicago producers started to use cheap synthesiser and drum machine technology to create their own dance tracks, which imitated a number of disco's bass lines and rhythmic patterns, and, in 1984, the term house music was reappointed to designate Chicago's electronic offshoot of disco. The new genre started to receive play in New York clubs in 1985. Sally Sommer's use of the term house music is more general than my own, and her use of the term house dancing is used interchangeably with the style of dancing at the Loft, which she calls "Lofting" (and which I label "individual free-form dance").

22. Jeremy Gilbert and Ewan Pearson, *Discographies: Dance Music, Culture and the Politics of Sound* (London: Routledge 1999), 134.

23. Sarah Thornton, *Club Cultures: Music, Media and Subcultural Capital* (Hanover, NH: Wesleyan University Press, 1996), 29.

24. Philip H. Dougherty, "Now the Latest Craze Is 1-2-3, All Fall Down," *The New York Times*, February 11, 1965.

25. Kai Fikentscher, *You Better Work! Underground Dance Music in New York City* (Hanover, NH: Wesleyan University Press), 101.

26. See, for example, Hillegonda Rietveld, "Living the Dream," in *Rave Off: Politics and Deviance in Contemporary Youth Culture,* ed. Steve Redhead (Aldershot, U.K.: Avebury, 1993), 54.

27. Edmund White, *States of Desire: Travels in Gay America* (London: Picador, 1986), 270–71.

28. Walter Hughes, "In the Empire of the Beat: Discipline and Disco," in *Microphone Fiends: Youth Music and Youth Culture,* ed. Andrew Ross and Tricia Rose (New York: Routledge, 1994), 151–52.

29. Richard Dyer, "In Defence of Disco," *Gay Left,* Summer 1979, reprinted in Hanif Kureishi and Jon Savage, eds., *The Faber Book of Pop* (London: Faber and Faber, 1995), 518–27.

30. Ibid., 523.

31. Gilbert and Pearson, *Discographies,* 102.

32. Sheila Weller, "The New Wave of Discotheques," *New York Sunday News,* August 31, 1975.

33. William Safire, "On the Hustle," *The New York Times,* August 4, 1975.

34. Shapiro, *Turn the Beat Around,* 184–85.

Section III

Theatrical-izations of Social Dance Forms

12

"A Thousand Raggy, Draggy Dances"

Social Dance in Broadway Musical Comedy in the 1920s

Barbara Cohen-Stratyner

When the Charleston became a fad with the white public, colored people were hoofing the Black Bottom. Now, when the Gay White Way, Fifth Avenue, Riverside Drive, and Long Island are turning to the Black Bottom, Negroes from coast to coast are going wild over the latest dance known as Messin' Around.

—Lester A. Walton, *New York Age* (October 17, 1925)

Consumption is not a thing of needs but a matter of choice freely exercised.

—Paul Cherington, director of research at the J. Walter Thompson Co., 1922[1]

In 1920s New York, you were what you danced. People defined themselves through choice and consumption of popular song and dance rhythms. When, whether, with whom, and where you did the fox-trot or the Charleston reflected your actual place in society and your self-definition. Both real social status and self-definition were changing daily, especially for women, due to suffrage, the Prohibition-era shock of common illegality, and economic realities and fantasies of the stock market. Concurrently, Broadway developed musical comedies that reflected their audiences, their social places, and self-definitions. These shows, like popular magazines, songs, and etiquette books, enabled the audiences to learn how to find and conduct a romance and, later, a marriage while maintaining independence and a wine cellar.

The place of social dance into modern-dress musical comedies was reflected in the integrated industries of Broadway, sheet music publishing, and recorded sound. One model was set in 1900–1919, when vaudeville intersected with the inexpensive rotogravure and recorded sound industries. Sheet music publishers advertised vaudeville performers on the cover page, recordings on the title page, and their own catalog on the back cover; vaudeville houses and record shops provided pianos for song pluggers. Songs and piano arrangements bore the images of exhibition ballroom dancers with, often, dance instructions. Popular numbers were frequently recorded twice—once as a song and again in a three- to four-minute "Fox Trot Medley"—suitable for dancing at home. Tin Pan Alley printers sold compilations of the year's best in arrangements for fox-trots and waltzes. The best way to bring attention to a song was to attach a dance number to it. As well as serving the plot, the shows' creators aimed at making the social dance numbers top-selling songs and recordings. This chapter will define the dances and the different genres of musical comedies before analyzing how the dances fit into the shows.

The Dances

The social dance scene became a staple of the musical in the mid-1910s as a result of the exhibition ballroom craze. Most musical comedies had a variety of dance scenes representing different genres. Social dances in the 1920s shows were variations either on the fox trot (or a similar holdover from the couple ballroom styles of the 1910s) or on the Charleston or Black Bottom, which were predominantly frontal dances, adapted from tap techniques. An occasional show, predominantly those set in Europe, replaced the Charleston with a tango or apache. Any of those genres could be staged for solos, couples, and choruses. In addition, most shows had a variety of dances and production numbers not using or referencing social dance (not discussed here).

As often happens in popular dance and music, those holdovers from the 1910s had moved from radically new to acceptable and established. Ragtime rhythms had been absorbed into the standard Tin Pan Alley repertory. Simi-

larly, the fox trots, one-steps, two-steps, and their so-called animal variations were still called "modern" dances, most popular with young adults,
but they no longer represented sophistication and advanced social behavior.
They were still the most frequently seen dances in stage representations of
modern life for multiple character types. Unlike the Grizzly Bear and Turkey
Trot, which had aged so quickly, they could only represent passé, the fox-trot
and generic one-steps could be updated each season. The fox trot, especially,
could be presented as appealing to both the social elite and upwardly mobile
middle class.

Choreographers retained these holdovers because they were so flexible
and adaptable. The different positions that determined where the male and
female dancers stood and how they held each other could radically change
how the standard dance steps looked to the audience. Even the following
social dance positions listed by social dance master Albert W. Newman show
the range of a standard fox-trot: "Closed position . . . the one in general use;
tango position . . . virtually standing side by side . . . in the same direction;
American position . . . partners very much at each others' side, right shoulder
almost touching."[2] Characterizations could easily be applied by performers
to show devoted love, couth, pretensions, and eccentricities.

The historiography of the dances the Charleston and the Black Bottom
remains complex and embedded at the fractious intersections of mainstream
and African American popular entertainment. It is most likely that they
were based on performative movements that we now know as tap and soft-
shoe steps. Similar steps were probably developed by more than one African
American dancer in vaudeville and were presented to the Broadway audiences in the many musicals and revues by African American songwriters.
The African American touring shows from 1900 to the 1920s were revues,
generally by companies headed by vocalists such as the Hyer Sisters or the
Whitman Sisters, or scripted musicals by companies headed by comics or
comic teams, among them Bert Williams and George Walker, Ernest Hogan,
and S. H. Dudley. Almost every vocalist or dancer in the 1920s shows had
been on one of these tours.

The 1920s era of popularity for the African American shows is generally
thought to begin with the Sissle and Blake revue *Shuffle Along* (1921) and the
musical *Liza* (1922, music by Maceo Pinkard). But, apart from Eubie Blake,
who had already had a long successful career as a pianist and composer, it
is important to remember that the songwriters considered themselves as
the third generation of African American ragtime composers, lyricists and
comics. They recognized Will Marion Cook and the team of Bob Cole, James

Weldon Johnson, and J. Rosamond Johnson as the first to focus on writing cohesive shows, rather than piano rags or individual songs. The next generation was Tin Pan Alley regulars, writing for African American shows and white vaudeville performers. They included Shelton Brooks, W. C. Handy, Billy Johnson, Cecil Mack (R. C. McPherson), Alex Rogers, Chris Smith, Henry Troy, Clarence Williams, and Spencer Williams, as well as arranger Ford T. Dabney and arranger, composer, and conductor Charles "Luckey" Roberts. They were widely recognized because they had performed in both the African American circuit Theatre Owners' Booking Association and white or integrated urban vaudeville. That group was augmented by veterans of the two, widely publicized World War I infantry bands, led by James Reese Europe and Tim Brymn.

The names given to dance numbers in musicals and revues clued the audience to the style and rhythm. Trots, one-steps, walks, and dances named for animals referred to exhibition ballroom styles introduced in the 1910s. They tended to be unstressed rhythms (1, 2, 3, 4, or 1, 2, 3, 4, 5, 6), in the style that became associated with the strumming of a ukulele. Dances with geographic references to the Southern port cities and, especially, areas on the Mississippi River were faster, syncopated, and based on the Cakewalk rhythm (1 & 2 & 3 & 4 &), its cousin the habanera (1&-a 2 & 3 &-a 4 & or 1–a &-a, etc.), or ragtime, a piano-based form with a Cakewalk in the left hand and the more complex habanera in the right. These included Charlestons, Black Bottoms, stomps, and todalos (spellings vary). References to the rural South tended to be minstrel-style nostalgia, such as "Swanee" or "Mammy."

The Charleston: The Dance that Defined the Decade

The song that everyone appropriately associates with the dance is by James P. Johnson and Cecil Mack and was included in the musical *Runnin' Wild* (October 1923), a vehicle for comic stars Flournoy E. Miller and Aubrey L. Lyles. Composer Will Marion Cook was the conductor; dances were by Lyda Webb. It was misspelled in the program and therefore reviewed as "The Charston." As usual in Broadway shows of the period, it was sung first (by Elizabeth Welsh) and then danced with the chorus. Most of the morning-after reviewers in Washington, DC, and New York focused on the "Red Caps" number, featuring eccentric dancers Tommy Woods, Ralph Bryson, and George Stamper, "whose elastic bones seemed utterly lacking in chalk." On October 30, 1923, the *New York Herald* critic, who described the Red Caps, praised "sprightly Elizabeth Welsh [who] stopped the show with a 'Charston' number in which the phenomenally agile chorus agitated around a syncopated waterfall."[3] Jazz historians Marshall and Jean Stearns assign "The Charleston" to the Red Caps, although this is not validated by the morning-after reviews in Washington or on Broadway. It is possible that the Red Caps reprieved the song later in the show.[4]

Within this chapter, I am defining the Charleston as including at least these three steps: the spiraling cross kick (step L and kick R, step R and kick L, while swinging arms in opposition), the jaybird or knee-in as a pose or side step, and the instep touch/knee raise to the side. Most Charlestoners added shoulder and hip-shaking movements from the Shimmy. The famous White Studio photograph of *Runnin' Wild* shows Welsh and the chorus in the knee raise. The equally famous still of Joan Crawford alone on the table in *Our Dancing Daughters* (MGM, 1927) showed the cross-kick.

Different origins for the Charleston were attributed in contemporary dance periodicals. The December 1925 issue of *The Dance* featured an article by frequent contributor Nanette Kutner about Broadway dance director David Bennett. It is primarily about two chorus effects in his *Rose Marie* but includes his claim that three years previously (i.e., 1922), he had observed "colored urchins" in Alabama "dancing and chanting in an inimitable manner. . . . The rhythm entered into Bennett's blood and he suddenly realized that here was a valuable find. Why not bring this Charleston dance to Broadway, ever seeking with bored eyes for something new—something different—something original?" Although he commissioned lyricist Irving Caesar to write a Charleston song for Bennett's revue at the Club Alabam in New York, this origin myth is highly unlikely because Bennett's expertise as a dance director was in stage pictures and chorus movement, such as the falling domino effect now associated with the Rockettes.[5]

An edition of the "New York Letter" in the January 1926 *Dancing Times* credited Ned Wayburn with the ballroom Charleston (the couple-dance version), introduced in the *Ziegfeld Follies of 1923* (act 1 finale), after he had been introduced to the dance by the songwriting/performing team of Noble Sissle and Eubie Blake.[6] Their 1923 "That Charleston Dance" was included in *The Chocolate Dandies,* staged by Wayburn's archrival Julian Mitchell in 1924. In the summer and tour editions of the 1923 *Follies,* Gilda Gray performed "Come Along," by the African American songwriting team of Henry Creamer and Turner Layton.[7] It is not certain whether Wayburn was misquoted or misremembered or that Sissle and Blake realized that they had double-booked their Charleston and substituted a song by their equally famous colleagues. As often with Wayburn, the specific innovation credit became generalized. His accurate claim to have developed the ballroom Charleston (which remained popular in England) should not be taken as a claim to be the inventor of the stage Charleston.

Alternative Charleston introduction theories were posited in *The New York World* in October 1923, which credits "little negro boys" outside the Winter Garden Theater; a "runaway sailor from New Orleans"; a chorus boy from *Liza;* a "colored maid in Chicago who taught it to Bee Jackson" ("the first white girl to do the Charleston"), but who appeared at the Club Alabam; and a "colored maid in Chicago" who taught it to Frances Williams.[8] The one person not credited was Lyda Webb.[9] The "little negro boys" is similar to the story cited by the Stearns, although they say that Irvin C. Miller saw them in front of his Lincoln Theater.[10] *The New York World* article also quotes Wayburn as having learned "the step" (the spiraling arms and alternating kicks) from "a Negro youngster" introduced to him by Aubrey Miller (or possibly his brother Irvin C.). The most useful information in the article is the analysis by (white) eccentric dancers. They recognized that parts of the Charleston were derived from functional steps in tap and soft shoe. Harland Dixon said that the side step was like "[shuffle] off to Buffalo" and entrance or exit sequence. Jack Haskell was quoted linking it to "over the top," which is a popular finale step in tap.

The persistence of the Charleston sets it off from the other social dances of the decade. More than any other dance, it defined the performer as young and willing to take chances on modern life. It managed to be both trendy and individualistic because it was concurrently hard to dance and easy to self-choreograph. In fact, the multiple movements that define the Charleston could be emphasized, deemphasized, or even dropped by different choreographers (for stage) and people (for social situations). In addition, the Charleston looked great in mid-1920s fashions. The slip dress emphasized shimmying shoulders and facilitated knee movements. Similarly, men could Charleston in soft jackets and pleated trousers or full dress formal wear.

Vaudeville and popular songs of the period were often referential, carrying themes and characters from different performers and creators. In musical comedy and revue scores, the references were often to social dances. For example, 1920 shows featured "I Love to Fox Trot" (A. von Tilzer, from *Honey Girl*) and "Keep a Fox Trot for Me" (by Ivan Caryll, from *Kissing Time*). The easiest way for shows to rip off "The Charleston" was to treat the song and dance as if they were generic. So Irving Berlin wrote "They're Blaming the Charleston" (1925) and "Everyone in the World Is Doing the Charleston" (1926, from *The Cocoanuts*), and the *George White Scandals of 1925* featured "Give Us the

Charleston" (by DeSylva, Henderson, and Brown). Similar vaudeville songs by Tin Pan Alley regulars included "I'm Going to Charleston Back to Charleston" (1925, by Roy Turks and Lou Handman) and "Yiddishe Charleston" (1926, by Billy Rose and Fred Fisher).

The Black Bottom

Unlike the Charleston, which developed into a couple and circle dance, the Black Bottom, named for a Nashville port area, remained a frontal performance solo. When a social dance referenced the Black Bottom, it was either the basic locomotion (in which each deliberate step begins with a toe touch then a swivel on the ball of the foot) or the stance, in what is now known as "jazz hands" with knees bent outward. That stance (also associated with the messin' around social dance) was a signature move for Ann Pennington, a featured dancer in the *Ziegfeld Follies* and *George White's Scandals*. The Perry Bradford song "The Original Black Bottom Dance" was introduced to theater audiences by Ethel Ridley in *Dinah* (1923, by Irvin C. Miller and Tim Brymn) and then by Alberta Hunter in vaudeville. African American theater critic Lester A. Walton wrote about the "etymology of the Black Bottom and Charleston" in an article on Luckey Roberts and cited lyrics from the Bradford's "The Original Black Bottom Dance":

> Hop down front and then doodle back.
> Mooch to your left and then you mooch to the right;
> Your hands on your hips and do the messin' around,
> Break a leg until you're near the ground.[11]

Ann Pennington presented a version of the dance to a different, now better-known song (by B. G. DeSylva and Lew Brown, with music by Ray Henderson) in the 1926 edition of *George White's Scandals* and is generally credited with popularizing it. Her version, in shimmy pose, emphasized what Marshall and Jean Stearns described as "a genteel slapping of the backside."[12] It evolved into the gesture more like striking a match on the hips but was the primary defining movement of the dance. The Black Bottom was not as pervasive as the Charleston, possibly because it was so associated with Ann Pennington's stage persona that it was not translated into a couple dance.

To be cast as the flapper with a Charleston or Black Bottom solo was good news for a performer. It was, for a time, the quickest route to stardom. Those dances provided opportunities to display balance, skill, and personality. Alan Dale proclaimed his discovery of Zelma O'Neal in his September 7,

1927, review of *Good News* in the *New York American*: "Little Zelma was the leading spirit of 'The Varsity Drag' and, you may believe it or not, but Zelma was 'it' with a vengeance. She pounds on the stage, she stamped her points, she wriggled her anatomy—that youthful, almost unformed anatomy—and little Zelma was 'made' in a night."[13] Once the Charleston and Black Bottom were introduced, performers rushed to learn them. The place to go was the Seventh Avenue and 133rd Street studio of African American dance teachers Billy Pierce and Buddy Bradley. At the time of his death in 1933, Pierce was credited with training Broadway and vaudeville dancers in both the Charleston and Black Bottom as well as serving as a tap coach.[14]

Social Dance in the Musicals

The Musicals

The modern-dress musical comedy was developed in the mid-1910s, concurrent with the exhibition ballroom dances. The two sets of Broadway productions that are generally credited as "first" are the summer musicals produced by Lew Fields and directed by Ned Wayburn and/or the Princess Theatre musicals written by collaborators Guy Bolton, Jerome Kern, and P. G. Wodehouse. Both genres featured characters in situations that reflected the audiences' experiences; they were about the people who were likely to be in the audience.

The Fields and Wayburn shows were large productions focusing on the adventures of middle-aged men and married couples divided by summer activities—*The Midnight Sons* (1909), *The Summer Widowers* (1910), and *The Hen-Pecks* (1911). Because Fields and Wayburn were in control, the domestic plots stretched to accommodate some spectacular elements, such as scenes at the circus. The three titles refer to contemporary slang—"midnight sons" were otherwise sober businessmen with nocturnal activities, "summer widowers" were men whose families were vacationing in summer homes at the shore or mountains, and "hen-pecks" were married men with nagging spouses. These male types constituted the primary audience for summer performances.

The size of the Princess Theatre determined the scale of those musicals. Although the Fields and Wayburn shows were in the (Thirty-ninth Street) Broadway Theatre, which seated thirteen hundred and included a full orchestra pit, the Princess Theatre could seat only three hundred, what would now be considered the size of an Off-Broadway house. The pit could accommodate only eleven musicians, so Kern wrote for an enhanced dance band rather than a full pit orchestra. The shows—*Very Good Eddie* (1915), *Oh, Boy* (1917), *Leave It to Jane* (1917), *Oh, Lady Lady* (1918), and *Oh My Dear* (1918)— were about and aimed at "twenty-somethings" with occasional middle-age couples to provide contrast and story complications. Designers made the already small stage area look like living rooms, so social dance seemed at home. The Princess Theatre comedies modeled appropriate behavior in romance and marriage and were targeted at dating couples and the newly married.

Plots and Characters in 1920s Modern-Dress Musicals

[Women were in] a mighty struggle towards differentiation and individual direction. [They were] demanding recognition as individuals first, and as wives and mothers second. [They were] claiming the right to dispose of themselves according to their own needs and as wives and mothers second.

—Beatrice M. Hinkle, "The Chaos of Modern Marriage," *Harper's* 152 (December 1925): 9.[15]

Modern-dress musicals of the 1920s served both needs. Despite women's new rights, choice of spouse was the major life decision that caught the attention of the young adults in the audience. As in operetta, dividing into appropriate couples was the raison d'être and finale of most musicals. They focused on the courtship of the younger couples and the matrimonial conflicts of the middle-aged characters. These shows provided opportunities for the older characters to accept compromise and for the young couples or potential couples to experience conflicts and separations in a separate reality: a learning experience expressed in dance and music. In terms of dramatic function, a social dance scene could be used to mask exits and entrances in service of disguised identities and marital complications. For those few shows with not wholly romantic plots, the social dance scene could also serve as a suspense mechanism, extending the stage time before characters were unmasked or discovered with the wrong partner.

The traditional "boy meets girl, boy loses girl, boy gets girl back" plots were varied somewhat to accommodate the generations. In a Cinderella variation, the specialty of Marilyn Miller and Mary Eaton, working girl meets rich boy, his family objects, girl wins over family, girl gets boy. There were two middle-aged couples—generally representing her employer and his parents. For the postsuffrage juvenile couple of similar economic status, the 1920s variation became boy meets girl, girl asserts her independence, boy and girl get back together. To this was added middle-aged man asserts independence and becomes foolish, middle-aged woman asserts independence and becomes wise, they decide to remain a couple. The topical plot complications generally served to reunite both couples.

The main female character was often an orphan (in a Cinderella plot) or relative from the country, as in *Mary* or *No, No Nanette*. In either case, her being unused to society provided the opportunity to serve as an "other," observing and learning appropriate social behavior. That character had been a fixture in advisory fiction and song throughout the nineteenth and early twentieth centuries, especially in so-called girls' novels. Unlike the heroines of those books, who struggled to become teachers and writers, the 1920s musical heroine worked in fashion or millinery and used social dance to mix with her customers and gain her idealized future. The hero was either as exemplar of society who gains heart and the courage to choose love over family or an outsider who gains access to society and the heroine. These musicals also often have secondary juvenile couples, who could be comics or dance specialists. On Broadway, these roles often went to established vaudeville dance teams. Ballroom dance teams who could not manage comic dialogue were cast as themselves or as guests at the social dance scene, performing their most up-to-date specialty. The male and female chorus members were always young. They served both script and choreographic functions as friends for the characters and to provide plot information. They also provided two dance roles: forming the physical frame for featured players and transforming featured dance solos into social dances forms. Many of the shows also had secondary dance roles for servants, who provided plot continuity and commentary and often performed eccentric or comic versions of the dances.

Integrating Dance Scenes into Musicals

Most plotted musicals maintained a basic pattern: The complications were set up in act 1 and solved at a social dance in act 2. For example, the Princess Theatre show *Leave It to Jane* (book and lyrics by Guy Bolton and P. G. Wodehouse, based on *The College Widow* by George Ade), set at a coeducational college obsessed with football, can be seen as a model for modern-dress musicals.[16] The various romantic plots established in act 1 culminate in the act 2 moonlit faculty reception. The authors prepare the audience by integrating the dance into dialogue and song introduction in act 1, with male students competing to make Jane commit to dancing with them that evening (i.e., in act 2):

Pearson: You're going to give me the first dance tonight, aren't you?
Hopper: Don't do it! He can't dance. Now, I've been taking lessons.
Pearson: You needed them.
McAllister: Give it to me, Jane! I can dance rings 'round both of them.

The dancing in act 2 occurs offstage, although the band can be heard by the characters onstage (and by the audience). College President Witherspoon defines himself as an elderly comic foil with his comments on dance: "You may call me an old fogy, but I maintain that the ballroom dance is an immodest performance. . . . If it were not for the accompaniment of music, I should say that the young men were embracing the young women. . . . I see no harm in rectangular dances . . . but they don't dance them any more."[17]

Successive characters facilitate the plot resolution in act 2 by getting one another off the stage to dance. *Good News* (1927) was one of the many variations on the elements of *Leave It to Jane*. In this well-remembered show, the act 1 plot setup (scene 3) was a preview of the dance, introduced by the line: "Let 'em worry about their dusty old books. We'll make Tait [College] famous for the 'Varsity Drag.' (Cuing Number 6 "The Varsity Drag")."[18] The offstage dance model was used in so many musicals because it could accommodate scenes in which many pairs of characters speak short spurts of dialogue, such as *Follow Thru!* (1929, act 1, scene 4). Interior variations of these scenes were generally set in rooms with multiple French doors so that characters could be smoothly foregrounded or backgrounded as the dialogue required.[19] During the later 1920s, "sit one out" shifted from its original meaning of not dancing to become a euphemism for necking or slipping away to obtain a drink, adding potential humor to the dialogue.

The dance craze was often the vehicle for the act 1 plot setup. In *Good Morning Dearie*, a 1921 musical by Jerome Kern and Anne Caldwell, a thief (an acquaintance of the characters who work in a fashionable dress shop) brags that he uses his ability to dance to get into homes of the wealthy:

Chesty: Say, you know me when it comes to that dancing stuff—there's many a swell house I danced my way into, and danced the night out with the pickin's in my pockets!
Margie: Well, gotta hand it to you, Chesty, for head work, and footwork!
Chesty: If I'd stuck to me dancin' stunts, they'd never a'nipped me! No matter how much mazuma was misin' they never suspected the professional entertainers! (act 1, 1–14, 1–15)

This dialogue introduces the first dance sequence, "Way Down Town," in the dress shop. The act 2 dance sequence is in an anteroom at the ball. As dancing couples sweep across the rear stage, the juvenile lead, Billy, delays his escape to dance "The Blue Danube Blues" with shopgirl Rose Marie. They perform the song, with encore refrain, and are followed by the (non-plot-related) specialty dance by superstar exhibition ballroom dancer Maurice Mouvet and his partner.[20]

The canonic iconography of the 1920s includes a *Life* magazine cover by John Held Jr. (for the February 16, 1928, issue) that shows a young, bobbed-haired flapper dancing with an elderly man in full tails. The caption is "Teaching old Dogs new tricks" [*sic*]. Held's focus was generally the youth of the 1920s: flappers and college joes in raccoon coats.[21] In this cover, the woman's string of pearls is flying off to graze the *L* of *Life;* her arms, legs, shoes, and garters epitomize the word "akimbo." He is bent forward, with his arms swinging back. They are doing the knees together, feet apart step that can be found in the Charleston and Black Bottom. The message of the cover is that youth, signified by the flapper, can be off balance and look dynamic, whereas the elderly man is just off balance.

The Charleston, Black Bottom, and similar dances were selected or adapted for scenes featuring straying, middle-aged and elderly men. These featured roles were often played by former dancers or physical comics. They were able to exaggerate the movements that seemed to push them off balance. The off-balance dances were introduced and popularized in revues. They entered musical comedies as signposts separating young from age and/or maturity. In one particularly overt example, in act 1 of *Mary,* the heroine's guardian is convinced that she has become poor and has to "take in floors to scrub!" To cheer her up, Tom, the secondary juvenile, enters "to show her the cutest dancing step," "The Tom, Tom Toddle."[22]

In musicals, the young can do the Charleston; when older couples try, they are literally off balance. In most plots, older women do the Charleston to show their ability to communicate with the young and serve as mentors in the rules of courtship. *No, No Nanette* (1925, music by Vincent Youmans, lyrics by Irving Caesar and Otto Harbach) follows a standard pattern in contrasting the courtship woes of the juvenile leads with the marital tension of the two middle-aged second couples (Nanette's aunt and uncle and a Bible publisher and his wife). It deserves closer analysis for the distribution of its vocal and dance numbers (figure 12.1). The older couples get the most memorable songs, among them "I Want to Be Happy," "Tea for Two," and "You Can Dance with Any Girl At All." In the latter song, the wife releases her husband to flirt but steps back from the risqué: "You can dance . . . as long as you come home with me." Although it is not a challenge to conventional morality, it follows the contemporary lineage of the usual message of the red hot mama vocalists like Sophie Tucker, who was more likely to sing "Mama goes where Papa goes or Papa don't go out at all."

The culture of Prohibition was reflected in the modern-dress musicals. Both songwriters and audiences seem to have memorized all of the provisions of the Eighteenth Amendment and related Acts of Enforcement. Songs and scripts referenced the common experience of illegally obtaining alcohol and individual clauses in the Acts. Although it was not common for characters to drink onstage, the frequent exits built into dance scenes could imply imbibing. Comic characters could appear more and more tipsy with each entrance. "Being tipsy," was easy for eccentric dancers. As Prohibition and

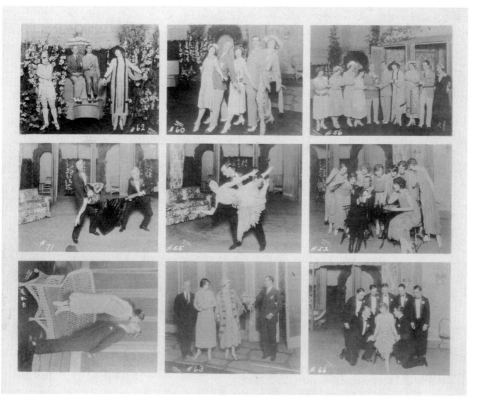

Figure 12.1: Photographs by White Studio of dance sequences in the original Broadway production of *No, No, Nanette* (1925), included with the prompt script. Billy Rose Theatre Division, The New York Public Library for the Performing Arts, Astor, Lenox and Tilden Foundations.

the general refusal to obey the laws of Prohibition progressed, it became more common for sympathetic secondary characters to be criminals: thieves or, as in the Gershwins' *Oh, Kay,* bootleggers.

Social Dance in Subgenres of Musicals

Within vaudeville and musical theater were many variations or subgenres that easily accommodated social dance scenes. Musical comedy and vaudeville, for instance, were obsessed with real twin or sibling acts and tandem teams that simulated twinness. The quick entrances and exits of a social dance setting facilitated switches of performer or character, as in *Two Little Girls in Blue* (1921), starring the Fairbanks Twins.[23] A subgenre developed in the late 1920s to accommodate the huge popularity of solo comedians and comic teams wooed from vaudeville. In these shows, the romantic entanglements of the juvenile couples and their older mentors were subsumed by the machinations of the comic leads. The plot complications of act 1 still set up a social dance scene, but it now existed only to be interrupted by the entrances of comics like Eddie Cantor, Skeets Gallagher, or the Marx Brothers. Dave Bennett's choreography for Gallagher's vehicle *The City Chap* (1925, by Jerome Kern and Anne Caldwell, from a book by James Montgomery) served its plot by setting act 1's finale in a village festival, providing opportunities for "rube" dances, and act 2's in a Saratoga ballroom, where George Fontana and Marjorie Moss danced to George Olsen and His Orchestra, Mary Jane "scored as a Charleston-ing soubrette," and George Raft "tied the show in knots as devious as he ties up his incredible legs."[24] In Irving Berlin's *The Cocoanuts,* written for the Marx Brothers, act 2, scene 1 was set at a tea dance in the lounge of the Cocoanuts Hotel in Cocoanut Beach, Florida. It opened with the song "Five O'clock Tea" and a specialty dance by Antonio and Nina DeMarco. The vocalists Three Brox Girls then sang "Everyone in the World Is Doing the Charleston," cuing a (different) specialty by the DeMarcos, and four national Charlestons, each represented by four chorus dancers: the English Charleston, a Spanish Charleston, a Lenox Avenue Charleston, and a Russian Charleston.[25]

Social Dance in Operetta and Plays

The other major function of social dance in 1920s Broadway musicals emerged in the operettas that persisted in popularity through the decade and into the 1930s. Romantic meetings on the dance floor remained the most common function, but historical and contemporary dances were also used as signals of chronology. This was vital in stories that followed as characters aged, such as *Show Boat,* whose plot stretches from 1887 through 1927 (the year that it opened). Composer Jerome Kern made brilliant use of subliminal social dance rhythms and included two preexisting popular songs to establish time frames: Charles K. Harris's ballad "After the Ball" and Joe Howard's Cakewalk "Hello My Honey," Tin Pan Alley's most successful rag. Social dance steps and appropriate music offered recognizable vocabularies to assist audiences in grasping the plot's chronology.

Dance served a similar function in modern-dress nonmusical theater. *Nice People,* Rachel Crothers's popular 1921 play about well-bred but aimless flappers, was typical of nonmusical social comedies dealing with courtship, marriage, and the conduct of women from "nice" people in "good" society.[26] In the first act, the principal female character pushes the limits of behavior by lying to her father and sneaking out of the apartment for a night with friends. The opening scene, introducing the three flappers and their escorts, includes short sequences of dance in and out of the room, with dialogue references to dancing with and without corsets. In the play synopsis in *Everybody's Magazine* (November 1921, illustrated with photographs from the Broadway production), it is made clear that the bad behavior of one of the escorts, Teddy, will include dancing.[27] Crothers did not interrupt the dramatic flow to include the dance scene in the play but cuts to the morning after. When Clara S. Beranger adapted the play as a film (1922, for William De Mille), however, she added an on-screen dance scene in the Lotus Blossom, "where no line marks the world from the half-world . . . a combination of society people, Bohemian and fast people."[28]

Conclusion

The insertion of social dance in the modern-dress musicals and plays followed America's obsession with consumption and choice. Just as they supported contemporary magazines, novels, and narrative films, the audience consumed musicals about people like themselves. From the stage, they adopted and copied new dances, as they did jokes, songs, and fashions. In the 1910s, social dance was a challenge to stagnation. People attended cabarets and Broadway revues to learn about the new steps, rhythms, and gender politics. In the 1920s, social dance had become a common experience in life, common in the sense of frequently occurring and in the sense that the audience shared the knowledge and experiences of the characters. They easily read social dance's vocabulary: the clues to character inherent in tempo, stance, and steps. Although the musicals were fixated on choice and forming couples, the dances could be performed as solo improvisations of self-identification.

Notes

"A thousand raggy, draggy dances" is a lyric from the introduction to "The Baltimore Buzz," by Nobel Sissle and Eubie Blake, from *Shuffle Along* (1921).

1. Simone Weil Davis, *Living Up to the Ads: Gender Fictions of the 1920s* (Durham, NC: Duke University Press, 2000), 9.

2. Albert W. Newman, "The Fox Trot," description of the dance, probably from *Dances of To-day* (Philadelphia: Penn Publishing, 1921), 2–3.

3. *Runnin' Wild* clipping file, Billy Rose Theatre Division, The New York Public Library for the Performing Arts.

4. Marshall Stearns and Jean Stearns, *Jazz Dance: The Story of American Vernacular Dance* (Schirmer Books: 1968), 145–46.

5. Nanette Kutner, "How the Charleston Came to Broadway," *The Dance*, December 1925, 16, 23, Jerome Robbins Dance Division, The New York Public Library for the Performing Arts.

6. "New York Letter," *The Dancing Times*, January 1926, 475, 477, Jerome Robbins Dance Division, The New York Public Library for the Performing Arts.

7. By 1924, Creamer and Layton had already written the jazz standards "After You've Gone" and "Way Down Yonder in New Orleans."

8. "The World-Wide Conquering Strut of the Charleston, Jazziest of all the Dances," *The New York World*, October 25, 1923, the Charleston (dance) clipping file in the Jerome Robbins Dance Division, The New York Public Library for the Performing Arts.

9. A recently discovered column by Billy Pierce in the national edition of the *Chicago Defender* (December 19, 1925) only confuses Webb's credit. Pierce, whose "Hittin' Here and There" column covered New York's entertainment scene, questioned it: "Well, since when did Lawrence Deas's name change to Lila Webb?" adding a paragraph of insults directed at her. There is no independent evidence that Deas, who staged *Shuffle Along*, was associated with *Runnin' Wild*. As the best-known African American director/producer of the period, he would have received an appropriate credit. Pierce's excoriation of Webb as a "little girl" may have been related to their rivalry as principal teachers in dance studios aimed at entertainers; cf. the column "Across the Pond" by the *Defender*'s Berlin correspondent, Ivan H. Browning, May 22, 1927.

10. Stearns and Stearns, *Jazz Dance*, 145.

11. Lester A. Walton, "Luckey Roberts Autographs Songs for the Prince," *The New York Age*, October 17, 1925.

12. Stearns and Stearns, *Jazz Dance*, 111.

13. Alan Dale, "New Musical Play Is Riot of Melody and Mirth," *New York American*, September 7, 1927; *Good News* clipping file, Billy Rose Theatre Division, The New York Public Library for the Performing Arts.

14. "Billy Pierce," obituary, *New York Herald*, April 13, 1933; "Stars Trained by Billy Pierce, Dead in Harlem," unidentified newspaper (possibly *New York Age*), April 13, 1933; and "Billy Pierce," obituary, *Variety*, April 25, 1933. Bradley, who was a source for the Stearns, claimed to be the principal teacher.

15. Cited in Dorothy M. Brown, *American Women in the 1920s: Setting a Course* (Boston: Twayne, 1987), 32.

16. Jerome Kern (composer), Guy Bolton, and P. G. Wodehouse, *Leave It to Jane*,

1917; Billy Rose Theatre Division (NCOF + Bolton), The New York Public Library for the Performing Arts.

17. *Leave It to Jane,* unpublished promptbook, Billy Rose Theatre Division (NCOF + Mandel, F), The New York Public Library for the Performing Arts.

18. Lawrence Schwab and B. G. DeSylva, lyrics by DeSylva and Lew Brown, music by Ray Henderson, *Good News,* 1927; unpublished typescript, Billy Rose Theatre Division (NCOF+ Schwab), The New York Public Library for the Performing Arts.

19. For example, act 2 of *No, No, Nanette;* floor plans included in unpublished typescript, 1925, Billy Rose Theatre Division, The New York Public Library for the Performing Arts.

20. Jerome Kern (composer) and Anne Caldwell, *Good Morning Dearie,* 1921; promptbook, Billy Rose Theatre Division (NCOF + Kern), The New York Public Library for the Performing Arts.

21. Carolyn Kitch cites this Held illustration in *The Girl on the Magazine Cover* (Chapel Hill: University of North Carolina Press, 2001), 126–27, but focuses on the economic relationship between a gold digger and her sugar daddy. See a similar study of *Saturday Evening Post* covers in Elizabeth Stevenson's "Flappers and Some Who Were Not Flappers," in *Dancing Fools and Weary Blues: The Great Escape of the Twenties,* ed. Lawrence R. Broer and John D. Walther (Bowling Green, OH: Bowling Green State University Press, 1990), 123–24.

22. Frank Mandel, Otto Harbach, and Louis Hirsch (composer), *Mary,* 1920; promptbook, Billy Rose Theatre Division (NCOF + Mandel), The New York Public Library for the Performing Arts.

23. *Two Little Girls in Blue* clipping file, Billy Rose Theatre Division, The New York Public Library for the Performing Arts.

24. "'The City Chap' Full of Dances and Fun," *New York Times,* October 27, 1925; in *The City Chap* clipping file, Billy Rose Theatre Division, The New York Public Library for the Performing Arts.

25. *The Cocoanuts* program file, Billy Rose Theatre Division, The New York Public Library for the Performing Arts.

26. Rachel Crothers, *Three Plays by Rachel Crothers* (New York: Brentano's, 1924).

27. The photograph captions read "Teddy [the heroine] and her friends, late in the evening, talk about going somewhere to dance" and "The above picture shows a group of apparently well-bred young people of New York's wealthy set planning to go somewhere at eleven o'clock at night, un-chaperoned, to dance"; *Nice People* clipping file, Billy Rose Theatre Division, The New York Public Library for the Performing Arts.

28. Rachel Crothers, *Nice People,* film adaptation by Clara S. Beranger, 1922; Billy Rose Theatre Division (MFLM + 1922), The New York Public Library for the Performing Arts.

13

From Bharata Natyam to Bop

Jack Cole's "Modern" Jazz Dance

Constance Valis Hill

What we used to see in the dance halls in the twenties and thirties is what real jazz dance is. A group of kids who did all those dances that were in then: the Camel Walk, the Charleston, the Lindy Hop . . . all stemming from African dance and all filled with authentic feeling. And the root of all these elaborations was the Lindy. Whatever is danced in the name of jazz dancing must come from the Lindy, necessarily theatricalized and broadened for the stage, of course.

—Jack Cole, "It's Gone Silly," 1963

In 1947, Jack Cole created "Sing, Sing, Sing" to the recording made famous by "King of Swing" Benny Goodman and his Big Band.[1] "[We] kicked, spun, slammed and slid on our knees for seven minutes in true Jack Cole style," said Rod Alexander about the dance performed by the Jack Cole Dancers when it premiered in New York at the Latin Quarter.[2] "Everyone came off the floor, gasped, and threw up. It was a ball-breaker, a number that asked the impossible."[3] Described by critics as "a dance in the style of Harlem" and "a primitive dance of primitive ecstasy," "Sing, Sing, Sing" was a stylized Lindy Hop, or jitterbug, that popular swing-era social dance that flung and flipped partners into breakaway solos and daring "air" steps.[4] More than a step, the jitterbug was a style, a state of mind; a violent, even frenzied athleticism made it hazardous, exciting, sexual, cathartic. The jitterbugger became synonymous with the "hepcat," a swing addict.[5] "Sing, Sing, Sing," however, was not a pat reproduction of the jitterbug. Cole had captured and distilled its energetic spirit. He codified its movement, disciplined its form, and tamed and readied it for the stage.

The post–World War II period saw a radical transformation in American jazz dance as the steady and danceable rhythms of 1930s swing gave way to the dissonant harmonics and frenzied rhythmic shifts of 1940s bebop. A postwar federal tax on dance floors closed down most big ballrooms, and the big swing bands that played them were eclipsed. The fading of swing bands instigated a virtual blackout of jazz dance in its traditional form of tap dancing on the popular stage. Many vaudeville houses converted into movie theaters. Popular tastes on Broadway turned from tap dance to ballet. And jazz musicians moved into small clubs, playing a new and virtually undanceable style of jazz called bebop.

Lindy Hoppers at the Savoy Ballroom by the late 1940s danced the jitterbug to the frenzied tempos of a bebop-inflected swing as well as other popular dances, including the mambo, rumba, and cha-cha-cha fueled by the Cuban migration into New York. To combat the near impossibility of dancing to the schizophrenic tempos of bop, Savoy dancers slowed their movements to half-time, absorbing into their undulating bodies the percussions that were formerly reserved for the feet.[6] Jazz tap dancer "Baby" Laurence Jackson matched the speed of bebop with taps that were explosions, machine-gun rattles, and jarring thumps and then moved these rhythms from the feet up, playing his body like a percussion instrument. On the concert stage (and quite apart from the jazz scene), the sinuous upper-body movements of Asadata Dafora, a native of Sierra Leone, soared free over the drum rhythms of the accompaniment and his rapid-beating feet. These dancers were the progenitors of a "modern" style of jazz dance in which rhythms, previously reserved for the feet, were absorbed and reshaped in the body.

"Sing, Sing, Sing" is an early example of this "modern" jazz dance. "I remember him [at the Rainbow Room]," Walter Terry said about Cole, "doing not only the oriental dances to jazz, but also Harlem dances, in brown chinos with bare feet and bare torso. He must have been the first to use Harlem rhythms that weren't done in terms of tap."[7]

Jack Cole—white, Catholic, and from New Brunswick, New Jersey—was a dance artist who was feared, misinterpreted, and often misunderstood.

Because he performed in nightclubs, his work was often dismissed as being merely commercial. Wrote John Martin: "In the type of dance he has created for nightclubs . . . he has no opportunity to concern himself with content and substance, but if he were really to turn his head to the creation of a ballet or serious repertory of the concert field, his almost fanatical concentration and creative power would probably result in some pretty staggering things."[8] Descriptions of Cole's dance style are nebulous. Margaret Lloyd's was that "Hindu-Swing is his own invention, stylized Boogie Woogie a specialty, and formalizations of Caribbean and South American rhythms his trademark."[9] Reconstructions of Cole's dances distort impressions of his style. From Deborah Jowitt thirty years later: "Cole strikes me as immensely aggressive; almost every gesture is delivered with maximum force."[10] Cole, furthermore, has been heralded as the "Father of Modern Jazz Dance." As Matt Mattox claims, "I learned his style of dance, which leaned toward modern as well as going in his own direction, and which I refer to as jazz dance—*real* jazz dance."[11] But that, too, was a title Cole would have abhorred and blatantly rejected. "The idea that some people have that I am in some way responsible for the 'modern jazz dance' movement of today is in itself a distortion," Cole wrote in an article in which he exploded on the subject of modern jazz dance.[12]

Titles notwithstanding, "Sing, Sing, Sing"—in its eclectic mix of American modern and African American social dance forms and classical East Indian dance technique and danced to the rhythms of swing in the tempos of bop—is illustrative of a postwar style of modern jazz dance that would be emulated by choreographers of the concert and musical stage, commercialized in the Hollywood musical film, and codified into a dance technique that would to this day be taught to jazz and musical theater dancers. I will explore the origins and influences of this style of modern jazz dance.

In 1934, one year after Prohibition came to an end, Cole left the concert world of modern dance for Manhattan's Embassy Club, a cabaret run by mobster Dutch Schultz. At twenty-one years old, he had already trained from the age of sixteen with Ruth St. Denis and Ted Shawn at Denishawn, danced with Ted Shawn's Male Dancers (1930–33), and performed with the Doris Humphrey-Charles Weidman dance group.[13] Cole's act at the Embassy with partner and former Denishawn dancer Alice Dudley borrowed the same formula of lush costumes and exotic renditions of dances from the Far East that had made Denishawn so appealing to popular audiences. Although some diners were annoyed by the sounds of bare feet slapping against the polished stage floor, Cole—determined to make "art dance" palatable to blasé supper-club habitués—stopped his audience from eating and drinking through the sheer intensity and variety of moods he evoked in each of his dances. "Appassionette" had violent and decadent jerking and posturing; "Dance for a Pack of Hungry Cannibals" "interpreted" oriental rhythms; "Japanese Lanterns," a solo for Cole, was inspired by Ted Shawn's "Japanese Spear Dance" (1919); and "Love Dance" offered interpretations of Bali.[14] Exotic to its core, Cole's club work won him critical acclaim.

By the late 1930s, Cole began an intensive study of "authentic" East Indian dance with the American-born dancer La Meri, who states, "From me he wanted the *adavus* of classical Bharata Natyam, and these I gave him."[15] Cole mastered the technique: the cobra head movements, undulating arms, subtle hip-shoulder isolations, precise mudra hand gestures, and darting eye actions. Then, without changing a beat or a line of the classical lexicon, he wove them into intricate routines and danced them to swing music (figure 13.1). *Swing Impressions of an East Indian Play Dance,* which Cole performed with partners Florence Lessing and Anna Austin, used the big-band swing arrangements of Larry Clinton and Raymond Scott. Hindu-swing? It seemed outrageous, but Cole was dead serious. According to Shirada Narghis, "Exponents of Natya generally refuse to depart from the original purity of altering the essential standards of performance. An exception is Jack Cole, who performs authentic Indian dance technique to swing tempos without losing the general dignity of the art."[16]

The strict discipline of Bharata Natyam technique enabled Cole to tilt, shift, and isolate the head, shoulders, ribs, and hips into dozens of small, sharp changes of direction. It was a powerful tool to rivet focus as well as to sexually titillate his audience. He commanded attention, not only through strong physical actions but also by doing nothing. Florence Lessing says, "We walked a bit, stood or sat, but we never lost eye contact. There was a very intense, personal thing going on that held the audience."[17] In 1939, Cole formed Ballet Intime with dancers Ernestine Day, Leticia Ide, Fe Alf, George Bockman, and Eleanor King as his ethnic tastes spread to the Caribbean and Latin America. "West Indian Impressions," danced to Cole Porter's "Begin the Beguine," threw the attention to Cole's slow-grinding hips doing his version of the Cuban rumba. And "Babalu," one of his so-called Latin impressions, borrowed the arched stance and rapid-tapping heels of flamenco dance.[18]

Cole's melting pot of "ethnic impressions" shifted from Spain and Cuba to Spanish Harlem, U.S.A., in 1942. "Wedding of a Solid Sender," performed at the Rainbow Room to Benny Goodman's "Yes, Indeed," characterized wartime zoot-suiters as young, urban, black, and Hispanic gangsters. The dance saw Cole strutting tough in a sharkskin suit with big shoulders and

Figure 13.1: Jack Cole in his "East Indian Dance" performed in a nightclub. Circa 1930. Photograph by Maurice Seymour. Courtesy of Ronald Seymour.

wide lapels, the whole of it vibrating with bold, vertical stripes. As the hero, Cole danced the role of the Solid Sender, a "Hep Cat of the First Water," who, not able to pass through the pearly gates of matrimony, is pronounced a "Square." Tap dancer Leticia Jay wrote that "Wedding of a Solid Sender" was "the first modern jazz dancing" she had ever seen: "It employed the principles of sharp dynamics and clarity of line characteristic of Bharata Natyam technique, without in any way suggesting East Indian type of dance."[19]

Although during this period Cole was reportedly concerned with "choreographic accounts of Negro life based on newspaper clippings and works of promised sociological import," it is more likely that his Harlem impressions, like "Reefer Man" and "Reefer Joint, 4:00 A.M.," came from his midnight jaunts to Harlem dance halls and nightspots.[20] As for the flashy splits and acrobatic knee slides that became Cole's movement signature, he quite possibly saw them performed by such class, flash, and acrobatic tap dance acts as the Nicholas Brothers and the Berry Brothers at the for-whites-only Cotton Club in the 1930s.

What is ironic about Cole's evolving style during the mid-1940s is that it was neither pure Harlem nor pure Hindu and fit into no easy category. Transcriptions of Harlem nightlife and social dances were not intended as veracious pictures but were instead used as springboards for his own creative output. John Martin said, "He is not of the ballet, yet the technique he has established is probably the strictest and the most spectacular. He is not an orthodox 'modern dancer,' for though his movement is extremely individual it employs objective material from the Orient, from the Caribbean, from Harlem."[21] The materials of Cole's jazz style can best be seen in the daily routine he subjected his dancers to in Hollywood during this period as resident director of the first permanent house ballet troupe at Columbia Pictures.[22] Working six hours a day, six days a week, the company began with Humphrey-Weidman–styled stretching and strengthening exercises on the floor and progressed to the drilling of routines in Cole's so-called Indian, Latin, and swing styles. La Meri taught Bharata Natyam technique, and a so-called jazz expert was brought in each afternoon to teach tap dance. When a major studio strike in 1946 brought film productions to a halt, canceling the renewal of dancers' contracts, Cole took his show on the road with many of his Columbia Pictures dancers, who included Florence Lessing, Rod Alexander, Carol Haney, Buzz Miller, and Gwen Verdon. "Jack Cole and His Dancers" opened at Chicago's Chez Paree in January 1947 with a program of four dances: two East Indian and two Afro-Cuban. It was in Chicago that

Cole began to work on a "swing dance" for himself and three men, using the Benny Goodman's big band's 1937 recording of "Sing, Sing, Sing."

The week Cole opened at the Latin Quarter in New York (the last week of March 1947), Ragini Devi presented a program of Hindu and Afro-Cuban dances at her Indian Dance Theatre; Leticia performed Hindu, Balinese, Siamese, Burmese, Javanese, and modern dances at the Barbizon Plaza Theatre; La Meri created a Hindu version of *Swan Lake* that was presented at the Ethnologic Dance Center; and Mura Dehn's show *Masters of Jazz* (which included Al Minns and Willie Posie) was seen in a program of traditional jazz dances ("Evolution of Lindy," "Shim Sham," and "Lonesome Blues"). One had only to go to the Latin Quarter for "The First Cafe Appearance of Jack Cole and His Company" to encounter translations of these ethnic dance forms in one show.

Cole opened with a suite of East Indian dances, performed by Florence Lessing and an ensemble of six to a jazz arrangement, and closed with a suite of Latin American dances to a Latin-swing arrangement. Sandwiched in between was the premiere of "Sing, Sing, Sing," "a dance of Jitterbug derivation" performed by Cole and an all-male trio to a small-band arrangement of the tune recorded in 1937 by the Benny Goodman big band.[23] The opening was electrifying: A flashy drum solo in the style of Gene Krupa introduced three male dancers, dressed in brown suits and porkpie hats, and the dapperly clad Cole as the star soloist.

There is a Labanotated score of "Sing, Sing, Sing" that was prepared by Billie Mahoney for the American Dance Machine's "Jack Cole: Interface Project."[24] The score for seven dancers is based on the recollections of Cole dancers Bob Hamilton, Buzz Miller, and Gwen Verdon, all of whom took part in the "Interface Project." Although the Labanotated score for "Sing, Sing, Sing" is not complete—Buzz Miller said, "No one could remember it all at the American Dance Machine, the score wasn't complete"—sections of the dance that were notated, along with an accompanying glossary, are extremely valuable in discerning Cole's evolving jazz style.[25]

The opening of the Labanotated score for "Sing, Sing, Sing" has the chorus of six (three women and three men) moving in unison with long-gliding jazz walks and riff walks. (A riff walk, from tap dance, is a step making four sounds on the toe-ball-heel, with a final accent on the ball of the foot.) Whether moving in single file along the diagonal or gliding past one another on their own horizontal paths, the lines are straight, the turns sharp, the curving spatial designs as precise as the inner workings of a clock. From glides to running slides, they suddenly "stop on a dime" to frame the entrance of the male soloist, who dances a stylized Lindy as the chorus keeps time by snapping fingers and slapping thighs.

One section of the score, annotated "Basie Vamp" (an obvious reference to Count Basie and His Orchestra, one of the leading swing big bands that played the Savoy Ballroom, "Home of the Lindy Hop"), begins with three male dancers moving downstage in a triangular unit, strutting and snapping, gliding and sliding, and altogether replicating, in sound and percussive gesture, the parts of the snare, tom-tom, and bass of a drum set. As the tempo accelerates, the men and soloist (this would have been Cole in the 1947 "Sing, Sing, Sing") make a group of four to form a square, strutting in slow motion around three female dancers. Riding over the measures of the music, the women make small and sharp isolations in staccato, accenting the steady four-beat with offbeat jerks of the head, ribs, and hips. Then all of them burst into jitterbug solos, moving from catch steps and snapped kicks in place to lateral gallops and weaving crossover steps, pivot turns, and slides across the floor. In the finale of "Sing, Sing, Sing," the group moves downstage in unison. With isolations reminiscent of East Indian technique, they fuse small, tight pulses and tilts of the head, shoulders, and chest with loose-legged shimmies and kicks, as arms circle in and out in figure-eight shapes. They create, in effect, a polyrhythmic drumming orchestra.

The layering, juxtaposition, and counterpoint in this last section of "Sing, Sing, Sing" invites comparison to Asadata Dafora in *African Dance Festival*, a concert presented at Carnegie Hall in 1943, about which Edwin Denby wrote: "Dafora only now and then called attention to his percussive foot beats. Though they were continuous, you watched the upper part of his body, the brilliantly rapid, darting, or sinuous arms, the strangely mobile shoulders, the slight shift of the torso. . . . The way he phrased the rhythmic patterns in these movements and so heightened the meaning of the dance resembles the way a blues singer phrases her song and heightens its meaning against the steady beat of the orchestra."[26]

As Dafora was concertizing traditional West African dance forms, so Cole was making art dances, using materials from the African American vernacular. Also like Dafora, whose dance rhythms soared freely over the drum rhythms of the accompaniment and over his own steady foot beats, Cole played intricate body rhythms over the steady propulsions of swing. There is another aspect of Cole's performance that resonates African, which Jerome Robbins articulates in describing the variants of Cole's style: "Packed into [Cole's] body were fierce discipline, controlled furies, exuberant sexiness, immaculate clarity, athletic ardor. . . . His movements, though rhythmically and kinetically complex, were exceptionally clear to the eye, spectacular whether gigantic or minuscule, tight without being restrictive, tense without being full of tension."[27] Put simply, the high degree of control in Cole's movement was aligned with a cool detachment in his performing style.

The use of the word *cool* in English is a basic reference to "moderation in coldness," extended metaphorically to include "composure under fire," and implies a state of calmness, especially in times of stress. The West African meaning of cool denotes the ability to be nonchalant at the right moment and places value on the ability to do difficult tasks with an air of ease and silent disdain. Dancers are admired for their cool, detached expressions when they dance. "Manifest within this philosophy of the 'cool,'" Robert Farris Thompson explains, "is the belief that the purer or cooler a person becomes, the more ancestral he becomes . . . mastery of self enables a person to transcend time and elude preoccupation . . . to concentrate upon truly important matters of social balance and aesthetic substance, creative matters full of motion and brilliance."[28]

John Martin recognized the high degree of control and cool detachment in Cole's performing style when he wrote that Cole was "not afraid of the floor, of falling or sliding on foot or knee or back. But for all his prodigious expenditure, he always has a smoldering reserve of energy." The Cole dancer was "a depersonalized being, an intense, kinetic entity rather than an individual."[29] This "mask of coolness," denoting a sense of purpose and self-control, concentration and transcendence, is the mask that Cole donned in performance. It was not a mask of cold detachment. For Cole, the essence of his jazz dance was the passion that was released through being totally engaged in the act of moving. Wrote Cole, "The ballet kids, with their dedication to and orientation toward linear designs, do the whole thing from the outside; they assume feeling. It [jazz dance] seems to require a less formal person . . . someone more concerned with individual expression."[30] From behind the mask of cool, the Cole dancer riveted every ounce of concentration on the preciseness of the movement, consumed in a state of technical preparedness that amounted almost to possession. With the dancer's face quieted, with concentration on the immaculate precision of a movement, the rhythms that were being subtly played in the body were brought into greater relief. Cole's dances, as Walter Terry observed, had "both the power and the ritualized quality of an incantational rite, apparent in many tribal dances of Africa."[31]

It can be argued that Cole's mask of cool also derived from East Indian sources as well as from his own immense powers of concentration, which had been sharpened from his intense study of world dance forms, many of them classical. But no matter from where in the world the raw materials of Cole's dance movement was absorbed, borrowed, or appropriated, "Sing, Sing, Sing" was a quintessential American jazz dance expression because of the way it was danced to jazz music (in Cole's words, "Jazz dance is anything that is danced to jazz music, so long as the movement corresponds in style"). Although "Sing, Sing, Sing" was a straight-ahead swing tune (its rhythm giving equal weight to the four beats of the bar, with a forward-moving propulsion imparted to each note through the manipulation of the timbre, attack, vibrato, and intonation), Cole's choreography was bop-inflected in terms of its attitude, dynamic, and movement style. He creatively played off the two rhythmic feels of swing and bop. Although swing was played in medium tempo, Cole (like bop musicians) both slowed down and sped up the beats in his phrases. Where choirs of instruments in the big swing band harmonized, bop musicians played in unison, as did Cole's dancers. Over the screeching and serene dynamics of swing, Cole's movement, like bop's melodic lines, was lightning-quick and compact. To the steady four-four rhythm of swing that chugged along like a steady locomotive, Cole contrasted with phrasings that allowed for more complex accents. He himself was not a bebop dancer; few were. The frenetic tempos of bebop made dancing to it too restrictive. But Cole had the temperament of a bebop musician. As Martin observed, "His art was strictly high-tension; nervous, gaunt, flagellant, yet with an opulent sensuous beauty that sets up a violent crosscurrent of conflict at its very source."[32] More important, the manner in which Cole's East Indian and Latin American movement rhythms were "played" over swing created a crosscurrent of rhythmic textures that was certainly bop in feel.

For Cole, bebop was an aesthetic: It was an attitude that expressed itself in Cole's habit of language and movement behavior. Cole's swing choreographies adapted a certain quality of "hip," as in hipster, the wise guy who knew what was under the surface of things. Hipness was a silent knowingness, and the hipster knew how the levers were pulled: He said nothing, however, but kept his cool; he eschewed anything that smacked of emotionalism. "The hipster was sophisticated, in the sense that his emotions appeared to be anaesthetized. His face was a mask and few things moved him."[33] Cole was well acquainted with the hipster, from his zoot-suited "hepcats" in "Wedding of a Solid Sender" to "Sing, Sing, Sing's" strutting street men in dapper suits and porkpie hats. In that dance, Cole himself played the quintessential hipster, looking strikingly similar to Marshall Stearns's description of the hipster as "the Jitterbug of the thirties in a Brooks Brother suit and a crew-cut."[34]

Cole's "Sing, Sing, Sing," then, descends from an unbroken line of African American vernacular dance, from the Strut (Cole's basic jazz walk), Grind, and Texas Tommy (forerunner of the Lindy Hop), to boogie-woogie, jitterbug, and jive. Still, "Sing, Sing, Sing" was not "pure" Harlem dance. Cole's choreography was informed by East Indian, Latin American, and Caribbean musical traditions and dance forms as well as by the modern American dance traditions of Denishawn and Humphrey-Weidman. I am not sure that Cole should be hailed the "Father of Modern Jazz Dance"—what a dubious distinction to father the mongrel hybrid of a dance that was postwar jazz. But Cole's extraordinary, although highly idiosyncratic, contribution to the jazz continuum is how he played the movement rhythms of Indian Bharata Natyam, Cuban rumba, and American jitterbug over and *against* jazz swing. Strutting in slow motion, sliding over the measure, pulsing in double and triple time, flick-kicking off the beat, and snapping out precision-timed isolations to the beat, Cole drummed the body. Dancing the jitterbug in a Brooks Brothers suit, his hair crew-cut, Cole's updated and cooled-down movement aesthetic distinguished "modern" jazz dance from anything that had come before it.

Notes

1. "Sing, Sing, Sing," written by Louis Prima and arranged by Jimmy Mundy, was recorded by Benny Goodman and his orchestra on July 6, 1937; the musicians included Goodman on clarinet and Gene Krupa on drums.

2. Glenn Loney, *Unsung Genius: The Passion of Dancer-Choreographer Jack Cole* (New York: Franklin Watts, 1984), 85.

3. Buzz Miller, telephone interview with the author, April 8, 1992.

4. John Martin, "This Week's Programs," *The New York Times,* April 6, 1947; Walter Terry, "The Dance," *New York Herald-Tribune,* October 26, 1947.

5. Joseph Mazo wrote that the "driving athleticism of the Lindy was an expression of self and of creativity for people who did not live on the same scale as F. Scott Fitzgerald's self-destructive heroes and heroines"; Joseph H. Mazo, "Jitterbug," *Dance Magazine,* May 1992, SC-20. Walter Terry suggested that Cole had somehow harnessed the frenzied jitterbug into a kind of jitterbug incantation: "Actions expand in pattern and dynamics, mirroring the generation of self-induced, hypnotic passion. Thus it resembles, while retaining American form, the Egyptian zakir and numerous other dances of personal ecstasy"; Terry, "The Dance."

6. In Mura Dehn's documentary film *The Spirit Moves,* Jeff Asquew and LeRoy Appins's dancing of "Bebop Time" at the Savoy Ballroom in the 1950s gives the clearest example of rhythms from jazz tap being absorbed up into the body; Mura Dehn, *The Spirit Moves,* ca. 1950, The Jerome Robbins Dance Division, The New York Public Library for the Performing Arts.

7. Glenn Loney, "The Legacy of Jack Cole: Rebel with a Cause," *Dance Magazine,* February 1983, 42.

8. John Martin, "The Dance, Jack Cole," in *Anthology of American Jazz Dance,* 2nd

ed., ed. Gus Giordano (Evanston, IL: Orion, 1978), 28; originally published in *The New York Times*, 1948.

9. Margaret Lloyd, "Swinging the Hindu Dance," *Christian Science Monitor*, February 13, 1943.

10. Deborah Jowitt, "Presenting Pizazz on a Platter," *The Village Voice*, September 13, 1976.

11. Matt Mattox, interview with the author, Paris, May 8, 1980.

12. Jack Cole, "It's Gone Silly," in *Anthology of American Jazz Dance*, 2nd ed., ed. Gus Giordano (Evanston, IL: Orion, 1978), 72–73; originally published in *Dance Magazine*, December 1963.

13. Concurrent with performing with the Humphrey-Weidman dance group (where he took classes and slept in the studio), Cole was studying classical ballet with Luigi Albertieri.

14. Descriptions of "Dance for a Pack of Hungry Cannibals" are so scanty, it is impossible to know which "oriental rhythms" Cole was attempting to interpret.

15. La Meri, "Encounters with Dance Immortals," *Arabesque*, January-February 1984, 18.

16. Shirada Narghis, "India's Dance in America," *Dance*, August 1945, 10.

17. Loney, *Unsung Genius*, 79.

18. During this time, Cole studied flamenco dance by day and frequented rumba clubs with Florence Lessing by night. Lessing says she first met Cole at Paco Cansino's Spanish dance class: "He was twirling a shiny red cape which looked flammable while smoking a cigarette"; William Daniel Grey, "A Conversation with Florence Lessing," *Dance Pages*, Spring 1990, 22.

19. Loney, *Unsung Genius*, 85.

20. Helen Dzhermolinska, "A Gallery of American Dancers," *Dance*, August 1942, 28.

21. Martin, "The Dance, Jack Cole," 28.

22. The group of dancers at Columbia were selected and trained by Cole and under studio contract to work on such films as *Cover Girl, Tonight and Every Night, Eadie Was a Lady,* and *Tars and Spars*.

23. According to Walter Terry's review of the Latin Quarter opening, "Sing, Sing, Sing" was performed by Cole and three male dancers, whereas John Martin reported that it was performed by an all-male quintet. The American Dance Machine's reconstruction of the dance had seven dancers, three women and four men. Buzz Miller says, "It was done originally just for boys. . . . [W]hen I joined the group in 1948, it was danced by boys and girls"; Walter Terry, "Dancing in the Supper Club: Jack Cole and His Dance Group," *New York Herald-Tribune*, March 30, 1947; John Martin, "This Week's Programs," *The New York Times*, April 6, 1947; Buzz Miller, telephone interview with the author, April 8, 1992.

24. In 1976, the American Dance Machine's "Jack Cole: Interface Project," under the direction of Lee Theodore, attempted to reconstruct Cole's choreography and technique by bringing together members of his company, including Bob Hamilton, Buzz Miller, Ethel Martin, Gwen Verdon, and Rod Alexander. From their recollections, Cole's "In a Persian Garden," "Macumba," and "Sing, Sing, Sing" were taught to a group of selected dancers. In addition, the reconstruction of these dances, plus a glossary of Cole's style, was committed to a Labanotated score and compiled by Billie Mahoney. The observations I make about Cole's choreographic style in "Sing, Sing, Sing" come from a reading of the score, registered with the Dance Notation Bureau.

25. Buzz Miller, telephone interview with the author, April 8, 1992.

26. Edwin Denby, "Asadata Dafora," *Dance Writings,* ed. Robert Cornfield and William Mackay (New York: Knopf, 1986), 183–86.

27. Jerome Robbins, "Knockout Numbers," *Vanity Fair,* December 1984, 115.

28. Robert Farris Thompson, "An Aesthetic of the Cool," *African Arts* 7, no. 9, (Fall 1983): 41.

29. Martin, "The Dance, Jack Cole," 281.

30. Cole, "It's Gone Silly," 73.

31. Terry, "The Dance."

32. Martin, "The Dance, Jack Cole," 281.

33. Marshall Stearns, *The Story of Jazz* (New York: Oxford University Press, 1956), 223.

34. Ibid., 159.

14

From Busby Berkeley to Madonna

Music Video and Popular Dance

Sherril Dodds

It is hardly surprising that the dancing body is a ubiquitous presence in pop music video. In both social and performance arenas, popular dance and music are inextricably linked. Dance frequently operates as a means to express musical mood and content. In public spaces, such as clubs, discos, dance halls, and bars that feature popular music, people gather to dance. In domestic settings, too, young people can respond to recorded music and dance in the privacy of their homes. Although this type of embodied expression to popular music can be spontaneous and improvised, it can also be highly structured and rehearsed, such as the instructional dances that accompanied early-twentieth-century ragtime music or novelty songs like "Macarena," which are marketed through a specific dance motif. In the presence of live music, the dance takes place both by the artists onstage, as an extension of their performance, and by audiences in response to the gig. Specific popular dances can also illustrate alliance to a particular music subgenre. Punks slam dance, metal fans headbang, and indie kids mosh. This close relationship between popular music and dance transcends to the screen, as well. One only has to think of popular television programs such as *American Bandstand* in the United States and *Top of the Pops* in the United Kingdom to conjure images of performers and audiences simultaneously engaged in dance.

The relationship between dance and music video is a similarly symbiotic one: Popular dance styles, both from vernacular and other screen traditions, serve as a visual illustration of the music; the music and visuals, meanwhile, inform and influence the dance practices of spectators who seek to embody the images that they see on screen. The dance component may be performed by on-screen audience members, professional backing dancers, or the singers and musicians of the band and can range from loose, improvised movement to tightly choreographed routines.[1] In this chapter, I set out to examine the way that music video appropriates and reconceives popular dance traditions for its own purposes. This is not a straightforward process of borrowing, however. The desire to sell images frequently results in the dance undergoing various transformations in order to suit the promotional requirements of the particular recording artists. Consequently, the dance may be distorted, simplified, glamorized, or loaded with meanings that may bear little relevance to its earlier form. It is clear that the creation of music television arose through a specific political economy, and in the following section I examine more closely the commercial intent of music video and its structural organization. I then follow this with a discussion of Fred Astaire and Busby Berkeley, important precursors to music video, and illustrate how the music videos of Michael Jackson, Madonna, and others contribute specifically to the idea of celebrity promotion.

The Rise of Music Video in the 1980s

Although there is considerable debate concerning the earliest example of music video, many scholars agree that particular socioeconomic conditions gave rise to a proliferation of music videos and the development of music television in the 1980s. Communications scholar Andrew Goodwin notes that popular music has always employed a range of media to promote itself; although records, cassettes, and CDs constitute the specific commodities produced by the music industry, popular music is reliant on other forms, such as television, posters, magazines, radio, and live performance to circulate meanings about itself.[2] Specific circumstances within the television and music industries, however, led to the music video explosion. The late 1970s marked a slump in music recording: Rock groups, which favored albums over singles as the primary source for selling music, were caught up in long promotional tours, resulting in lengthy breaks between albums and thus less opportunity to stimulate musical innovation.[3] It was the development of "new pop" in the early 1980s that prompted a seismic shift in music production and promotion. The "authentic musicianship" of the 1970s rock band was succeeded by new pop, a genre marked by a blurring of boundaries between human and technologically enhanced performance.[4] Because music could be created only in the studio (the bands were unable to play live), other performance opportunities became necessary. Music video offered an alternative form of promotion that produced a circuit for rapid innovation. Cultural theorist Will Straw details how videos were strategically employed to market specific singles, which partly explains the comeback of the top-forty hit parade in the 1980s.[5]

Pop music historian Simon Frith describes how music television developed out of the deregulation of broadcasting; the influx of cable and satellite television stations led to the creation of so-called narrowcast television with specialist channels aimed at niche markets.[6] He suggests that music television channels were quick to appeal to the youth market, which had largely remained uncatered to. MTV was launched in 1981, and due to its capacity to reach a global audience instantly, it prompted a desire for increased creative output as producers and consumers sought to keep up with new musical and visual innovations.[7]

The Function and Structure of Music Video: An Overview

The inception of music television initially resulted in a rapid increase in music sales as a slot on MTV stimulated a more immediate market response.[8] Music television stations needed to develop a dedicated audience, and this meant appealing to consumers who might not necessarily engage in live music performance but who would be content to watch music in the comfort of their homes.[9] Frith suggests that music television fundamentally operates as an advertising service in that it constructs a "community of consumption."[10] The music television audience is the "product" that appeals to advertisers, and although there has been a waning of youth interest in music television, this has been superseded by the development of a more affluent over-thirty audience.[11] It is therefore hardly surprising that music television charges a high premium for its advertising slots.

Music video is clearly a promotional tool and consequently seeps into the arena of advertising. Music video and advertising enjoy a reciprocal relationship in that they trade in shared visual ideas and techniques.[12] Marketing scholar Stephanie O'Donohoe conceptualizes this connection in terms of "leaky boundaries" to describe the way in which these popular forms merge and overlap.[13] Indeed cultural theorist Andrew Wernick proposes that the "intertext" of promotion has gone radically beyond the advertising media into all aspects of cultural life.[14] He states that promotion is a signifying system applicable to commercial and noncommercial phenomena and that cultural goods are situated in a vast network of consumer lifestyles. The appropriation of popular and social dance styles by music video, then, becomes a means to maximize audience interest and to construct a distinctive image for the recording artist.

The promotional capacity of music video is closely tied to its structural organization; therefore, any study of music video requires close attention both to musical and image analysis. Whereas some scholars argue for a postmodern reading of music video as it appears to present a random flow of eclectic images, others argue that this perspective fails to address the popular music context from which music video emerges.[15] Goodwin stresses that the images of music video are designed to illustrate the sound (rather than the reverse), and to avoid a purely visual bias he has conceptualized a "musicology of the image" as a methodological tool of analysis.[16]

According to Goodwin, music is made up of various components, such as tempo, rhythm, arrangement, harmonic development, acoustic space, and lyrics, which he then identifies in relation to the images of music video. He suggests that the arrangement of a song is dependent on the relationship between voice, rhythm, and backing, elements that may be carried through to the choice of images. For example, the voice can be foregrounded through close-ups of the singer's face, key rhythmic moments focused on through shots of the musicians, and the lyrical content depicted, either literally or metaphorically, through on-screen events.

The aim of music video is to create the impact of live performance on the small screen. Frith suggests that "movement" becomes a metaphor for sound, through such devices as fast cutting, swirling bodies, and visual excess.[17] Media theorist Carol Vernallis is equally insistent that any reading of music video should not be divorced from the codes and conventions of popular music. In contrast to analyses that promote the essentially narrative character of music video, she states that "videos follow the song's form, which tends to be cyclical and episodic rather than sequentially directed. More generally, videos mimic the concerns of pop music, which tend to be a consideration of a topic rather than an enactment of it."[18] For the purposes of analysis, it is possible to make links between the promotional function of music video and the organization of sound and image. I argue that the relationship between sound and image is never arbitrary and that the meanings invested in this interaction produce a set of ideas that are used to identify and brand the artist.

Pioneers of the Hollywood Musical

Before looking at some specific music videos, it is useful to examine screen-dance traditions that have informed the dance content of music video production. Two pioneers of the Hollywood musical approached the filmic representation of dance in distinct ways. The end of the silent era in 1928 marks the advent of the Hollywood musical; a proliferation of film musicals over the next two decades poured out of the major studios, such as MGM, RKO, and Warner Brothers.[19] These films, including *Dames* (1934), *Shall We Dance* (1937), *The Harvey Girls* (1942), and *An American in Paris* (1951)—performed by stars such as Fred Astaire, Ginger Rogers, Gene Kelly, Eleanor Powell, and Cyd Charisse—are notable for their spectacular song and dance routines.

Busby Berkeley was one particular innovator who choreographed specifically for the film medium. Berkeley's dance routines draw on a tradition of Broadway revue featuring grand stairways, revolving platforms, thrust walkways, and choruses of dancers that privilege visual experience over physical expression.[20] Berkeley is best known for choreographing complex geometric dance routines filmed in such a way so as to create abstract, mobile patterns.[21] He manipulated scores of female dancers in precise military motifs in which the movement content generally depended on a series of poses rather than any established dance techniques. In Berkeley's work, the camera is very much a participant in the dance. For instance, he often used tracking shots that moved along the lines of women and sometimes employed close-ups to show off each woman's face. His signature mark, however, was the so-called top shot. Berkeley regularly placed the camera overhead so that his circular designs could be viewed as elaborate, kaleidoscopic effects.[22]

Another key individual who exerted a considerable influence on the relationship between dance and film was famed dancer-choreographer Fred Astaire. Unlike Berkeley, Astaire came from a musical comedy stage tradition and worked with solos and duets rather than choruses.[23] Astaire drew on an eclectic movement vocabulary that included ballroom, tap, jazz, and, at times, a trace of ballet. Reputedly a perfectionist, Astaire developed some specific ideas on the way in which dance should be choreographed and filmed. According to film historian John Mueller, "[T]he idea was to put the [film] medium at the service of the dance."[24] Mueller describes how Astaire constructed full-length dance numbers, unlike some choreographers who would simply edit together a series of short phrases. The dance was of paramount importance to Astaire, and for this reason he insisted on full-body shots, the dancers being captured in a tight frame, and a limited number of cuts. As Mueller notes, he rarely employed special effects or "arty perspectives" and used "reaction shots" sparingly.[25] The result is that the dance is seen as clearly as possible without being distorted through the filmic apparatus (figure 14.1).

In various ways, the screen-dance concerns of these two pioneers share similar territory to the dance imagery of music video. Berkeley's manipulation of the filmic apparatus to create eye-catching and opulent screen-dance images ties in with music video's desire to attract audience attention through innovative and dazzling film techniques. In much the same way that Astaire used social dance to accompany popular song in Hollywood musicals, music video producers draw upon the latest dance crazes to promote pop music singles. As with Astaire's reputation as a showcase dancer, the record industry promotes specific music artists as star talents through their dance expertise.

Music Video: Showcase Dancers and the Hollywood Musical

Michael Jackson and Madonna, multimillionaire celebrities who have enjoyed long recording careers, have attracted both mainstream and scholarly interest.[26] Jackson, a designated "megastar," has been performing since childhood and his dancing prowess likened to that of James Brown. As cultural critic Kobena Mercer has noted, "[T]he emotional and erotic expressiveness of the voice is complemented by the sensual grace and sheer excitement of Jackson's style."[27] Madonna is similarly positioned as a multitalented superstar known equally as a singer, dancer, fashion icon, and actress.[28] Significantly, Jackson has been linked to Fred Astaire in that he is reputedly an admirer of Astaire, draws frequently upon the codes and conventions of the Hollywood musical tradition, and is admired for his awesome dance performance.[29] In the video for "Beat It" (1983), the establishing scenes depict two street gangs congregating for a fight along with shots of Jackson located alone in what appears to be a low-budget bed-sitter or motel room. As the gangs enter into battle, with the two leaders poised with knives, their movement is reminiscent of the choreographed fight scenes from the Jerome Robbins film musical West Side Story (1961). At this point, Jackson

Figure 14.1: Fred Astaire dances in the 1955 movie musical *Daddy Long Legs*. Circa 1955. © John Springer Collection/CORBIS.

enters into the frame and resolves the fight peacefully, leading a unison dance routine that uses sharp, street-dance moves that include Jackson's trademark spins, kicks, pelvic thrusts, and shoulder isolations. The notion of "beat it" is a clever pun that plays upon the combative idea of attack, the imperative instruction to "clear off," and the musical concept of counting rhythm. These ideas are then carried through into the events of the music video. For instance, the pace at which the gangs walk mirrors the meter of the music, and as Jackson sings, "It doesn't matter who's wrong or right," he pulls the two gang leaders apart. Thus the idea of "beat it" simultaneously refers to the fight, his pacifist message, and the music.

Dance historian Beth Genné makes the connection between the street-scene dances that Jackson has employed and the tradition of street numbers used in Hollywood musicals.[30] Unlike the safety of the home or the respectability of the workplace, the street carries with it a degree of the unknown with its potential for excitement and danger. Indeed, one fantasy of music video is played out as the star performer appears to be from the street and therefore possesses a concomitant urban savvy.[31] The idea of looking "at home" on the street offers the artist admiration and respect. So, too, within the Hollywood musical, the star persona and dancing ability of the lead performers is often played down so that they appear more accessible as individuals: Dance routines take place in everyday spaces, hence the ubiquity of street-scene numbers. The characters are not glamorized as professional performers but featured as everyday workers, such as soldiers, sailors, and farm hands.[32] Similarly, within "Beat It" Jackson is simultaneously promoted as an everyday guy, peacemaker, and star dancer, and his body becomes a receptacle for both audience identification and aspiration.

Jackson's music video "Thriller" (1983) also takes place on the "street," but this time it is styled as a "B-movie horror," and his performing self offers further ambiguity as he plays a 1950s teenage sweetheart, werewolf, "present day boyfriend," and zombie. Significantly, the economic function of selling records was somewhat redundant for this music video as Jackson's album *Thriller* (1982) had already achieved monumental commercial success; the video's primary purpose was to promote Jackson as a star.[33] The main dance section of the video occurs when Jackson appears to his "movie date" as one of the living dead. Again, he executes a carefully drilled routine of street dance, similar in movement content to that of "Beat It," while shadowed by a unison chorus of backing dancers, also dressed as zombies. It is at this point that the horror story is temporarily suspended to showcase his spectacular dance routine. As Kobena Mercer states, "[T]he dance breaks loose from the narrative and Michael's body comes alive in movement, a rave from the grave: the scene can thus be seen as a commentary on the notion that as star Jackson only 'comes alive' when he is on stage performing."[34] Vernallis furthers this idea in musical terms. She notes how the "live bass and guitar riff," as opposed to the earlier mechanical bass line played on keyboards, is more "warm-blooded" in sound and matched by the energy of the dance.[35] In both "Beat It" and "Thriller" Jackson's dancing body allows him to occupy multiple personas, which play into the ambiguity of Jackson as a celebrity.[36]

Madonna is similarly known for multiple changes of image. Philosophy scholar Douglas Kellner describes this as a strategy that perpetuates a consumer mentality: "[S]he encourages experimentation, change, and production of one's individual identity . . . which offers the possibility of a new commodity 'self' through consumption."[37] In the video of "Material Girl" (1985), the central dance sequence is a pastiche of the Marilyn Monroe musical number "Diamonds Are a Girl's Best Friend," from the Howard Hawks film *Gentleman Prefer Blondes* (1953). Dressed in a red evening gown and dripping in diamonds, Madonna toys with a group of male admirers in black tuxedos who fall at her feet, carry her around, present her with jewels, and lavish her with affection. The reference to Marilyn Monroe in "Material Girl" could be read as a means for Madonna to associate herself with the meanings that circulate around Monroe as a "screen goddess" and "cultural icon." Yet even if, as Goodwin suggests, many readers have no prior knowledge of the intertextual link to *Gentleman Prefer Blondes,* the opulence of her dancing body emits clear messages about Madonna's star status.[38] Although the "material girl" image is challenged within the video as Madonna is charmed by a film producer who offers her a bunch of crumpled flowers and collects her in an old pickup truck, Kellner argues that "the most attractive images in the musical production numbers do celebrate high and expensive fashion, diamonds, and other costly ornaments as keys to a successful image and identity."[39]

In the video for "Vogue" (1990), Madonna once again borrows from an existing dance tradition. Here she uses voguing, a vernacular dance form that developed in the gay dance clubs of New York by African and Latin American males. The video is shot in stark black-and-white frames, and Madonna is styled in an homage to Hollywood movie stars, a list of whom are recited in the lyrics. At the beginning of the video, Madonna and various backing dancers hold a series of positions as if from a fashion shoot while she commands, "Strike a pose." Later, she executes a more complex dance routine flanked, again, by a group of men in stylish suits. They perform a geometric sequence of movement, typical of voguing, in which limbs articulate from the spine through sharp lines and right angles. Further on, still, she dances a duet that incorporates elements of voguing with a more bouncy street-dance style of skipping on the spot and a fleeting Charlie Chaplin pose.

Significantly, there is no reference to the origins of voguing within this appropriative act, which dance scholar Jonathan Jackson describes as "the commodification and distortion of black vernacular dancing for mainstream white Euro-American consumption."[40] Indeed, Madonna continues to borrow from other cultural communities, as in her video "Hung Up" (2005), in which she incorporates krumping, a bewilderingly fast style of L.A. hiphop dance. The use of cutting-edge social dance styles is clearly a means to position herself as an innovator close to underground street culture, yet this neatly sidesteps the issue of cultural appropriation. As Kellner argues, on the one hand her use of African American popular dance and musical styles is a means to promote black artists and their traditions; on the other hand, as a wealthy white woman it conveys her position of power as she controls and takes center stage within the music and dance imagery.[41] Hence, the transition of popular dance styles from street to screen clearly takes on a political as well as aesthetic dimension.

In addition to Michael Jackson and Madonna, there are numerous recording artists whose music videos, in the tradition of Hollywood musicals, employ lavish musical numbers to promote their dancing ability and star status. Yet not all music videos that pay homage to a musical tradition necessarily feature recording artists who are showcase dancers. The video for Bjork's "It's Oh So Quiet" (1995) employs a big dance number, and although it is clearly a playful homage to the Hollywood musical and draws upon all kinds of Hollywood clichés, it is obvious that Bjork possesses no formal dance training. This nod toward the heritage of the Hollywood musicals of the 1930s and 1940s is perhaps not surprising given that "It's Oh So Quiet" is a cover version of the 1940s Betty Hutton song "Blow a Fuse." In the video, during the quiet and toned-down verses, which Bjork commences with a "shhh," the movement consists of simple walking or singing toward the camera. Notably, it is in the riotous choruses, in which both the volume and energy of her voice are audibly raised, that the dynamic and elaborate dance sequences occur. In her vivid orange dress, Bjork accompanies tap-dancing mechanics and then kicks over a pile of tires. A Busby Berkeley–style top shot focuses on well-dressed ladies twirling around with brightly colored umbrellas; Bjork somersaults up a wall (presumably via a body double) and dances with a mailbox that miraculously comes to life. Her raw and almost girlish style of movement is set in contrast to the slick expertise of the backing dancers; yet her lack of ability speaks more of her willingness to join in with this postmodern play on tradition than any kind of failings as a "star performer."

Indeed, there are even instances when the recording artists have little or no presence in the video clip itself, although the dance content still operates in a promotional way. The Bluetones's video for "After Hours" (2002), for instance, styles itself on the film musical *Bugsy Malone* (1976), which features children playing adult roles in a 1920s-style gangster story. The video uses a single Steadicam shot to focus on the children who sing and dance in place of the band. The camera follows the young boy singer, dressed in classic mobster pinstripes, as he interacts with a pianist and jives with a glamorous girl; a cleaner tap-dances, and the "gang" of children then execute a slick jazz Charleston sequence. It is only in the final few seconds of the song when the real band, also dressed as gangsters, actually appears and shoots white foam at the children with their "splurge guns." The video ends as Mark Morris, the lead singer, winks at the camera. Again, through the use of homage the band is placed in a playful and knowing position in relation to the original film. In another music video, "Let Forever Be" (1999) by the Chemical Brothers, a young woman is regularly multiplied into identical clones. This effect is achieved by a clever play between electronic image modification and in-camera tricks that employ complex set designs and multiple dancers. For instance, at one point the protagonist runs up an escalator. As she turns to face us, the camera moves into an overhead shot and, through digital means, the image is divided into triangles to produce a kaleidoscopic effect. The viewer is duped, however, as this electronic device is dissolved into a shot in which the image is a material reality: There are now six duplicate women, lying on six staircases, who suddenly get up and dance. Although the band features only briefly in crude disguise, the innovative allusions to Busby Berkeley both through digital and "material" means ties in with the band's musical image, which is based on "anonymous" electronic dance music.[42]

Music Video and Vernacular Dance

Although the music videos discussed so far make reference to popular screen and stage musicals, other music videos use everyday vernacular dance practices as a promotional strategy. Ricky Martin's "Livin' La Vida Loca" (1999) draws on the theme of Latin America both in the content of the song and the style of the music. Throughout the video, Martin's backing dancers perform a generic and rather stereotypical Latin American movement vocabulary of flicking heads, sharp turns, pelvic isolations, and fast footwork. Although some of the sequences take place on a dimly lit club dance floor with Martin singing on stage, others are situated on a street in the middle of a rainstorm as a group of female dancers strip off items of clothing and gyrate their bodies wildly. Hence, the dance content not only positions Martin as a key exponent of Latin-influenced pop, but it also associates him with the essentialist notion of a passionate and sexually charged Latin American body. In this instance, a selected dance genre is strategically used to link the artist and his music with a particular style and image. Thus, it is Latin American social dance that bridges the relationship between Martin and a "hot heterosexuality."

Another music video that purposefully employs a vernacular dance idiom to correspond with the music is Nirvana's "Smells Like Teen Spirit" (1991). In keeping with the band's grunge image, the video takes place in a musty old hall. The shots cut simply between a janitor cleaning the floor, the band executing an energetic performance of the song, an incongruous set of cheerleaders set just to the left of the band, and an audience of young people seated on raised seating who, as the song progresses, move into the performance area to dance to the music. The audience movement primarily consists of moshing, a dance style that mixes jostling, barging, jumping, and headbanging, which developed alongside 1990s indie rock. The charged and aggressive movement sits well with the power behind this thrusting rock anthem. The video is actually pedagogical in the sense that it demonstrates to viewers how so-called indie kids should behave. Again, there is a clear association between movement content and music style.

In Fatboy Slim's "Praise You" (1998), the video is shot in the style of a home movie depicting a group (operating under the name of Torrance Community Dance) performing in a shopping mall. The look is very amateurish due to the badly executed mix of hip-hop, disco, jazz, and modern dance. There are hints of a well-meaning Christian fellowship suggested through the title of the track, the nerdy clothes and hairstyles, and the team pep talk that has overtones of a prayer meeting. Whether they are indeed a genuine community dance group or just a well-observed fabrication by the director is unimportant. Although other artists resort to slick dance routines and glossy images, Fatboy Slim differentiates himself through embracing all that is uncool, thus positioning himself as cutting edge.

Clearly, music video employs a complex process of appropriation, transmission, and dissemination of popular dance practices from stage, street, and screen that are transmitted back and forth from local vernacular contexts through to the mass-mediated screen of the global television audience. Music video is a platform both for the dilution and innovation of popular dance forms. Although, on the one hand, it operates through a form of cultural theft as it feeds off existing popular dance traditions as a means to promote its artists and attract "commodity viewers," it also serves as a pedagogical tool that circulates and distributes dance styles that audiences are keen to adopt and develop. Thus, a sophisticated circuit of reinvention takes place. I do not want to overlook the ideological work of music video producers in their uncritical desire to borrow from other dancing communities to satisfy a primary consumerist urge. Yet it is important to recognize that audiences have a powerful degree of agency in deciding whether to choose any of the commodities offered, be it the music itself, the lifestyle of the artist, the dance style, or the body image on display. Music video is clearly an important site for creative investigation into dance; it has served as a wealth of choreographic innovation during its twenty-five-year existence. This is certainly an anniversary to be celebrated.

Notes

1. Theresa Buckland, "Dance and Music Video," in *Parallel Lines: Media Representations of Dance*, ed. Stephanie Jordan and Dave Allen (London: Arts Council of England, 1993), 53.

2. Andrew Goodwin, *Dancing in the Distraction Factory: Music Television and Popular Culture* (London: Routledge, 1993), 25–26.

3. Will Straw, "Popular Music and Postmodernism in the 1980s," in *Sound and Vision: The Music Video Reader*, ed. Simon Frith, Andrew Goodwin, and Lawrence Grossberg (London: Routledge, 1993), 7.

4. Goodwin, *Dancing in the Distraction Factory*, 32.

5. Straw, "Popular Music and Postmodernism in the 1980s," 8.

6. Simon Frith, *Music for Pleasure: Essays in the Sociology of Pop* (Cambridge. U.K.: Polity, 1988). 208.

7. Straw, "Popular Music and Postmodernism in the 1980s," 8.

8. Frith, *Music for Pleasure*, 210.

9. Goodwin, *Dancing in the Distraction Factory*, 40.

10. Frith, *Music for Pleasure*, 209.

11. Goodwin, *Dancing in the Distraction Factory*, 44; Frith, *Music for Pleasure*, 211.

12. Ann Kaplan, *Rocking Around the Clock: Music Television, Postmodernism and Consumer Culture* (London: Routledge, 1988), 12; Stephanie O'Donohoe, "Leaky Boundaries: Intertextuality and Young Adult Experiences of Advertising," in *Buy This Book: Studies in Advertising and Consumption*, ed. Mica Nava et al. (London: Routledge, 1997), 258.

13. O'Donohoe, "Leaky Boundaries," 257–58.

14. Andrew Wernick, *Promotional Culture: Advertising, Ideology and Symbolic Expression* (London: Sage, 1991), 95.

15. For critiques of postmodern readings of music video, see Goodwin, *Dancing in the Distraction Factory;* and Straw, "Popular Music and Postmodernism in the 1980s."

16. Goodwin, *Dancing in the Distraction Factory*, 49–71.

17. Frith, *Music for Pleasure*, 216.

18. Carol Vernallis, *Experiencing Music Video: Aesthetics and Cultural Context* (New York: Columbia University Press, 2004), 3.

19. James Monaco, *How to Read a Film: The Art, Technology, Language, History, and Theory of Film and Media* (Oxford: Oxford University Press, 1981), 208–9.

20. Jerome Delameter, *Dance in the Hollywood Musical* (Ann Arbor: University of Michigan Research Press, 1981), 27–48.

21. Monaco, *How to Read a Film*, 248.

22. Delameter, *Dance in the Hollywood Musical*, 32.

23. Ibid., 49.

24. John Mueller, "Watching an American Screen Original: Astaire-style Film," *Dance Magazine* 58, no. 5 (May 1984): 132.

25. Ibid.

26. See Goodwin, *Dancing in the Distraction Factory*; Kaplan, *Rocking around the Clock*; Douglas Kellner, *Media Culture* (London: Routledge, 1995); Kobena Mercer, "Monster Metaphors: Notes on Michael Jackson's *Thriller*," in *Sound and Vision: The Music Video Reader*, ed. Simon Frith, Andrew Goodwin, and Lawrence Grossberg (London: Routledge, 1993); and Carol Vernallis, *Experiencing Music Video: Aesthetics and Cultural Context* (New York: Columbia University Press, 2004).

27. Mercer, "Monster Metaphors," 93.

28. Kellner, *Media Culture*, 263.

29. See Beth Genné, "'Dancin' in the Street': Street Dancing on Film and Video from Fred Astaire to Michael Jackson," in *Rethinking Dance History: A Reader*, ed. Alexandra Carter (London: Routledge, 2004), 140; and Mercer, "Monster Metaphors," 104.

30. Genné, "'Dancin' in the Street,'" 140.

31. Goodwin, *Dancing in the Distraction Factory*, 116.

32. Jane Feuer, *The Hollywood Musical* (London: BFI, 1993), 1–22.

33. Mercer, "Monster Metaphors," 96.

34. Ibid., 104.

35. Vernallis, *Experiencing Music Video*, 167.

36. Mercer, "Monster Metaphors," 93–107.

37. Kellner, *Media Culture*, 263.

38. Goodwin, *Dancing in the Distraction Factory*, 22.

39. Kellner, *Media Culture*, 274.

40. Jonathan David Jackson, "Improvisation in African American Vernacular Dancing," *Dance Research Journal* 33, no. 2 (Winter 2001/2002): 42.

41. Kellner, *Media Culture*, 291.

42. I use the term *anonymous* in that the band does not promote itself through pinup imagery. Also, photographs of them are never used in official publicity.

15

The Dance Archaeology of Rennie Harris

Hip-Hop or Postmodern?

Halifu Osumare

Rennie Harris is a hip-hop concert choreographer. If this sounds like an oxymoron, then you have not seen his critically acclaimed dance works. Harris shatters the high art (read ballet and modern dance) and low art (read popular street dance) paradigm in a definitive style that challenges our notions of modernism in dance. "I like to manipulate time, where now, past, and future are at the same time."[1] And so Rennie Harris does in his exquisitely crafted dances that play with the time signature of movement: attempting to dance outside of time into eternity.

Harris has unintentionally contested the concert dance world in a fundamental way by establishing Rennie Harris Puremovement as the first American concert dance company to solely utilize the vibrancy, virtuosity, and showmanship of hip-hop dance as its launching pad, employing street dance to probe the human psyche as well as to make poignant personal, cultural, and even epochal statements. It is precisely the *informality* of street dance manipulated by a creative artist that can challenge the status quo of modern, ballet, and modern jazz dance as the only legitimate concert forms capable of compelling choreographic content. Harris explicates: "Urban dance is not formal. It's an experience. It's social. That's what allows it to denounce what tends to control."[2] Indeed, Harris has taken the experience of street dance, in all its unceremonious, improvisational, at-the-moment creation, and transformed it into poignant choreography that is on the cutting edge of today's dance and theater worlds.

At the foundation of Harris's aesthetic are his deep concerns with the human condition, his own spiritual development, and the state of the world. Using hip-hop dance to explore these age-old issues, Harris has become an archeologist of sorts, digging up relics of the past that have proved to be persistent, remaining just below the surface: racism, misogyny, classism, and neocolonialism. These extant bugaboos of humanity, exorcized through his oeuvre, are laid raw and bare through his adept use of hip-hop elements and contemporary theatrical devices. These vital concerns are made clear in the body (hip-hop dance), text (rapped verse and recorded narratives), sound (DJing, beat-box, and aural soundscapes), and visuals (video collages), all allowing the audience to deconstruct gripping social issues while probing their personal relationship to them. Rennie Harris's particular use of form and content is the reason I ask the question: Are his dance creations hip-hop or postmodern? I explore the complex answer to this question in this chapter.

Rennie Harris Puremovement (RHPM), founded in Philadelphia in 1992, is the brainchild and lifeblood of Lorenzo "Rennie" Harris. Beginning in his North Philadelphia community as a stepper—a precision style of rhythmic unison dancing made famous by African American fraternities and sororities—Harris is well versed in many styles of the black-Latino vernacular dance that fall under the large rubric we call hip-hop dance: popping, locking, electric boogie, house, and b-boying/b-girling (break dancing). From street stepping he graduated to the Scanner Boys as a b-boy in which his tags, or names, became Disco ("because I was always dancing") and PSK or Prince Scare Krow (because of his penchant for the popping and electric boogie styles of hip-hop dance) as well as the one that really stuck, Prince of the Ghetto. He was discovered by the larger world when the Smithsonian Institution's Folklife Center came mining for American folk culture in his Philadelphia community in the late 1970s.[3] At age fourteen, he began teaching hip-hop dance for the Smithsonian, which had recently discovered the new phenomenon of hip-hop culture around the same time the first rap tune, Sugar Hill Gang's "Rapper's Delight," was broadcast nationally. Harris was, therefore, one of the first hip-hop dancers to be legitimized by a preeminent U.S. cultural institution.

Once he was "discovered," his career skyrocketed. Having established himself as a precocious authority on street dancing in his teens, Harris went on to teach workshops at UCLA, Columbia College, and Bates College. He also has credits within the world of rap, having toured with famous old-school rappers like Run-DMC, the Fat Boys, and Kurtis Blow. He worked for a while in commercial music videos but quickly realized that he wanted more creative freedom to offer an alternative to hip-hop's commercial side. Today, he brings these dynamic styles to the concert stage in powerful statements that have mesmerized audiences throughout the world. Notably, he has won three Bessies (New York Dance Performance Award) for his choreography while simultaneously becoming a leading spokesman for the positive and creative aspects of hip-hop culture. As dance critic and scholar Sally R. Sommer recognizes, "Since Harris has survived into his forties he has taken the mantel of elder statesman, historian, teacher, and defender of Hip-hop's best values. Harris experienced guns and death, and he is tired of the Hip-hop that glorifies violence."[4] Harris has definitely earned the right to be hip-hop culture's moral conscious and to "represent," in the hip-hop sense, its regenerative and evolutionary side.

The Hip-Hop Dance Aesthetic

Harris's choreography conceptualizes hip-hop as a cultural extension of the Africanist dance continuum, from traditional West African dance through American tap and early jazz dance to the 1970s street corner b-boy competitions. B-boying/b-girling is embodied text just as rap music is oral poetry. Dance in hip-hop culture, as a part of the African diaspora, can be likened aesthetically to a Séné-Gambian village *bantaba* circle, where a griot, or oral historian, sings the genealogical lineage of the people along with symbolic gestures and often spontaneous dance by the people that serve to focus the expressive energy of the entire event. Today, Harris makes each of his dances collaborations between him and his dancers through their engagement with the improvisatory tradition. In his choreography, Harris celebrates this Africanist dance and cultural continuum through funky black American social dance, drill marching, choreographed unison electric boogie steps, and the all-important improvised b-boying.

Harris's choreography testifies to the eloquent articulation of both direct (text) and subtle (subtext) nuances through dance. Dance as narrative that indicates, identifies, imagines, and subverts in hip-hop culture was made lucid early on in hip-hop's development by Sally Banes's description of the potential of the freeze in b-boying: "Another important set of motifs in the freeze section was the exploration of body states in a subjunctive mode—things not as they are, but as they might be—comparing and contrasting youthful male vitality with its range of opposites: women, animals (dogs, horses, mules) babies, old age, injury, and illness . . . and death."[5]

Innovative freezes and the stop-on-a-dime syncopated breaks in the fast-paced rhythmic phrasing are a part of the masterful b-boy or b-girl's solo. In true Africanist style, movement dialogue of the soloist with the other dancers on the stage and the audience creates the community of the b-boy circle. This "conversation" is made audible through the shouts and taunts on stage, along with the audience's hand clapping and screams, all of which challenge each b-boy to surpass the last skilled bodily display. Each improvised rhythmic step and swift change of direction masterfully attempts to keep up with today's fast-paced MTV-BET pastiche lifestyle. Hip-hop dance mirrors the intricacies of our interwoven lives in urban America, reflecting the synergy and complexity of dancers of various ethnicities creating within this Africanist dance style.

Knowledge of the components of a skilled b-boy/b-girl solo is necessary to understand Harris's oeuvre. Following the entrance into the dance circle, four basic sections of b-boying are the tools of good improvisation: (1) top rock or uprock, standing feet work of rapid weight shifts: (2) six-step, fast feet and hand rhythms working together while crouched close to the floor; (3) power moves or improvised acrobatics containing a myriad of spins and flips; and (4) an ending "freeze" pose. The third section may contain traditional moves such as flares (spinning on the back with legs above the head), the turtle (rhythmic hopping on both hands while the rest of the body is suspended close to the floor), one-handed hand spins, or back flips and are interspersed with the second section, or six-step. The masterful combination of these two b-boy components renders more of a dance style as opposed to pure acrobatics, utilizing the subtle textures of the music. All b-boys or b-girls take their turn soloing, but the energy builds in just the right encoded manner, partially because each dancer knows the etiquette of just the moment to enter the circle when current dancer executes his or her final freeze. Because of its highly skilled, exhibitionist style, Harris has dubbed this branch of hip-hop dance the "ballet of hip-hop dance."[6] Harris has been able to transform a dance form meant as virtuosic spectacle into an often delicate and subtle, pared-down, concert-oriented movement vocabulary that explores the human condition.

In order to reproduce the spontaneity and in-group rules, Harris cannot always control these b-boy circles that he inserts into his choreography. Although he attempts to retain the structure and social process of good b-boy form, his choreographic works become a give and take between choreographic structure and the at-the-moment creation of the dancers. "Because it's on the stage, people think community does not exist. My dancers will change my choreography [to fit their needs at the moment], sometimes to the point that I don't even recognize it. We have actually had b-boys come up on stage from the audience and represent."[7]

In his form of dance, Harris must be ready for anything. The democracy of the b-boy circle demonstrates how individualism of dance style works with what Robert Farris Thompson calls the "looking smart" aesthetic to create the necessary communal social context.[8] In the end, it is the collective energy of the circle to which each individual has contributed that is evaluated as a successful performance. The socializing process promoted by this communal aesthetic becomes salutary for the traditional concert dance audience.

Hip-Hop Dance in Historical Context

Improvisational emphasis and the "looking smart" aesthetic are a part of a long history of black popular dancing that has permeated the Americas through the Atlantic slave trade. Because the Africanist aesthetic in dance and music has become so all pervasive, Harris has easy access to this historical dance continuum, as do American audience members who view his choreography. My earlier comparison between the Séné-Gambian *bantaba* and hip-hop dance circles is a far-reaching association across the globe that encompasses the history of an approach to the body, community sensibilities, and ultimately to life itself. Dance scholar Jacqui Malone explains, "Africans' strong attitudes toward music and dance—and the links between them—set the stage for the dance and music-making cultures to come in North and South America."[9] Malone further explains, "African-American dance serves some of the same purposes as traditional dances in Western and Central African cultures: On both continents black dance is a source of energy, joy, and inspiration; a spiritual antidote to oppression, and a way to lighten work, teach social values, and strengthen institutions."[10] Dance carries social values in all cultures, but the role of improvisation and the individualist style promoted by the embodying of group values in African-based dance is particularly instructive for the outsider audience member.

American popular dances of the twentieth century are rife with this Africanist dance aesthetic through the influence of African American culture.

The turn-of-the century cakewalk, even with its Europeanist mocking allusions, the 1920s Jazz Age Charleston with its relaxed torso and polyrhythms that freed the American body publicly, the 1930s Lindy Hop's frenetic and showmanlike quality that complemented the big band sound, all the way to the world dance craze of the 1950s twist that freed the European pelvic girdle, as well as the youth-oriented dances of the 1960s that led to the 1980s break dance craze are all a part of this historical dance continuum in which I situate the dance foundation of the choreography of Rennie Harris. American audiences that view his work are already socialized into this aesthetic as part of the American dance legacy.

Beyond American shores, black American social dance forms also influenced Europe. British dance scholar Belinda Quirey reflects on this aesthetic's influence in England: "The Americans soon put an end to any stodginess. We have never looked back since. From Jitterbug to Jive, from Jive to Rock 'n' Roll, from Rock 'n' Roll to the Twist, and from then on to the more recherché items of Afro-American culture it has all been one way traffic. . . . As far as body mechanics go, the important thing is the different use of the foot and of the pelvis. The latter change has been seen most obviously in the Twist, but it has been there from the start of the Jitterbugging."[11] This historical dance legacy came from Africa to the Americas, where African-diasporic dance cultures merged European partnering styles and African improvisational "apart dancing" to create vibrant fusion dance styles in the United States, the Caribbean, and South America that have all affected the rest of the world. Rennie Harris's adept use of the skilled b-boy solos in the African apart dancing tradition is exactly where his choreography merges with this dance history (figure 15.1).

I agree with Jonathan Jackson's appraisal of the place of improvisation in the African American dance repertoire: "The central principle on which my analysis is based is that in African-American vernacular dancing improvisation *is* choreography."[12] Rather than antecedent, improvisation, with its riffing, repeating, layering, and ritualization, according to Jackson, is choreographic creation in the moment that is predicated on the summoning of individual and collective energies in the act of dancing. What he calls dance "vamping" (so prevalent in music) or "jockeying" is the antecedent to choreographic inspiration that can lead to the inspired improvised solo. In hip-hop, uprocking or top rocking is the vamp that precedes the six-step and power moves of the b-girl. Vamping establishes the "groove, or a sense of repetitive on-goingness."[13] As Jackson explains, the groove is the communal beat that contains the collective rhythm from which inspired impro-

Figure 15.1: Rennie Harris in "Scarecrow" (1998). Photo by Bob Emmott.

vised choreography will emerge. Harris's adroit use of his dancers' skilled improvised bodily texts is a great part of what makes his choreography so compelling and appealing. As I will explore, Harris is well aware not only of improvisation as choreography but also of the African dance continuum from which it comes.

Early Repertoire Sets the Stage

Within this aesthetic context, one of Harris's earlier works, "Students of the Asphalt Jungle" (1995), made his artistic statement and established Rennie Harris Puremovement as a new kind of concert dance company based on the power of street dancing. Making the Africanist cultural continuum clear, Harris incorporates specific West African dance movements into his choreography, which to the novice viewer could be mistaken for hip-hop dance. For example, in "Students of the Asphalt Jungle" he uses movements from *Ekonkon,* a celebration dance of the Djoba people of the Casamance region of Senegal. This quoting of specific West African dance is situated within basic dance torso isolations as well as popping, locking, and funk movements that create a rich intracultural text of dance. Then, suddenly halfway through the precise choreographic patterns of audience-facing dance lines, diagonals, and cannons, one by one the six male dancers, bare chest and dressed in white pants and sneakers, come down stage center to "throw down" in nuanced polyrhythmic movement statements that not only demonstrate skilled athletic solos but also subvert our high art notion that they do not have anything to actually "say." Here rhythmic virtuosity is celebrated as dialogic process between self and body, dancer and community, soloist and audience. This, in other words, is a kind of contemporary *African* American dance, developed over five hundred years in the black Atlantic.

Yet even in this celebration of the New Age African dance circle and the continuation of Africanist movement styles, Harris makes an explicit *political* statement. The opening soundscape is of Rev. Martin Luther King Jr.'s voice expounding on justice and freedom. In using this recorded speech at the beginning of the dance, Harris illuminates the sociopolitical context of this male bravado dance ritual, and thus he cojoins his aesthetic with its social context. The last syllables of King's resounding words are technically slowed to allow a seamless segue into the beginning musical rhythms, reminding us that ubiquitous celebratory R & B, soul, funk, and blues, produced in working-class black communities, were created in spite of social containment and personal pain. As the title alludes, Harris positions "Students of the Asphalt Jungle" in a *specific* place: urban America with all of its seething, shifting, overlapping of race and class. The U.S. asphalt jungle is his "dance studio," a kind of training ground for these male dance "students" using the streets to prove their triumphant manhood, despite the mean situations in which they often dodge the police and each other.

Yet, it is "Endangered Species," his 1994 tour-de-force solo that set the direction of Harris's use of hip-hop as a concert form. "I'm not interested in entertaining anymore. I have personal issues to deal with, and I have to deal with how they affect me."[14] The centrality of Harris's personal issues, as an impetus for his choreography, became apparent within two years after he began Puremovement. "Endangered Species" became his first attempt at inserting his personal life as a black male growing up in a Philadelphia ghetto into his developing artistic corpus. A sole black male figure, danced by Harris himself, enters a smoke-filled center stage spotlight, using a slow mime-electric boogie run that turns in the four sacred directions. It is as if he is both blessing the stage for the story that is about to be told and running for his life, in slow motion, at the same time. He wears black pants and a long-sleeved sweatshirt, sporting dread locks that drape his anguished face. The entire effect transports one out of time.

The solo male figure is every (black) man, but he has a particular family story to tell. Again, the textual soundscape becomes crucial to this solo work and carries the spoken statement that Harris wishes to make in "Endangered Species": "Two of my brothers are hustlers, aka gangsters," the prerecorded text of Harris's voice begins.[15] The soundtrack breaks his story down for us, including the violence against his lesbian sister by one of his brothers. "Maybe he thought he could beat it out of her." Harris reveals the violence from which he comes, from which many us emerge onto life's stage. "It sounds crazy, but maybe we're all guilty. . . . I didn't have a choice. I had to adapt. . . . My identity was lost. It was taken from me. As a kid I wanted to be white. I guess that was because of that European concept." As the sound text positions this black everyman into a specific story—a particular family in a particular urban ghetto—ambiguity, fear, and despair ripples through his body with the hip-hop dance techniques of the "snake" and "ticking," allowing us to literally see his anguish in the adeptly executed isolations of his muscles.

Scholars and social critics such as Cornel West have articulated black male angst within the realities of urban ghetto life. In delineating the taxonomy of sociological explanations of urban problems of unemployment, poor housing, unequal education, gang violence, and the like, West examines the *personal* in relation to these sociological indexes: "[P]eople, especially degraded and oppressed people, are hungry for identity, meaning, and self-worth."[16] This is exactly what the recorded text of Harris's "Endangered Species" alludes: "My identity was lost. It was taken from me." The soundtrack continues: "If I'm for my race, does that make me a racist? I don't hate anyone, so I guess I'm not a racist. Racism! That's a funny word. Yet that is what America was built on."

Racism and its insidious effects is what he is trying to exorcize through the use of his body and soul. West gives us further reflection on the complexity surrounding the victimization process in black urban ghettos: "Although black people have never been simply victims, wallowing in self-pity and begging for white giveaways, they have been—and are—victimized. Therefore, to call on black people to be agents makes sense only if we also examine the dynamics of this victimization against which their agency will, in part, be exercised. What is particularly naïve and peculiarly vicious about the conservative behavioral outlook is that it tends to deny the lingering effect of black history—a history inseparable from though not reducible to victimization."[17] Harris allows us an up close and personal view of one black male victim in this history, and this dance work is his exercising personal agency against it through dance. In "Endangered Species," form and content are poignantly made inseparable as Rennie Harris's dance aesthetic.

Harris has been able to step outside of insidious U.S. racism, with dance as his vehicle of vision and personal salvation. In "Endangered Species," he stands, he crouches, he kneels, and he lies down in desolation. He cries out in pain of it all. Each robotic pop that he does technically appears as a fractured image of a man, as if he feels every lash of the slave master's whip, every continued overt and covert racist act against his people. But it goes far deeper than that. As he writhes on the floor, he cries out: "Ma, help me, help me!" He bridges the pain of the historical, social, and personal, all in one heartfelt cry.

Harris's Postmodern Dance

Given the particular symbiosis of Harris's form and content, an examination of postmodernism in dance and his hip-hop aesthetic is in order. Contemporary postmodernism is a general challenging affront to previous sacrosanct modernist paradigms of conceptual representations of reality. Yet postmodernism means different things in different disciplines.[18] In dance, as in other performing arts, postmodernism has meant a redefining of previous conceptions of form, with a different emphasis on the body, while critiquing perceived clichéd modernist conventions. Sally Banes's *Terpsichore in Sneakers: Post-Modern Dance* (1977, 1987) first laid out the dance landscape, starting in the 1960s, that developed out of the classic modern dance era. She delineates a typology of a postmodernist movement in dance over the second half of the twentieth century that included the use of gravity (crucial to hip-hop dance), dissonance, and a horizontality of the body, as opposed to the verticality of classical ballet and what became defined as classical modern dance. Underpinning this "new" physicality was a simultaneous interest in both primitivist and other disciplines' modernist approaches and an engaging of the stridency of modern life in the twentieth century.[19] "The body itself became the subject of the dance, rather than serving as an instrument for expressive metaphors."[20]

Replacing the sacrosanct establishment of modern dance became the raison d'être of dance postmodernism. Banes discusses choreographers who challenged the era of Martha Graham, Doris Humphrey, José Limón, Katherine Dunham, and Alvin Ailey with the postmodern choreographers of the 1960s and 1970s: Judson Dance Theatre artists, such as Yvonne Rainer, Simone Forti, Steve Paxton, Trisha Brown, David Gordon, and others who began to explore what she considered true modernism. Some postmodernists did eventually return to narrative content in the 1980s—the period she calls the "re-birth of content"—such as Lucinda Childs, Laura Dean, and Karole Armitage. Banes also established a general rubric of "new" approaches to dance that bind these sequential but overlapping camps: pastiche (radical juxtaposition), emphasis on irony, playfulness, historical references, the use of vernacular materials, and process over product, breakdowns of boundaries between art and life, and between artists and audiences.[21] Banes goes on to elucidate the use of narrative text and the language of gesture that also emerged in the postmodern era of the1980s. "One method of installing meaning in dance, the most nonverbal of the arts, is in fact to appropriate language and language-like systems. . . . Not surprisingly, the interest in verbal language has been accompanied by a rekindling of interest in narrative structures. . . . [T]he narrative, whose death seemed a certainty in the sixties and seventies, has been reborn in the eighties."[22]

Given this typology of postmodern dance characteristics, Rennie Harris's aesthetic becomes quintessentially postmodern at the turn of the twenty-first century. Although Harris may not have been aware of the convolutions of the shifting postmodern concert dance scene, his natural instincts as a creative artist, coming of age in the hip-hop era, fit naturally into these explorations. In "Endangered Species," he engages hip-hop gestures, such as both arms extended to the side with a tilt of the head that has come to mean a challenge ("You want a piece of this?"). He introduces this gesture in the section of the soundtrack that alludes to guns. It becomes indicative of the gestural, languagelike features of the postmodern aesthetic in dance. His use of recorded text as an ongoing narrative, often instead of music, is another device introduced into concert dance during the postmodern era of the 1980s. Harris is intent on telling stories of the ghetto, but *how* he does it corresponds to the concert dance era into which he inserted his hip-hop aesthetic.

Yet dance scholar Brenda Dixon Gottschild situated the entire postmodern aesthetic within a ubiquitous Africanist aesthetic in American culture: "So much of what we see as avant-garde in the postmodern era is informed by recycled Africanist principles and parallels traditional, characteristic Africanisms that we all grew up with as Americans, black, white, and brown. . . . The coolness, relaxation, looseness, and a laid-back energy; the radical juxtaposition of ostensibly contrary elements; the irony and double entendre of verbal and physical gesture; the dialogic relationship between performer and audience—all are integral elements in Africanist arts and lifestyle that are woven into the fabric of our society."[23]

Rennie Harris's entire approach draws from this rich range of the Africanist aesthetic. Harris explains, "From the ring shout to the cakewalk to the camel walk (one of the early hip-hop dances) to the moonwalk. This is the black dance legacy."[24] Viewed from Gottschild's revisionist perspective, Harris does not, in fact, borrow from a postmodern concert-dance aesthetic developed by white dance artists. Instead, it is the evolving field of contemporary concert dance that consciously and unconsciously borrowed from the pervasive Africanist aesthetic within which Harris was already socialized. Gottschild further elucidates: "Irony, paradox, and double entendre, rather than the classical European, linear logic of cause, effect, and resolution are basic to the Africanist aesthetic and offer a model for postmodernism subconsciously and at times, deliberately. It is probable that Dunn, Rainer, and others were not aware that in traditional Yoruban performance modes, the categories of play, ritual, and spectacle are fluid, multidimensional, multicentered concepts that put to shame the Europeanist idea that Africanist ritual is rigid and static."[25]

Postmodern dance and the Africanist aesthetic are therefore inseparable. Given the fact that hip-hop jams were starting in New York during the 1970s, at the height of the Judson Dance Theatre movement, spanning contact improv "jams" that borrowed from the freestyling of the b-boy circle and earlier forms such as the jazz jam sessions, the "parallel processes" and the lack of "coincidence," to which Gottschild refers, are made salient in Harris's work. American artistic production would not be what it has become without the all-pervasive Africanist aesthetic. Hence, my discussion of Harris's work within a postmodern dance context is from this understanding of his centrality to one of its antecedents and mainstream culture's partial appropriation of an aesthetic that was second nature to his sense of physicality, aesthetic principles, and overall approach to performance.

Rome & Jewels: *One Foot in the Streets and One Foot in the Universe*

Radical juxtaposition of Harris's developing aesthetic was clearly established with the summer 2000 premiere of his first evening-length, critically acclaimed, dance-theater work, *Rome & Jewels*. Harris says about himself: "I have one foot in the streets, and one foot in the universe."[26] The production toured for two years internationally, and *Rome & Jewels* brought his two feet together in a dynamic reenvisioning of Shakespeare's classic *Romeo and Juliet*, a tale of young love, an interfamily feud, and premature death. The Philadelphia press assessed, "Harris and his local hip-hop troupe Puremovement have launched a remarkable project, not always easy to understand but accumulating force and power from its fusion of Shakespeare and African American cultural forms. Both street kids and scholars will find themselves laughing at familiar codes."[27] By the time *Rome & Jewels* made its New York premiere that fall at the prestigious Joyce Theater, the critics had boned up on hip-hop culture and were ready for Harris's innovative new dance-theater challenge. *The New York Times* highlighted Harris's adroit juxtaposition of various hip-hop dance styles to represent the rivaling gangs: "These battles are portrayed through competing hip-hop dance styles, with the Caps as 'b-boyers' and the Monster Q's as hip-hoppers (popping and electric boogie boys). . . . In Mr. Harris's schema, these competing dance styles function as both identifying gang colors and as weapons of gang warfare." The critic goes on to reinforce my earlier point about his use of staged improvisation: "But even while their dancing declares their allegiance to their gangs, the members are most respected for their ability to improvise—to assert themselves as individuals—within these dance forms."[28] Through his creative genius, what was considered low art is now revolutionizing how we even conceive concert dance and theater, and in the process he blurs the lines between lowbrow and highbrow, a dichotomy about which the United States has always been ambivalent.[29]

Harris, therefore, was armed with aesthetic "permission" to experiment with one of the most famous stories in Western theater. From the obvious influential theatrical antecedents like *West Side Story* (1957) and Baz Luhrman's film *Romeo + Juliet* (1996), he was fortified to privilege his own background as context to make his unique statement about this continuing human theme. In fact, the issues of the hip-hop generation are perfectly suited for Shakespeare's vision of love and hate in the drama of societal antagonisms. The mid-1990s so-called West Coast–East Coast rap wars, which some say resulted in the deaths of Tupac Shakur and Christopher "Biggie" Smalls, are proof of the ripe fodder hip-hop culture provides for the tensions in the plot. Harris needed to look no further than his North Philadelphia origins for inspiration. Harris reflected to an audience before an Ann Arbor, Michigan, performance of *Rome & Jewels* in 2002, "This piece made me realize I had issues. In working through them in *Rome & Jewels,* I knew I was doing something right."[30]

Harris truly makes us question our sense of what is high culture with his use of the battling styles of hip-hop dance, the poetics of rap, and the radical juxtapositions of sound that have always been at the center of hip-hop sampling and DJing since Afrika Bambaataa's electrofunk sound in the culture's early days in the Bronx. He sees rap as having iambic pentameter, just as Shakespeare's poetic form. Harris also views Shakespeare as violent and scandalous as some hip-hop cultural forms are today: "What makes them so great together is that they're one and the same. There's nothing different. Some people will ask me if their kids can come to the show: Is it vulgar, is it violent? Shakespeare was vulgar and violent."[31] He goes on to elucidate more about the cutting-edge nature of rap and its connections to classic Shakespearean text in a *St. Louis Dispatch* interview: "Rappers are juxtaposing all kinds of mad [crazy] stuff coming out of everywhere. Shakespeare did that. I made all these small connections when I was preparing to do the work, familiarizing myself with it to take the edge off of being nervous about messing with the world treasures, so to speak. Once I made those connections, I was inspired."[32]

Human beings continually configure ourselves around some form of difference and otherness. Yet creative geniuses like Harris deconstruct difference to lay bare human commonalties. Creating *Rome & Jewels* ultimately becomes a catharsis for him, allowing Harris to coordinate his two feet, one in the streets and one in the universe, theatrically pointing him in the direction of his next major evening-length work.

Facing Mekka: *Confronting the Self*

Facing Mekka, Harris's next mammoth undertaking, premiered at Lafayette College in fall 2003. The company describes the work as being exploratory of human commonalities that are often reflected in the dance and music of various cultures. In today's global-cosmopolitan era, contemporary choreographers are engulfed in a fusion of cultures and styles that reflect the United States as a center of world culture. Rennie Harris's *Facing Mekka* is a deep exploration of this cultural fusion through the human body and spirit via the African diaspora. *Facing Mekka* is unlike any of Harris's other works because he attempts to show global connections, a concept underpinning his work with Shakespeare's poetry. Musically, this newer Herculean work is a vivid aural cacophony of DJing, a recorded soundtrack, and East Indian tabla. The multiple-image video collage made by Tobin Rothlein serves as a visual bricolage of world cultures and events, from brutal images of the Civil Rights movement and World War II to scenes of Islamic pilgrimages to the holy city of Mecca.

Again, in this work, form is based in hip-hop dance; however, b-boying, popping, and the robot are broken down even further to their essential movement phrasings and contrasted with traditional African dance and a Japanese Butoh aesthetic. The internal muscular work of Butoh connects with the skillful muscular isolations of popping, becoming a point of exploration to reveal deep cross-cultural connections through the body. As Suzanne Carbonneau notes, "[F]or Harris, extending hip-hop means expanding the possibilities for the form to achieve meaning, depth, and significance, rather than to simply increase its physical thrills and acrobatics."[33] In *Facing Mekka,* one views the minute changes in movement from a West African stomp or jump with a graceful throw of the arm, to a sensual Caribbean hip movement, to a familiar power move of a b-boy, to the slow, meditative gestures of his female dancers, all in the service of probing the potential of the human spirit.

Facing Mekka is essentially structured in an overture and nine sections, within two distinct parts. Three elements bind the piece into a coherent whole: Harris himself, as a sagelike elder who inserts himself periodically within the multicultural musings of the dance, a rectangular white mat area center stage that serves as focal performing point for soloists and small groups, and the live musicians (DJ turntablist, African drummer, Indian tabla player, cello, and singers) always visible on stage right. Part one is like a community ritual of cleansing that tries to exorcise that which ails us as a planet. Harris's elder figure briefly appears on the center mat crouched over in a dim light, seeming to be emerging from something, but can hardly stand upright. As he finally stands and begins to reach upward, the lights fade. A man appears, dressed in an African caftan, singing/praying like a West African griot who chants the ancestral lineage or an Islamic muezzin who calls the faithful to prayer from the minaret of the mosque. This figure calls to the spirit in us all through slow, pleading, melodic phrasings in a non-English language, as the dancers of the ensemble appear behind him, standing stoically and looking straight ahead. This overture ends as the praise singer fades behind them and as the dancers begin to move in a fierce rhythmic manner. The piece is now in full force.

In the first section, the community, equally charged by women and men, begins the cleansing ritual necessary for transformation. Here, the women and men perform an Afro-jazz, African dance. The rhythm-heavy musical ensemble, led by the *djembe* drums, sometimes in unison, provides the driving and sometime droning center for the energy-charged dancing, interspersed with Egyptian angular motifs. This opening dance makes clear the continuities between West African and African American dance styles as having the same root. During this fast and furious rhythmic section, a female dancer carrying a white handkerchief appears, waving it at the floor and throughout the general space. She is the ritual cleanser, ridding the community and this sacred and theatrical space of all negativity. Harris's sage figure enters, executing his crouched-over, scarecrowlike popping style, and then quickly exits, leaving the dancers moving to a slower African-based rhythm that eventually embraces Cuban songs that call orisha (Yoruba) deities inherited from Nigeria. This new dimension of spiritual invocation with Caribbean influences, which revise African religions, leaves two men center stage on the white mat. Their sequence contains slow b-boy movements that are low to the ground and appears to leave them struggling. They are trying to heal themselves.

The next four sections demonstrate Harris's use of hip-hop dance as a part of his arsenal to achieve meaning, depth, and significance. Although some male dancers deconstruct b-boy moves into their simplest components through slow-motion technique, others are often moving at the expected virtuosic full speed of hip-hop power moves. Again, the sage (Harris) enters briefly with his hunched-over, spastic, popping movements and quickly exists. During this section, dancers take the six-step into various time signatures, all the while dancing to a droning melodic singer who again pleads for spiritual redemption within a subdued lighting that puts the audience in another time zone. As the women enter with b-girl slow-motion acrobatics, they introduce Butoh-like movements on the central white mat. The sensual arms, hip, and mimelike walks are executed to a soft flute, in contrast to the previous, more intense section with the singer. It is here that Harris introduces beat-boxing, another hip-hop element, through the verbal dexterity of the original male African singer, and at the same time the women move out of abstract movement and into recognizable b-girl moves. As the dancers fade away, they leave the singer, who takes center stage with his beat-boxing, accompanied by the scratch beats of the DJ, segueing back into his Arabic prayer that ends the first part. The cleansing and community ritual is now complete.

Part two opens with a solo female dancer whose painted face is reminiscent of African initiates undergoing a spiritual rite of passage. She is a kind of New Age initiate of the future. She is crouched down on the floor struggling to arise. With slow-motion b-girl moves and abstract movement, she reflects the pain of growth. She never fully stands throughout the whole piece but hangs over after standing, with her hands scraping the ground as she moves. When she is joined by other female dancers, a unison motif privileges a hunched-over aesthetic that is simian-like in its effect. Finally, the original dancer stands upright and reaches upward while the chorus moves in the background with a popping style laced with Egyptian-like poses. After the male dancers join the females, the full community is constituted again as the deconstruction of b-boying moves continues with a sense of going in and out of real time. Musically, the tabla becomes prominent, and as the dancers fade into the background, what Harris's musicians do musically underpins and echoes the multicultural amalgam of the dance. A long tabla solo blends into the other instruments as they enter the intense rhythmic soundscape; the night I was present, the experience was transcendent.

The second half of *Facing Mekka* is considerably different in mood and furthers Harris's intent of confronting the self both individually and collectively. After the cleansing communal ritual of the first half, the latter part of the work is an intense probing of the possibilities of healing ourselves from both personal and collective global obstacles. The individual and the social are conflated in an obvious layering of meaning through movement choices, music, and the stunning visual-paneled backdrop that projects epoch scenes of world events, placing us in various time periods and cultures. In the concluding scene, all of the dancers onstage exit by walking slowly backward off stage left, leaving the elder sage alone, still crouched over. He begins his spastic, popping, jerky movements again, but slowly they become more articulate and coherent, and as he moves to the center white mat we see the human possibility of all of this personal, cultural, and global exploration—a full-blown man that is everyman. He has been there all the time, and the community had to move through the cleansing, healing, and personal probing in order for this every human to be born. The dimensions that *Facing*

Mekka encompasses as a process of confronting the self is rife with traditional African religion, Eastern meditations, as well as Islamic allusions through the focal, unifying point of the Kaaba of Mecca's Great Mosque, to which Muslims face no matter where they are in world. This is Harris facing Mecca, facing himself for world salvation.

In our hip-hop-rock-reggae-garage-new wave times, Harris explores what binds us as human beings in a post-9/11 world that sorely needs to understand and move to that which unites rather than divides. And if the music, rhythms, and movements that fused and permeated the world through the cultures that emerged from the transatlantic slave trade could possibly lead us to a more united space, what more appropriate movement form than hip-hop. Hip-hop's street vernacular, as it evolved from the Africanist aesthetic continuum, becomes a launching pad into this exploration of global humanity that is *Facing Mekka*. Harris's ending solo as sagelike elder, who has inserted himself periodically within the multicultural musings of the dance, is called "Lorenzo's Oil." When one knows Harris's canon of work, one realizes this is actually a reworking of "Endangered Species." In *Facing Mekka,* Harris has moved far beyond the mesmerizing rhythmic acrobatics of hip-hop dance, taking us on a vertical dive into the collective human soul. His stage oeuvre is so street—colloquially layered with signifying, radical juxtaposition and social commentary—that it becomes postmodern by definition. As Harris often says to his audience, "Race means competition—there's only culture."[34] In plumbing the archaeology of the human spirit, *Facing Mekka* becomes a metaphor for Harris facing himself while forcing us to face our potential that waits just below the surface of human culture at every moment. Throughout his career, Harris has privileged the creating of community, whether onstage, in his workshops, or in the projection of his philosophy. He implores the best of hip-hop culture: free choice and skilled individuality within the context of community. As he expounds, "In my choreographic process, individual identity is first and foremost. Once I let go [with my dancers], I was able to keep it hip-hop because the dancers change it, taking the risk factor up, which makes it more exciting for the audience. The black/Latino community has always had to have voice [as oppressed people]. Hip-hop is just the latest part of that story."[35] He has come full circle: After he has traveled around the globe, he returns to his origins, his own self, where any artist lodges his or her work. As in his previous dances, Harris starts and ends with the urban streets, making no detours to the ballet or modern dance methods to speak his movement truth.

From "Students of the Asphalt Jungle" to *Facing Mecca,* Harris's aesthetic is simultaneously black vernacular and postmodern. The implicit use of physical gravity and horizontality in breaking, along with Harris's use of radical juxtaposition and direct and indirect movement texts, positions his choreography right in the center of the postmodern aesthetic. Yet this same style and approach is based in the Africanist aesthetic that is as old as African apart dancing and as "new" as avant-garde jazz riffing. Given this dual way of perceiving Harris's choreographic canon, he is developing perhaps a new form of theatrical ritualization that is both basic and futuristic, with one of his feet in the street and the other in the universe.

Notes

1. Rennie Harris, interview with the author, Ann Arbor, MI, January 11, 2002.
2. Ibid.
3. Brenda Dixon Gottschild, *Digging the Africanist Presence in American Performance: Dance and Other Contexts* (Westport, CT: Greenwood Press, 1996), 158–59.
4. Sally Sommer, "Prophets in Pumas: When Hip Hop Broke Out," *Dance Magazine,* July 2004, 31.
5. Sally Banes, "Breaking," in *Fresh Hip Hop Don't Stop,* ed. Nelson George (New York: Random House, 1985), 97. For one of the most complete theoretical texts on the languagelike semantic features of dance, see Judith Lynne Hanna, *To Dance Is Human: A Theory of Nonverbal Communication,* 2nd ed. (Chicago: University of Chicago Press, 1987).
6. Rennie Harris, interview with the author, Tallahassee, FL, March 4, 2005.
7. Ibid.
8. Robert Farris Thompson first explicated specific aesthetic principles of African-based performance in his "ten canons of fine" form and his "aesthetic of the cool" in *African Art in Motion: Icon and Act in the Collection of Katherine Coryton White,* exhibition catalog, National Gallery of Art, Washington, DC, for the Frederick S. Wight Art Gallery, University of California, Los Angeles (Los Angeles: University of California Press, 1974).
9. Jacqui Malone, *Steppin' on the Blues: The Visible Rhythms of African American Dance* (Chicago: University of Illinois Press, 1996), 22.
10. Ibid., 24.
11. Steve Bradshaw, Belinda Quirey, and Ronald Smedley, *May I Have the Pleasure: The Story of Popular Dancing* (London: Dance Books, 1987), 88–89.
12. Jonathan David Jackson, "Improvisation in African-American Vernacular Dancing," *Dance Research Journal* 33, no. 2 (Winter 2001/2002): 42.
13. Ibid., 47.
14. Rennie Harris, "Dance and the Community," plenary session, Congress on Research in Dance Annual Conference, Tallahassee, FL, March 4, 2005.
15. Rennie Harris Puremovement, "Repertoire," video recording, 1998.
16. Cornel West, "Nihilism in Black America," in *Black Popular Culture,* ed. Gina Dent (Seattle: Bay Press, 1992), 38.
17. Ibid., 39.
18. In social theory, Frederic Jameson's classic neo-Marxian analyses in *Postmodernism, or, the Cultural Logic of Late Capitalism* (Durham, NC: Duke University Press,

1992) interrogates the concept of postmodernism and challenges its very existence. Far from accepting the most common definition that postmodernism is "the end of meta narrative," Jameson views the idea that the present historical juncture is defined by the *lack* of an organizing grand paradigm is itself a self-referential grand theory. This neo-Marxian perception of the confluence of our contemporary times and a kind of late capitalism is key for Harris's evening-length hip-hopera, *Rome & Jewels*, which I investigate in this chapter.

19. Sally Banes, *Terpsichore in Sneakers: Post-Modern Dance* (Hanover, NH: Wesleyan University Press, 1977, 1987), xii. I am aware of the continued debate, spawned by Susan Manning's challenge to Sally Banes's *Terpsichore in Sneakers* (1987), about what exactly constitutes postmodern dance; however, Manning's concerns with Banes's "partisan" periodization of dance history and postmodernism's place in it ("Modernist Dogma and Post-modern Rhetoric," *The Drama Review* 32, no. 4 [1988]: 32–38), as well as Banes's own rejoinder upholding her delineation of postmodern dance choreographers based in their own self-description ("Terpsichore in Combat Boots," *The Drama Review* 33, no. 1 [1989]: 13–16), has little relationship to my concerns with what I call Harris's postmodernist hip-hop aesthetic. Three years later, several choreographers and dance scholars (including Sally Banes) in Ann Daly's "What Has Become of Postmodern Dance" (*The Drama Review* 36, no. 1 [1992]: 48–69) thankfully extended the debate. In this article, Banes observed that the second generation of postmodern dancers, emerging in the 1980s, following the analytic and metaphoric postmodernists of the 1960s and 1970s, made more use of the "avant/pop music world . . . and its use of narratives and the traditions of dance history" (60). By the 1990s, we had established dance makers using pop music and a new engagement with ballet and modernists styles, such as Bill T. Jones, Susan Marshall, and Bebe Miller. My point is that Rennie Harris takes use of the vernacular to a new dimension by *ignoring* ballet and modern dance by invoking a parallel Africanist vernacular dance tradition only utilized in fragments by previous choreographers (e.g., Bill T. Jones with his pop-locking inserts within modern balletic phrasings and Doug Elkins's forays into hip-hop styles). But no one completely privileged a black-Latino street dance form, as does Harris, as the basis for serious concert choreography to comment upon both the form itself and to make poignant narrative statements about the interior, social, and global spheres we inhabit.

20. Banes, *Terpsichore in Sneakers*, xviii.

21. Ibid., xxiii.

22. Ibid., xxix.

23. Gottschild, *Digging the Africanist Presence*, 50–51.

24. Rennie Harris, interview with the author, Tallahassee, FL, March 4, 2005.

25. Gottschild, *Digging the Africanist Presence*, 51.

26. Harris, "Dance and the Community."

27. Elizabeth Zimmer, "Fusing Shakespeare, Hip-Hop Dance," *Philadelphia Inquirer*, June 16, 2000.

28. Suzanne Carbonneau, "This Shakespeare Is a Hip-Hop M.C.," *The New York Times*, September 24, 2000.

29. For one of the early definitive studies of this issue in U.S. popular culture, see Lawrence Levine's *Highbrow/Lowbrow: The Emergence of Cultural Hierarchy in America* (Cambridge, MA: Harvard University Press, 1988).

30. Rennie Harris, preperformance audience address, Power Center, Ann Arbor, MI, January 11, 2002.

31. Rennie Harris, interview with the author, Ann Arbor, MI, January 11, 2002.

32. Kevin C. Johnson, "The Bard in Hip-Hop," *St. Louis Post-Dispatch*, September 21, 2000.

33. Suzanne Carbonneau, "Facing Out, Facing In: Facing Mekka," http://www.puremovement.net/rhpub.html (accessed May 2004).

34. Rennie Harris, preperformance audience address, Power Center, Ann Arbor, MI, January 11, 2002.

35. Ibid.

Section IV

The Contemporary Scene

16

"C'mon to My House"

Underground House Dancing

Sally R. Sommer

Underground house dancing is a name given to varied dance forms that evolved in New York City and Chicago clubs during the 1970s and are danced to house music.[1] A distinctly urban form, underground house flourishes in the club atmosphere and a convivial communal vibe. House parties travel internationally with the popular house DJs who tour the world with their vinyl and great dancers. Even as it is enjoying a fresh popularity in Japan, South America, and Europe, and students are clamoring for house to be taught in the studios, the American clubs that nurture it have been closing at an alarming rate. Paradoxically, since the aftershocks and wars following the September 11, 2001, terrorist attacks, the longing for the safe respite and the reassurance of nonviolent congregations has intensified.[2]

Of all the formal qualities that constitute the essentials of house, nothing could be more ephemeral or more powerful than the vibe, the defining building block of the underground house scene. The vibe is an active communal force, a feeling, a rhythm created by the mix of dancers, the balance of loud music, the effects of darkness and light and physical/psychic energy. Everything interlocks to produce a powerful sense of liberation. The vibe is an active, exhilarating feeling of "nowness" that everything is coming together, that a good party is in the making.

House is performative, always "in-the-making." Central to the dancing and the vibe are the improvisational exchanges between DJ and dancer, between dancer and dancer—playfulness, fast-moving exchanges and game structures, imaginative sonic and physical dialogues—all realized through the actions of dancing. Music maker and dance maker exist concomitantly as producer and consumer, subjective and immediate. The sound has been engineered (equalized) so that some of the deep bass lines are not heard but felt as vibrations in the sternum, so the dancer literally embodies the music.

The vibe is constructive, a distinctive rhythm and groove that carries the party psychically and physically. "[H]ouse is a feeling and no one can understand really unless their feet moved to the sound of our house. 'Can-you-feel-it?'"[3] Because rhythm coheres the whole, the vibe is mutable, in flux, controlling the ebb and flow of the night. The beat means safety. It pulses through bodies, causes the floor to bound and rebound, and, because everyone is moving in synchrony, it avoids disharmony, eschews collisions and fights.

House music has been specifically created as *dance* music: Nonstop music drives nonstop dancing. Underground house encompasses a wide range of musical and dance styles. Its fundamental premises, however, are baseline tempos that hover around 125 to 130 beats per minute, versus the slower 100 beats per minute of hip-hop or the faster 150 to 180 beats per minute of electronic-techno rave music, "speed nuts." An important characteristic of house music is that the vocals (if any) ride the music and enhance the beat. Words are not as important as the sound of the voice, the prolonged high wail of rapture. The lyrics tend to be self-referential to the underground scene, "C'mon to my house, my house on the hill" or "I'm Living my Life Underground," or lyrics can also insistently repeat a single upbeat idea, such as "Stay Together." A few of the variations are jungle house, hip-hop house, deep house, and Jersey house, which Brahams La Fortune describes as featuring uplifting vocals like "the sun will come out tomorrow" delivered in repetitious, gospel-like incantations. The insistent repetition of a few words, the fixed rhythm, and the song wailing obscure meaning. Decontextualized, the lyrics seem decidedly flaccid. When coupled with the high emotionality of the music, however, the words take on a rhythmic intensity and meaning, turning into a narrative exhortation that propels the dancers. This sonic/tactile fusion situates the receiver in a space very different from the everyday. This is the "*communitas*" that anthropologist Victor Turner theorizes and is explicitly stated in underground house music and inscribed by the dancing bodies.[4]

House exists as a dialogic interaction. House music is meant to be *danced to* not listened to. "The skill and art of the DJ are based, partly, on an ability to be attuned to the moods of people and to play with those emotions until the crowd allows itself to be taken on a trip of rhythms, sound bites, audio textures and lyrics."[5] Kai Fikentscher—scholar, househead, and DJ—describes the DJ's compositional transactions from his insider sites. "[T]he response from the dance floor, in the form of the sum of individual responses, is continually evaluated by a DJ who, for hours on end, is involved in structuring his or her musical program. Thus, the uniqueness of underground dance music lies not only in a particular combination of musical mediation and musical immediacy, but also in the positioning of mediated music at the heart of a complex whole in which music and dance, performance and reception, production and consumption are inextricably intertwined, and simultaneously, and often spontaneously, enacted."[6]

Following Victor Turner's theories further, several aspects of *communitas* (both "spontaneous" and "normative" *communitas*) apply to the nature of club gatherings and the community of dancers. His formulations of initiates as "liminal or marginal people" (he calls them "edgemen") striving "to rid themselves of the clichés associated with status incumbency and role-playing and to enter into vital relations with other men in fact or imagination" aptly describe hard-core househeads and why they come together to dance.[7]

Although the rave and underground house share some of the same sensibilities, major distinctions exist in the dancing and in the nature of the altered state of mind, the "zone." The house dancer does not fall into the protracted, hours-long dance trances characteristic of the raves, in which the individual relinquishes self-identity to the collective. "[A]utonomy is no longer the issue. Spectators see only the surface, but the ravers are already part of the scene, in the machinery."[8] Submerged in the crowds and sonic washes, ravers dance alongside one another while maintaining the introverted concentration necessary to savor the perceptual-physical sensations heightened by Ecstasy, the raver's drug of choice.

Sidestepping the luscious loss of self of the raves, the goals of the househead are to be a part of the group yet still maintain a sense of individuality: to seek the good vibe and hit the zone through the physical rapture of intense hard dancing. Because the forms of underground house dancing are interactive and improvisational, the dancer strives to keep a sense of objectivity. This is not to say that there is no drug use. But for experienced, hardcore house dancers who come to the clubs to "work" (i.e., dance hard), drugs and alcohol are viewed as "very expensive dehydration."[9] The heavy demands of the virtuosic competitive dancing in a tight circle dictate sobriety, and so do the other dancers. In the body dives and the sweeping floor work, the dancer must be able to judge speed, distance, and attack within millimeters.

A couple of well-established and tacit rules affirm that dancing is the prime identifier. Clubbers can dance together for years and not know one another's given names or family names nor their addresses or phone numbers. "Do not ask about my job. Do not ask what I do. Judge the way I dance."[10] No one is assessed on outside accomplishment, no expectations transfer from the outside world. The only worthy thing is what one can add to the party. Underground house clubs and dance practices represent contemporary, "liminoid" *rites of passage,* with vivid stages of *separation* and *liminality* in which a "leveling," "denuding," or the "stripping" of the ritual subjects occurs in the *rites de passage.* "[S]igns of the preliminal status are destroyed and signs of their liminal non-status applied. I have mentioned certain indicators of their liminality—absence of clothing and names."[11] Several redemptive transformations are contained in the social/physical paradigm: the redemption of *communitas,* the redemption of total body sensuality without rampant sexuality fostered by protracted dancing that engages body and mind, and the redemption of the vital aliveness of playfulness and fun. In underground house, playfulness and fun *cannot* be overemphasized. These are the magnetic forces that draw the dancers to the club and hold the groups together. In Turner's strategies, play and fun exist most fully in the transitional states of *ludic liminality* (*ludic,* meaning playful, out of the everyday), which are "potentially, and in principle, a free and experimental region of culture, a region where not only new elements but also new combinatory rules may be introduced."[12] Mikhail Bakhtin writes about folly's corrective power: "Folly is, of course, deeply ambivalent. It has the negative elements of debasement and destruction . . . and the positive element of renewal and truth. . . . It is the other side . . . of official laws and conventions . . . a form of wisdom . . . free from all laws and restriction."[13]

A close parallel also exists to Sigmund Freud's theories about games and play in prepubescent latency. In underground house, the physical interactions are an adult version of play, and the dancers are forthright in talking about play as a primary structure. According to Freud, "Should we not look for the first traces of imaginative activity as early as in childhood? The child's best-loved and most intense occupation is with his play or games. Might we not say that every child at play behaves like a creative writer in that he creates a world of his own, or, rather, re-arranges the things of his world in a new way which pleases him? It would be wrong to think he does not take that world seriously; on the contrary he takes his play very seriously and he expends a large amount of emotion on it. The opposite of play is not what is serious, but what is real. In spite of all the emotion with which he cathects to his world of play, the child distinguishes it quite well from reality."[14]

The terms "underground" and "house" are replete with multiple allusions. Adding to the confusion is the fact that in dance/club circles, "underground" and "house" tend to be used interchangeably. The word "house" signifies homey feelings, and in the original parlance of gay clubs, the dancers were sometimes referred to as "children." Some view the DJ as a priest, a shaman who musically ministers to the dancers enjoying a temporary regression from adult strictures. Others view the DJ (especially in the gay clubs) as a sexualized mother to the whole-body, sensual state of the dancer. But the good family feeling is central. "The club is family. The club is safe haven. The club is everything home is *not*. It's the kind of family you wish you had."[15] Well-known house DJ Tony Humphries states, "When I spin music at the club [it] should be as comfortable for you as being at my house."[16]

Underground is the name given to the clubs where house dancing takes place; it also signifies a way of life. This life takes place after dark, out of sight, and has its own codes and transactions. The name carries historical implications: The Underground Railroad was the secret path of escape for slaves seeking freedom. Merging the historical into the hip, Ejoe Wilson says, "House is some freedom dancing, that's what house is!"[17] People go underground to hide. Underground figures are thought of as gangsters, lawbreakers, pimps, and whores or, simply, the marginalized. And since 1999, under the U.S. Drug Enforcement Agency's expanded interpretations of the "crack house" laws, clubs and dancing can be and have been criminalized. *Village Voice* writer Frank Owen reports on the scene: "'I'm beset by the hounds of City Hall,' adds Jim Chu who owns Den of Thieves, a progressive music bar on the Lower East Side. Last year, inspectors from the Department of Consumer Affairs issued several summonses because people were dancing in the bar which has no cabaret license. 'People dance at Taco Bell if there's a good tune on,' Chu insists. Nevertheless, he remodeled the entire bar to discourage dancing."[18]

The golden age of underground house in New York City lasted from the mid-1970s through the early 1990s. The most famous club was Paradise Garage (1976–87). Affectionately pronounced "Gay Raj," it primarily catered to the gay crowd, although it was not exclusively gay. Even today, the Garage has recognizable cachet (a London club and a recent form of rave music are called "Garage" in homage). In addition to dancing, the Garage was a "scene," a style, a fashion, a place to scope and be scoped. Certain designated nights featured special parties: pajama parties, toga parties, beach parties, fifties parties, and so forth, in addition to all the holidays.

For the serious dancers, however, there was another place to go: David Mancuso's Loft. Less expensive than the Garage and less visible, the Loft began, literally, as a party in Mancuso's living loft. It was famous for attracting dancers as well as a more mixed crowd of blacks, Latinos, whites, gays and straights, men and women, and dancers of all ages.[19] "It was my first experience in a very cool atmosphere," says Archie Burnett, who began his club life as a Lofter. "Not too white, not too black, not too straight, not too gay, you know—truly cool."[20] Unlike the Garage, the Loft was not a place to display, to dress up, or pick up: "You came to dance your brains out."[21]

In contrast to the Garage, with its gorgeous scrutinizing doorman who determined who could and could not enter, the Loft had bouncers. "Loft bouncers were just *big*. Not mean—just tall. All those guys had to do was just stand there." Entering the Loft was simple. A friend vouched for you. "The philosophy was that friends of friends don't fuck up, that someone you call a friend will act in a proper manner and add to the party rather than detract from it."[22]

The Loft style was sensible. Dancers wore work clothes that could take sweat and dirt and were comfortable to move in: sneakers, loose pants (elastic waist and cuffs) in army green or workman blue or subway orange, topped with T-shirts or tank tops. Little idiosyncratic "flavors" like a hat, colored shoes, hot socks, or colorful underwear lent individuality to the clothes. Lofters carried duffel bags with a change of clothes, a towel, and baby powder (to speed up the floor or dry the body), signifying they were in for the long haul and big sweat (figure 16.1). In the powerful and tacit codes of the club, however, participants had to arrive clean and cologned. Clothes got soaking wet, and the rule was and still is that you could sweat, but do not stink.

At the Loft's biggest, longest-lasting location (in Manhattan's SoHo district), there were two huge floors for dancing, with black walls and black ceilings covered with flotillas of multicolored balloons. Each floor had its own DJ, distinctive musical sound, and mood. By the early morning hours, however, the cream of the crop, the hardest of the hard-core dancers, headed to the basement, the deepest underground, where the best dancing took place. To this day, the dedication to inclusiveness, attracting a mixed crowd, the dedication to the music, the dancing, the inexpensive balloon decor, and the practical styles of dress and demeanor serve as models of production and consumption for the underground house.

Figure 16.1: House dancer Barbara Tucker in a toe stand. Photo by
Andrew Eccles.

In the 1980s, house was exported to Europe, where it provided a valuable matrix of material and production for the music, dancing, and social
discourses of the clubs. Transmogrified through the European (especially the
English) sensibility, house got exported back to America as raves in the early
1990s. Around 1997, raves became large-scale mainstream dance events, with
massive gatherings in the thousands. These could take place in legitimate
clubs or in moveable "secret" outdoor and indoor venues whose locations
were broadcast through an underground network of phone numbers and
the Internet that everybody seemed able to access.

Subsequently, a flurry of articles and TV reports highlighted the phenomenon by explaining the "new" dance craze or by warning about the dangers

of the drug Ecstasy. For example, during a brief six-month period, from December 1999 to July 2000, *The New York Times* published eighteen articles about raves (mostly positive). During the same period, three rave films were released. Given the adversarial position that hegemonic moral and political forces have always taken toward social dancing, what is surprising is that so many positive responses to the raves were actually written. Ironically, the positive social factors that elicited favorable responses in 2000 had originated thirty years earlier in the underground house movement, when they were dismissed or reviled.

During the same six-month period in 1999 and 2000, many New York City clubs were closed. Indicted under Mayor Rudolph Guiliani's "Quality of Life" laws of the 1990s, clubs were targeted as unlawful and immoral. But this was only a recent example of the continual intracultural efforts by the mainstream to colonize the marginalized "edgemen."

At least since the 1830s in New York City, dancing and dance halls have been voyeuristically scrutinized with curiosity and condemnation. Moralizing "tourist" reports from the 1830s describe nefarious underground clubs in the rough Five Points district of Manhattan (the area around Foley Square) where hundreds of beer and dance hall joints existed in the cellars of tenement buildings. Just as in present-day clubs, these early clubs attracted mixed groups. More disturbing to the reformers, however, was that they attracted mixed races of sailors from around the world whose ships unloaded at the docks surrounding the neighborhood. *An Account of Colonel [Davy] Crockett's Tour to North and Down East,* anonymously written in 1835, said the "cellars was jam full of people, and such fiddling and dancing nobody every [*sic*] saw before in this world . . . black and white, white and black, all hug-em-snug together. I do think I saw more drunk men and women, that day, than I ever saw before. . . . I thought I would rather trust myself in an Indian fight than venture among these creature after night."[23] Seven years later, Charles Dickens visited Five Points and in *American Notes for General Circulation* described "lanes and alleys paved with mud knee-deep; [and] underground chambers where they dance and game."[24] Carolyn Cooper, recounting the suppression of Jamaican culture in the nineteenth century, describes the same transaction: "The pornographic impulse to simultaneously expose and conceal the prurient exotic facts of native life [substitute "club life"] is barely suppressed. Travel writing of this age is essentially a colonizing fiction, civilizing savage landscapes—but only so far. Domesticating difference . . . feeds the eroticized *conquistador* fantasies of the voy(ag)eur/reader safe at home . . . and tames the feminized, alien landscape."[25]

The 1997 crackdown on clubs focused not only on the illegal social clubs but also on "the hundred or so licensed clubs that dot Manhattan, identified by police as a magnet for drug sales, underage drinking, loud music, and other conditions which create an atmosphere conducive to crime."[26] Most disturbing, however, was when the war on clubs got merged with the war on drugs. Local sanctions were transformed into a national antidrug campaign aimed at nightlife and dancing, which criminalized the clubs and the people who danced in them. According to a 2001 *Village Voice* article:

> In January [2001], as part of the DEA's new Operation Rave Review, promoter James D. Estopinal, a.k.a. "Disco" Donnie, and Robert and Brian Brunet, part owners of the State Palace Theater in New Orleans, were indicted under a 1986 "crack house" statute created to target drug dens where owners "knowingly and intentionally" allowed drug use to take place. The feds claimed that the sale of over-priced bottles of water (which kept a person on Ecstasy from dehydrating) and the presence of drug information groups like Dance-Safe and on-site private ambulances . . . were evidence that the State Palace Theater operated as a crack house. . . . The New Orleans plea states that glow sticks and dust masks, as well as vapor rubs and inhalers—all typically associated with raves—can be considered drug paraphernalia. The feds also nixed massage tables and "chill rooms," or "areas in the theater which are purposely kept 15 degrees cooler than the rest of the theater."[27]

In backlash to the closings, and disgusted by expensive, slicked-up mainstream clubs, a nostalgia movement sprung up in New York City. Clubbers are "Bored Shitless with the Club Scene," the *Village Voice* announced. They want to experience "house roots" and return to the positive feelings and identifications associated with the origins of the house "family." Along with a good number of Japanese and European underground house purists, these new nostalgic clubbers seek out everything old-house and try to recreate the old feeling in new parties.[28] This nostalgia represents a major paradox of social dance culture. Although it is completely fascinated by the futuristic (summarized in one 1999 rave film's cyborg technobionic title, *Better Living through Electronic Circuitry*), dance culture feels equally drawn toward the past:

> It's obsessed with roots, origins, and all things "old school." Reinvoking the "original principles" of the New York dance underground, nights like Body & Soul, Together in Spirit, Journey, and Soul-Sa [different house parties that take place at various clubs] appeal both to disenchanted veterans of the original scene and to neophytes who feel the romance of a lost golden age they never actually lived through. With clubbing tourists coming from all of the world to experience "the real thing" as a sort of

time-travel simulacrum, New York's 70's style dance underground has become a veritable heritage industry similar to jazz in New Orleans. . . . [W]hat exactly is the allure of this period? "It's that whole mythic aura thing," says Hill. "None of these people went to the Loft in the 70s or the Garage in the 80s [two famous house clubs] so the spell can't be broken. It's like some mad idyllic party that they can't ever have attended.[29]

Befitting their position in a disapproving society that legislates against them, underground clubs are located in unattractive, nonresidential, light-industry districts. Unremarkable and anonymous from the outside, underground house clubs do little advertising beyond the postcards or flyers handed out on the sidewalks. Although they open at 10:00 P.M., they remain empty until midnight or 1:00 A.M. Outside there are no signs, no visible addresses, no fancy lighting—just a couple of black doors. What makes them recognizable is the barely discerned thump of the bass penetrating the brick walls plus the cluster of people in front. Seeking to stay below the radar, the clubs are elitist and secretive, or they are fluid events, whose organizers throw special "parties," hosted by well-liked DJs, that move from club to club. The dancers also shift and navigate through a series of clubs on a single night, staying in one place until it closes or until they get bored. Avoiding the well-known touristy mainstream clubs, they move to another club that stays open later or has a better vibe. Recently, a lot of the parties have moved to Brooklyn, and as the night progresses, the dancers move deeper into the heart of the borough: "By eight o'clock in the morning—or two in the afternoon if you're lucky—we'll be deep in Brooklyn," says Brahams La Fortune.[30]

An important part of the underground house rite of passage is the body check at the door, emblematic of cleansing, of releasing weapons and the combativeness of the streets before entering the safe haven. "It means I come in peace. I am open to what the DJ has to offer me."[31] This formally separates the outside from the inside, demarcating the secular from the sacred, marking the transition from a secular-temporal space to an untemporal place. The newly frisked and denuded initiate makes the transition by moving either through a metal-detector arch, entering a poorly lit foyer or darkened hallway, and/or by actually going through a set of doors in order to reach the inner sanctum of the dance floor. "That's when I begin to smell the familiar smells of reefer, sweat, and feel the heat. The bass drums flutter in my stomach like butterflies and I am about ready to jump out of my skin."[32] Inside, the outside world drops away. One crosses into a place with different codes, rules, judgments, and games, into an environment that is acoustic, olfactory, and tactile.

Once inside, the body vibrates as the bass resonates in the bones. On the floor, strobe lights pixilate space and action, light cones probe the darkness, and whirling light flecks reflect off mirrored balls to produce visual and physical disorientation. Perceptual modes shift, sensing with the skin and seeing in the dark. Everything is in motion. The only way to get balanced and centered is to move your feet. House music is "produced so that it must be 'listened to' *with the body.*"[33] As the song lyrics say, "[N]o one can understand really unless their feet move onto the sound of our house. 'Can-you-feel-it?'"[34]

Terry Eagleton notes, "Aesthetics is born as a discourse of the body," and in underground house the body is not a metaphor for something else, it is the object.[35] "The whole thing—the sweat, the pain, the gasping for air—works as a systems check, lets me know I'm alive."[36] Because it is impossible to talk or to hear, movement and gesture become language, become identifiers.

What keeps the floor alive and dancers alert are the improvised dialogues of movement that define the vibe of a house party. Interactions arise then disappear throughout the evening. They can be as simple as an exchange between the music and a dancer or maybe just two people dancing or as big and rambunctious as a circle of dancers in fierce competition. Whatever the modality of relating, interactive, improvisational play is always present. It is manifested in acute attentiveness (something less merged, perhaps, than Turner's "direct, immediate and total confrontation of human identities" in *communitas,* which shatters the boundaries of *"I-thou,"* as Martin Buber termed it) and in a respect for another's invention.[37] It is that thrill of recognition when one dancer gets topped, then retaliates by topping one better.

Precisely because househeads maintain a sense of individuation and observation and engage in genial competitions, house produces extremely sophisticated and varied dancing. Club dancing is not only thrilling physical virtuosity and improvisational play, it is also an extremely serious expression. Club dancers dance to worship on Sunday mornings when dawn hits outside and the DJ decides to spin some "gospel-house" mixes. When his father died, Archie Burnett escaped to the club and the solace of dancing as a way of working through pain and loss. Brian "Fast Footwork" Green and friends danced hard the night a dancer got shot for a jacket: "Without dancing and the club there would have been a lot of violence that night."[38] Conrad Rochester memorializes the dead in his dancing: "I took their moves . . . and changed them up in my own little way. And when I do those moves, it's the way I show my love for them . . . to let them know we are still out there rockin' for them and the dance, and to let them know that their spirit is still strong, and will never die."[39]

The ways in which the dancers use challenge circles, improvisations, and humor mediate and censor the shifting modalities that assist them in maintaining a balance between "zoning" and interactive dancing. This process reflects Freud's concepts about how the creative process functions, which is explained and elaborated by psychoanalyst Ernst Krist's work, "Regression in Service of the Ego": "This form of regression . . . can also be regarded as controlled realization of the censorship between the present unconscious and consciousness. It is by no means a psychological regression, but rather one in which contact with reality is readily accessible (to the artist)."[40]

Something edgy yet grounded is created by the competitive nature of circles. In 1842, Charles Dickens wrote in his *American Notes* detailed descriptions of a dancer and dance hall in Manhattan's Five Points district, in which the circle formed the prime structural element (a common underground house practice familiar to any clubhead today):

> [T]he sport [the dancing] begins to languish, when suddenly the lively hero dashes in to the rescue. Instead the fiddler grins, and goes at it tooth and nail; there is new energy in the tambourine, new laughter in the dances. Single shuffle, double shuffle, cut and cross-cut; snapping his fingers, rolling his eyes, turning in his knees, presenting the back of his legs in front. Spinning about on his toes and heels like nothing but the man's fingers on the tambourine; dancing with two left legs, two right legs, two wooden legs, two wire legs, two spring legs—all sort of legs and no legs—what is this to him? And in what walk of life, or dance of life, does man ever get such stimulating applause as thunders about him, . . . he finishes by leaping gloriously on the bar-counter, and calling for something to drink, with a chuckle of a million of counterfeit Jim Crows, in one inimitable sound.[41]

A soloist separates from a group, a circle (aka "cipher") forms, and, if he is good, he is acknowledged ("does man ever get such stimulating applause as thunders about him?") (figure 16.2). Today there would be less applause and more whoops of approval. And, if the solo were extraordinary, the watchers would slap the floor to show honor and respect. Then, without a break, another dancer would enter and the cipher would continue.

"Cipher" is a term rich in connotations. It denotes fast-moving, interactive riffs (verbal, physical, sung, or percussive) that can spring up anywhere, any time—in the street, in a car, in the subway, or at the club. The word also applies to the actual circle that forms around the action or person when

Figure 16.2: William "Quick" Reynolds, at the Vienna Volksgarten club in Vienna, Austria, performs within the circle, 1996. Photograph by Raphael Barth.

something creative is happening. The circle is the most important structure in the liminal and spontaneous *communitas* of the club, inscribing the essential interpersonal exchange. The circle forming around and supporting the good performer (and, conversely, a circle not formed) is the physical emblem of important social and aesthetic mediations, described by Robert Farris Thompson: "Thus call-and-response, and solo-and-circle, far from solely constituting matters of structure are, in actuality, levels of perfected social interaction. The canon is danced judgment of qualities of social integration and cohesion."[42]

Humor exists in several layers. In interactive social settings, because humor is productive and speculative, it invents strategies to enact alternative human realities. Analyzing house interactions, Hillegonda Rietveld writes, "Fun, as well as celebrating the body rather than the mind, can have an undermining effect on any unitary belief of a particular kind of hierarchial world order."[43] Among househeads, humor is most pointedly made by mimicking and commenting, in dance, on the other guy's style. Yet, although the quality of the humor can be wickedly on point, it is rarely cruel. Humorous exchanges often involve props: a roll of toilet paper, a balloon, and so forth. For example, someone's shirt gets swiped and is passed around in a contest of keep-away.

It becomes a handkerchief to blow the nose on, a dress, a wig of long hair tossing in the breeze, a waiter's towel.

Immediately recognizable material and characters are appropriated from popular sources: Kung fu movies, circus, capoeira, video games, television advertisements, famous people, movies, and magazine ads are speedily encrypted into the funny, furious language of iconographic gestures or phrases. As dancers radicalize images, they recontextualize the familiar in unconventional ways. The connections must be perceived, then instantly physicalized in order to keep the flow of the image exchanges.[44] The art is to keep the response rhythms fast (as in Dirty Dozens) or, better yet, accelerate the tempo. The most important mode of demolition is a quick wit, literally thinking on your feet. The choices must be apt, well coded, readily readable, and executed in a nanosecond with physical-mental agility that display the players' easy familiarity with popular images and all their multivocal significances. This is a rapid game of wit that resets meanings, transforming the mundane into the extraordinary.

The body is instrument, signifier, and site of regeneration in underground house styles. In this subculture, winning space inside and against the hegemonic order is articulated in the symbolic challenges of dancing: dances of imitation, derision, and parody. As it moves away from the norm and toward a new condition, it asserts a promise. It also poses a threat. Still, in many ways, underground house is an archaic throwback, idealistic even, in its circles and gamesmanship, in its physical states of preverbal exchanges. As signified by its name, house denotes a place of life and interaction, a sense of safety and play.

Freud wrote, "When the child has grown up and has ceased to play, and after he has been laboring for decades to envisage the realities of life with proper seriousness, he may one day find himself in a mental situation which once more undoes the contrast between play and reality."[45] When people mature, they cease to play, to their detriment. But whosoever understands the human mind knows that nothing is harder to give up than a pleasure once experienced. Actually, we can never give anything up; we only exchange one thing for another. Hard-core househeads have re-created that liminal and almost ideal transitional world in which they experiment with multiple states of mind and shifting identities through total body and athletic endeavor. This is not a display of the person, clothes, or status but of movement and imagination. They gather to dance, and underground house provides them with a redemptive social space in which to attain individual and communal harmony.

Notes

1. I use the labels "house," "lofting," and "loft" dancing as the dancers do, following their looser time frames and definitions. This differs, for example, from the way Tim Lawrence dates and defines "house," based on dates of music publications or club openings and closings. In truth, the names or labels that dancers use to define what they are doing are flexible. Because dancing has no hard-copy way of dating itself, it crosses other boundaries and definitions. The information in this chapter is based on my research on social dance and the clubs, which has been ongoing since the mid-1970s. More specific to this chapter is the research done since 1992, which has concentrated on a group of dancers from the underground house scene in New York City who were the main subjects of an hour-long video documentary, *Check Your Body at the Door* (2001, created and produced by Sally R. Sommer). Although the majority of these dancers are African American and/or Hispanic American, together they form a multigenerational, multiracial group of exceptionally stable, self-defined househeads who have been, since very early ages, serious club dancers devoted to their chosen craft. All of the dancers are people the author has known for years (some for as many as twenty, others for as few as six). The subject and the focus of *Check Your Body at the Door* is to record something of the lives and dance craft of these extraordinary dancers and dances that make up the vibrant underground house scene of New York City during the 1990s.

2. As anecdotal evidence, Archie Burnett, Chris Buxenbaum, and Brahams La Fortune all said they were noticing an increase in club attendance since "9/11" (the terrorist attacks of September 11, 2001). As Burnett observed, "People need to bust out more than ever, now"; see *Check Your Body at the Door,* video documentary, directed by Sally R. Sommer, 2001.

3. Song lyrics from "Can You Feel It?" by Larry Heard and Chuck Roberts (London: Desire Records, 12-inch vinyl, 1988); quoted in Hillegonda Rietveld, *This Is Our House: House Music, Cultural Spaces and Technologies* (Aldershot, England: Ashgate, 1998), 5.

4. Turner's work is inconsistent in its italicizing of key words. For the sake of consistency throughout this chapter, I have chosen to italicize these words. Turner has eloquently refined and extended the premises of Arnold Van Gennep's initial work, *Rites de Passage* (1908), with its three stages of seclusion, transition, and incorporation. Although it is difficult to separate the parts from the accumulative gestalt of Turner's writings, two sections have been particularly useful: one about *communitas*, liminality, and low status, and the second "Liminal to Liminoid: In Play, Flow and Ritual"; see Victor W. Turner, *Ritual Process* (Chicago: Aldine, 1969), 125–41; Victor Turner, *From Ritual to Theatre: The Human Seriousness of Play* (New York: Performing Arts Journal, 1982), 20–60.

5. Rietveld, *This Is Our House,* 191.

6. Kai Fikentscher, *"You Better Work!" Underground Dance Music in New York City* (Hanover, NH: University of New England/Wesleyan University Press, 2000), 79–80.

7. Turner, *From Ritual to Theatre,* 27–29.

8. Sadie Plant, quoted in Rietveld, *This Is Our House,* 194.

9. Archie Burnett, video interview with the author, April 24, 1998.

10. Archie Burnett, video interview with the author, October 1996.

11. Turner, *From Ritual to Theatre,* 26.

12. Ibid., 28–29.

13. Mikhail Bakhtin, quoted in Rietveld, *This Is Our House,* 202.

14. Ethel Spector Person, Peter Fonagy, and Servulo Augusto Figueira, eds., *On

Freud's "Creative Writers and Day-Dreaming" (New Haven, CT: Yale University Press, 1995), 3–5.

15. Brian Green, "Fast Footwork," video interview, New York City, June 1996 and November 23, 1996.

16. Tony Humphries, video interview, New York City, December 12, 1995.

17. Ejoe Wilson, interview, New York City, August 1, 1994.

18. Frank Owen, "Crackdown in Clubland," *Village Voice*, February 18, 1997, 38–39.

19. Lewis Vargas is a proud, "real" Loft baby, brought to the Loft in the 1980s by his mother, Josie, when he was eight years old. "I loved it! And I'm still clubbing today." Archie Burnett confirmed this, saying that he used to babysit Lewis and his brother at the Loft, "Yeah, we used to play with the balloons"; Sommer, *Check Your Body at the Door*, 2001; Burnett, telephone conversation, December 31, 2001; Burnett, video interview, July 31, 1993.

20. Archie Burnett, telephone conversation, New York City, July 14, 2000.

21. Brahams La Fortune, video interview, New York City, August 1, 1993.

22. La Fortune, interview, New York City, August 1, 1993; Burnett, telephone conversation, New York City, July 14, 2000.

23. Quoted in Luc Sante, *Low Life* (New York: Vintage Books, 1992), 291.

24. Ibid., 293.

25. Carolyn Cooper, *Noises in the Blood: Orality, Gender, and the "Vulgar" Body of Jamaican Popular Culture* (Durham, NC: Duke University Press, 1995), 21.

26. Owen, "Crackdown in Clubland," 39.

27. Tricia Romano, "Rave Robbers," *Village Voice*, July 17, 2001, 35, 39.

28. Frank Owen, "Private Pandemonium: As Clubs Flounder, Clandestine House Parties Flourish," *Village Voice*, July 17, 2001, 37, 38.

29. Simon Reynolds, "Disco Double Take: New York Parties Like It's 1975," *Village Voice*, July 17, 2001, 43–44.

30. Sommer, *Check Your Body at the Door*, 2001.

31. Archie Burnett verbally plays with the pun and multivocal meaning of "rites of passage," which he also uses as a "right" of passage (i.e., the right to pass must be earned).

32. Archie Burnett, video interview with the author, New York, April 24, 1988.

33. Rietveld, *This Is Our House*, 10, emphasis mine.

34. Song lyrics from "Can You Feel It?" by Heard and Roberts, quoted in Rietveld, *This Is Our House*, 5.

35. Quoted in Rietveld, *This Is Our House*, 2.

36. Archie Burnett, video interview, New York City, August 1, 1996, and October 1997.

37. Turner, *From Ritual to Theatre*, 46.

38. Green, "Fast Footwork."

39. Conrad Rochester, "SP," video interview, New York City, July 31, 1994, and August 1, 1994.

40. Krist quoted in Person et al., *On Freud's "Creative Writers and Day-Dreaming,"* 65.

41. To emphasize that the establishment was a dancing place, Dickens referred to it as "Almacks," an allusion familiar to his readers, because Almacks was a famous London dancing assembly; Dickens quoted in Sante, *Low Life*, 293–94.

42. Robert Farris Thompson, *African Art in Motion: Icon and Act* (Berkeley and Los Angeles: University of California Press, 1974), 28.

43. Rietveld, *This Is Our House*, 201.

44. Turner's discussion of Mihaly Csikszentmihalyi's "flow" theory appears in Turner, *From Ritual to Theatre,* 20–60.

45. Quoted in Person et al., *On Freud's "Creative Writers and Day-Dreaming,"* 3–5.

Selected Readings

Lipsitz, George. *Time Passages: Collective Memory and American Popular Culture.* Minneapolis: University of Minnesota Press, 1990.

Maestro. DVD, dir. Josell Ramos. Disc 1: Theatrical Release (77 min.); disc 2: Supplemental Material (144 min.). Additional footage: "Paradise Garage Footage"; Behind the Scenes, "Making of *Maestro,*" with Josell Ramos; director's documentary, "Ron Hardy: A Look into the Chicago House Music Legend"; "Sound Systems," with David Mancuso, featured DJ; "The Dancers," interview (July 26, 2006).

Thomas, Helen, ed. *Dance in the City.* New York: St. Martin's Press, 1997.

Village Voice. 1997–2003, with special attention to authors Frank Owen and Tricia Romano.

Werde, Bill. "No Love: KTU Jock Louie De Vito Outsold Paul Oakenfold, but Why Can't He Get Any Respect?" *Village Voice,* July 17, 2001.

17

Dancing Latin / Latin Dancing

Salsa and DanceSport

Juliet McMains

The following conversation transpires between two characters in the 1998 film *Dance with Me*. Rafael (Cheyenne), a Cuban recently arrived to work as a handyman at a Texas ballroom dance studio, approaches Ruby (Vanessa Williams), an American ballroom dance champion, as she practices by herself with only the music of her feet scraping the floor for accompaniment.

Rafael: How can you dance without music?
Ruby: It's choreography. Cha-cha.
Rafael: That's cha-cha-chá? I never seen a Latin dance that looked like that.
Ruby: Stick around. I compete professionally in the Latin Dances.
Rafael: How can you dance without music? It comes from the music. I'm sure that's why you look so stiff. You should put on music. Then I'm sure you would feel better.
Ruby: What do you know about professional international style Latin dancing?
Rafael: I'm Latin, but I never heard of that.
Ruby: Then I wouldn't talk to professionals about it.

A radical disjuncture between Ruby and Rafael's conception of "Latin" dance forms the foundation for such conflict throughout the film. This early scene captures many of the major issues at stake: Latin dance as predetermined choreography versus improvisational movement inspired by music, the professionalization of Latin American social dance by a dance industry not located in Latin America, and disputes over who has authority to judge the quality of Latin dance (does coming from a Latin culture trump being a professional Latin dancer?). Ruby and Rafael's contrary expectations are the result of their membership in different communities of Latin dance practitioners, each with distinct aesthetics, techniques, goals, and histories. Ruby is a professional ballroom dance competitor specializing in the Latin division. She shares the biases of the ballroom dance industry in which she has been trained, including belief that precise footwork, choreographed rhythms, long body lines, and competition judges define good Latin dancing. Rafael's assumptions are similar to those of many other Latinos and Latin Americans who regard Latin dance as an expression of cultural identity commonly used to build social bonds in everyday life. Although the characters in this film are fictional, the community of Latin dancers each represents is not.

Conflict and confusion commonly result from use of the phrase "Latin dance" because this refers to so many different practices. Beyond their common emphasis on hip movement and a sexually charged interaction, many so-called Latin dances share little in aesthetic or technical character. This film dramatizes many points of opposition between two traditions of Latin dance: social salsa and competitive International Style Latin. Although these are not the only Latin dance styles to find themselves in contention, salsa and ballroom have both enjoyed such international popularity over the past decade that they are continually forced to define themselves in relation to each other. In this chapter, I will compare these two dance styles, their histories, and the communities in which they are practiced in order to draw out some of the issues arising from use of the word "Latin" to describe such dissimilar dance practices. I will demonstrate how ballroom Latin dances signal Western performers' difference from stereotypes of Latin-ness projected by hip-swinging seductresses, a distancing that simultaneously reinforces the stereotype.[1] I will also examine the corollary reclamation of Latin dance by salsa dancers as a means of affirming membership in a pan-Latino community. I will challenge dichotomies commonly employed to categorize salsa and ballroom Latin by arguing that both have specific and rigorous techniques of movement. And I will illustrate how commercialization has virtually eliminated improvisation from ballroom dancing, whereas salsa dancing, even in its commodification, maintains its improvisational character. Through my comparison, I hope to encourage reconceptualization of Latin dance as a constellation of loosely related but distinct dance traditions whose varied histories have chiseled artistic expression layered with complexity and nuance.

Migration, Proliferation, and Hybridization

The expression "Latin dance"generally refers to dances of Latin America, meaning countries of the Americas, including Central and South America as well as the Caribbean, whose residents speak romance languages (derived from Latin). Although some definitions of Latin America include countries in which the population speaks French, most uses of "Latin" to describe dance refer only to dances from Spanish- or Portuguese-speaking regions.[2] Use of one term to describe dance practices emanating from such diverse geographic and cultural regions appears problematic in itself. This ambiguity has been exacerbated, however, by classification of several American and English ballroom dances as "Latin." Although the ballroom Latin dances were inspired by social practices from Latin America, they were defined and developed in the United States and England, where they diverged starkly from concurrent practices in Latin America. The ballroom forms tend to be characterized by a straight spine, movement that is produced through complete transfer of weight from foot to foot, poses and body shapes in which the entire body is extended, extreme toneness throughout the body, foot positions that are clearly articulated, and the prevalence of predetermined steps. Although Latin American social dance practices comprise specific techniques that are particular to each, several commonalities are consistent across many forms. For example, Latin American versions of rumba, samba, and salsa utilize a more dynamic and flexible spine, weight shifts propelled by core body movement often resulting in weight suspended between the feet, flexed knees and a lower center of gravity, centrality of polyrhythms over body lines, and improvisation closely linked to musical structures.[3] I focus on these distinctions between ballroom Latin dances and those practiced in Latin America (including Latin American communities living outside its geographic borders), even though substantial variation is prominent within each group because of their opposing relationships to the concept "Latin."[4] For the predominantly white ballroom dance community, "Latin" is about Otherness; for Latin American and Latino communities dancing salsa, "Latin" is a label of cultural pride. Whereas ballroom dancers are "dancing Latin" as a means of affirming their distance from Latin ethnic identity through consciously donning a mask of Latin-ness, many salsa dancers participate in "Latin dancing" in order to assert their membership in a Latin community.

Since the first Latin dance boom swept Europe and the United States in the 1910s, the ballroom dance industry has capitalized on stereotypes of Latin as hot, passionate, and sexy in order to market and sell Latin dance.[5] Western consumers dancing "Latin" could borrow some of the excitement associated with Latin stereotypes without the burden of racial discrimination. For example, Latin identity could be worn for the duration of a rumba, a dancer siphoning off positive associations without fear that his or her identity would be reduced exclusively to the realm of sexual desire. Many Western consumers even today find comfort in assuming a mask of Latin-ness in order to perform movements exceeding Western standards of propriety. They can enjoy pelvic thrusts or lustful embraces judged to be too wild, sexual, or vulgar within their own cultural frame under the guise of "Latin" dance. The fact that the ballroom Latin dances have little in common with actual dance practices in Latin America has been of little relevance to their success in the West. Their marketability depends on the fantasy of Latin-ness they enable Westerners to sustain, one that allows them to project their own anxieties about sexuality and physicality onto an exotic Other.[6]

Even ballroom dancers of Latin American descent may participate in this masquerade as a means of aligning themselves with a Western cultural position. For example, Mexican American celebrity contestant Giselle Fernandez explained on the popular television show *Dancing with the Stars* that she assumed an alter ego by the name of Rosarita in order to prepare herself for the ballroom rumba performance. Although on the one hand she claims a privileged access to the character of Rosarita because of her ethnicity, the fact that she gives her alter ego a different name indicates the distance at which she needs to hold this eroticized Latin identity from her core public persona. In her clever ploy, Fernandez both capitalizes on the "authenticity" advantage she gains by claiming her identity as a "real" Latina while simultaneously distancing that sexualized image from the serious public identity she has cultivated as a journalist. In mainstream American culture and in a ballroom dance industry dominated by non-Hispanic whites, Latin dance signals an exotic Other that relies on a stereotype of excessive and deviant Latin sexuality that even Latin Americans may disavow.

Latin Americans outside ballroom dance circles, however, use the same word "Latin" to describe dance practices closely connected to their heritage and identity. Salsa, in particular, proudly embraced as a Latin dance by Latin American and Latino communities, has become a vital source for fostering cultural identity within and across various ethnic and national groups. Because salsa celebrates contributions from so many different Latin cultures as vital to its creation, the dance floor is often a site at which particular national and ethnic identities are affirmed and pan-Latino coalition is forged. Many practitioners find salsa offers them a link to their particular cultural background (Cuban, Puerto Rican, Dominican, Columbian, etc.) at the same time it allows them entry into a much larger Latin community. In spite of the ballroom dance industry's continued use of Latin dance as a symbol of exotic difference and perhaps in direct response to it, Latinos have reclaimed Latin dance as a vital expression of their own identity. Salsa affirms that Latin dance is sexy but also that it is rhythmic, alive, rebellious, clever, creative, and constantly in flux.

Salsa emerged as a distinct genre of music and dance in the late 1960s when Latin American musicians living in New York began to market their music, updated variations on Cuban mambo, under the label "salsa."[7] The music, which in the 1950s was primarily a hybrid of Cuban *son* and African American jazz, began to reflect an even wider range of influences, mirroring the multiethnic constitution of its musicians who hailed from disparate Caribbean, South American, and American cities.[8] The dance likewise continued to mature and change as new generations and populations embraced it. The staccato, rebounding movements of mambo gave way to the continuous rolling body action and weight shifts of salsa. Partnering became more prominent as turns from swing, hustle, and ballroom dancing worked their way in between rhythmic body isolations. Early salsa lyrics were often political, exposing oppression, poverty, and violence. Boricuan writer Mayra Santos Febres argues that salsa engendered a "translocal" community because the common local experiences of oppression and rebellion described in salsa lyrics and echoed in the movement cut across national boundaries. Although this translocal community shares a common spoken language in Spanish, it might be better defined by the values and experiences encompassed by salsa: skill at improvisation, mixed origins, polymetered rhythms that coexist and fuse, economic deprivation in *el barrio,* and feet that constantly shift in unpredictable patterns in response to the environment.[9] Even as salsa has expanded to include love ballads with no explicit political content, the sustained popularity of salsa music and dance across different national and ethnic groups that feel a sense of propriety over the genre (Latin Americans from almost every country will refer to salsa as "our music") encourages pan-Latino coalition.[10] Furthermore, the physical contact enabled by the dance among individuals from diverse Latin American backgrounds produces alliances (friendly and romantic) that attest to salsa, even *salsa romantica,* as a vital mechanism for creation of pan-Latino identity.[11] This tradition of salsa as a means of cultural identification contrasts sharply with the history of Latin dance as signifier of cultural difference in the ballroom dance industry.

International Style Latin dance is part of DanceSport, the name adopted to describe competitive ballroom dancing in the late 1980s in order to facilitate an international effort to secure its acceptance as an Olympic sport.[12] Unlike social dancing in Latin America, which is commonly practiced by nonspecialists as part of everyday communal life, DanceSport requires intensive study and devout commitment for success at either the amateur or professional level. DanceSport competitions are held throughout North America, Europe, Asia, and in former English colonies (e.g., South Africa, India, Australia), although they are virtually unknown in Latin America. American participation in DanceSport has grown steadily since the early 1990s, in part due to immigration of dancers from Eastern Europe (where DanceSport is a popular activity for children) and in part to media exposure in film and television. DanceSport includes two major divisions: Standard (which is comprised of waltz, tango, Viennese waltz, fox trot, and quickstep) and Latin (which consists of cha-cha, samba, rumba, paso doble, and jive). Even a cursory examination of this list is bewildering to most who do not understand why tango (a dance from Argentina) is excluded from the Latin division and jive (an American dance) is classified as Latin. The inconsistent categorization has more to do with historical timing than it does with the national origin of each dance. Competitive ballroom dancing was developed in England in the 1920s. When the dances were codified in these early years, tango was already an accepted and popular ballroom dance and was standardized alongside the waltz, fox trot, and quickstep (Viennese waltz was added to the Standard division in the 1960s). The dances included in the Latin division were codified much later by the English dance societies and were not added to competitions until the 1950s.

The newly accepted dances were grouped together in a new competition category called "Latin and American," which was eventually shortened to "Latin American" (or often just "Latin"). If the grouping together of dances originating (at least in name) in Cuba (cha-cha and rumba), Brazil (samba), Spain (paso doble), and the United States (jive) into a single category were not misleading enough, omission of the conjunction *and* from the title has led most people to assume that the Latin category of DanceSport encompasses dances of Latin American origin.[13] The mere fact that two of these four countries (Spain and the United States) are not in Latin America should be enough evidence to dispel this misconception, but Latin is a powerful insignia. The Latin American category of DanceSport is commonly confused with dance from Latin America.

All Latin American dance is, in the words of eminent Cuban scholar Fernando Ortiz, the product of "transculturation," the merging of elements from two or more cultures to create a new cultural phenomenon.[14] African rhythms, brought to the Americas by slaves, transformed as they met with European melodies and indigenous instruments, resulting in numerous and varied musical styles throughout the Caribbean, Central America, and South America. New dances likewise evolved that combined elements from African dances, such as pelvic and torso isolations and the primacy of improvisation, with European closed-couple partnering techniques. Over the course of the twentieth century, specific Latin American social dances, including the tango, rumba, samba, cha-cha, and mambo, enjoyed periods of popularity in Europe and America.[15] In the new Western context, the Latin dances were transformed once again in response to the values, abilities, interests, and experiences of their new practitioners. The migration of dances such as the samba or rumba to Europe and America, and their subsequent synchronization with previously established ballroom dances, was hardly a new or isolated event. It was merely another instance of transculturation, the process through which these dance were created in their countries of origin. The problem I highlight here is not that Latin dance continues to grow and change in new locations but that the new forms keep the same name. From the moment each Latin dance was accepted into European and American ballrooms, at least two distinct practices continued to develop under the same name: one in the Western ballrooms and another in Latin American communities. Although there has always been some contact and overlap between the two groups, the styles developed relatively independently until the end of the twentieth century when increased globalization, multicultural awareness, and the cachet of Latin as a popular style in the West helped bring the two practices into dialogue, contention, and dissension.

The film *Dance with Me* accurately captures common tropes used by both communities in their struggle to gain validation for their form of Latin dance. Discipline and control characterize DanceSport Latin in this film as Ruby attempts to master her body through hours of structured practice in the studio. Salsa is portrayed as the expression of emotion through a spontaneous physical response to music. Whereas the practice of DanceSport Latin functions as the means by which Ruby earns a living and fulfills an American work ethic in which personal satisfaction must be subjugated for professional success, salsa dancing becomes the vehicle through which she falls in love and recognizes the value of community. These two forms of Latin dance are diametrically opposed in the film: the structured, technical form for competition dancing versus the spontaneous, free form for social interactions. The world of DanceSport brings professional recognition and financial success but lacks emotional honesty. The world of salsa clubs and parties offers personal interactions of friendship, community, and romantic love but no economic stability. This dichotomy can be largely explained by the different contexts and contrasting goals of salsa and DanceSport. Salsa is a social practice in which the social, interactive experience for the participants is the primary focus. DanceSport is a theatrical representation of social dance in which the main concern of the activity is its effect on the viewers. Whereas the social priority of salsa has lead to emphasis on play, musicality, subtlety, exchange between partners, leadability of vocabulary, and the feeling of the moves for the dancers themselves, none of these skills are highly valued in DanceSport Latin. Seduction is practiced on the audiences and judges, not within the partnership. As in the ballet pas de deux, preference for long body lines often supersedes any tendency toward realism in these passionate embraces. Preset DanceSport choreography foregrounds visual readability of body positions and rhythms, expansive presentational movement directed toward an audience as well as a partner, contrast in movement dynamics, speed, control, dramatic tricks, and visual effect (figure 17.1).

Ruby's choice of a romantic relationship with Rafael over a career as a DanceSport champion implies that the values embraced by salsa dancing (including friendship, love, familial responsibility, community) win out over those of DanceSport (including competition, professional development, financial success). In the final scene of the film, however, Ruby and Rafael are pictured teaching in the ballroom studio. They have brought some of the salsa dancers and musicians from the club scenes into the studio, but love and salsa are not enough to shield the happy couple from the necessity of earning a living. Although the film champions the values Rafael brings from his Latin culture, the couple does not return to Cuba but attempts to sustain these values as they continue to live in capitalist America.

Their choice parallels that facing many Latino *salseros* in the United States who are now earning a living teaching, performing, and competing in salsa. No longer is salsa merely a social form shared between family and friends. Its burgeoning popularity has precipitated (and been precipitated by) an ever-growing salsa dance industry, which, although not named in the film, was absolutely crucial to the film's production. Los Angeles area salsa dancers and teachers were used extensively as cast and choreographers. Yet the

Figure 17.1: DanceSport Latin competitors Valentin Chmerkovskiy and Valeriya Kozharinova execute elegantly crafted choreography at the Yankee Classic in Boston in June 2005. Photo © 2005 by Jonathan S. Marion.

term *salsa* was not mentioned once in the film, nor was the varied ethnic and national makeup of its cast acknowledged. Instead, the film represents a generic Latin dance embraced by a generic Latin community whose nominal identity as Cuban must have been undermined by the fact that the "Cuban" lead was played by a music star readily identifiable to the American public as Puerto Rican. Although on the one hand this elision underscores how salsa can enable Latino identity that transcends national identity, the failure to name or distinguish among different Latin dance styles falsely implies that Latin dance enjoyed by Latin people exists outside structure, education, and commerce.[16] The prominence of salsa dance business, however, can no longer be overlooked.

Technique and Sabor

Still emergent when this film was made, the new salsa dance industry may constitute the largest percentage of social dance commerce worldwide. Consumers from Anchorage to Zagreb are salsa mad, purchasing salsa dance classes, videos, magazines, shoes, and music as well as entrance to clubs, congresses, and shows at a fever pitch. Salsa dancers who acquired their skills by growing up in a culture in which salsa music and dance are part of everyday life cannot rely on the methods by which they learned as the basis of a successful teaching business. Because, until recently, there was little precedent in Latin America for teaching social dance in formal classes, salsa professionals have relied heavily on models created by the ballroom dance industry for counting their rhythms, breaking down actions, and naming their steps. Even Eddie Torres, New York's "King of Mambo" and its most influential mambo and salsa teacher, credits ballroom dancer June Laberta with teaching him music and dance theory.[17] Although *salseros* have readily borrowed from the ballroom dance industry, they have simultaneously struggled to distinguish salsa from ballroom Latin. Celebrating the African roots of salsa and incorporating movements from Afro-Cuban rumba have emerged as popular strategies for marking salsa's difference from white-washed, Western Latin dance.[18] Although embrace of Latin dance's African heritage is a powerful move that counters corollary erasures by the ballroom dance industry, the polarization of the "colored" practice of salsa and the "white" ballroom dances leads to unintended consequences.

Less politically charged words tend to stand in for the unspoken racial difference, which is often condensed onto two terms: technique and *sabor*.[19] The ballroom Latin dancer has technique: training and corporeal discipline. The salsa dancer has *sabor,* a word that could be poorly translated as "flavor," "fire," "feeling," or "soul." This distinction is also reflected in the terms "studio" and "street" dancer. Salsa is usually referred to as a street dance, a name acquired because its early practitioners could not afford to dance on the polished sprung floors of the ballrooms and developed their dances, literally, on the street. Latin dancers who have little formal training but acquire their skills by experience in nightclubs and at private parties and family gatherings are still referred to by members of both the salsa and ballroom communities as street dancers. The difference between studio and street dancers is a class distinction embedded in racial difference, but it is greater than mere economics.

The fact that street dancers do not have formal dance training in structured classes does not mean that they have no training. It is a different training system, one that relies on immersion in the culture. Someone who is formally trained in studio dancing appears, by some interpretations, to have not only the money to pay for lessons but also the moral restraint to appreciate strict codes of bodily control and emotional expression and the intellectual ability to understand its syntactic structures. Following this same line of reasoning, street dancing signals a community of people not only who cannot afford structured lessons but also whose emotional and sexual impulses cannot be contained by discipline and whose intellectual capacities are not sufficiently developed to grasp rules dictated by a dancing teacher. It is this moral and intellectual hierarchy implied in the distinction between studio and street Latin dancing that continues to sustain harmful racial stereotypes and to reinforce the perception of Latin as Other.[20]

Just because it has been less well articulated does not mean that salsa dancing has no technique. In fact, the myth that street salsa dancing has no technique is used as both a put-down by the ballroom community and a marketing strategy by salsa dancers. Because it is less technical—that is to say, less strictly bound by rules and detailed muscular analysis—salsa dancing appears to be a more "genuine" dance experience. The absence of the strict structure dictated by official dancing organizations appears to allow for a more natural response to the music and one's partner. Salsa dancing is uninhibited emotional expression, argue many of its proponents (figure 17.2). I counter, however, that it is not the lack of technique in salsa social dance practices that enables people to feel a more authentic expressive experience. It is actually the specific technical structure of salsa dancing that creates space for more individual improvisation, creative expression, and *sabor.* So, although both ballroom Latin and salsa dancers tend to use the word "technique" to signal a specific kind of technique, one that has been theorized through the study of physiology and taught through careful verbal explanation, I use the term to describe the particular methods utilized to produce any kind of movement, whether or not its practitioners can articulate their process.[21]

In ballroom Latin, the major muscle groups in the stomach, back, pelvis, legs, and feet are always connected. Although the muscle groups do not always move in the same direction at the same time, movement in any one area always affects the others. For example, a weight shift through the feet and bending of one knee enables a rotation of the pelvis and subsequent movement across the ribs and back, which then produces a tiny pressure change in the man's hands on his partner's back, indicating to her the precise moment at which she should shift her weight. This strict interconnectedness of major muscle groups allows for the kind of speed in partnering dynamics that gives ballroom Latin its unique appeal. What it does not encourage, though, is the kind of polyrhythmic movement that is popular in salsa danc-

Figure 17.2: Salsa dancers Edgar Martinez and Florabelle Moses playfully improvise at the West Coast Salsa Congress in Los Angeles in May 2006. Photo © 2006 by Juliet McMains.

ing. Because salsa music is based on many different rhythms interacting to produce its complex structure, dancers often mimic the different instruments with different parts of their bodies. For example, salsa dancers may move their feet in rhythm with the congas, thrust their rib cages forward in time to the clave, and shimmy their shoulders between hits of the cowbell. The disconnection of the muscle groups and their ability to initiate independent movements give salsa its particular movement style. This technique of poly-rhythmic body articulation links salsa dancing most closely to West African dance practices from which both the music and the movement draw much of their inspiration.[22] Thus, the defining characteristics of these two move-ment forms are clearly linked to raced movement practices: the black West African dance practices that foreground multiple points of articulation and the white Western concert dance traditions, particularly ballet, that privilege bodily cohesion and control.

The two practices also use different partnering techniques. Ballroom Latin dancers maintain a consistent connection throughout the course of dancing so that every shift of weight is clearly communicated from one body to the other. They accomplish this tight connection by maintaining a stable frame in the arms and moving the rib cage and back within this frame to com-municate movement choices. Salsa dancers maintain a looser connection through the hands, initiating leads by moving the arms or the entire body weight. Strong body-to-body connection through the hands is only used to initiate turns, not to coordinate each step. Though ballroom Latin dancers shun this loose connection because more dynamic and faster changes of energy are not possible, it enables more spontaneous improvisations. Perfect coordination of movement is not expected between partners, so missteps become new steps rather than mistakes.

Improvisational skill is highly esteemed by *salseros*. Excitement is gener-ated out of uncertainty. Not being able to predict precisely the next moves of the musicians or one's partner makes each decision that brings all three into harmony deliciously rewarding. The best social dancers are not only skilled at responding to a human partner but also know equally well how to part-ner the music. Many dancers are masterful musical interpreters, matching percussion accents and melodic crescendos with their own physical repartee. Such skills are revered not because a dancer has planned in advance which movements will complement which measure of music but precisely because he or she has not. The expert improvisational dancer can instantaneously recognize musical patterns, evaluate the available spatial parameters, and seamlessly communicate with his or her partner in order to perform stunning combinations of grace and dexterity that an inexpert observer might swear had been rehearsed beforehand.

Audience-driven performance dance practices, on the other hand, do not usually value improvisation to the same degree. Although improvisation may dazzle onlookers in a social dance club, it rarely works as a successful strategy for staged performance of social dance. The stage and competition frame sets up different audience expectations from those produced by the frame of a nightclub. An audience of performance expects a well-rehearsed routine, neatly worked out to match the music. Whereas in the social setting spectators may have just witnessed the dancers' introduction and can be assured that their interactions are unrehearsed, an audience of theatrical performance has no similar validation that significant movement choices are being made in the moment of execution. DanceSport competitors thus employ minimal improvisation during a competition. Spontaneous creation of new combinations and moves on the competition floor seems too risky when dancers have only a few seconds to convince each judge of their superior skill.

Improvisational dexterity sets salsa dancers apart from most DanceSport competitors. The sophistication of this skill is not, however, usually recognized by audiences because improvisational structure is difficult to decipher unless the viewer is also a practitioner.[23] A spectator must be able to compare the dancers' spontaneous decisions against a range of other possible choices in order to appreciate the ingenuity of each selection.[24] Because so few observers of improvisational social dance recognize the level of skill displayed and dancers themselves may not be able to articulate their method because the speed of the dance requires them to bypass conscious thought, improvisation is rarely recognized as the complex, precise, and demanding technique that enables salsa's *sabor*. Failure to recognize improvisation as a technique continues to reinforce the dichotomy between "natural" salsa dancing and "disciplined" ballroom Latin.

Genealogies of Improvisation

Although salsa and ballroom dance are both practiced in social and theatrical settings (including performance and competition), each form has been shaped by a history that privileges one venue over the other. These contrasting histories have led to the primacy of improvisation in salsa, which remains predominantly a social practice, and the absence of significant improvisation in ballroom dance, which, even in its social expression, is mainly concerned with its effect on viewers. A brief outline of these histories will help to illustrate this distinction.

The advent of modern ballroom dancing in the early twentieth century coincided with the emergence of a dance industry, a network of related businesses that included dancing teachers and schools, exhibition performers, cabarets, dance manuals, records, and clothing. The appearance of social dance commerce led to radical changes in the nature of social dancing, which increasingly became mediated and spread by businesses with economic motivations. Dance historian Julie Malnig has linked the emergence of the ballroom dance industry in the 1910s with the contemporaneous growth of advertising, which enabled entrepreneurs to foster associations between dance products and unrelated desires (i.e., romance, wealth, popularity, social ease).[25] As advertising and consumer culture increasingly defined American culture throughout the twentieth century, social ballroom dance became something to be purchased from an industry, rather than a social exchange between individuals.

Codification of social dancing into a salable product resulted in elimination of improvisation from social ballroom dance practice. Multiple factors including marketability, racial prejudice, and its upper-class image contributed to the crystallization of social ballroom dance as a series of predetermined steps rather than a set of techniques for creating a dynamic physical dialogue. Movements and rhythms that emerged as variable and mutable constellations in early versions of each ballroom dance were codified by the ballroom dance industry in part because standardized dances proved much easier to sell. In addition to the practicality of marketing a single correct version as superior, attempts to distance the dances from their lower-class and black origins were equally significant in the expulsion of improvisation from ballroom dance floors. Catering to a primarily white and upwardly mobile clientele, the American ballroom dance industry has profited from "refining" dances not previously practiced by its elite patrons. Such a project required distinguishing between refined and unrefined dancing, resulting in common beliefs about the right and wrong way to execute the socially elevated ballroom dances. This hierarchy led to less variation, individual choice, and improvisation by ballroom dancers who followed the specific instructions of star ballroom dance teachers like Irene and Vernon Castle and Arthur Murray.

Adoption of the English system of competition dancing in the 1960s, however, played an even larger role in excising improvisation from American ballroom dance. The British style of ballroom dancing was nationally standardized by committee in the 1920s and had, by the 1960s, enjoyed a forty-year period of development as a competitive form in which improvisation was rarely utilized. When this English system of national and international competition was adopted by U.S. dance schools in the 1960s, regional variation and improvisation were almost entirely purged from the ballrooms. When techniques like those promoted by Arthur Murray studios had been distributed nationally but enacted locally, there was still some room for regional variation. Once dancers were traveling to compete together in nationally organized competitions, sharing space with one another, and mimicking the winners of each competition in hopes of improving their own rankings, there was little incentive to cultivate individual style.

When interest in social ballroom dancing started to revive, fueled by the disco craze of the mid-1970s, and then soared in the 1990s, few teachers or studios recognized the incongruity of teaching social dancing based on the new teaching methods designed to produce successful competition results. Although confusion between theatrical and social dance had been a marketing tool of the ballroom dance industry throughout the twentieth century, the current obfuscation runs deeper than merely public perception. Teachers of social ballroom dance are primarily DanceSport competitors, rarely participating in social dancing themselves. Many studio teachers are immigrants from Eastern Europe, where DanceSport is a popular youth activity. Although superbly trained dancers who excel in the competition style, these immigrants rarely have any experience or exposure to social ballroom dance, further exacerbating conflation of the two. Whereas competitive ballroom dancing was once a polished and flamboyant version of the popular social form, social ballroom dance has now become a stylization of DanceSport. As a result, the low priority placed on improvisation in DanceSport is also transposed to social ballroom dance, once again driving improvisation off social dance floors.

Salsa, in contrast, has remained first and foremost a social form. Although the ballroom dance industry codified and simplified the mambo in the 1950s, mambo and *son* continued to evolve into salsa outside ballroom dance studios. As it developed through the 1970s and 1980s, distinctly different styles emerged in various cities within the Latin diaspora, each group of practitioners folding local dance traditions into the mix. Movements from *santería, plena,* tango, hip-hop, and even ballet became fair game for the salsa melting pot. This radical regional variation encouraged the understanding of salsa as a mutable dance practice, not a fixed series of steps. Salsa's close association with the evolving music, which was defined by improvised interaction between its musicians, also encouraged dancers to maintain improvisation as paramount in their practice.

When national and international salsa dance congresses were organized in the late 1990s, no single salsa style had emerged as predominant. The New York style was admired for its suave partnering, sophisticated poise, and commitment to breaking on the second beat. Los Angeles dancers became renowned for their speed, acrobatics, and attack. Intricate footwork was the hallmark of Puerto Rican dancers. And casino style from Cuba and Miami was distinctive for its pretzel-like turns and the group *rueda,* in which the women are passed around a circle of men executing moves simultaneously in response to called or signed cues. The convergence of *salseros* with such different strengths fueled innovation. Rivalries heightened the dancers' drive to outdo one another through improvisational interplay on the social dance floor, cross-fertilization strengthening, and proliferating the diversity of salsas. As this borrowing and blending has intensified, the tradition of improvisation through social practice remains strong. Unlike the creation of national and international networks of ballroom dance competitions that stifle improvisation, salsa congresses encourage it. Such a distinction is reflected in (and enabled by) the structure of salsa congresses, which do not generally include competition. Instead, the congresses are comparable to ballroom competitions as the forum at which enthusiasts from various geographic regions converge to share and show off their skill, enjoy workshops and performances, and dance until dawn. Because social dance remains the central activity at the salsa industry's most prominent public events, improvisation remains crucial to the practice.

Would the Real Latin Dance Please Stand Up?

As the popularity and visibility of both salsa and DanceSport continue to climb, neither is likely to relinquish claim to the name "Latin dance." How do we proceed, then? Is there a right and a wrong, a real and a fake Latin dance? Attempts to privilege salsa as so-called authentic Latin dance may draw attention to earlier Western appropriation, but they simultaneously reinforce binaries that have lead to racial stereotyping. The relationship between ballroom and salsa is much more complex than that suggested by dichotomies of *sabor*/technique, natural/trained, colored/white. A more productive approach might be a rigorous examination of the histories of various Latin dance traditions in their specificity, calling attention to the points at which they cross and are altered as a result of their meeting. I also hope that wider recognition of the context in which salsa and DanceSport developed (social floor versus competition floor) and the corollary role of improvisation (primary versus minor) in each will lead to understanding of their differences in terms beyond race and ethnicity. Although salsa may have developed in primarily Latino communities and the annals of DanceSport history belie its white, Western past, neither remains so homogenous. Non-Latino *salseros* from the United States, Japan, Israel, France, and Korea flock to salsa congresses, and Latinos now number among DanceSport champions.

Ultimately, the challenge to which both writers and readers of history must rise is to maintain an awareness of the history of cultural imperialism in which Latin dance is enmeshed without reproducing the power imbalance upon which that history is based. We cannot naively assume that a celebration of all forms of Latin dance as equally valid will enable everyone to live in peace and harmony, nor should we focus so exclusively on the injustices of the past that we reinforce their racial logic. These two extremes must be held in constant balance as we strive to build a new understanding of Latin dance that both maintains awareness of its troubled past and enables us to move beyond it.

Notes

1. I use the term "Western" to describe dominant Euro-American cultural values. I recognize that continued use of language that situates the West at its center may on some levels reinscribe the global hierarchies I seek to disrupt. I choose to use this imperfect vocabulary, however, because these are the terms in which the discourse I critique has been forged, both in the academy and in the media. For a discussion of use of the terms "Western" and "non-Western," see Georgina Born and David Hesmondhalgh, "Introduction: On Difference, Representation, and Appropriation in Music," in *Western Music and Its Others: Difference, Representation, and Appropriation in Music,* ed. Georgina Born and David Hesmondhalgh (Berkeley and Los Angeles: University of California Press, 2000), 47.

2. For why Brazilian dance should be categorized as Latin dance, see Karen Backstein, "Taking 'Class' into Account: Dance, the Studio, and Latino Culture," in *Mambo Montage: The Latinization of New York,* ed. Augustín Laó-Montes and Arlene Dávila (New York: Columbia University Press, 2001), 449–72.

3. My descriptions of Latin dance styles here and elsewhere in the chapter are based on extensive observation of and participation in multiple forms of Latin dance. I have been practicing ballroom forms of Latin dance since 1991 and salsa since 1997. I began teaching both forms in 1997. My role as a teacher of both styles has contributed substantially to my ability to differentiate between the techniques and aesthetics of each.

4. Given that salsa was largely developed by Latinos living in the United States, my use of the term "Latin America" will include U.S. Latin American communities.

5. See, for example, Marta Savigliano, who traces Western appropriation and sale

of tango as part of the "economy of passion" that relies on and reinforces Latin stereotypes of "exotic," "primitive," and "uncivilized," in *Tango: The Political Economy of Passion* (Boulder, CO: Westview Press, 1994). For more general discussions of Latin stereotypes reproduced by media, see Clara E. Rodríguez, ed., *Latin Looks: Images of Latinos and Latinas in the U.S. Media* (Boulder, CO: Westview Press, 1997).

6. My use of the concept *Other* to mean different from and implicitly less than the normative Western subject follows that of key postcolonial scholars. See Edward Said, *Orientalism* (New York: Vintage Books, 1978); and Homi K. Bhabha, "The Other Question: Difference, Discrimination and the Discourse of Colonialism," in *Out There: Marginalization and Contemporary Cultures*, ed. Russell Ferguson et al. (New York: New Museum of Contemporary Art; Cambridge, MA: MIT Press, 1990), 71–87.

7. Music historian Max Salazar actually dates the first use of the word "salsa" to describe Latin dance music to 1933, although the word was not commonly used as a music label until the late 1960s; Max Salazar, "Salsa Origins," in *Mambo Kingdom: Latin Music in New York* (New York: Schirmer Trade Books, 2002), 255–59.

8. Histories of salsa music have been written and debated by numerous scholars. See Jorge Duany, "Popular Music in Puerto Rico: Toward an Anthropology of *Salsa*," *Latin American Music Review* 5, no. 2 (1984): 186–216; Vernon W. Boggs, ed., *Salsiology: Afro-Cuban Music and the Evolution of Salsa in New York City* (New York: Greenwood Press, 1992); Peter Manuel, "Puerto Rican Music and Cultural Identity: Creative Appropriation of Cuban Sources from Danza to Salsa," *Ethnomusicology* 38, no. 2 (1994): 249–80; and Lise Waxer, ed., *Situating Salsa: Global Markets and Local Meanings in Latin Popular Music* (New York: Routledge, 2002).

9. Mayra Santos Febres, "Salsa as Translocation," in *Everynight Life: Culture and Dance in Latin/o America*, ed. Celeste Frazer Delgado and Jose Esteban Muñoz (Durham, NC: Duke University Press, 1997), 175–88.

10. Peter Manuel argues that recent gains in the civil rights movement created an environment in which Latinos were able to overcome national difference to form a coalition to fight common discrimination. He suggests that salsa enabled (and was enabled by) this political awareness of Latino identity; Peter Manuel, "The Soul of the Barrio: 30 Years of Salsa," *NACLA Report on the Americas* 28, no. 2 (1994): 22–29.

11. I follow many other scholars who likewise argue that Latin dance is a crucial means through which Latin identity is created and political rebellion enacted. See Celeste Frazer Delgado and Jose Esteban Muñoz, "Rebellions of Everynight Life," in *Everynight Life: Culture and Dance in Latin/o America*, 9–32; Frances R. Aparicio, "Salsa, Maracas, and Baile: Latin Popular Music in the Poetry of Victor Hernandez Cruz," *MELUS* 16, no. 1 (1989/1990): 43–58; Patria Román-Velázquez, *The Making of Latin London: Salsa Music, Place, and Identity* (Aldershot, U.K.: Ashgate, 1999); and Priscilla Renta, "Salsa Dance: Latino/a History in Motion," *CENTRO Journal* 16, no. 2 (2004): 139–57.

12. The effort was partially successful. DanceSport received official sanction as an Olympic sport by the International Olympic Committee in 1999 but has yet to be included on the schedule for the Olympic Games. DanceSport is one of dozens of officially recognized sports waiting to be added to the already crowded Olympic roster.

13. Because so many Latin Americans speak Spanish, "Latin" is often confused with "Spanish" or "Hispanic," resulting in the assumption that Spanish dances like the paso doble are Latin dance.

14. Fernando Ortiz, *Cuban Counterpoint: Tobacco and Sugar* (New York: Knopf, 1947), 102–3.

15. For a history of the Latin dances in English ballrooms as imported by M. Pierre and Doris Lavelle, see Irene Evans, *A Concise History of Latin American Dancing in the U.K.* (United Kingdom Alliance of Professional Teachers of Dancing, 1992). See also the technique book Pierre, *Latin and American Dances for Students and Teachers* (London: Thomasons, 1948).

16. Rafael is pictured dancing Cuban rumba in the opening scenes as well as Los Angeles–style salsa and Cuban *casino rueda* later in the film.

17. Eddie Torres, interview with Diane Duggan, August 30, 2001; transcript, The Jerome Robbins Dance Division, The New York Public Library for the Performing Arts.

18. Although the casting of African American actor Vanessa Williams in the role of DanceSport champion may obscure the actual demographics of the sport, Dance-Sport has very few black participants. White dancers from a variety of countries and ethnicities (particularly Eastern Europe), Asians (and Asian Americans), and a growing number of Latinos constitute the competitors and audience at any DanceSport event.

19. I am grateful to Jesús Morales for suggesting this comparison.

20. Anthropologist Néstor García Canclini makes an analogous argument about attempts to reify Latin American as "traditional," contending that opposing pressures to modernize Latin America while preserving its "tradition" reproduce the hierarchies and inequalities that have thus far defined Latin America's relations with the West; Néstor García Canclini, *Hybrid Cultures: Strategies for Entering and Leaving Modernity,* trans. Christopher L. Chiappari and Silvia L. Lopez (Minneapolis: University of Minnesota Press, 1995).

21. My use of the word "technique" to describe all movement practices rather than just those with well-articulated pedagogical models is indebted to the early work of Marcel Mauss, "Body Techniques," in *Sociology and Psychology: Essays,* trans. Ben Brewer (London: Routledge, 1979), 97–123; and subsequent development of his ideas by dance scholars such as Cynthia Novack, *Sharing the Dance: Contact Improvisation and American Culture* (Madison: University of Wisconsin Press, 1990); and Susan Leigh Foster, "Dancing Bodies," in *Meaning in Motion: New Cultural Studies of Dance,* ed. Jane C. Desmond (Durham, NC: Duke University Press, 1997), 235–57.

22. Dance scholar Yvonne Daniel writes about the Cuban *son,* which is the basis for both the music and movement of salsa, that "the emphasis on moving hips permits the torso to divide its movement potential, and to create separate visual rhythms, polyrhythms between the upper and lower torso. The 'divided' torso of *son* is African as opposed to European dance of the period, which generally used the entire torso as a stabilizer for arm and leg movement"; Yvonne Daniel, "Cuban Dance: An Orchard of Caribbean Creativity," in *Caribbean Dance: From Abakuá to Zouk,* ed. Susanna Sloat (Gainesville: University Press of Florida, 2002), 43. For characteristics of West African dance, see also Jacqui Malone, *Steppin' on the Blues: The Visible Rhythms of African American Dance* (Urbana: University of Illinois Press, 1996).

23. Margaret Thompson Drewel also argues that improvisation cannot be readily appreciated by audiences who are not themselves trained in the movement genre they observe; Margaret Thompson Drewel, "Improvisation as Participatory Performance: Egungun Masked Dancers in the Yoruba Tradition," in *Taken by Surprise: A Dance Improvisation Reader,* ed. Ann Cooper Albright and David Gere (Middletown, CT: Wesleyan University Press, 2003), 119–32.

24. Susan Leigh Foster similarly describes the pleasure of watching improvisational concert dance by stating, "Unanticipated trajectories, landings, and traversals create

stunning kinesthetic paradoxes as one compares what the body might have done with what it actually did"; Susan Leigh Foster, *Reading Dancing: Bodies and Subjects in Contemporary American Dance* (Berkeley and Los Angeles: University of California Press, 1986), 179.

25. Julie Malnig, "Two-Stepping to Glory: Social Dance and the Rhetoric of Social Mobility," in *Moving History/Dancing Cultures: A Dance History Reader*, ed. Ann Dils and Ann Cooper Albright (Middletown, CT: Wesleyan University Press, 2001), 271–87. For discussion of the early commodification of ballroom dance, see also Danielle Anne Robinson, "Race in Motion: Reconstructing the Practice, Profession, and Politics of Social Dancing, New York City 1900–1930" (PhD diss., University of California, Riverside, 2004).

18

Louisiana Gumbo

Retention, Creolization, and Innovation in Contemporary Cajun and Zydeco Dance

May Gwin Waggoner

"Do you know who made you?"
"Nobody, as I knows on," said the child, with a short laugh.
The idea appeared to amuse her considerably; for her eyes twinkled,
and she added, "I spect I grow'd. Don't think nobody never made me."
—Harriett Beecher Stowe, *Uncle Tom's Cabin*[1]

South Louisiana is a study in contrasts and contradictions. Moss grows in the air, swamp maples turn red in the spring, and bayous flow in two directions. The region's public radio station devotes Saturday mornings to zydeco music and Saturday afternoons to Metropolitan Opera broadcasts, four-year-olds play accordion, and older couples who can hardly walk nonetheless manage a turn on the dance floor. From the hot, muggy days when slaves' work songs rang out in the humid Louisiana sky, from the cold winter nights when early Acadians gathered around the fireplace to sing and dance, through physical suffering and exile and isolation and neglect and economic hardship and war, music has been one constant, a way to keep the past alive, to mark events, to mourn and rejoice.

History books tell us that during the seventeenth and eighteenth centuries, the New World welcomed explorers and colonists who built a nation. These books neglect, however, the fact that the nation was also built by unwilling immigrants. Among them were two very dissimilar groups transported to the nascent colonies against their will. Thousands of miles apart, Africans and Acadians alike were forced into the holds of overcrowded ships, their families divided and destroyed.[2] The bodies of those who died of illness or dehydration or starvation were thrown overboard.[3] After weeks and months at sea, the human cargo was unloaded in the colonies. The Africans, in chains, were treated as commodities; the Catholic Acadians were shunned as pariahs. In some Southern colonies, the Acadians were taken directly from the boats to the fields, where as indentured servants they worked alongside the slaves. In some northern colonies, many died in the streets, neglected by those who had fled religious intolerance in England. The slaves and the exiles eventually found a home in Louisiana. Their parallel experiences produced two different musics, "separate but equal," each imbued with its own flavor.

To outsiders, the word Louisiana conjures up exotic images of moss-draped live oaks, bayous, alligators, and accordions. The terms "Cajun," "Creole," and "zydeco" are often used interchangeably, and misconceptions abound. Restaurants in the United States and in Europe advertise as "Cajun" or "Creole" food that is merely charred or peppered, and New Orleans advertises the Cajun identity as its own. Those who discovered Cajun music in the 1970s celebrate the resurrection of a phenomenon that never died; those who discovered zydeco at the same time ignore three centuries' worth of tradition. The story of Louisiana dance is not the story of a series of dances but rather the story of one long dance, a river that swept up the new and deposited the superfluous at every bend.

It is tempting to compartmentalize Louisiana dances neatly into Cajun and zydeco. However, the truth is more complicated. Though an awareness of a black style existed as far back as the 1920s, black and white musicians all played what they called "French music." There was no detailed nomenclature; blacks often referred to their style as lala or Creole music.

The Cajun culture is in many ways atypical of the Protestant Anglophone Deep South; however, in one essential way the two cultures are similar. Though Southern segregation was imposed by law, blacks and whites worked side by side in the fields and learned from one another for two centuries. Unlike the situation in the North, where laws promoted interaction but where de facto segregation separated the races, a camaraderie born of familiarity developed in Louisiana and all over the South. Custom transcended laws; music transcended artificial barriers. Musicians of both races performed together, and contacts and friendships encouraged the exchange and incorporation of ideas and musical styles. The radio made no racial distinctions. Just as an Anglo-American boy from Tupelo synthesized his unique style from white popular music, blues, rock, R & B, and what was known in the 1950s as "hillbilly" music, descendants of slaves and exiles contributed to one another's musical styles. Lawrence Levine's characterization of zydeco as "a hybrid with a strong African base" can be applied equally well to Cajun music.[4]

A definition of terms is definitely in order. The word Cajun derives from the American pronunciation of the word *Acadien,* which refers to settlers who colonized the Canadian Maritime Provinces beginning in the early seventeenth century. The name zydeco has given rise to debate and disagreement,[5] but the term generally refers to music created by Louisiana's black Creoles after World War II, when the a cappella *juré* tradition was instrumentalized and used as dance music.[6] The term Creole has the most definitions, often contradictory. The word comes from the Spanish *criollo,* "native to America." The first definition refers to descendants of Old World stock born in the New World but kept "pure" of New World blood. The second definition is just the opposite; it describes that which has adapted to the climate of Louisiana and includes creole tomatoes and creole horses which were suited to the Louisiana climate. Later, the term served to differentiate French-speaking black people, called Creoles of color, from Anglophone African Americans.[7] Today's white and black Creoles are conscious of their shared French heritage. Although this South Louisiana communality may create confusion in the minds of outsiders, it is the very mixing of traditions that has ensured their cultural survival.

For the past fifty years, an enthusiasm for taxonomy has artificially compartmentalized dance music into pop, rock, R & B, blues, swamp pop, jazz, soul, hip-hop, rap, gospel, rock 'n' roll, heavy metal, country, reggae, and others and has differentiated Cajun from zydeco.[8] This fragmentation may satisfy ethnomusicologists but not musicians, who have always vigorously resisted labels. Canray Fontenot, for example, supposedly disparaged the term zydeco, stating "I don't play that zodiac music."[9] At a time when Yo-Yo Ma records Appalachian folk music with other classical musicians and jazz violin is a recognized instrument, perhaps we, too, should refuse artificial musical boundaries. Like a Venn diagram, traditions overlap;[10] the descendants of musicians of both races who worked together centuries ago in the fields now play together onstage.

Any cultural manifestation must adapt or die. Creolization, or adaptation to New World conditions, infused a hybrid vigor to contemporary Cajun and zydeco dances. Innovation was a means to cultural survival. The theories of creolization and retention can be applied equally to Louisiana; dances adapted to Louisiana continue to carry their European past in them. What forms the unique character of social dance in contemporary Louisiana is the ethnic blending that continues to redefine the culture.

The Acadians and Their Dances

In a culture obsessed by food, South Louisianans like to describe their culture as a gumbo. This thick, spicy soup begun with a French roux includes fowl and game from the Louisiana bayous and prairies, rice and garlic from Spain, and okra from Africa, often spiced with Caribbean tasso and peppers and washed down with German beer! In contrast to European cultures in the United States that either assimilated or isolated themselves, the Acadians' very survival depended on cooperation and interaction. Those hardy souls from Poitou and the Vendée who arrived in New France (Canada) in 1604 were joined thirty years later by colonists from other regions of France and Europe. Freed from feudal constraints, they experienced their first taste of personal freedom and depended on one another and on the indigenous Micmacs. At the time of their brutal expulsion four generations later, the only things they shared with France were their language and their religion.[11] Ironically, these first northern Europeans to settle North America were also the first victims of ethnic cleansing there.[12] By 1765 when the Acadians arrived in Louisiana, the colony had become Spanish.[13] In New Orleans, the dominant French culture absorbed the new arrivals from Malaga and the Canary Islands more easily than it accepted the Acadians.[14] New Orleans white Creoles, descendants of colonists who arrived as early as 1699, cherished their ties to France and considered themselves superior to the rural Acadian peasants. As the result of generous land grants, the Acadians settled along the Mississippi River in what would be called the Acadian Coast.[15] Many Spanish colonists moved westward with the Acadians; families named Romero and Miguez settled in the town of New Iberia. After the 1803 Louisiana Purchase and Louisiana's transformation to statehood in 1812, the Acadians continued to live along the bayous and on the prairies in relative isolation and were even fairly uninvolved in the Civil War.[16]

Substantial immigrant waves at the end of the eighteenth century and during the nineteenth century added new ethnicities to Louisiana. An Afro-

Creole population arrived in Louisiana as early as 1791 as a result of a revolution in the island of St. Domingue, and a group of refugees from Cuba doubled the population of New Orleans in 1809. A number of Napoleon III's soldiers settled in Avoyelles Parish after their disastrous defeat in Mexico in 1862, French journalists sought refuge in New Orleans after the revolutions of 1830 and 1848, young men left Germany to avoid forced conscription at the time of the Franco-Prussian War in 1870, Irishmen fled starvation, and other hardy souls sought their fortunes in the New World. And the Louisiana Acadians continued to plow their fields, set their traps, live simply off the land, and quietly absorb new settlers with names like McGee, McCauley, Reed, Schexnayder, Huber, and Dubcek.[17] In the prairies and swamps, they lived as they had lived since their arrival, despite the social upheavals engendered by the war. Their dances reflected their European heritage; many a couple courted to a waltz, a quadrille, a square dance, a Virginia reel, a polka, a "Put-your-foot-right-there."[18]

Meanwhile, in New Orleans and surrounding areas, the French language languished for fifty years before its death in the early years of the twentieth century. The military occupation of the South, ironically referred to as "Reconstruction," destroyed both the Francophone and Anglophone economies of the region.[19] Both blacks and whites realized that their children's economic security depended on their knowledge of English and embraced the language of the Anglophone conquerors. By World War I, despite efforts to preserve it, the French language was dead.

As the twentieth century dawned, the Louisiana Acadians' isolation began to evaporate due to Teddy Roosevelt's melting-pot philosophy, the discovery of oil in 1901, and American military service. In 1916, a federal law established mandatory schooling to be effected in English. The Great Depression saw the exodus of many Louisiana Acadians to East Texas, where they worked in the shipyards and the oil industry. There they spoke English, were called "Cajuns," and were exposed to new music. Louisiana soldiers returned from World War II with a broader worldview and a more sophisticated musical ear.

Mandatory schooling in English dealt a blow to the French language. The social stigma attached to children who failed first grade because they could not understand their teachers added to the humiliation of being Cajun, and at least two generations of parents refused to teach French to their children. As in New Orleans, many parents stopped using French at home, believing that success for their children depended on their assimilation. Ironically, the Acadians were exiled in the very region they had claimed 150 years before.

The intrusion of the outside world into the Acadian community resulted in a series of changes in music and dance on several levels. The first change was social. Nineteenth-century *bals de maison,* or house dances, had been family affairs held in private homes where behavior was closely monitored.[20] These house dances disappeared in the 1920s as public dance halls opened. There, young people were less supervised, and group dances gave way to couple dances.

The second change was a natural simplification in the dance tunes and steps that European peasants had brought to America. In a loose cultural application of Gresham's law, either the simpler Cajun steps drove complicated figures out of existence or the dances were modified as different ethnic groups sought a common denominator on the dance floor.[21] Circle dances became couple dances, complicated figures disappeared, the polka evolved into the familiar two-step, and the mazurka was influenced and modified by the waltz.

The third change was one of musical structure. Like their European ancestors, the Acadians had generally separated dance music and vocal music except during Lent, when they interpreted the Catholic church's ban on "music" as a ban on orchestral music alone and danced to a cappella vocal melodies.[22] In contrast, traditional African music present in Louisiana for two centuries had always combined movement with vocals. As the twentieth century dawned, these European and African traditions began to blend, and in the 1930s, musicians started alternating verses and instrumental interludes. Elements from the blues tradition entered the mix, and dance bands eventually adopted a sixteen-bar instrumental bridge from popular and bluegrass music.

The fourth change occurred as musicians added instruments from their own musical traditions. The traditional Acadian orchestra composed of fiddle, triangle, and sometimes harmonica grew to include Spanish guitar, African and Caribbean percussion, and German diatonic accordion. A more complex timbre resulted. At the same time, the accordion's limits in keys and notes resulted in simpler and less chromatic tunes. Because the accordion's volume made it the dominant instrument, vocalists were forced to sing in its key and on a higher pitch in order to be heard.

The fifth change of the twentieth century was technological. With electric amplification, the fiddler no longer had to bear down on the strings, and the style became less forced. The electric guitar and the steel guitar entered the orchestra from country-western music; the drum set reinforced strong African rhythms. Elements of rock 'n' roll and the new sounds of bluegrass, rhythm and blues, jitterbug, rock, and pop blended into what became known as "swamp pop."

The Festival that Started a Revolution

Cajun dances would no doubt have remained simple, and perhaps they would have been lost, had it not been for a shift in the region's cultural equity, defined by folklorist Alan Lomax as the balance between preservation and innovation. In the middle years of the twentieth century, innovation, tradition, and fortunate circumstances combined in a serendipitous way to alert the outside world to the existence of a lively regional music that defied classification. Rooted in music, the consequences of this new awareness extended far beyond dance halls, and repercussions were felt even forty years later as far away as Buckingham Palace.

The Newport Folk Festival of 1964 was a turning point in Cajun music and dance. The overwhelming success there of both black and white musicians not only made the outside world take notice of South Louisiana's vibrant sound, it also awakened its own citizens to the unique music they had always taken for granted and had sometimes disparaged as "chanky chank." A grassroots return to original heritage music followed, and the rest of the country responded. Tourism increased. Area restaurants began to feature Cajun bands every night.[23] Cajun French activists pressured the state legislature to establish the Council for the Development of French in Louisiana in 1968 to preserve the French language, to add it to school curricula, and to restore it as an official language of the state.[24] Francophone militants established Cajun French as a literary language by writing poetry and producing plays for the French-speaking population.[25] In addition, one young Louisiana attorney's thirty-year campaign against the British Crown finally resulted in the formal acknowledgement on December 9, 2003, by Queen Elizabeth II of the role Britain had played in the exile of the Acadians.[26]

Anyone listening to Dewey Balfa recordings from before this festival and afterward will notice a distinct fiddling-style change toward complexity, as the musicians responded to audience attention and interest, in what Barry Ancelet characterizes as contextual change.[27] As bands experimented with complex sounds and timbres, young dancers' movements followed suit. Most had grown up with traditional French and German dances, several had learned folk dances from other cultures or festivals, and all of them knew swing, pop, jitterbug, and rock 'n' roll. Unconcerned with the lofty mission of preserving old traditions, they simply wanted to dance. They invented new movements and steps on the dance floors of newly opened restaurants and dance halls, incorporating arm movements from German traditional dances as well as from swing and jitterbug, giving rise to the arm pyrotechnics seen in some of today's Cajun dances.

An interesting anecdote concerns the invention of the dance now known as *la patte cassée* or "crippled chicken." In the early 1970s, newly formed bands like Coteau and Beausoleil performed at dance halls and student hangouts close to the campus of the University of Southwestern Louisiana (now the University of Louisiana at Lafayette). One evening, a particularly talented young dancer arrived with a sprained ankle. He took to the dance floor anyway but favored one leg. One observer likened him to a chicken with a broken leg, and several other couples joined in, laughing at themselves. The next week, these dancers were astonished to see couples executing the crippled chicken. This dance, basically a variation of the jitterbug, remained popular and is now a mainstay of the Cajun repertoire, though it is a pure invention, an example of Stephen J. Gould's punctuated evolution on the dance floor![28]

Another dance was invented at this time, as young dancers provided entertainment for the tourists who came to see dancing turned into a performance. In the *danse à trois,* one man dances with two women using twirls, turns, and intricate arm movements. Many Cajuns today would swear that this dance is traditional, though it would have been ludicrous to dance it in the past, when the point of social dance was to meet one-on-one.[29]

It was in the 1970s and 1980s that the Cajun jig, yet another example of hybrid vigor, entered the dance scene. This jig was influenced by the Irish jig, which in turn is based on step dancing as opposed to complicated figures.[30] It combined the two-step, swing, and jitterbug, which are all in duple meter. As opposed to the traditional waltz and two-step, the couple is connected by only one hand and dances apart as in the traditional jig.

Nowadays in dance halls almost anything goes. Certain bands are more traditional, others more country-western, others incorporate rock 'n' roll. Savvy dancers know which band is playing at which dance hall on which night. The traditional Cajun repertoire includes smooth waltzes, zydeco, jigs, line dances, and two-steps played by instruments that come from Cajun, country-western, and zydeco traditions (figure 18.1). Southwest Louisiana may be one of the few regions in the country where a woman buys new ankle boots to go dancing!

Never has Cajun music been so varied, so open to innovation. Professional troupes perform the *bourrées, contredanses,* and *mazurkas* of the past.[31] Musicians like David Greely are determined to find their voice inside the harmonies and instruments of the culture itself. Other bands, like Beausoleil, start

Figure 18.1: Dancers at Randol's Cajun Restaurant and Dance Hall, Lafayette, Louisiana, 1988. © 2006 PhilipGould.com.

from old sources but add Caribbean rhythms. New songs appear in Cajun French, normative French, English, or all three, influenced by musical trends. Some compositions resemble Cajun music in little but their instrumentation. These are all perfectly legitimate ways to create.

Zydeco

Like the music of the Cajuns, the origins of zydeco, "a joyous work in progress,"[32] were drawn from three continents, creolized and tempered by the flames of hardship and exile. It is common knowledge that African Americans in the bayou country are the descendants of slaves brought from Africa and the West Indies. What is not generally known, however, is that many slaves were freed well before the Civil War, some because of military service, some as a reward for faithful employment, some according to a Spanish ban on native slaves, and some at their owners' deaths. In 1788, 1,701 freed slaves were registered in the census of lower Louisiana.[33] Free black communities all over South Louisiana and extending eastward and including New Orleans were home to people of mixed race, known as *gens de couleur libres,* or free people of color.

Like branches of the same tree, Cajun and zydeco traditions are rooted in the same soil; the music of one has its origins in the traditions of the other.[34] The creators of both traditions shared the same experiences in the early and middle years of the twentieth century; young speakers of French or Creole at home were equally marginalized at separate segregated Anglophone schools. Both Cajun and zydeco music were first performed in private homes. Both fell into disuse as "old folks' music" in the 1960s,[35] and the leap into public consciousness affected them equally. Simple instruments appear in both traditions; the Cajun *'tit fer* (triangle) is fashioned from the tines of a harrow, the percussive zydeco *frottoir* from the ordinary washboard, and both traditions may incorporate spoons and bones.[36] A cappella vocal lines appear in the form of *musique à bouche* and the *danses rondes* from the Acadians, field hollers and *juré* from the Afro-Creoles.[37] The beat was provided by feet in the *musique à bouche,* by claps and shouts in *juré.*

However, these branches separate and grow in different directions. Instrumentation is similar but not identical. Though the accordion is the dominant instrument in both, Cajun music is usually played on a diatonic accordion, whereas zydeco favors the chromatic piano accordion that can play flatted, bluesy notes. The Cajun fiddle is usually absent in zydeco music, which may even use saxophone or trumpet. The Cajun *'tit fer* is replaced by the zydeco *frottoir.* One could say that the melody dominates Cajun music, whereas the rhythm, often syncopated, dominates Creole music.[38] Zydeco music is more often duple than triple; Cajun may be both. Zydeco is linked more directly to courtship and its results than its Cajun counterpart. This characteristic may shock those who make their first visits to zydeco clubs in the area. Historically, African dances celebrated fertility, and the African dancers were considered less inhibited than white dancers. Some slave owners banned the kalinda. Early zydeco, with less stylized complexity than Cajun dances, was a sexy dance. It was toned down in the 1930s and 1940s to conform to community expectations, but following societal changes in the 1980s and 1990s that permitted more open expression of sexuality, it returned to its roots (figure 18.2).[39] Elements of the Delta Stomp are present in zydeco from the beginning but appear in Cajun dances only later from rock 'n' roll. Cajun dancing is smooth and horizontal, with emphasis on forward movement and an erect upper body carriage. Zydeco's more vertical movements involve the whole body.[40] Arms may be held up and stiff. Unlike contemporary Cajun dances, no simplification was involved in zydeco. Its steps were always simple; there were no stylized figures that disappeared.

Could zydeco have been born anywhere else but in French Louisiana? Conditions favored a synthesis of social and musical elements from three continents, in a region where Africans and Acadians had known and respected one another for more than two centuries. In nowhere else but South Louisiana could French have been a vehicle to unite the two with the Mississippi Delta's blues tradition serving as catalyst. Perhaps the best we can do is to state that zydeco is poised at the confluence of rock 'n' roll, rhythm and blues, Cajun, and *juré*. Who knows where the currents will take it.

Let me return to the favorite South Louisiana preoccupation with food. If two people are given the same ingredients and asked to create a meal, chances are that those meals will be different. Today's Cajun and zydeco dances continue to evolve, as diverse as the myriad traditions that formed them. This is good; whatever does not evolve dies. The evolution of dance is

Figure 18.2: Dancing under an old tent at the Grand Marais, Louisiana, zydeco trail ride dance, 2003. © 2006 PhilipGould.com.

an organic one. Artificial controls are both useless and ludicrous.[41] Tradition is a process, not a product. Despite individual efforts to control or dominate them, Cajun and zydeco will become what they become.

Notes

1. Harriett Beecher Stowe, *Uncle Tom's Cabin*, ed. John Woods (Oxford: Oxford University Press, 1965), 277.

2. Every schoolchild learns of the nightmare of slavery. Slaves were imported into Louisiana as early as 1719, along with smugglers, inmates of debtor prisons, indentured servants, and colonists. One must also remember that the Native Americans were also enslaved. The history of the Acadians is less well known. French settlers arrived in the Maritime Provinces as early as 1604 and lived as neutrals for a century and a half; however, the Acadians were pawns in the numerous wars between the French and the English. According to the Treaty of Utrecht, Acadia was a British colony; Barry Ancelet, Jay Edwards, and Glen Pitre, *Cajun Country* (Oxford: University of Mississippi Press, 1991), 8–9. Historians differ in their interpretations of the motives for the forced deportation of the Acadians by the British: Some say the peninsula on which they lived was important strategically, some say the Acadians were peace-loving farmers who posed no problem, some say they were feared as possible saboteurs. In any event, this expulsion of unarmed civilians resulted in the deaths of half of the Acadians and the forced resettlement of thousands more. For more on this history, see Ancelet et al., *Cajun Country;* Carl Brasseaux, *Scattered to the Wind: Dispersal and Wanderings of the Acadians, 1755–1809* (Lafayette: Center for Louisiana Studies, University of Southwestern Louisiana, 1991); Glenn Conrad, ed., *The Cajuns: Essays on Their History and Culture* (Lafayette: Center for Louisiana Studies, University of Southwestern Louisiana, 1978); James Dormon, ed., *Creoles of Color of the Gulf South* (Knoxville: University of Tennessee Press, 1996); and Gwendolyn Hall, *Midlo-Africans in Colonial Louisiana: The Development of Afro-Creole Culture in the Eighteenth Century* (Baton Rouge: Louisiana State University Press, 1992).

3. Usually typhus or smallpox; Brasseaux, *Scattered to the Wind,* 9.

4. Lawrence Levine, *Black Culture and Black Consciousness: Afro-American Folk Thought from Slavery to Freedom* (Oxford: Oxford University Press, 1977), 24.

5. For a discussion of the terms, see Barry Ancelet, "Zydeco/Zarico: The Term and the Tradition," in *Creoles of Color of the Gulf South,* ed. James Dormon (Knoxville: University of Tennessee Press, 1996), 126–44.

6. The word *juré* refers to a tradition of songs sung to the accompaniment of hands and feet. Alan Lomax called *juré* "the most African sound I found in America"; Ben Sandmel, *Zydeco!* (Jackson: University Press of Mississippi, 1999), 34. Some *juré* songs drew inspiration from the Cajun repertoire; Sandmel, *Zydeco!,* 33.

7. Another definition concerns Creole languages, which grew up as lingua francas between slave traders and their cargo. There are Dutch Creoles and English Creoles; Louisiana Creole is based on French. The word "Creole" does not necessarily imply racial mixing; the sine qua non for *la créolité* is adaptation.

8. The coining of the name "zydeco" was a part of this trend. The term was first used in 1960 by Mack MacCormack, a record producer in Houston; Barry Ancelet, *Cajun and Creole Folktales: The French Oral Tradition of South Louisiana* (Oxford: University Press of Mississippi), xix.

9. Susan Kiefer, personal interview with the author, July 26, 2005.

10. For example, a newly formed band called Keljun mixes Celtic and Cajun sounds, and the band Zydecajun mixes zydeco and Cajun.

11. The deportation began in September 1755 and ended in 1762.

12. The British, at war with the French, needed the Acadians to produce food and to maintain the dikes constructed to reclaim the land. Fearing their unity, the English evicted them and dispersed them by force among their colonies. The term *ethnic cleansing* is not too strong. The entire nation of Acadia simply disappeared.

13. The treaty that ended the Seven Years' War required that France cede her possessions in New France to Britain. Spain received the territory that would become Louisiana.

14. Wrought iron appeared on New Orleans balconies, architectural styles changed, and rice, olive oil, and green peppers appeared in New Orleans cuisine. The famous French Market beignets are plainly Spanish sopaipillas!

15. The Acadian Coast comprises the present-day parishes (counties) of Ascension and St. James to distinguish the settlements from those of the German coast and present-day St. Charles and St. John the Baptist parishes, which were settled as part of John Law's colonization scheme. "German" referred to the entire Holy Roman Empire; May Waggoner, *Le plus beau païs du monde: Completing the Picture of Proprietary Louisiana, 1699–1722* (Lafayette: Center for Louisiana Studies, University of Louisiana at Lafayette, 2005), 19.

16. Many exiles eagerly fought the British during the American Revolution and the War of 1812. Fifty years later, however, they merely wanted to farm, and their loyalties lay neither with the Confederacy nor with the Union, both alien cultures. Desertion rates were high.

17. Some Cajuns refer to themselves today as "Swamp Irish." Just as earlier Rodriguez and Dominguez families had become Rodrigue and Domingue, many German family names were Gallicized: Huber to Oubre, Dubcek to Touchet, Himmel to Himel.

18. Corinne Saucier, *Traditions de la paroisse des Avoyelles en Louisiane* (Philadelphia: American Folklore Society, 1956), 52.

19. Other important Louisiana Creole settlements included Donaldsonville and St. Martinville, where descendants of old families still boast of aristocratic ancestors fleeing the French Revolution.

20. The origin of the term *fais-dodo* to describe a party lies in this tradition. Parents brought their children and babies to the house dances, put them all together in one room, and told them "Fais dodo" (Go to sleep), so the parents could dance.

21. Gresham's law, formulated in the sixteenth century, states that bad money drives good money out of circulation.

22. These circle dances were referred to as *danses rondes*. Women also sang narrative songs and ballads during *veillées*, evenings spent with friends. An older tradition was the *musique à bouche*, an a cappella solo vocal line accompanied only by foot taps to mark the rhythm. This *bottine souriante* is also present in Quebec music. When the Acadian exiles arrived in St. Domingue on their way to Louisiana, the Acadian exiles are reported to have danced to *reels à bouche*, wordless dance music made by their voices alone; Ancelet et al., *Cajun Country*, 164.

23. Traditional dance halls had been open only on weekends.

24. Beginning with the 1864 state constitution, the use of French had eroded in legal documents. The 1921 constitution was amended to prohibit the use of all languages other than English in education; Carl Brasseaux and James Wilson, personal interviews with the author, July 13, 2005.

25. See also explanation in May Waggoner, *Une fantaisie collective: Anthologie du drame louisianais cadien* (Lafayette: Center for Louisiana Studies, University of Louisiana at Lafayette, 1999); Jean Arceneaux, *Cris sur le bayou* (Quebec: Les Editions Intermède, 1980); Jean Arceneaux et al., *Acadie tropicale* (Lafayette: Center for Louisiana Studies, University of Southwestern Louisiana, 1983).

26. Warren Perrin, *Acadian Redemption: From Beausoleil Broussard to the Queen's Royal Proclamation* (Erath, LA: Acadian Heritage and Cultural Foundation, 2004), 115.

27. Barry Jean Ancelet, "'T'en as eu t'en auras plus': The Effects of Changing Contexts on Cajun Music" (paper presented at the American Folklore Society, Rochester, NY, 2002).

28. Punctuated evolution, or punctuated equilibrium, states that most morphological evolution occurs during relatively brief episodes of rapid change that punctuate much longer periods of stasis.

29. Barry Ancelet, personal interview with the author, Lafayette, LA, June 29, 2005.

30. Simone Voyer, *La gigue: Danse de pas* (Sainte Foy, QC: Les editions GID, 2003), 13.

31. The troupe Renaissance Cadienne researches and performs the older dances so that future generations will know the old ways, http://www.RenaissanceCadienne.org.

32. Sandmel, *Zydeco!*, 168.

33. Carl Brasseaux, "Creoles of Color in Louisiana's Bayou country," in *Creoles of Color of the Gulf South,* ed. James Dormon (Knoxville: University of Tennessee Press, 1996), 67–68.

34. For example, one of the most popular of the Cajun songs, "Allons danser Colinda," probably refers not to a woman named Colinda but to an African dance, the kalinda.

35. Sandmel, *Zydeco!*, 12.

36. The washboard has been redesigned to be worn over the shoulder.

37. See note 6 for the definition of *juré* and note 22 for definitions of *musique à bouche* and *danses rondes*. Hollers were used in the fields to transmit information; the rhythm derived from clapping, foot stomping, or occasional shouting.

38. This syncopation derives from hambone syncopation (juba), a type of body percussion in a 3–3–2 rhythm in which the chest and thighs are slapped to keep the beat. Hambone syncopation also appears in the related Delta Stomp.

39. Barry Ancelet, in Dormon, *Creoles of Color of the Gulf South,* 138.

40. Levine, *Black Culture and Black Consciousness,* 16.

41. One well-intentioned South Louisiana organization dedicated to the preservation and promotion of Cajun music even voted in the 1990s to outlaw the Cajun jig as "inauthentic." Needless to say, the dance is still a popular one, and the artificial controls were as effective as the suggestion by some feminists during the 1970s that the plural of the word "woman" be changed to "womyn" in order to remove the offensive syllable "-men."

19

The Multiringed Cosmos of Krumping

Hip-Hop Dance at the Intersections of Battle, Media, and Spirit

Christina Zanfagna

The circle of the dance is a permissive circle: it protects and permits. At certain times on certain days, men and women come together at a given place and then, under the solemn eyes of the tribe, fling themselves into a seemingly unorganized pantomime which is in reality extremely systematic in which by various means—shakes of the head, bending of the spinal column, throwing the whole body backwards— may be deciphered as in an open book the huge effort of community to exorcise itself, to liberate itself, to explain itself. There are no limits—inside the circle.

—Frantz Fanon[1]

Expanding the Circle

The circle of the dance that Fanon speaks of can be found not only in African contexts but also in powwow dances, the ring shout of slave times, the Italian tarantella, the Brazilian *samba de roda,* and other dances spanning the globe. The circle of the dance is mobile and can form in multiple situations and environments. Ronald Radano, writing about the recurring figure of the circle in African American music scholarship, notes that the "tenacity of this historical icon," aside from its cross-cultural and even universal significance, reflects the desires of some scholars and artists to reproduce notions of a coherent Africanist black America.[2] The challenge "is to tell the story of the circle so as to resist claims of continuity and uncomplicated racial whole-ness while at the same time recognizing socially generated coherences that emerge within the logic of race."[3] The importance of the circle in locating meaning in black expressive forms does not lie solely in its existence as a thing—a black thing or direct African offspring—but rather as a discourse. To dance in or into a circle is to engage in a performative and discursive process through which people transform chaos into order. It is an opportunity for discussion and interaction between seemingly disparate arenas of life. In this chapter, I will use the metaphor of the circle to link fighting and dancing, the worldly and the otherworldly, the underground and the mainstream, spirituality and commercialism. Radano continues, "The circle coheres as it is born out of incoherence."[4] The circle is a way for hip-hop dancers to assert their wholeness even as the edges of their lives may seem frayed and unbounded—a way to build a world within a world.

Furthermore, the challenge is to tell the story of the circle as an expanded tale of multiple and overlapping circles. After outlining the similarities be-tween circles of battle and circles of dance in hip-hop culture, I will give a brief history of krumping and explain how it is practiced in two different ringlike contexts: one competitive, one spiritual. For the circle can also be talked about as a ring. The ring is an arena of physical combat, competition, and artistry. It is also place of spirit(s), of God, of holy dance and religious trance. At early religious gatherings of enslaved Africans in brush harbors—often referred to as the "invisible church"—the ring shout was performed. Among the trees, they shuffled counterclockwise in a circle, swaying, clap-ping, stomping, and tapping their heals but never crossing their feet so as not to confuse the sacred ritual with social dancing. Accompanied by chant, this rhythmic walk moved increasingly faster until "shouters" (dancers) worked themselves into a quivering, trembling trance.[5] The hip-hop dance styles of clowning and krumping embody both the competitive and spiritual aspects of the ring, as manifested in the boxing ring and the ring shout. In an era of holy wars, jihads, genocide, and the war on terror, violence and religion often go hand in hand. But the more meaningful linkages between battle and spirit can be seen in the daily artistic practices of individuals. Competition and spiritual practice involve the interactive, embodied, dialectical pursuit of something greater, inspirational, and lasting.

Focusing on adolescent hip-hop dancers from Los Angeles, California, I will remodel Victor Turner's concept of "liminality" into a multidimensional condition of being in order to examine krumping as a phenomenon and experience within and in between multiple spheres of society.[6] Turner provides a singular vision of liminality that must be opened up in order to understand the way krumping is experienced in the public space of commercial culture. He states, "If our basic model of society is that of a 'structure of positions,' we must regard the period of margin or 'liminality' as an interstructural situation."[7] Krumping, in the midst of this "structure of positions" or at the center of many related spheres, creates a paradoxical situation of being between and within many interrelated, multidimensional structures of society. Reshaping Turner's argument, young hip-hop dancers occupy states of liminality while also being incorporated into the multiple spaces of the mainstream, the market commodity, and the commercial music industry. (And yet, many of them do not enjoy the material benefits of the mainstream.) There is not just one "interstructural situation"; rather, there are myriad cross-sections in which one experiences the state of being "in-between."

Thus, within liminality, there are many circles; there is a fluidity of identity in which one can cross normally "policed" boundaries of urban space and commercial culture. Krumping, in the varying spatial contexts of competitive battle, spiritual practice, and commercial media—in overlapping and concentric circles of personhood, community, culture, and society—takes on multiple meanings. My analysis also reflects the circular geometry of black vernacular dance, specifically krumping, as I use a multilens approach. I will explore the multiringed cosmos of krumping through not only the voices of krump dancers but also the sometimes oppositional voices of people from the varied contexts with which krumping intersects (i.e., scholars, journalists, filmmakers).

Dancing the Fight, Fighting through Dance

Break dancing, one of the four elements of hip-hop along with emceeing, DJing, and graffiti, developed in the 1970s in the Bronx and Los Angeles. Dance critic Sally Banes describes the urban vernacular dance as a "fusion of sports, dancing and fighting" that combines Latino and West Indian influences and aspects of the electric boogie, uprocking, and aerial gymnastics.[8] Break dancing busted into the spotlight in movies like *Wild Style* and cameos on Burger King commercials. Glorified (and sometimes patronized) as an alternative to gang activities, the media painted break dancing as a bona fide ghetto savior—part dance, part sport, part pantomimic drama—to keep brown and black youth away from crime, violence, and other related evils. To the uninitiated, especially cops, it looked like street fighting. Legend has it, New York City policemen were about to arrest a group of young guys for violent behavior until they explained they were "just dancing" and proceeded to demonstrate each dance move to the cops. Young people developed artistic means to claim territories, negotiate boundaries over territories, and fight for their status among and against rival clans, each with its own name and color. Paul Spencer's description of Trobriand dance as an "idiom of confrontation" and "equivalent to fighting" offers insight into the link between dance and dispute: "To the extent that such a display led to the dispersal of a weaker group, direct encounters were avoided."[9] The "display occurs at the most sensitive point," the boundary between territories, at the crossroads of life and death, and in moments of spiritual insecurity.[10]

The thing is, there is a blurry line between dancing and fighting (e.g., capoeira, bullfighting, Trobriand warrior dances, and even *West Side Story*) as there is between artistic innovation and battle. There are also significant similarities between hip-hop dancing and boxing. They are both intimate arts, requiring the close proximity of human bodies, often flesh to flesh, often involving sweat. They are based around moves, moves that are responded to by those present. Toasting and boasting, taunting and flaunting play prominent roles in the ritual. Think Mohammed Ali with his rhymed, rhythmic rants. Each man and woman has his or her own unique style and, if they are good, a few tricks up the sleeve. And finally, both boxing and hip-hop dancing take place in a spatial complex known as "the ring." Although hip-hop dancers may not refer to their arena of dance as the ring, most break dancing battles or freestyle sessions are organized in a circular formation, in which dancers move along the outside edge of the ring while other dancers break in and out of the center.[11]

Hip-Hop Dance in South Central, Los Angeles

In the wake of the Rodney King riots of 1992, Thomas Johnson—founder and father of clown dancing—found himself behind bars and looking for a way to make a positive change in his community in South Central. After a religious epiphany while in prison, he started performing hip-hop dance at little kids' birthday parties donned in a clown suit, a rainbow-colored Afro, and clown face paint. Blasting hip-hop beats through his boom box, he created the first moves of what he then called "clown dancing." Eventually, it would just be called "clowning," a highly versatile and varied form of black street dance that combines local styles such as G dance or gangsta boogie and stripper dancing, referring to the sexual and dynamic performance style of black strippers. It also fuses elements of popping and locking, two older forms of competitive, illusory hip-hop street dance associated with funk dance and break dancing, and Jamaican dance hall moves such the butterfly and the rodeo.[12] The bobbling bodies, contracting chests, and liquid limbs of clown dancers led Shaheem Reid of MTV News to write, "If you look like Bozo having spasms, you're doing it right."[13] Under the name Tommy the Clown, Johnson began to gain a sizable following of youth around the neighborhood who were dubbed the Hip-Hop Clowns. Dancers paint their faces like clowns in an act of masking that allows them the invisibility to express themselves without self-consciousness and restraint (figure 19.1).

Figure 19.1: Tommy the Clown and the Hip-Hop Clowns, Los Angeles, February 25, 2005. Photo permission by www.tommytheclown.com.

As one of the krumpers, Dragon, elucidates in the acclaimed documentary *Rize*, by filmmaker David LaChapelle, "If you know there's a mask covering your face, you feel that it's just you by yourself and that your identity is hidden . . . and you can dance as freely as you want to."[14] Tommy the Clown describes his painted face as a "weapon."[15] Masks also involve magic; dance theorist Lois Ellfeldt has remarked: "The wearer of the mask takes on supernatural or sacred powers."[16] The painted clown mask speaks to the element of play and goofiness in clowning. (Goofy is one of the funny and energetic styles pioneered by the dancer Goofy himself.) Play is about doubleness; play masks the seriousness and the sacredness behind the playfulness. It is both tragic and comic, improvisational and orderly, everywhere and nowhere.[17] It opens up a space of reversals in which violence becomes spiritual, art becomes battle, oppression transforms into liberation (and vice versa). Says Richard Schechner, "Play is the improvisational imposition of order, a way of making order out of disorder."[18] The clown, like the jester and harlequin, is an outsider engaged in the tragicomic play of life and death.

From Clowning to Krumping

It was not long before the circus clown element soon expanded into a harder, more aggressive and personal solo style called krumping, a style that allowed dancers to confront and work through the more difficult emotions of pain and anger.[19] The play became more serious—that is, it became serious play—and the face paint became more "tribal" and warrior-like as South Central, particularly Watts and Compton, again started to resemble the police state atmosphere of the 1990s. Former New York City Police Commissioner William J. Bratton was appointed chief of the Los Angeles Police Department in October 2002 and began employing the same police tactics as he did under Mayor Rudolph Giuliani. He targeted petty crime, graffiti, and minor violations such as loud radios and disorderly conduct. It is clear to see how African American youth engaged in the often-misunderstood expressive behaviors of hip-hop culture would be under attack.

Krumping developed and flourished within this atmosphere of constraint, surveillance, and brutality. With little or no funding for arts programs, after-school activities, and opportunities to express themselves, South Central youth took it upon themselves to create a proactive (not just reactive) outlet through hip-hop dance. The krumper Dragon elucidates: "We don't have after-school programs. . . . In the inner city we're all thought to be sports players. . . . Everybody does not play basketball and everybody does not play football. Is there something else for us to do? So a group of us got together and invented this." The dance movements reflect this type of physical release of pent-up emotion and aggression, a hyperkinetic "ghetto ballet" danced by both males and females that looks like a combination of street fighting, moshing,[20] sanctified church spirit possession, and aerobic striptease. It is volatile and warrior-like, spastic and quaking, an ecstatic and cathartic dance that involves the vigorous bending of the spine and the thrusting/popping of the chest. LaChapelle makes overt connections between krumping and traditional African dance as well.[21] In line with Los Angeles gangsta ethics and aesthetics, the style is hard and intense. The moves are strong and masculine and the speed of delivery mind-blowing.[22] One journalist describes the movements as "rapidly flailing appendages."[23] Krumping is danced to hardcore, beat-heavy hip-hop tracks, sometimes with no vocals. With preaching, as with rapping or "spitting," sometimes it is not what one does but how one does it. Style is a means to substance and pleasure, a way to engage the physical, emotional, and the spiritual.[24]

Similar to the b-boy and b-girl break dancing crews, krump dancers form structured and organized crews or families, a tight-knit group of individuals whose loyalties and commitment extend beyond the circle of the dance. These rings or bands of krump brothers and sisters can provide the support and stability many of the dancers do not receive from their own families at home, Each family is organized around a mentor, lead krump dancer or king, who is often referred to as a "Big Homey" and trains, teaches, and counsels "Lil' Homies" in both dance and life. Most of the initial families comprised African American youth, but soon Asian American crews such as Filipino Rice Track formed, and dancers of different racial and ethnic backgrounds began krumping as well.[25]

Krumping on the Streets: Spirit in the Ring of Dance

Dragon explains, "There is a spirit in the midst of krump-ness. There is a spirit there . . . most people think, they're just a bunch of rowdy, ghetto, heathen thugs. No, what we are is oppressed." Whereas the religious imagery of the slave spirituals masked the underlying call to protest, the sacred has been the "hidden transcript" beneath the rebellious, supposedly secular performance of hip-hop dance.[26] Mark Anthony Neal identifies the Black Public Sphere as a collection of covert social spaces hinged around two main centers of black life: the church and jook joint or club.[27] The club has always been in contest and concert with the black church as a vehicle for expression, producing a discordant marriage between the sacred and the secular. I would also add the "streets" as a third spatial center marked by liminalities, a place of the betwixt and between, of literal intersections and corners, of the crossroads, of the sacred and the profane.[28] Adolescent hip-hop fans often occupy a liminal moment in their lives as well as a multiliminal status in society. Youth on the streets do more "house wrecking," spirit conjuring, and pelvic gyrating than either the church or the club could imagine.[29] Many hip-hop dancers undergo churchlike experiences, an enduring hallmark of black popular music such as soul and jazz. Los Angeles, long touted as a diffuse concrete sprawl epitomizing the ethics and aesthetics of car culture, immortalized by the G-Funk inspired gangsta rap of Dr. Dre and Snoop, is often overlooked as a place of sociality and artistic communion.

The sacredness of krumping is captured during a krump session in *Rize*. During a collective dance gathering in a South Central school yard, one of the female dancers, Daisy, falls under the spirit and loses consciousness. Those who are not soloing or dancing play a vital supportive and interactive role for the soloist or featured dancers. They help create a mood of submergence, simultaneously celebratory and sepulchral. They respond to the dance through gestures, arm waving, head rocking, forward lurching inclinations, and visceral exclamations. Dancers sometimes hoist one another up into the air, tug on one another's clothing, kick and push at one other to rile themselves up, awakening the aggression within as if it was some sleeping lion, provoking their own spirits into being. Although it may look combative, they say that fighting is the last thing on their minds.

Collapsing into the arms of a fellow dancer, a nearby youth explains that Daisy has just fallen under the spirit, "She just struck . . . that's what we've all been waiting on." Another voice chimes in, "She has reached the inevitable." When Daisy is asked what happened, she answers, "I don't know . . . I just let go." Under the dome of the night sky, young krumpers gather in informal, amorphous circles, dance to hip-hop tracks made of heavy, repetitive, rhythmic loops, under basketball hoops that hang over their heads like holy halos. In the labyrinth of the city, at paved crossroads, rings abound. This play of circles makes up the larger circle of the krump dance session, which is a ritual of serious play. The energy and vigor of hip-hop provides the aesthetic means to exorcise the demons and conjure spirit. But though it looks wild and out of control to outsiders, it is actually self-governing/ordering and defies claims that hip-hop youth are inherently violent and disruptive. Not only is this dance not violent, it is also organized healing and cathartic release. Krumpers talk about it as channeling their anger in a positive way. That said, krumping is more than a coping mechanism and reveals that hip-hop culture is not just about criminal behaviors and mentalities, thuggin', and nihilistic street life.

Similar to the forest sanctuaries of the rural South, krumping provides a street sanctuary of the urban city. It relocates the "invisible church" of the brush harbor to the streets, the school yards, and the blacktops as the dancers transform certain musical practices and rituals found in the black church to fit their hip-hop lifestyles. Dragon and Miss Prissy even perform krump-inspired praise dancing in the church, and many of the dancers proclaim that they "get krump for Christ." The abrasive nature of krumping makes it difficult to locate its sacred undercurrent; the spiritual forces brewing within it are often secreted in moves that convey sexuality, violence, and suffering. But in the circle of dance when the "spirit in the midst of krump-ness" is present, the dancers' experience of the world is circular: They can, as hip-hop fan, scholar, and producer Daniel Hodge says, "see the sacred in the profane," they can love and hate simultaneously, they can span earth and sky.[30] Dragon explains, "This is the only way we see fit of storytelling. This is the only way of making ourselves feel like we belong." In the circle of the dance, which is animated by mythic energy and the twin experience of fantasy and reality, people can break everyday rules. Boundaries between this world and the otherworld are blurred.

Krumping at the Battle Zone: Competition in the Ring of Combat

The Battle Zone, an annual krumping competition judged by the barometer of audience applause, takes place at the Great Western Forum in Inglewood, Los Angeles. The Forum was formerly the home arena for the Los Angeles Lakers and now houses the megachurch congregation of Faithful Central, where hip-hop-inspired gospel star Kirk Franklin runs the musical program on Sundays.[31] Already, the arena fuses elements of sport, competition, and religion. In front of thousands of children and parents, Tommy the Clown, wearing a heavy weight belt and his normal clown attire, starts off the night with a prayer and then launches into the dramatic battlelike atmosphere. He is master of ceremonies, ringmaster (directing the circuslike events), and ringleader (encouraging the battle). The dance battles take place in a boxing ring and unfold in a series of rounds between two individuals matched by age, size, and gender. Each round lasts approximately ten to fifteen seconds; dancers have to execute their routine quickly and efficiently, making sure they get to their best moves before the music stops. Improvisatory flare is critical.

The spirit of serious play is present in the boxing ring as well. Part clowns, part warriors, dancers jostle for prestige among rival clans. One dancer sits in a chair while the other performs to the seated opponent, aggressively approaching his or her prey with boastful moves of pantomimic intimidation: a flip of the cap, a tug of the shirt, a pop of the collar, an expression of utter disgust, a thrust or pop of the hips. Fellow crew members of the competitors line the ring in support. Although dancers are not allowed to touch each other, they get as close as they can—close enough to feel the breath and sweat of their opponent, close enough to make someone's blood boil and burn. The dancer sitting tries to be as stoic as possible, maintaining a stone-cold, deadpan face in the midst of the flurry of movement within and around the ring. As the battle warms up, dancers—men and women alike—rip off pieces of their clothing, inciting a raucous reaction from the audience. During these moments, the dance becomes a contest of physical and emotional revealing, the ripping and stripping of clothes a metaphor for the unveiling of spirit and raw emotion that krumping demands. Who can get their soul more naked? Who can tap that vital flow coursing through the human veins, that divine spark within?

The ring is a resource, refuge, and strategy at the crossroads of adolescence and adulthood, of roads of life and roads of death, of victory and defeat, of turf and territory, often at moments of spiritual insecurity. *The circle coheres as it is born out of incoherence.* Rings form out of necessity, because the stakes are high. They open up a space, create a stage, and make a center where there was not one before. Krumping, in various circles and rings, is a unique response to a specific set of circumstances, not just a product of behavioral norms.[32] Different metaphors are at work as krumping enters different kinds of rings and circles. In the boxing ring, krumping is sport and artistic battle, a creative, resistant display of one's own power and prowess. In the padded, roped-in world of the boxing ring, young krumpers are both *protected* and *permitted* to release aggression through fierce, competitive dance. Although there may be victors and losers, there does not necessarily have to be destruction. As a locus of spirit possession—as a ring shout–styled event—krumping is religious ritual. It is the means through which to bring the spirit(s) down. *There are no limits—inside the circle.* As Dragon has said, "Krump is a state of being, a mindset of no boundaries, no lines, no limitations, just to be free. I think it will bring a lot of people back to Christ and back to what life is really about."[33]

Rize: *Krump Rising above and/or into Mainstream Circles*

The ring shout gives way to polite applause.
—Paul Gilroy[34]

The documentary *Rize* is credited with bringing mainstream awareness to the dance form and movement. LaChapelle, a fashion photographer known for his flashy, glossy style, first saw krumping on the set of Christina Aguilera's music video "Dirrty" and was compelled to find out more about the dance form. The documentary opens with apocalyptic black-and-white footage of the 1965 Watts riots and 1992 Rodney King riots, announcing South Central as the crucible-like setting for krumping's inception and advancement. LaChapelle never explores krumping beyond its inner-city setting, enforcing the claim that krumping is an "authentic" art form in direct opposition to the excessive materialism and bedazzling commercialism of mainstream hip-hop culture. By confining krumping to (ghetto) urban space, he feeds into a kind of segregation that black people have experienced historically and continue to experience even today around space. At the beginning of *Rize*, Dragon forcefully reiterates, "This is not a trend. Repeat, this is not a trend." But revolts against the mainstream quickly become mainstream themselves. According to dance scholar Debra Cash, the real spin move of the film (not to be confused with the head spin of break dancing) is that "these young men and women have transcended commercialism."[35] Krumping is simultaneously a heroic, artistic, proactive expression born out of the deplorable conditions of the inner city and an economically viable commercial endeavor, transcendent in its ability to spiritually and morally rise above oppression and literally transportive as a professional route out of the ghetto.

Since *Rize* was released in 2005, krumping has received a significant amount of media attention. It has been featured in Missy Elliot's video "I'm Really Hot," Black Eyed Peas' video "Hey Mama," and Madonna's music videos "Hung Up" and "Sorry." Female krumper Miss Prissy is reportedly touring with rapper The Game. Countless videos have cropped up on krumping battles, including one in which a crew of krumpers takes on a crew of break-dancers. Instructional videos, which break down specific moves and styles, may be ordered from the Internet. (Of course, such videos become obsolete in the blink of an eye as the styles change on a daily basis). The Debby Allen Dance Studio in Culver City, Los Angeles, offers krumping classes and hosts krump battles with Tommy the Clown. Robin D. G. Kelley warns that "the explosion of interest in the inner city cannot be easily divorced from the marketplace."[36] Clearly, in commercial rings, krumping becomes a commodity that can be bought and sold. As much as mainstream society wants to distance itself from black youth, krumping is not separate from society but is in many ways central to the construction of how mainstream society sees itself. What does it mean when krumping, as a black cultural production, enters this space? How does it get policed? What limits are placed on it when it enters the commercial ring? Who are the victors and victims? Ironically, hip-hop artists' critique of dominant society often supports the structures of dominant society; they sometimes end up glorifying and reinscribing their ghettoized status as they attempt to overcome it.

Krumping's status as a trend and commodity or as creative, resistant act changes depending on in which circle it is being danced; each sphere of culture assigns different meanings to the dance. What are the possibilities and limitations within each circle? Krumping is dazzling, trendy entertainment and a source of income in commercial circles and yet subject to the power dynamics of the mainstream. It is a stylized "idiom of confrontation" in the boxing ring of the Battle Zone, a conduit of catharsis in the street rings of krump brothers and sisters, and a tool to praise God when dancing in the outer circle of the pulpit. These are but a few circles in which krumping operates within a larger, multisphered constellation; krump dancers move back and forth between these worlds depending on the particular project they are working on, depending on the needs and desires of their spirits. Riding the tension between fluidity and fixity, krumping is bound to the streets of South Central as it extends beyond and circulates through various circles of culture (reaching as far as the United Kingdom, Germany, and Japan). Ultimately, krumping is a sonic and physical force that challenges notions that there is one identifiable, authentic, "ghetto" culture relegated solely to the inner city.

The Magic of Commodity: Spirituality within Commercialism

How do krumping and hip-hop at large, as a highly commercial mass-mediated art form, manage to induce an authentic spiritual ecstasy? Despite the music industry's ostensibly homogenizing, devouring force, both hip-hop youth and mainstream media turn consumer culture into something akin to religion. Hip-hop's musically "elemental" nature—the basic human coupling of spoken words over beats, breath over heartbeats—keeps it bound to the spirit of the masses. Like other black popular expressions before it, even as krumping goes mainstream, practitioners struggle to keep it from being co-opted. African American art forms often have an underground status even when they are immensely popular, as if they are telling a different tale. Hip-hop culture still gives the appearance of marginality and liminality, an appearance based on a discouraging reality that many young hip-hop followers do not enjoy in the benefits of "mainstream" life. For all its bling-bling overindulgence and absurd parody, hip-hop maintains a serious and almost ominous quality. The double voice or double vision of hip-hop uses flashiness and material goods to mask a deeper struggle that is moral and spiritual. It uses play and competition to mask and transform pain into prestige and pleasure.

Consumer capitalism also deifies hip-hop stars and rap music as charismatic, quasi-religious forces in American culture. Ronald Radano states, "The initial magic of the commodity 'slave' creating its own possession to assert a basic freedom takes modern form in the interplay of black music with the magical powers of mechanical reproduction and consumer capitalism."[37] The spiritual and ritual events in hip-hop are extended and enhanced by mainstream media. Hip-hop may be one of those "modern forms" Radano refers to; its status as commodity and its formidable selling potential "texture the very flesh" of the hip-hop subject with "the mark of capitalist exchange," textures it with the "magic of the commodity."[38] Gilroy speaks to the particular way commodities link melanin, memory, myth, and magic: "Similar investments in the magic of black vitality are associated with the views of the body as confirmation of racialised particularity that have taken root inside the black communities themselves."[39] Epitomizing the experience of black expressive freedom for many youth, hip-hop is often linked to a particular type of transcendence; its artistic otherness becomes almost otherworldly. The real battle in krumping is to resist the essentialist racializations around the black body that already exist in commercial media (e.g., MTV, BET, and ESPN).

Fruitful Darkness: Hip-Hop's Underground Railroad to Spirit

> No thanks to the slaveholder nor to slavery that the vivacious captive sometimes dances in his chains; his very mind in such circumstances stands before God as an accusing angel.
> —Frederick Douglass, "Speech on American Slavery," 1850[40]

Although the commercial music industry tends to reduce hip-hop to a shallow glorification of the liminality many dispossessed youth occupy, its sacred function is to mediate the perplexity of the in-between, to live out the questions regarding the limits of life, which necessarily remain mysterious.

Offering up a musical, meaningful, and ecstatic framework through which to experience life, hip-hop allows listeners to "dwell poetically" in multiple liminalities and uncertainties.[41] Krump dancers lose themselves in the sensuousness of temporal and physical play—the play of beats, the play of movement, and the play of real and unreal—while confronting the difficulties of their everyday lives. Paradoxically, it is the pain and the struggle that allow them to rise. They acknowledge that they are politicized subjects and yet do not allow that externally imposed construction to limit their artistic and spiritual vision. They recognize that there are both limits and no limits within the circle(s) of dance. The ecstatic experience in krumping, then, is a true paradox, encompassing the pleasure in the pain, the tragedy in the comedy, the moral poverty of material wealth, the spiritual riches available in utter despondency, and the capacity for ecstasy within liminality. Paradox approximates the extremity of life that is too difficult to describe. And art, especially dance, approaches that paradox.

As Michael Eric Dyson states, "Hip-hop reaches out and speaks to that person in pain, in suffering, facing death, who reaches out to something greater—whether that be God or spirit—to battle through the forces that attempt to dehumanize us."[42] It articulates the capitalist and religious spirit of the present times—the chaos, the contradiction, the mess—in a uniquely brutal and human way. To borrow a song title from Aretha Franklin—the "Queen of Soul"—krumping pulls down the "Spirit in the Dark."[43] It dances into broader fields of possibilities and potentials, reclaiming public space and acquiring multiple meanings as it enters new rings of culture and power.

Notes

1. Frantz Fanon, *The Wretched of the Earth* (New York: Grove Press, 1963), 57.
2. Ronald Radano, *Lying Up a Nation: Race and Black Music* (Chicago: University of Chicago Press, 2003), 54. Radano then expands on the universal importance of the circle: "Beyond the African correlates described above, we find in the historical record similar configurations in which circularity signifies tangible forms of coherence, from the circles of hell through which Dante and Virgil proceeded to the Pawnee nest figure in Native American symbolism; from the celestial wheel of Hindu cosmography to Aristotle's 'unmoved mover,' who generates the circular perfection of heavenly spheres and in turn sublunar motion." For examples of the way the ring shout has been theorized in scholarship on African American music and culture, see Sterling Stuckey, *Slave Culture: Nationalist Theory and the Foundations of Black America* (New York: Oxford University Press, 1987); and Samuel Floyd Jr., *The Power of Black Music: Interpreting Its History from Africa to the United States* (New York: Oxford University Press, 1995).
3. Radano, *Lying Up a Nation*, 55.

4. Ibid., 54.

5. Sally Banes and John F. Szwed, "'Messin' Around' to 'Funky Western Civilization': The Rise and Fall of Dance Instruction Songs," in *Dancing Many Drums: Excavations in African American Dance*, ed. Thomas F. DeFrantz (Madison: University of Wisconsin Press, 2002), 193–94. See also Sterling Stuckey's idea of the ring shout as ideology and religious vision in "Christian Conversion and the Challenge of Dance," in *Dancing Many Drums*, 42.

6. See Victor Turner, *The Ritual Process: Structure and Anti-Structure* (Chicago: University of Chicago Press, 1969).

7. Victor Turner, "Betwixt and Between: The Liminal Period in Rites of Passage," in *Reader in Comparative Religion: An Anthropological Approach*, 4th ed., ed. William A. Lessa and Evon Z. Vogt (New York: Harper & Row, 1979), 234.

8. Sally Banes, "Breakin'," in *That's the Joint: The Hip-Hop Studies Reader*, ed. Murray Forman and Mark Anthony Neal (New York: Routledge, 2004), 14. For a more extensive discussion on the history and cultural influences of break dancing and hip-hop dance at large, see also Michael Holman's "Breaking: The History" and Katrina Hazzard-Donald's "Dance in Hip-Hop Culture" in *That's the Joint*. For further discussion of the stylistic elements of breaking, graffiti, and rap and the social factors that led to their emergence, see also Tricia Rose's second chapter in her book *Black Noise: Rap Music and Black Culture in Contemporary America* (Hanover, NH: Wesleyan University Press, 1994).

9. Paul Spencer, ed., *Society and the Dance: The Social Anthropology of Process and Performance* (Cambridge: Cambridge University Press, 1985), 22.

10. Ibid.

11. The circle or ring—an important symbol in many of the world's cultures—plays a particularly vital musical and spiritual role in African American culture dating back to the ring shout. At a KRS-One concert at the Temple Bar in Los Angeles (2005), he abandoned the stage to perform from the middle of the dance floor. The crowd enveloped him in concentric circles, forming a mandala-like image on the dance floor. The force of his testimony undulated out from his center while the crowd's energy pushed in toward him with their arms raised to the sky, and their mouths spit his lyrics right back at him. Another example of the ring complex in hip-hop culture is the cipher. A cipher is formed when a group of people stands in a circle and engages in the art of freestyling. Participants take turns freestyling (performing spontaneous rhymes) over the beat-boxing (vocal percussion) of one or more of those present. The rules of conduct are unspoken and self-ordering. Ciphers are generally assembled informally, on street corners, in back alleys, parking lots, school yards, subway trains, outdoor basketball courts, at hip-hop concerts, or occasionally in people's homes.

12. The Electric Boogaloos are often credited with popularizing popping and other related styles on the television show *Soul Train* in the late 1970s.

13. Shaheem Reid, "Krumping: If You Look Like Bozo Having Spasms, You're Doing It Right," MTV, 2004, http://www.mtv.com/news/articles/1486576/20040423/index.jhtml? (accessed July 14, 2006).

14. Quote taken from David LaChapelle's documentary *Rize*, Lionsgate Films, 2005. All succeeding quotes by krump dancers are from LaChapelle's film, unless otherwise noted.

15. Georgina Harper, "Rize," 2005, http://www.londondance.com/content.asp?categoryID=1921 (accessed July 14, 2006).

16. Lois Ellfeldt, *Dance: From Magic to Art* (Dubuque, IA: Wm. C. Brown, 1976), 26.

17. Radano, *Lying Up a Nation*, 343.

18. Richard Schechner, *Performance Theory* (New York: Routledge, 1988), 98.

19. Mandalit del Barco writes, "The word 'krump' evolved from the lyrics of a song in the 1990s, but the young dancers have given it another meaning: 'Kingdom Radically Uplifting Might Praise'"; Mandalit del Barco, "'Rize': Dancing above L.A.'s Mean Streets," *NPR*, June 27, 2005, http://www.npr.org/templates/story/story.php?storyId=4718456 (accessed July 14, 2006).

20. Moshing, done in a mosh pit formed near the stage, is often associated with crowd surfing and stage diving at heavy metal or rock music concerts. It involves pushing, shoving, jumping, and bumping into other people in the circular pit.

21. In *Rize*, the juxtaposition of archival footage from a traditional African (Nuba) dance ritual reveals the remarkable similarity between African dance forms and krumping in style, movement, and function. In both contexts, the dancers paint their faces to create masks, arrange themselves in circle formations, and achieve trancelike states. Their movements appear violent and aggressive at times, but no real fighting occurs, and both scenes contain moments of boastful, more controlled posturing. (Strangely, the scene features Afro-Cuban *bata* drumming instead of the music they normally dance to.) No commentary is made about the pairing of these two practices; the audience is forced to intuit the connection between Africa and South Central, the tribal and the urban, the ancient and the modern.

22. LaChapelle puts a disclaimer at the beginning of *Rize*, assuring viewers that none of the footage has been sped up in any way.

23. Richard Harrington, "Moving 'Rize' Has Legs," *Washington Post*, 2005, http://www.washingtonpost.com/wp-dyn/content/article/2005/06/23/AR2005062300653.html (accessed July 14, 2006).

24. When someone is clowning or krumping, he or she is often said to "get krump" or "clown out."

25. Milk, a well-known Caucasian krump dancer, performed at the Battle Zone in December 2005.

26. To refer to the masked meanings in black music, Mark Anthony Neal borrows the term *hidden transcript* from James C. Scott, *Domination and the Arts of Resistance: Hidden Transcripts* (New Haven, CT: Yale University Press, 1992); Mark Anthony Neal, *What the Music Said: Black Popular Music and Black Public Culture* (New York: Routledge, 1999).

27. Neal, *What the Music Said*, 6–7.

28. Realizing that *communitas* and "liminality" in the modern world are different from the liminal phase in Ndembu ritual, Victor Turner introduced the term "liminoid" to denote the quasi-liminal character of cultural performances, entertainment, and leisure activities in industrial society; Victor Turner, "Liminal to Liminoid in Play, Flow, and Ritual: An Essay in Comparative Symbology," *Rice University Studies* 60, no. 3 (1974): 53–92. Liminoid phenomena occur outside the boundaries of normal economic, political, social structures and are, in effect, decontextualized. The liminal and the liminoid, as existential situations, open onto a "realm of primitive hypothesis" that juggles the factors of existence and juxtaposes the "categories of event, experience, and knowledge, with a pedagogic intention"; Turner, "Betwixt and Between," 241.

29. "The Corner," a hip-hop track by Common featuring Kanye West and the Last Poets on *Be* (2005), speaks about the social, cultural, and spiritual significance of the corner in African American culture and the inner city.

30. Daniel Hodge, interview with the author, Los Angeles, April 24, 2005.

31. Kirk Franklin is one of the pioneers of the gospel rap style, which developed in the early 1990s in conjunction with the increasing popularity of contemporary Christian music and the commercial success of his 1997 hit "Stomp." (Franklin's 2005

"Looking for You" single spent seventy-four weeks on Billboard's Hot 100.) Gaining a sizable following among America's youth, the holy hip-hop movement now has its own record labels, awards ceremony, apparel, and radio shows. The past few years have also witnessed an explosion of hybrid institutions, organizations, and events that integrate hip-hop aesthetics and ethics with overt spiritual objectives.

32. Robin D. G. Kelley, "Looking for the 'Real' Nigga: Social Scientists Construct the Ghetto," in *That's the Joint!*, 123.

33. "Film Focus: *Rize*," 2005, http://www.bbcworld.com (accessed July 14, 2006).

34. Paul Gilroy, "Exer(or)casing Power: Black Bodies in the Black Public Sphere," in *Dance in the City*, ed. Helen Thomas (New York: St. Martin's Press, 1997), 27.

35. Debra Cash, "Dance: Spin Crazy," 2005, 90.9 WBUR, http://www.wbur.org/arts/2005/50519_20050808.asp (accessed July 14, 2006).

36. Kelley, "Looking for the 'Real' Nigga," 121.

37. Radano, *Lying Up a Nation*, 167. The slave songs and, more important, the discourse surrounding the origin of slave songs territorialize and essentialize blackness as an exclusive category ultimately impossible to mimic or appropriate. Thus, it gains a certain type of intangible, magical capital.

38. Ibid., 149.

39. Gilroy, "Exer(or)casing Power," 27.

40. Frederick Douglas, "The Nature of Slavery," extract from a lecture on slavery at Rochester, NY, 1850, in *My Bondage and My Freedom* (New York: Random House, [1855] 2003), 266.

41. Martin Heidegger, ". . . Poetically Man Dwells . . .," in *Poetry, Language, Thought*, trans. Albert Hofstadter (New York: Harper & Row, 1971), 216–56.

42. Michael Eric Dyson, *Open Mic: Reflections on Philosophy, Race, Sex, Culture and Religion* (New York: Basic Civitas Books, 2003), 271.

43. Refers to the Aretha Franklin song "Spirit in the Dark," on *Spirit in the Dark* (Atlantic Records, 1970). Perhaps we can understand this idea as an inversion of Plato's allegory of the cave, where enlightenment is found in things profane and things hidden in the flickering shadows, in a "fruitful darkness"; Turner, *The Ritual Process*, 243. Some kind of subliminal metaphor of an underworld is at work here—the belly of the beast, the horrifying pit of the slave ship—that lies at the heart of the struggle young hip-hoppers confront as they engage with the music, the dance, and the culture.

Contributors

Elizabeth Aldrich is known for her work in period dance and has provided choreography for nine feature films, including *The Age of Innocence* and *The Remains of the Day*. She has presented performances, workshops, and lectures throughout North and South America, Europe, and Asia and has written extensively on dance. She was responsible for the Library of Congress's American Memory Internet project, "An American Ballroom Companion, c. 1490–1920," and currently serves as dance curator at the Library of Congress.

Barbara Cohen-Stratyner serves as Judy R. and Alfred A. Rosenberg Curator of Exhibitions, The New York Public Library for the Performing Arts. Her more than sixty exhibitions and Web sites have included Vaudeville Nation, JAZZ, Popular Music of the Caribbean, and Touring West. Among her books are *Popular Music: 1900–1919* (Gale, 1988) and *The Dance Direction of Ned Wayburn: Selected Topics in Musical Staging, 1901–1923* (University of Wisconsin Press, 1996). She holds a PhD in performance studies and an MFA in theater design from New York University.

Yvonne Daniel is professor emerita of dance and Afro-American studies at Smith College. Her books include *Rumba: Dance and Social Change in Contemporary Cuba* (Indiana University Press, 1995) and *Dancing Wisdom: Embodied Knowledge in Haitian Vodou, Cuban Yoruba, and Bahian Candomblé* (University of Illinois Press, 2005). She has also edited four documentary videos on Caribbean dance: *Cuban Dance Examples, Cuban Rumba, Public Vodou Ceremonies of Haiti,* and *Sacred Choreographies of Cuba and Haiti* (Insight Media). Daniel holds an MA and PhD in anthropology from the University of California, Berkeley.

Sherril Dodds is a senior lecturer at the University of Surrey, England. She holds a PhD in dance studies from the University of Surrey and is the author of *Dance on Screen: Genres and Media from Hollywood to Experimental Art*

(Palgrave, 2001). She has also contributed essays on such topics as female striptease, postmodernism and popular culture, and pop music video for *Dance in the City* (St. Martin's, 1997); *Dancing Texts: Intertextuality in Interpretation* (Dance Books, 1999); and *Music, Sensation and Sensuality* (Routledge, 2002).

Lisa Doolittle, choreographer, dancer, writer, is professor in theater arts, University of Lethbridge. She is coeditor with Anne Flynn of *Dancing Bodies Living Histories* (Banff, 2001) and director of the award-winning documentary *Dancing Bodies* (2003), and her writing appears in *Right to Dance, Dance and Human Rights* (Banff, 2005) and in *Dance Connection, Canadian Theatre Review, alt.theatre,* and *Dance Research Journal.* Her current research on Canadian multiculturalism investigates connections between dance, citizenship, cultural policy, and human rights.

David F. García is assistant professor of music at the University of North Carolina at Chapel Hill. Garcia received a PhD in ethnomusicology from the CUNY Graduate Center. His publications include *Arsenio Rodriguez and the Transnational Flows of Latin Popular Music* (Temple University Press, 2006). He has done research in New York City, Miami, Los Angeles, Havana, and Curaçao. His current research interests include the early history of mambo and Latin jazz and the historiography of popular music.

Nadine George-Graves is an associate professor at the University of California at San Diego. Her research is situated at the intersections of critical race theory, gender studies, performance studies, theater history, African American performance history, and dance history. She is the author of *The Royalty of Negro Vaudeville: The Whitman Sisters and the Negotiation of Race, Gender, and Class in African American Theater, 1900–1940* (St. Martin's, 2000) and is currently completing her second book, *Working It Out with Urban Bush Women.* Additionally, George-Graves is an artist with extensive experience and training as a performer, director, choreographer, adapter, and writer.

Jurretta Jordan Heckscher is a research specialist at the Library of Congress and a former dance specialist at the National Endowment for the Arts who holds degrees from Harvard, Oxford, and the George Washington Universities. The recipient of a Marshall Scholarship from the British government and the Ralph Henry Gabriel Dissertation Prize from the American Studies

Association, she has published dance criticism in the *Washington Post* and other publications.

Karen Hubbard is an associate professor of dance and theater at the University of North Carolina, Charlotte. She was a Fulbright-Hays scholar at the University of Nairobi and has taught master classes throughout the United States, South Africa, Portugal, and the British West Indies. Hubbard has studied with Mr. "Pepsi" Bethel and performed with his fledgling Authentic Jazz Dance Theatre Company. Based in part on her work with Mr. Bethel, she has developed a curriculum on the cultural, historical, and aesthetic aspects of jazz, an innovative approach to teaching vintage jazz dance.

Tim Lawrence is program leader of the Music Culture: Theory and Production degree at the University of East London. He is the author of *Love Saves the Day: A History of American Dance Music Culture, 1970–79* (Duke University Press, 2004). He holds a PhD in literature from Sussex University.

Julie Malnig is an associate professor in the Gallatin School of Individualized Study at New York University, where she teaches courses in performance criticism, history, and theory. She is the author of *Dancing Till Dawn: A Century of Exhibition Ballroom Dance* (New York University Press, 1995) and has written on twentieth-century social dance, particularly social dance of the 1910s and 1920s, in numerous publications. She is a former editor of *Dance Research Journal* and has also served as editorial board chair for the Congress on Research in Dance. Malnig holds a PhD in performance studies from New York University.

Carol Martin is an associate professor of drama at Tisch School of the Arts, New York University. She is the author of *Dance Marathons: Performing American Culture of the 1920s and 1930s* (University of Mississippi Press, 1994). She is currently writing a book on documentary theater. Martin's guest-edited issue of *The Drama Review TDR* on documentary theater in the United States, the United Kingdom, and Israel, Lebanon, and Germany was published in fall of 2006. Her essays and interviews have appeared in anthologies, academic journals in the United States and abroad, and *The New York Times*.

Juliet McMains is an assistant professor in the Dance Department at the University of Washington. She has been competing in DanceSport for ten years, currently in the professional Latin division. She is coauthor, with Danielle Robinson, of "Swinging Out: Southern California's Lindy Revival," in *I See America Dancing: Selected Readings, 1685–2000* (University of Illinois Press, 2002), and the author of *Glamour Addiction: Inside the American Ballroom Dance Industry* (Wesleyan University Press, 2006). She holds a PhD in Dance History and Theory from the University of California, Riverside.

Terry Monaghan is the founder and producer of the U.K.-based Jiving Lindy Hoppers since 1984. His restaging of performance-quality Lindy Hop has been influenced by work with Mr. "Pepsi" Bethel and former Lindy dancers, including Frankie Manning, Norma Miller, "Mama Lou" Parks, and George and Sugar Sullivan. He is currently completing his PhD on Harlem's Savoy Ballroom at Goldsmiths College, University of London. He was a dance consultant for a recently completed BBC Television documentary on jazz and Latin dance.

Halifu Osumare is an associate professor of African American and African studies at the University of California, Davis. She has an MA in dance ethnology from San Francisco State University and a PhD in American studies from the University of Hawai'i. She writes and publishes about dance, African American performance, and the globalization of hip-hop and is the author of *The Africanist Aesthetic in Global Hip Hop: Power Moves* (Palgrave, 2007).

Sally R. Sommer is a professor in the master's program in American dance at Florida State University. She is the producer of the television documentary on New York City's club scene, *Check Your Body at the Door.* Her articles have appeared in *The Village Voice, The New York Times, Dance Magazine,* and *The Women's Review of Books,* among others. She is the author of *Ballroom* (Milkweed, 1989) and has contributed extensively to numerous dance and American history encyclopedias. Her PhD is in performance studies from New York University.

Constance Valis Hill is a Five College Professor of Dance at Hampshire College. She is a jazz dancer and choreographer and earned her PhD in performance studies from New York University. Her writings have appeared in numerous publications, including *Dancing Many Drums: Excavations in African-American Dance* (University of Wisconsin Press, 2002) and *Taken by Surprise: A Dance Improvisation Reader* (Wesleyan University Press, 2002). Her book *Brotherhood in Rhythm: The Jazz Tap Dancing of the Nicholas Brothers* (Oxford University Press, 2000) won the ASCAP Deems Taylor Award in 2001.

May Gwin Waggoner is Laborde-Neuner Board of Regents Professor of French and Francophone Studies at the University of Louisiana, Lafayette. Her specialty is Louisiana Francophone language and literature and Louisiana Acadian music. Her publications include *Une fantaisie collective: anthologie du drame louisianais cadien* (Center for Louisiana Studies, University of Louisiana, Lafayette, 1999); a critical and bilingual edition of *Les Vagabondes: Poésies Américaines,* by Camille Thierry, with Frans C. Amelinckx (Éditions Tintamarre, 2004); and *Le plus beau païs du monde: Completing the Picture of Proprietary Louisiana, 1699–1722* (Center for Louisiana Studies, University of Louisiana, Lafayette, 2005).

Tim Wall is professor of music and head of academic affairs in the Department of Media and Communication at the University of Central England (UCE). He is also the director of UCE's Urban Cultures Research Group and chair of the Radio Studies Network. He publishes on a range of topics in popular music culture, the music industries, and music radio and is the author of *Studying Popular Music Culture* (Arnold, 2003).

Christina Zanfagna is a PhD candidate in ethnomusicology at the University of California, Los Angeles. Her work has appeared in *The Beat, Roots, Afropop Quarterly,* and the *Pacific Review of Ethnomusicology.* Her doctoral dissertation explores themes of spirituality and commercialism in holy hip-hop music and culture. Zanfagna has performed with the Gospel Music Workshop of America (GMWA) mass choir in New Orleans and the batUCLAda Brazilian percussion ensemble and co-organized the first Hip-Hop Film Festival in Los Angeles.

Index

The University of Illinois Press
is a founding member of the
Association of American University Presses.

Composed in 9/13 ITC Stone Serif
with Poplar Black display
by Celia Shapland
at the University of Illinois Press
Designed by Dennis Roberts
Manufactured by Thomson-Shore, Inc.

University of Illinois Press
1325 South Oak Street
Champaign, IL 61820-6903
www.press.uillinois.edu